THE DEATH PENALTY IN CHINA

The Death Penalty in China

POLICY, PRACTICE, AND REFORM

Bin Liang and Hong Lu
EDITORS

Roger Hood
FOREWORD

 COLUMBIA UNIVERSITY PRESS   NEW YORK

COLUMBIA UNIVERSITY PRESS
Publishers Since 1893
New York   Chichester, West Sussex

cup.columbia.edu
Copyright © 2016 Columbia University Press
All rights reserved

Library of Congress Cataloging-in-Publication Data

Death penalty in China (Liang and Lu)
   The death penalty in China : policy, practice, and reform / edited by Bin Liang and Hong Lu ; foreword by Roger Hood.
      pages cm
   Includes bibliographical references and index.
   ISBN 978-0-231-17006-2 (cloth) — ISBN 978-0-231-17007-9 (pbk.) — ISBN 978-0-231-54081-0 (ebook)
   1. Capital punishment—China.   2. Criminal justice, Administration of—China.
I. Liang, Bin, 1972-   II. Lu, Hong, 1966-   III. Title.

HV8699.C6D434   2016
364.660951—dc23

2015020786

Cover design: Jordan Wannemacher

References to websites (URLs) were accurate at the time of writing.
Neither the author nor Columbia University Press is responsible for URLs that may have expired or changed since the manuscript was prepared.

CONTENTS

FOREWORD by Roger Hood VII
PREFACE AND ACKNOWLEDGMENTS XI

CHAPTER ONE
▸ China's Death Penalty Practice: Working Progress, Struggle, and Challenges Within the Global Abolition Movement
Bin Liang 1

CHAPTER TWO
▸ The Criminal Justice System and the Death Penalty
Hong Lu, Yudu Li, and Charlotte Hu 31

CHAPTER THREE
▸ Crimes of Counterrevolution and Politicized Use of the Death Penalty During the Mao Era
Ning Zhang 62

CHAPTER FOUR
▸ China's Death Penalty in a State-Power-Based Society
Yunhai Wang 97

CHAPTER FIVE
▸ From "Killing Many" to "Killing Fewer"
Susan Trevaskes 123

CHAPTER SIX
▸ The Abolitionist and Retentionist Debate
Zhigang Yu (translated by Charlotte Hu) 156

CHAPTER SEVEN

▶ Guiding Cases for China's Death Penalty: Analysis and Reflection
  Xingliang Chen (translated by Charlotte Hu)   187

CHAPTER EIGHT

▶ The Death Penalty After the Restoration of Centralized Review: An Empirical Study of Capital Sentencing
  Moulin Xiong   214

CHAPTER NINE

▶ Public Opinion and the Death Penalty
  Shanhe Jiang   247

CHAPTER TEN

▶ Between Deference and Defiance: Courts and Penal Populism in Chinese Capital Cases
  Hualing Fu   274

CHAPTER ELEVEN

▶ Chinese Capital Punishment in Comparative Perspective
  David T. Johnson and Michelle Miao   300

CHAPTER TWELVE

▶ China's Death Penalty in the Twenty-First Century
  Bin Liang and Hong Lu   327

LIST OF CONTRIBUTORS   351

INDEX   355

FOREWORD

▸ ROGER HOOD

AT THE TURN OF THE TWENTY-FIRST CENTURY, I was fortunate to be invited to China with my colleagues, Saul Lehrfreund and Peter Hodgkinson, under the auspices of the United Kingdom Foreign and Commonwealth Office, by the Ministry of Foreign Affairs of the People's Republic of China. The purpose, from the Chinese side, was to inform us about the justifications for the use of the death penalty in the context of China's social, cultural, and political development. From our side, we hoped to make our hosts more aware of the international movement to abolish the death penalty as a violation of the right not to be arbitrarily deprived of life or to be subject to cruel, inhuman, and degrading treatment or punishment, as established in Articles 6 and 7 of the International Covenant on Civil and Political Rights (ICCPR), which China had signed in 1998. We stressed that until the death penalty was abolished, China should move to restrict the scope of capital punishment to only the most serious crimes with lethal or other extremely grave consequences and to enforce the safeguards established by the United Nations to protect the rights of those facing the death penalty, particularly to receive a fair trial and to be presumed innocent until proved guilty by a competent, independent, and impartial tribunal.

We were received with courtesy, but the responses to our message were rigidly defensive. We were reminded how long it had taken the United Kingdom to abolish capital punishment since the issue had been raised early in the nineteenth century, and it was suggested by some that it would also take a century before full abolition would become possible in China. The developing international engagement, marked by European Union–China human rights dialogues and seminars, appeared to be having little impact. Indeed, I recall that during the European Union–China Human Rights Seminar to discuss the death penalty that was held in Beijing in May 2001, a major "strike-hard" (*yanda*) campaign was simultaneously being put into effect, resulting in at least 1,781 executions between April and July.

Yet changes were afoot, led by Chinese academic lawyers. At a conference held at Renmin University in 2005, the agenda was no longer "Should China abolish the death penalty?" but rather "How can China move forward to abolish the death penalty?"

Things have changed remarkably since then. The criminal policy of "blending leniency and severity to maintain social fairness and justice" has been firmly established. This has meant that the number of capital crimes has been reduced—first from 68 to 55 and then hopefully to 46 (proposed in the Ninth Amendment to the Criminal Law in November 2014, which is currently under review)—and China officially confirmed before the United Nations Human Rights Council in 2007 that its final goal is abolition. Several procedural safeguards have been introduced in the hope that they will improve the prospects of a fair trial, curb abuse of state power, and avoid wrongful convictions of the innocent arising from coerced confessions. A system of reviewing all immediate death sentences by the Supreme People's Court was reestablished in 2007, resulting in the introduction of guidelines to distinguish cases where the courts regard immediate execution as necessary from those for which the death penalty can be suspended; to try to remedy arbitrariness of decisions made by different courts; and to ensure that executions are limited to the gravest cases. Although statistics of the number of death sentences and executions remain, most regrettably, a state secret, there appears to be no dispute among China's academic community or foreign-based nongovernmental organizations that the number of executions has declined very substantially, even though it is still estimated that about 3,000 convicted citizens are executed annually. There is still a long way to go, but China is undoubtedly making strides along the road to abolition.

Thus the time is right for an assessment of what has been achieved and what barriers remain to limiting further the scope of capital offenses with the eventual goal of abolition. Hence, this excellent collection of essays should be greatly welcomed because it provides insights into the way in which Chinese scholars, both within and outside China, as well as foreign scholars who have studied the Chinese system in depth, explain the changes under way and assess their significance. It has been edited with great skill by Professors Bin Liang and Hong Lu, both natives of China now teaching and researching in the United States. Through their extensive contacts, they have been able to obtain contributions from the new generation of Chinese scholars, few of whom are well known in the West. Their reflections on the historical, legal, political, and cultural context within which death penalty reform in China is being pursued provide an authentic and fresh picture of how the debate on abolition is being pursued in that vast country. Particular significance is given to two factors. First, the historical legacy of using the death penalty as an instrument of political power and as a means of legitimating the state's claim to provide security is analyzed. Second, the role of public opinion—or, more accurately, public pressure, especially from the families of victims—is acknowledged as a restraining element on a judiciary that is still far from being politically independent.

One problem with writing about China's death penalty system, as mentioned earlier, is the lack of any published data on the number of death sentences imposed and executions that take place annually, and for which crimes. The shortage of empirical data is acknowledged, and although one study of the crimes for which immediate death sentences were imposed by the courts of first instance is reported, the editors and many contributors illustrate their essays with revealing and often dramatic case studies of wrongful convictions, as well as those where the Supreme People's Court has tried to establish guidance on where the line should be drawn between cases that the Court believes demand immediate execution and those where the convicted person could be spared by a suspended death penalty (in effect, life imprisonment). These vivid cases undoubtedly enhance the book.

The editors hope that the death penalty system will be much improved "20 years from now" so as to close the gap between China's practices and international standards. Like almost all the other contributors, they do not believe that there is a good prospect of abolition in the short term. Even those who say that they are abolitionist in principle proclaim that they are retentionist in practice, meaning that, in their view, the most realistic policy in the current political context is to press for progressive reform rather than abolition.

It is clear from these essays, taken as a whole, that whether this conclusion is too pessimistic will depend on political leadership as China increasingly takes on the mantle of a world superpower. This thought-provoking book implies that much will turn on whether and when Chinese leaders decide to ratify the ICCPR. That would surely undermine the political legitimacy of capital punishment and hasten the time when Chinese lawyers, public servants, and politicians come to accept abolition of the death penalty on the principled grounds that it cannot be enforced without breaching the fundamental human right not to be arbitrarily deprived of life nor to be subjected to cruel, inhuman, and degrading treatment or punishment.

The Death Penalty in China needs to be read by everyone concerned with the project of eliminating capital punishment throughout the world.

PREFACE AND ACKNOWLEDGMENTS

RIGHT AROUND THE TIME at which we put the finishing touches on this book, the Dui Hua Foundation (http://duihua.org/wp/) released news on October 20, 2014, that China executed approximately 2,400 people in 2013, compared with 778 people executed by the rest of the world combined (estimate by Amnesty International in March 2014). Although the Chinese number still appears very high, it actually represents a steady decline over the years due to reform efforts taken by the Chinese government. On the one hand, the Chinese legislature has taken measures to reduce the number of capital offenses in the law. The 2011 revised Criminal Law (the Eighth Amendment), for instance, abolished 13 previous capital offenses (with 55 remaining). The draft Ninth Amendment, currently under consideration by the Chinese National People's Congress, proposed further reduction of 9 more capital offenses. On the other hand, the Chinese judiciary also tightened its judicial review of death sentence cases (in particular the final review and approval by the national Supreme People's Court). The news released by the Dui Hua Foundation showed that 39% of all death penalty cases reviewed by the Supreme People's Court in 2013 were sent back to provincial high courts for additional evidence. Moreover, in an effort to increase judicial transparency, a total of 152 death penalty review decisions were published online by the Supreme People's Court from July 2003 to September 2014. However, defense lawyers participated in only 13% of all these cases. As a matter of fact, the Chinese Criminal Procedure Law mandates the assistance of defense lawyers for all capital offenders during both trials of first and second instances (Article 34) but stipulates that the Supreme People's Court shall listen to the opinion of the defense lawyers during its final review and approval phase only if they so request (Article 240).

News about China's death penalty practice, such as that from the Dui Hua Foundation, often draws people's attention and could generate further questioning and sometimes reinforce people's stereotyping of China's practice (e.g., the high execution numbers). To many people (Chinese citizens included), China's death penalty is still an enigma. For example, despite continued efforts to increase transparency, data on China's death sentences and executions are still not available publicly and remain a state secret.

To the Chinese leaders, the death penalty is probably not on their priority list. The new political leadership under Xi Jinping is already busy with a list of more urgent issues, such as how to continue sustainable economic growth, how to fight blatant official corruption, how to promote the "Chinese Dream" and maintain a harmonious society, how to deal with aggravating environmental and pollution problems, and how to handle international challenges from the Diaoyu Islands (also known as the Senkaku Islands), the South China Sea, and unstable and unpredictable North Korea, to name a few. Nevertheless, global human rights organizations repeatedly target China's death penalty system as part of China's human rights record, and the growing number of countries that have joined the abolition movement worldwide also puts increasing pressure on China.

Perhaps propitiously, the rekindled interest in building an effective system of the rule of law emphasized by the fourth plenary session of the Eighteenth Chinese Communist Party Central Committee in October 2014 may have an unexpected effect on China's death penalty reforms. Granted, criminal sanctions (including the death penalty) will likely continue domestically as an instrument to stabilize the unstable social development during the rapid expansion of the market economy. Nevertheless, the realization by the party-state of the importance of a stronger and more effective legal system brings hope for further restrictions on future death penalty use in China.

It is within this political, economic, and social context that we initiated this project. The goal of this collection is to comprehensively and systematically examine the current conditions and progress of the existing Chinese death penalty system and to analyze critical challenges faced by that system.

With contributions by leading scholars in this field from five countries and four continents, we hope that this collection will offer readers diverse perspectives on China's death penalty practice so that they can gain an appreciation of how much China has overcome and the necessary work required for more future reforms. Like many others, we are overwhelmed by problems that need to be addressed in China's legal reforms in general and death penalty reforms in particular; nevertheless, we remain optimistic about China's future. Twenty years from now, it is our hope that China will have a much improved death penalty system that addresses competing needs of justice and provides fundamental fairness to both the victim and the defendant, if it has not already become abolitionist in law or in practice.

During our work on this project, we have received assistance from many scholars and friends. First of all, we would like to express our gratitude to a number of scholars for their careful review of original contributions in this volume. Their comments and suggestions helped our contributors improve the quality of their works and stimulated more discussions. These reviewers (in alphabetical order of their last names) include Liqun Cao at the University of Ontario Institute of Technology, Qijun Duan at Hunan University Law School, Jonathan Hassid at Iowa State University, Bill Hebenton at the University of Manchester School of Law, Ming Hu at Zhejiang University Law School, Su Jiang at Peking University Law School, Margaret Lewis at Seton Hall Law School, Xiaobing Li at the University of Central Oklahoma, Siyu Liu at New Jersey City University, Terance Miethe at the University of Nevada–Las Vegas, Daniela Stockman at Leiden University, Caixia Su at the South-Central University of Economics and Law, Yuning Wu at Wayne State University, Jianhua Xu at the University of Macau, Yuexing Zeng at Kunming University of Science and Technology Law School, Lening Zhang at Saint Francis University, and Yue Zhuo at St. John's University.

Second, we would like to acknowledge tremendous help with our research and editing from a group of our colleagues and students, including Taylar Goike, Erin Moore, and Taylor Cunningham from Oklahoma State University and Tamara Madensen, Melissa Rorie, and Jason Mitchell from the University of Nevada–Las Vegas. In addition, we would also like to offer our appreciation to other colleagues and friends who assisted us with the preparation of this manuscript, including Xingliang Chen at Peking University Law School, Roger Hood at All Souls College, Oxford, Andrew

Scobell from the Rand Corporation, Ming Hu at Zhejiang University Law School, Kai Kuang at Hunan University Law School, Min Ge at China Agriculture University, and Shanshan Li from Beijing, China.

Third, we would like to thank both Jennifer Perillo and Stephen Wesley from Columbia University Press for their continuous encouragement and timely support throughout this project. Without their assistance, this project would not have been completed smoothly.

Last, we are indebted to the unwavering love and support from our family members, including Ying, Gloria, Jason, Shannon, and Selina. Love you all indeed.

1

China's Death Penalty Practice

WORKING PROGRESS, STRUGGLE, AND CHALLENGES WITHIN THE GLOBAL ABOLITION MOVEMENT

▸ BIN LIANG

FEW SOCIAL ISSUES have received more public attention and scholarly debate than the death penalty. Although the global abolitionist movement has made successful strides in recent decades, a small number of countries remain committed to the death penalty and impose it relatively frequently. In this regard, the People's Republic of China (PRC or China hereafter) no doubt leads the world in the numbers of both death sentences and executions. Nevertheless, usually missing from public discussion (in particular among Western nations and societies) are the tremendous changes that have already occurred to China's death penalty system. Such changes have become increasingly evident since China kicked off its legal reforms in the 1990s that aimed at building an effective Chinese legal system.

The main goal of this collection is to examine China's death penalty practice within the dramatically changing social, political, and legal context of China and under the influence of the global abolition movement. In this introductory chapter, I would like to draw attention to China's death penalty practice through two interrelated lenses, one domestic and the other international. The domestic lens focuses on internal changes to China's practice, while the international lens situates China's reforms within the context of the global abolition movement and examines whether and how China's reform measures have addressed concerns raised by the international community.

DOMESTIC LENS: WORKING PROGRESS IN DECADES

Although studies of China's death penalty have grown significantly in the past two decades, the world came to know about China's practices mostly through research and media reports from Western countries, many of which portrayed China's practices through negative or even vilified lenses (Lu & Miethe 2007:1). One major problem with such portrayals (which contain elements of truth) is that they fail to capture the complexity of China's death penalty system as a whole and its rapid evolution and changing nature, especially in recent years (see table 1.1). To highlight and reflect on these dramatic changes, five death penalty cases in different eras are discussed in this chapter. These cases are neither comprehensive nor representative of all capital cases of their times. Rather, they collectively form a collage that gives the reader a glimpse of China's death penalty practices at different times.

Politicized Use of Capital Punishment from the 1950s to 1970s

Zhang Zhixin was born in Tianjin in 1930, received her college education in the early 1950s, and became a member of the Chinese Communist Party (CCP) in 1955 and a cadre in the Communist Party Propaganda Department in Liaoning Province. Her fate, however, dramatically changed after the onset of the Cultural Revolution (1966–1976). In 1968, she was denounced for her critical comments about Chairman Mao and was sent to the "school for cadres" (reeducation camp) and ultimately labeled an active counterrevolutionary. Zhang was then arrested and imprisoned in 1969. In prison, she was tortured and raped, and her attempted suicide was deemed "confrontation and protest against the Party." In 1970, Zhang was condemned to death for having opposed Mao and Jiang Qing (Mao's wife) in favor of Liu Shaoqi (who was elected China's chairman in 1959 but was disowned by Mao in the late 1960s as "the number one capitalist roader and a traitor"), and her case was transferred to the Liaoning High People's Court and then to the Party Revolutionary Committee of the province for approval. Chen Xilian, then head of the province and military commander of the region, decided that Zhang be spared in order to "serve as a living (negative) example," and Zhang's sentence was reduced to life imprisonment. In 1973, during a meeting to criticize Lin Biao (who was named Mao's successor after Liu Shaoqi but was labeled a counterrevolutionary after

TABLE 1.1 Timeline of China's Death Penalty Legal and Policy Changes

YEAR	MAJOR CHANGE(S)
1949	The PRC was founded. No formal criminal law or criminal procedure law was passed.
1954	The NPC passed the Organic Law of the People's Court, which stipulated that death penalty cases were to be reviewed and approved by provincial high courts and the SPC (Article 11).
1958–66	The SPC reviewed and approved death penalty cases based on a NPC decision passed in 1957.
1966–76	The SPC's review and approval power became defunct during the Cultural Revolution period.
1979	The first Criminal Law and the first Criminal Procedure Law were passed; 28 death-eligible offenses were stipulated, and the SPC possessed the final review and approval authority for death penalty cases (Article 199). The Organic Law of the People's Court was revised: the SPC still possessed the final review and approval authority (Article 13).
1980	The SCNPC decided to delegate the final review and approval authority from the SPC to provincial high courts.
1981	The SCNPC passed the Decision on Review and Approval of Death Penalty Cases, which (1) extended the delegation of the SPC's final review and approval authority from 1981 to 1983 and (2) authorized that no SPC final review and approval would be needed in violent cases, such as murder, robbery, and arson. The Decree on Punishing Military Personnel Who Derelict Military Duty added 13 new capital offenses.
1982	The Decree on Severely Punishing Criminals Who Disturb National Economic Order added seven new capital offenses, including drug trafficking.
1983	The Decree on Severely Punishing Criminals Who Threaten Public Security added 10 new capital offenses. The SCNPC passed On Expediting Trial Procedure Against Criminals Who Severely Threaten Public Security, under which certain cases were no longer bound by stipulations of the Criminal Procedure Law (e.g., the statute of limitations for criminal appeals was shortened from 10 to 3 days). The Organic Law of the People's Court was revised to allow the SPC to delegate the final review and approval power (Article 13). The first strike-hard anticrime campaign kicked off; provincial high courts, instead of the SPC, exercised the final review and approval authority in certain cases (e.g., violent offenses, narcotics offenses).
1984	Six ministries (SPC, SPP, MPS, MJ, MPH, and MCA) jointly adopted Temporary Provisions on How to Utilize Corpses or Organs of Executed Offenders.

Continued

TABLE 1.1 *(Continued)*

YEAR	MAJOR CHANGE(S)
1986	The Organic Law of the People's Court was revised and continued to allow the SPC's delegation of the final review and approval power (Article 13).
1988	The Supplemental Regulations on Punishing Criminals Who Leak National Secrets added one new capital offense.
1990	The NPC adopted the Decree on Drug Control, which made the death penalty applicable to all narcotics offenses.
1991	The Supplementary Regulation on Punishing Illegally Digging and Robbing Ancient Remains or Tombs added one new capital offense.
	The Resolution on Severely Punishing Criminals Who Abduct and Sell Women and Children added three new capital offenses.
	The Resolution on Prohibiting Prostitution and Pimping added two new capital offenses.
	The SPC issued a notice to delegate the final review and approval power to the Yunnan High Court for drug cases.
1992	The Decree on Punishing Criminals Who Hijack an Aircraft added one new capital offense.
1993	The Resolution on Punishing Criminals Who Produce and Sell Fake and Shoddy Products added two new capital offenses.
	The SPC issued a notice to delegate the final review and approval power to the Guangdong High Court for drug cases.
1995	The Resolution on Punishing Criminals Who Disturb the Financial Order added four new capital offenses.
	The Resolution on Punishing Criminals Who Issue, Counterfeit, or Sell Special Value-Added Tax Invoices added two new capital offenses.
1996	The Criminal Procedure Law was revised: (1) the final review and approval authority still resided in the SPC (Article 199); (2) legal representation was mandated in death penalty cases; and (3) legal injection became one means of official execution.
	The SPC issued a notice to delegate the final review and approval power to the Guangxi, Sichuan, and Gansu High Courts for drug cases.
1997	The Criminal Law was revised, with a total of 68 capital offenses.
	The SPC's Notice on Granting the Final Review and Approval Authority in Certain Death Penalty Cases to Provincial High Courts and Military Tribunals still allowed the decentralized practice of death penalty review and approval.
2001	The SPC decided to implement legal injection nationwide as the means of execution.
2002	The SPC issued the Notice on Utilizing Lethal Injection in Executions to ensure standardized procedure.

YEAR	MAJOR CHANGE(S)
2005	The SPC issued the Notice on Further Improving Appellate Trials (i.e., trials of second instance) in Death Penalty Cases, mandating an open-court appellate trial after July 2006.
2006	The Organic Law of the People's Court was revised again and abolished the delegation of the SPC's final review and approval authority (Article 12).
	Over 6,000 judges received special training on death penalty trials in Beijing (National Judiciary College), the first such training ever organized by the SPC.
	The SPC and the SPP issued the Answers to Some Procedural Questions with Regard to Open-Court Appellate Trials in Death Penalty Cases.
2007	The SPC took back the final review and approval power.
	Four ministries (SPC, SPP, MPS, and MJ) jointly issued the Opinion on Further Strictly Enforcing the Law to Ensure the Quality of Death Penalty Cases, which, e.g., adopted rules against torture, demanded witness testimony in appellate trials, guaranteed lawyers' rights, and granted visitation by family members before execution.
2008	The SPC issued On Certain Issues with Regard to Execution Halt Procedure.
2010	The SPC issued Opinion on Certain Issues Concerning Implementing the Criminal Justice Policy of Balancing Leniency and Severity.
	Five ministries (SPC, SPP, MPS, MNS, and MJ) jointly issued the Rules on Certain Issues Concerning Examination and Judgment of Evidence in Death Penalty Cases and Rules on Certain Issues Concerning the Exclusion of Illegal Evidence in Criminal Cases.
2011	The Eighth Amendment of the 1997 Criminal Law was adopted: 13 previously capital offenses are no longer death eligible, but 55 death-eligible offenses remain.
2012	The Criminal Procedure Law was revised, and new measures were adopted to strengthen criminal defense: e.g., granting lawyers' early intervention in the investigation stage (e.g., Articles 33 and 36), simplifying procedures for lawyers to meet with detained clients (e.g., Article 37), adopting exclusionary rules against evidence illegally obtained through torture (e.g., Articles 50, 53, 54), and mandating that interrogations of criminal suspects be recorded or videotaped for suspects facing a potential death sentence or life imprisonment (Article 121).
2013	The SPC held an open-court hearing in its review of a death penalty case, its first-ever open-court hearing in death penalty reviews.

Abbreviations: MCA = Ministry of Civil Affairs; MJ = Ministry of Justice; MNS = Ministry of National Security; MPH = Ministry of Public Health; MPS = Ministry of Public Security; NPC = National People's Congress; PRC = People's Republic of China; SCNPC = Standing Committee of the National People's Congress; SPC = Supreme People's Court; SPP = Supreme People's Procuratorate.

a failed coup in 1971), Zhang, then suffering from mental illness, shouted a slogan against Mao. This was judged another counterrevolutionary crime, and her case was resubmitted for death sentence approval in 1975. This time, Mao Yuanxin, Mao's nephew and then the top person in charge, ordered her to be condemned to death with immediate execution. Zhang was executed in secret on April 4, 1975, at the age of 45. Before execution, her throat was slit, a method invented to prevent condemned prisoners from proclaiming their innocence or shouting political slogans considered unacceptable. Four years later, in the spring of 1979, her case was overturned, and Zhang was officially proclaimed a martyr.[1]

Zhang's case is one of the best-known cases during this historical period. As reflected in her case, the most dominant feature of this era was the politicized use of the death penalty against counterrevolutionaries (see chapter 3). From 1949 to 1979, no formal criminal codes (e.g., criminal law, criminal procedure law) were adopted. Rather, the Regulations on the Punishment of Counterrevolutionaries in the PRC was adopted in 1951 and served as the major guideline in identifying and punishing counterrevolutionaries. Although it is still a secret how many people like Zhang were convicted and executed as counterrevolutionaries, the estimated number is in the millions.[2] As a means to facilitate political movements during this era, the politicized use of capital punishment ended any slim hope of building a formal legal system and maintaining a standardized legal procedure for China's death penalty practice. For instance, although the Supreme People's Court (SPC) exercised the final review and approval power for death penalty cases after 1958, such review became defunct during the Culture Revolution period (see table 1.1). When the first Criminal Law of the PRC was adopted in 1979, counterrevolutionary offenses were written into the law, 15 of which carried potential capital punishment (Articles 91–97 and 100–101). It was not until 1997, when the Criminal Law was revised, that such counterrevolutionary offenses were replaced with offenses of endangering state security (subject to the death penalty).

"Strike-Hard" Campaigns in the 1980s

Born in 1957, Zhu Guohua came from a very privileged family. He is the youngest son of Zhu Qi, who is the only son of Zhu De, one of the pioneers of the CCP and top leaders of the PRC and the top general of the People's Liberation Army. After receiving a college degree in the early 1980s, Zhu

Guohua worked as an employee of the Tianjian railway system. As the grandson of Zhu De, good-looking Zhu Guohua was often favored by young ladies and indeed dated many of them. His easygoing sexual relationships were unfortunately deemed illegal as a form of "hooliganism" (*liumang zui*) after the first round of the "strike-hard" (*yanda*) campaign[3] was initiated by the government in 1983. What was worse in his case was that the Decree on Severely Punishing Criminals Who Threaten Public Security,[4] adopted by the Standing Committee of the National People's Congress (SCNPC) in September 1983, made a number of crimes death eligible, with hooliganism topping the list. Zhu Guohua was convicted of this crime,[5] sentenced to death, and executed promptly at the age of 25 (he was one of 82 people executed on the same day). Only after the 1979 Criminal Law was revised in 1997 was the offense of hooliganism officially abolished.

Zhu's case was exceptional at an exceptional moment. On the one hand, in the late 1970s and early 1980s, China had just started moving away from a series of political movements that had plagued the nation in the previous decades and had initiated its economy reform and "open-door" policies. Learning from its mistakes of the past, the CCP, under the leadership of Deng Xiaoping, began to build its system of the rule of law. Codification of major laws, such as the 1979 Criminal Law and Criminal Procedure Law, was promoted as a key signal of this move. On the other hand, crimes reportedly began to climb after the implementation of the economic policies. A number of infamous cases in the early 1980s shocked the conscience of the nation. Take the case of the two Wang brothers, for example. With stolen guns, Wang Zongfang and Wang Zongwei committed their first quadruple murder in February 1983 in Shenyang (in northeastern China) and killed six more people as they fled to the southern part of the nation, where they were eventually captured and killed by the police in September in Jiangxi Province.[6] Given the grave situation, Deng promptly ordered the onset of the first nationwide strike-hard campaign against crimes. The strike-hard campaign serves as a good example of the inferiority of law in China: law is often used as a tool to serve economic and political interests and is regarded as an inconvenience when it becomes an obstacle to the accomplishment of political and economic goals.

The strike-hard campaign seemingly exhibited a short-term effect in cracking down on crimes, but it also dramatically expanded the use of capital punishment against crimes that were not death eligible under the 1979 Criminal Law, mainly through new decrees adopted by the SCNPC in the early 1980s (see table 1.1). Caught in such a moment, Zhu's hooliganism became a target of the crackdown, and his prestigious family background could not save him from the most extreme punishment. The intermittent but continued strike-hard campaigns in the 1990s and in the new century have had a long-lasting impact on China's practice of the death penalty: they not only greatly expanded the scope of capital offenses (to a total of 68 by the time the Criminal Law was revised in 1997) but also circumvented and forfeited important safeguards that had been designed to correct potential mistakes and limit death sentences and executions, one of which is the SPC's final review and approval authority for death penalty cases. Although key laws, such as the Criminal Law, stipulated that the SPC exercise the final review and approval power, this power in practice was delegated to the provincial high people's courts in the 1980s either through the SCNPC's decrees (including the revision of the Organic Law of the People's Court in 1983) or through the SPC's own delegation (see table 1.1). This delegation in essence made the final review and approval procedure defunct because the provincial high courts now exercised both the appellate review power as the courts of second instance and the final review and approval power on behalf of the SPC. It took the SPC two and a half decades to retrieve its final review and approval power in 2007.

Wrongful Convictions in the 1990s

On April 22, 1998, two dead bodies were found in Kunming City, Yunnan Province. The deceased male, Wang Junbo, was the deputy chief of the Lunan (now Shilin) County police department, and the female, Wang Xiaoxiang, was an officer of the Kunming City police department. It appeared that both victims had been shot to death at close range by Wang Junbo's handgun, which was missing from the site of the crime. Very soon, Wang Xiaoxiang's husband, Du Peiwu (an officer working at a drug rehabilitation center), was viewed as the primary suspect on the theory that he committed the double murder because he had detected the affair of the Wangs. From June to July, Du was tortured repeatedly in police interrogation and finally "confessed" his crime and made up the story that he had thrown the missing gun into the famous Lake Dianchi. From December 1998 to January 1999, Du was brought to trial for the alleged double murder, where he recanted his confession and produced evidence of torture (e.g., photos of his injuries, clothes he had worn). Unfortunately, his defense was ignored, and Du was convicted and sentenced to death with immediate execution by the Kunming Intermediate Court. In October 1999, in the trial of Du's appeal (i.e., the trial of second instance), the Yunnan (provincial) High People's Court affirmed Du's conviction but reduced his sentence to the death penalty with a two-year suspension, and Du was sent to serve his time in Yunnan Number One Prison, despite his claim of innocence. The case, however, took a dramatic turn in June 2000, when the missing gun was found by the Yunnan police when they cracked another case in which the leading criminals confessed to the murder of both Wangs in 1998. In July, the Yunnan High Court finally announced Du's innocence in a retrial.[7]

The Du case is one of the best-known wrongful conviction cases in the 1990s, along with others, such as those of Sun Wangang,[8] Zhao Zuohai,[9] and She Xianglin.[10] As has been pointed out (e.g., Jiang 2013), these cases collectively exposed a number of problems of the existing system: first, the practice of the criminal justice system still leans heavily toward a presumption of guilt rather than innocence, even though the latter is officially stipulated by the revised Criminal Law and Criminal Procedure Law. When insufficient or problematic evidence is produced in court that generates reasonable doubt, judges often choose to side with the prosecution rather than find the defendant innocent. Second, police misconduct in general and torture in particular are widespread and tenacious problems in China, and as a result, overreliance by the courts on defendants' "self-confessions" often leads directly to wrongful convictions. Third, given the close relationship among the police, the procuratorate, and the court (the so-called *gongjianfa*), and the lack of meaningful checks and balances, cooperation among them works as an assembly line in criminal practice against powerless defendants and defense lawyers. Unless something fortuitous occurs (e.g., the "deceased" returns alive), wrongful convictions often have been (and still are) impossible to detect and correct. Nevertheless, exposures of wrongful conviction cases have triggered new waves of reform measures by the authorities, especially in the new century (see table 1.1). For instance, the SPC mandated open appellate court hearings (instead of closed-court record review) for all death penalty cases in 2006; in 2007, the SPC took back its final review and approval power to limit the use of the death penalty; and in 2010, five ministries collectively adopted two evidentiary rules to target illegal evidence extracted from torture, and such rules were later integrated into the revised 2012 Criminal Procedure Law. The effect of these new measures, however, remains to be seen, because new cases of wrongful conviction have continued to emerge in the new century and have shocked the conscience of the nation (see chapter 2).

Cautious Use and Formalized Procedure in the Twenty-First Century

The case of Dong Wei, in which an ordinary assault turned into a murder, would have gone unnoticed but for its dramatic ending. On May 2, 2001, 25-year-old Dong got into a fight with another man outside a dance hall in Yan'an City, Shan'xi Province, and allegedly hit the victim on his head repeatedly with a brick. The victim died a few days later in a hospital. In November, Dong was charged with murder and was convicted and sentenced to death with immediate execution by the Yan'an Intermediate Court in December. On appeal, Dong and his attorney, Zhu Zhanping (who was hired for the appeal only), challenged the insufficient evidence and contradictory testimony produced in the trial court and petitioned for a more lenient sentence, given the fact that the criminal incident was precipitated by the victim (who approached Dong and his two female friends first and initiated both the verbal and the physical fight). After a closed-session review, the Shan'xi (provincial) High People's Court affirmed both the conviction and the sentence on April 22, 2002, and Dong was scheduled to be executed on April 29. Moreover, Dong's attorney, Zhu, was not notified of the appellate ruling until April 27, as the clock was ticking. Zhu immediately traveled to Beijing and tried to appeal the case to the SPC. After being rejected at the front gate, Zhu finally managed to gain access under false pretenses on April 29 and persuaded Deputy Judge Li Wuqing to review the case. Judge Li made a phone call to the executing officers in Shan'xi and temporarily halted the execution minutes before it was to be carried out, and the SPC afterward issued an official stay of execution. The dramatic halt of the execution at the last minute caught the immediate attention of the media, and Zhu's brave effort was hailed as "saving a person under the gun/knife" (*qian/dao xia liu ren*). After a retrial per the SPC's order, nevertheless, the Shan'xi High Court once again sustained the original conviction and sentence in August 26, and Dong was executed on September 5.[11]

As dramatic as Dong's case is, people still debate whether his case was truly meaningful,[12] because such great effort seemingly ended with the loss of Dong's life anyway. Nevertheless, Dong's case showed China's struggle in the new century to tighten its use of the death penalty through formalized legal procedures in capital execution. Specifically, in 2008, the SPC issued On Certain Issues with Regard to Execution Halt Procedure to address issues presented in Dong's case.[13] Most recently, in May 2014, a defendant named Liu shouted "Injustice" right before his scheduled execution in Huizhou, Guangdong Province. On the basis of the SPC's Execution Halt Procedure, the execution was immediately stayed. Although the execution was resumed and carried out after another round of review of Liu's case, this temporary stay was hailed as a welcome safeguard measure to protect procedural justice.[14]

New Challenges in the 2010s

Compared with the majority of China's death penalty offenders (who commit violent crimes or drug offenses), Zeng Chengjie represented another type, the white-collar offender. Growing up in a poor family, Zeng managed to become a successful businessman and a CEO of a real estate company in Hunan Province before he was arrested in December 2008 for financial fraud. Zeng was convicted and sentenced to death with immediate execution by the Changsha Intermediate People's Court in May 2011. His conviction and sentence were affirmed by the Hunan High People's Court in December, and the SPC also reviewed and approved his death sentence in June 2013. On July 12, 2013, Zeng was executed by the Changsha Intermediate Court. An unexpected exchange occurred, however, after Zeng's execution. Zeng's daughter, Zeng Shan, complained in her blog that she had never received a notice about Zeng's execution and therefore had been unable to meet her father for "one last time." In response, the Changsha Intermediate Court posted on its official blog that "there is no legal basis for the relatives of the executed to demand a final meeting with the offender before the official execution." Facing heated discussion by Internet users triggered by its cold response, the court allegedly deleted its original message half an hour later and posted another message two days later, on July 14, saying that "the executing officer notified Zeng of his right to meet Zeng's relatives before the execution, but Zeng did not request such a meeting." Apparently, the court did post an official notice of the execution on the twelfth on its bulletin board at the courthouse (as a routine practice), but neither Zeng's family members nor his attorney received a notice in person.[15]

What makes Zeng's case interesting is neither his crime nor his capital punishment. Rather, it is the postexecution challenge by Zeng's family members of the alleged lack of timely notification of the execution and the failure by the court to arrange a final meeting for family members to say good-bye to Zeng. Although the Criminal Procedure Law does not contain specific stipulations on arranging a final meeting, the SPC's interpretation (of Article 423) and its joint opinion in 2007 (see table 1.1) seem to indicate that the people's court should notify defendants' family members about the pending execution and make arrangements when they request a final meeting.[16] On the one hand, Zeng's case may indicate heightened legal consciousness by the public in the new era that will lead people to demand more rights (in this case, to meet the soon-to-be-executed offender one final time before execution); on the other hand, Zeng's case may also represent new challenges to China's practice of capital punishment, especially when "maintaining social stability" and "appeasing the feelings of the public" still carry significant weight in death penalty cases.

INTERNATIONAL LENS: INTERNATIONAL CONCERNS AND CHINA'S REFORM MEASURES

In studying China's death penalty system and its reforms over time, it is also critical to examine China's practice within the international context, where dramatic changes in the movement to abolish the death penalty have been witnessed in recent decades. By the end of 2013, a total of 140 nations had abolished the death penalty either in law or in practice (including 98 nations that abolished the death penalty for all crimes), compared with 58 nations that retained the use of the death penalty (Amnesty International 2013). This represents a sharp contrast to less than four decades ago, when merely 16 nations had abolished the death penalty for all crimes by 1977.[17] This world trend has been well noted by Chinese scholars and politicians and has already affected China's reform measures over the years (e.g., Liu 2013; Miao 2013). However, supporters of outright and immediate abolition are still the minority among Chinese scholars, not to mention the general public, who seemingly favor retention and sometimes more expansive use of the death penalty (see chapter 9). Often, it is pointed out that almost all nations with a large population (over 100 million) have retained the death penalty, and it is simply not the right time for an outright abolition given the unique circumstances of China (see Chen 2006; Yu 2009; and chapter 6).

It is not the purpose of this opening chapter to discuss how China has responded to or countered this world trend (e.g., see chapters 6 and 11). Nevertheless, it is useful to contrast international concerns raised by the international community (e.g., foreign scholars, international and human rights organizations, and the media) with China's reform efforts in recent decades to highlight China's progress and further challenges ahead.

In table 1.2, international concerns about China's practice are succinctly listed, along with reform measures adopted by China. Although not exhaustive, the list here encompasses major concerns expressed about China's death penalty practice over the years.

First, because China is the largest executioner in the world, its extremely high death sentence and execution numbers often raise deep concerns in the international community. Although China never officially (or unofficially) discloses such information, conservative estimates by human rights organizations often put the number of executions in the thousands each year (see chapter 2), and other sources suggest that it has been as high as the tens of thousands (e.g., Johnson & Zimring 2009, chapter 7). In addition, China's broad coverage of death-eligible offenses raises concerns about potential abuse of such extreme punishment (e.g., against counterrevolutionaries and nonviolent criminals, such as drug traffickers).

As discussed in the Zhang Zhixin case, China realized the abuse of counterrevolutionary offenses after the Cultural Revolution was ended and officially replaced them with offenses of endangering state security in 1997 (when the Criminal Law was revised). Moreover, other controversial crimes, such as hooliganism, were also abolished (see the Zhu Guohua case). In the new century, prompted by the SPC leadership, new measures have been put into place to limit the use of death sentences and executions (e.g., Trevaskes 2012). Although information on China's practice in regard to the death penalty is still treated as a state secret, both official reports and scholarly investigation seemingly confirm that the numbers of death sentences and executions started to decline, especially after 2007, when the SPC took back its final review and approval power (see chapter 8). In 2011, the Eighth Amendment of the Criminal Law eliminated the death penalty for

TABLE 1.2   Contrast Between International Concerns and China's Reform Measures

CONCERNS ABOUT CHINA'S PRACTICE	REFORM MEASURES IN RECENT YEARS
High death sentence and execution numbers	Measures adopted to limit death penalty coverage and immediate execution: e.g., number of capital offenses reduced in 2011; expanded use of suspended death sentence
Broad coverage of death-eligible offenses (e.g., counterrevolution offenses, nonviolent capital offenses such as economic offenses)	Gradual reduction: e.g., counterrevolution offenses no longer exist; number of economic capital offenses reduced in 2011
Execution of protected groups (e.g., minors)	1997 Criminal Law exempted minors (under 18) and pregnant women; the 2011 revision exempted seniors (above 75 at trial unless the murder was "cruel and unusual") (Article 49)
Lack of due process rights in trials	1996 Criminal Procedure Law confers a number of key rights on defendants: e.g., legal representation (Article 34) and right to confront witness and evidence
	2012 Criminal Procedure Law: full recording of police interrogation is mandated for criminals facing a potential death sentence (Article 121)
Decentralization of death penalty decision making (i.e., the final review and approval authority)	Review and approval power retrieved by the Supreme People's Court in 2007
Lack of transparency: e.g., death penalty information treated as a state secret	Reliable information still not available, but emerging signs of increased transparency: e.g., more news reporting, open-court appellate hearings since 2006
Anticrime (strike-hard) campaigns leading to violation of legal requirements and procedures	Anticrime campaigns have become less frequent in the new century but are not completely gone

13 nonviolent and economic crimes but left 55 crimes eligible for the death penalty (see chapter 2 for a list of these capital crimes).

Amnesty International reported two executions of minors (under 18) by the Chinese government early in the twenty-first century,[18] although the 1997 Criminal Law officially exempted minors (under 18) and pregnant

CONCERNS ABOUT CHINA'S PRACTICE	REFORM MEASURES IN RECENT YEARS
Communist Party's intervention and influence in trials	Still possible, but its frequency is unknown; new measures adopted to reduce or limit external interference (e.g., the Fourth Five-Year Reform Plan of the People's Courts)
Use of torture to force confession as evidence against suspects and defendants	Preventive and corrective measures adopted: e.g., two evidentiary rules adopted in 2010 to exclude evidence illegally obtained through torture (incorporated into the 2012 Criminal Procedure Law)
Inhumane treatment on death row (e.g., death row inmates in shackles)	Death row inmates allowed visitation by family members before execution
"Cruel and unusual" execution style (e.g., shooting)	Viewed as "human and scientific," lethal injection was adopted in 1996 and has been widely used in the new century
Mass sentencing and execution rallies	Reduced and intermittent use, subject to regulations (e.g., parading criminals publicly atop trucks on streets prohibited)
Commercial use or selling of body organs of executed offenders	Prior consent required, subject to regulations: Temporary Provisions on How to Utilize Corpses or Organs of Executed Offenders (1984); Regulations on Human Organ Donation and Transplantation (2007)
Lack of domestic public criticism and overwhelming official rhetoric to appeal to "popular will and support"	Official rhetoric still powerful, but diverse and dissenting opinions have emerged (e.g., scholarly debate, public reaction, and media reporting in wrongful conviction cases)

women from the death penalty. The Eighth Amendment of the Criminal Law in 2011 further broadened this exemption to include seniors (above 75 years of age at trial) unless the murder was committed in an extremely cruel manner (Article 49).

Second, when defendants are charged with serious crimes eligible for the death penalty, lack of judicial due process rights and protection is always a major concern, especially given China's high criminal conviction rates and inadequate criminal defense. The 1996 Criminal Procedure Law conferred a number of key rights on defendants in general, such as the rights to request bail, to obtain the assistance of legal counsel, and to confront witness and evidence. With regard to the death penalty, the 1996 law specifically mandated legal representation for defendants facing a potential death sentence or life imprisonment (Article 34). The revised 2012 Criminal Procedure Law aimed to further broaden the scope of criminal defense rights. With regard to the death penalty, for instance, Article 121 of the new law provides that interrogations of criminal suspects may be recorded or videotaped, and for suspects facing a potential death sentence or life imprisonment, full recording of the interrogation is mandated.

As discussed earlier, the decentralization of death penalty review and approval power in the 1980s and 1990s raised deep concerns both domestically and internationally about lack of uniform and consistent standards in rendering death sentences nationwide and about lack of substantive and meaningful final review and approval because the provincial high courts exercised their power both as the appellate court and on behalf of the SPC. Finally, in 2007, the SPC took back its long-missing authority and resumed its role as the final gatekeeper of death penalty cases.

Another related critique of China's death penalty practice concerns the lack of judicial transparency. Not only is information about the total number of death sentences and executions a state secret, but also appellate reviews are often shrouded in secrecy because the appellate courts often choose a closed-court review based purely on the record instead of holding a full open-court hearing. Again, the SPC spearheaded a number of reform measures to increase judicial transparency. For instance, in 2005 and 2006, the SPC issued two key judicial notices to mandate an open-court appellate trial in death penalty cases after July 2006 (see table 1.1), and this open-court hearing requirement was added to the revised 2012 Criminal Procedure Law (Article 223). The 2012 Criminal Procedure Law further detailed the final review and approval procedure (Articles 235–240). In June 2013, the SPC held an open-court hearing in its final review of a death penalty case in Hebei Province, its first-ever open-court hearing in death penalty reviews.[19] Note that such an open-court hearing is not required by the Criminal Procedure Law, and it is probably unrealistic for the SPC to do so in every single death penalty review, but the SPC is setting an example for the lower courts to follow in tightening up the use of the death penalty. To further improve judicial transparency, the SPC has actively promoted the publication of judicial documents online in recent years and has encouraged the lower courts to follow suit. In July 2013, the first group of SPC judicial documents was published at its designated website (www.court.gov.cn/zgcpwsw), and it is reported that more publications are expected, including all SPC-reviewed death penalty cases.[20]

Third, another major concern about China's death penalty is extrajudicial interventions and their potential impact on death penalty practice. As discussed earlier, the strike-hard campaigns in the past three decades have had a tremendous impact on China's criminal justice system in general and death penalty practice in particular. Often, under the pressure of such campaigns, more death sentences and executions were witnessed, and legal requirements and procedures stipulated in laws were either circumvented or blatantly ignored in order to strike the criminals "severely and swiftly" (*cong zhong cong kuai*) (e.g., Liang 2005). In the 1996 anticrime campaign, for example, three men in Jilin Province were arrested for robbery on May 21 and executed on May 31. Their initial trial and sentencing, appellate trial, and the final review and approval all took place in five days between May 24 and 28 (Amnesty International 1997). During the 2001 campaign, one gang of bank robbers was executed in May only 15 minutes after they were sentenced to death (Gittings 2001). Although the policy of "balancing leniency and severity" gradually replaced the strike-hard policy as the new criminal justice policy in the new century (see chapter 5), the anticrime campaigns are not completely gone. The anticrime campaign initiated by Bo Xilai in Chongqing in 2009 and 2010 once again witnessed violations of legal procedures with massive convictions and sentences, including death sentences and executions.[21]

Other means of extrajudicial interventions (e.g., by the party and political-legal committees) are also well known in China because judicial independence is fundamentally missing. What is unknown is the frequency of such interventions as more and more new measures have been adopted to insulate the courts from external interference. In July 2014, the SPC issued its fourth Five-Year Reform Plan (2014–2018), in which some proposed measures are exactly aimed at further protection of judicial independent decision making from external interference (e.g., see Lubman 2014).

Fourth, a number of concerns have also been raised about the enforcement of the death penalty over the years, including, but not limited to, the use of forced confession (via torture) against defendants, inhumane treatment of death row inmates (e.g., death row inmates are shackled), the use of mass sentencing and execution rallies, and commercialized use of human organs of the executed. Police torture is a serious problem that plagues China's criminal prosecution and has been identified in almost all wrongful conviction cases (as seen in the Du Peiwu case). To curb such abuses of power, five ministries collectively adopted two evidentiary rules in 2010 to target illegal evidence extracted from torture, and such rules were later integrated into the revised Criminal Procedure Law in 2012. The effect of these new measures, however, remains to be seen (see, e.g., Chen & Spronken 2012).

In China, very little attention is paid to death row inmates (arguably the most vulnerable group in the criminal justice system), and very little information is openly available on their postconviction treatment. In 2007, four ministries (the SPC, the Supreme People's Procuratorate [SPP], the Ministry of Public Security [MPS], and the Ministry of Justice [MJ]) jointly issued the Opinion on Further Strictly Enforcing the Law to Ensure the Quality of Death Penalty Cases (hereafter Opinion on Death Penalty Cases), in which Article 45 introduced, for the first time, a requirement for the courts to contact and to arrange visitation by relatives of a soon-to-be-executed criminal (e.g., Trevaskes 2007). However, as seen in the Zeng Chengjie case, the actual implementation of the Opinion on Death Penalty Cases is far from satisfactory because many family members of the executed never receive official notice of the execution in time.

Lethal injection was first added as one option for the means of execution by the 1996 Criminal Procedure Law, and after a few years of experiment, the SPC began to push aggressively for the nationwide adoption of legal injection in 2001 and 2002. Contrary to being constitutionally challenged as a form of cruel and unusual punishment, as has happened in the United States, lethal injection is hailed in China as a scientific and civilized method of carrying out executions with little pain and high accuracy, and the only practical problem seemingly is the high cost of lethal injection (Lu & Miethe 2007:115–117; Trevaskes 2012:163).

Public condemnation and sentencing and execution rallies have been one of the dominant practices of socialist popular justice. They were intended to serve as an effective way of educating the public, amplifying the deterrence effect, and reinforcing the boundary of law and the sense of justice (Lu & Miethe 2007:97–98). Such rallies have often been widely used in anticrime campaigns. Nevertheless, concerns about the effects of such rallies and potential violations of individual privacy rights and basic human dignity began to loom in the new century. In 2007, the joint Opinion on Death Penalty Cases officially stopped the practice of exhibiting criminals or parading them publicly atop trucks on streets (*youjie shizhong*) (Article 48). Nevertheless, public sentencing and execution in an enclosed space (e.g., a stadium) still occur from time to time, especially during crime campaigns (see, e.g., Liu 2013:174, 255–256).

Another concern of human rights organizations is the commercialized use of organs of the executed because there is always a shortage of available organs and a high demand for their medical uses (e.g., Owen 1995). In 1984, six ministries (the SPC, the SPP, the MPS, the MJ, the Ministry of Public Health [MPH], and the Ministry of Civil Affairs) jointly adopted the Temporary Provisions on How to Utilize Corpses or Organs of Executed Offenders, which stipulated clearly that for a prisoner to be a donor, prior consent must be given by that person or the person's surviving family, unless the body is unclaimed. Nevertheless, it was pointed out that "since prisoners are often kept from communicating with family members, there is no one to claim the body, which is harvested and cremated almost immediately" (Baard & Cooney 2001). In 2007, China's State Council adopted the Regulations on Human Organ Donation and Transplantation, which further detailed the principle, scope, procedure, and management of human organ donation and transplantation. Unfortunately, the new regulations did not address issues related to executed offenders, and questions still exist on whether the regulations are applicable to executed offenders (e.g., whether death row inmates qualify as "citizens" [*gongmin*] legally). In practice, human rights organizations often criticized the heavy reliance by the Chinese government on executed offenders as the primary source of medically used organs (e.g., Amnesty International 2013). In response, China's answers seemed to be self-conflicting from time to time. For instance, refuting such an accusation, a spokesperson of the MPH announced at a news conference in 2006 that the primary source of donated and transplanted organs in China was consenting civilians;[22] nevertheless, in 2012, Huang Jiefu, deputy minister of the MPH, openly admitted that 90% of organs came from executed offenders, and that a shortage had occurred in recent years because the number of executions had declined after 2007. Huang also expressed his hope that China would be able to build an effective organ donation system to draw more civilian donors in three to five years instead of relying on organs from executed persons.[23]

Finally, given the nondemocratic nature of the Chinese government and the lack of strong dissenting opinions, questions can be raised about the official rhetoric of overwhelming support for its death penalty policies. It is true that the Chinese government has often turned to "public opinion" (based on official polls) to find support for its tough stance on the death penalty and to legitimize its claim that it is "not the right time for an outright abolition given the unique circumstances of China." However, it is also true that diverse opinions (including outright critiques) have begun to emerge in China, and this is evident in many aspects, such as scholarly debate (see chapter 6), media reporting of wrongful conviction cases, and public demand for further formalization of the laws, including protection of their emerging rights (as seen in the Dong Wei and Zeng Chengjie cases). Such emerging diverse opinions can be reasonably expected to grow in the future.

In sum, although substantial gaps still exist between China's death penalty system and international standards (see chapter 12), China has made tremendous progress, especially in the new century, in its practice and has tried to improve on many aspects outlined here. Further improvement of China's practice depends not only on domestic reform initiatives in its criminal justice system but also on the world trend in abolition of the death penalty.

UNIQUE FEATURES AND ORGANIZATION OF THE BOOK

Although the topic of the death penalty in general has been extensively studied within the context of Western countries or from a wide global perspective (e.g., Hood & Hoyle 2008; Sarat & Boulanger 2005), scholarly studies (academic books in particular) of China's practice of the death penalty remain rather limited, despite the existence of broad interests from a diverse group of audiences.

Studies of China's death penalty can be found in three primary sources. The first is studies published in academic journals. These studies provide information on different aspects of China's practice. Nevertheless, given the limitations of journal articles (e.g., length), these studies often focus on specific issues, not the overall picture of the death penalty in China. The second source involves nonacademic publications by a diverse group of organizations (e.g., nongovernmental organizations that focus on human rights issues). For example, Amnesty International collects and publishes relevant annual (or special) reports about China's death penalty and collected, tallied, and published estimates of death sentences and executions in China for over three decades until it ceased to do so in 2009 on the grounds that the data were misleading. Though not completely accurate and the numbers are often underestimated, such information is still widely cited as a major source by scholars.

In contrast to the first two sources, the third source, research monographs by academic publishers, often possesses some advantages, given the nature of this source (e.g., prestige, length, organization, market, readability), and monographs are able to systematically cover a subject in depth and reach a much broader base of audiences, both academic and nonacademic. The overwhelming majority of scholarly books that address China's practice of the death penalty manage to cover China's death penalty only partially, either within the global context of death penalty studies via an international comparison approach (e.g., Hood & Hoyle 2008; Johnson & Zimring 2009) or within studies of China's punishment and criminal justice system in general (e.g., Bakken 2005; Cao, Sun, & Hebenton 2013). In contrast, scholarly English works fully devoted to China's practice of the death penalty are extremely limited and have appeared only in recent years (see Brook, Bourgon, & Blue 2008; Lu & Miethe 2007; Trevaskes 2012).

While Brook, Bourgon, and Blue's book (2008) is a historical study of *lingchi* (death by a thousand cuts, a particular form of execution used in ancient China), both Lu and Miethe's book (2007) and Trevaskes's book (2012) are devoted to studies of the PRC's death penalty practice. Lu and Miethe's book (2007) is the first study to systematically trace the historical and legal development of the PRC's death penalty. It discusses the death penalty both in law and in books on the basis of empirical data and examines the content of narrative text in actual judicial rulings of a number of death penalty cases for contextual analyses of both death penalty theories and practices. In contrast, Trevaskes's book (2012) focuses on policy changes in the twenty-first century and contrasts the "kill many" policy typified by the crime campaigns in the 1980s and 1990s with the new "kill fewer" policy in the twenty-first century. Further, Trevaskes dissects how China's current criminal proceedings (e.g., guilt finding and sentencing) leave ample room for judicial discretional interpretations (which are therefore subject to the influence of the CCP's ideology and policies).

Given the paucity of academic works on this subject, there is ample room to further examine China's death penalty, in particular important developments in China's death penalty law and practice in recent years. For example, as discussed earlier, the SPC took back the final review and approval authority for all death penalty cases in 2007, the scope of capital-eligible offenses was reduced (especially for nonviolent, economic crimes) in 2011 when the Criminal Law was revised, and a massive effort has been under way to construct a more uniform sentencing guideline, particularly for death sentence decisions. These new developments call for a need to further update and carefully analyze key issues in this field.

In comparison to previously published works, this book presents the following unique features:

It is the first edited book in English on China's death penalty. We have been able to draw on expertise from a group of prominent scholars and experts in this field who have keen knowledge about the subjects that they are addressing in this collection. As a result, this collection is able to address multiple recent issues with regard to China's practice of the death penalty and give the audience a systematic analysis of China's death penalty system.

It is a collective effort by scholars and experts from five countries and four continents (Europe, Australia, Japan, the United States, and China). Contributors in this volume include Chinese domestic scholars, overseas Chinese scholars with Western training, and Western scholars who specialize in this topic. The diverse background of contributors of this collection offers different perspectives and lends validity and reliability to this project. Moreover, the inclusion of Chinese domestic scholars (often missing or marginalized in previously published works) adds a native flavor to our storytelling and increases its authenticity. Working at the front line, these Chinese domestic scholars often possess firsthand and insider information. It is immensely beneficial for the reader to look through these native Chinese scholars' lens in examining China's death penalty.

It covers a number of extremely understudied topics in this field, such as the roles played by public opinion and the media in China's struggle with its death penalty practice. Many of these issues have become prominent only in recent years, when the use of the Internet and microblogs (*weibo*) have continued to transform people's lives in China. Although public opinion and social media have not yet prompted major policy changes with regard to

China's death penalty practice, both have already made an impact on judicial decision making in individual cases. The interplay between media and public opinion and death sentences in China provides a unique sociolegal case study, particularly within the context of the formalization and legalization movement in China.

Empirical data on China's death penalty practice are often impossible to obtain or elusive because the Chinese government carefully guards its death penalty information as a state secret. Domestic scholars from China in this collection managed to collect invaluable information (though unsystematic) through their unique methodologies (e.g., analysis of judicial documents collected from multiple cities, analysis of individual death sentence cases). These empirical data allow them to address their issues in depth, and such empirically based discussions allow a Western audience to gain a glimpse of the actual situation regarding China's death penalty practices.

Through a comparative approach, many studies in this collection situate their examination of China's case in a broader context and compare China's practice and experience with that of other nations and societies. As a result, the audience will be able to relate what is ongoing in China to their own experience and knowledge about their own nations.

The major goal of this book is to examine China's death penalty practice within the dramatically changing social, political, and legal context of China and under the influence of the global abolition movement. The scope of this collection covers (1) dominant theories and policies regarding China's death penalty practice over time; (2) characteristics of China's current death penalty practices based on empirical data; and (3) ongoing challenges and potential future reforms of the death penalty system in China. Specifically, the remainder of the book is organized as follows:

In chapter 2, Hong Lu, Yudu Liu, and Charlotte Hu present a much more detailed examination of China's existing death penalty system. First, death-eligible offenses in the current Criminal Law and estimates of death sentences and executions are discussed within the overall context of crime and punishment. Second, criminal procedure in China under the current Criminal Procedure Law and roles of key players involved (e.g., judges, prosecutors, police, defense lawyers) are examined, followed by discussion of special procedures for death penalty cases. Last, through examination of a recent wrongful conviction case, this chapter analyzes existing problems of China's death penalty practice.

In chapter 3, Ning Zhang focuses on counterrevolutionary crimes and politicized use of the death penalty during the Mao era. In particular, Zhang analyzes historical records and examines in great detail judicial practices during the campaign of repression of counterrevolutionaries (1950–1953). As Zhang points out, a number of dominant features that arose from this era, such as politicized use of the legal system, criminalization of social behaviors, use of quotas in death sentencing and execution, decentralization of the power to impose death sentences, use of mass trials, sentencing, and executions, and the invention of the death penalty with reprieve (i.e., suspension), all left a significant imprint during this era, and some still continue to affect China's death penalty practice today.

In chapter 4, Yunhai Wang focuses on the nature of Chinese society as a state-power-based society, which is the key, Wang argues, to understanding and explaining the practice of the death penalty in China. Although China has witnessed significant transitions from the Mao era (in which the death penalty was mainly used to suppress political enemies) to the Deng era (in which the use of the death penalty was broadened to cover newly added economic crimes) and to the more recent Jiang, Hu, and Xi eras (in which more legal procedures and protections were added), the fundamental nature of China as a state-power-dominated society has not been changed. As a result, CCP leaders have consistently used the death penalty as a political tool to legitimize their governance against potential crimes, be they counterrevolutionary, economic, public official, or drug offenses, over the decades.

In chapter 5, Susan Trevaskes details the transition of China's death penalty practice from "killing many" to "killing fewer" in the new century. Analyzing the ambiguity of China's Criminal Law and the great effort led by the SPC leadership to expand the use of suspended death sentences in the new era, Trevaskes shows how the "severity" and "leniency" dialectic has played out in the new policy of "balancing leniency and severity." This delicate balance, pushed mainly through judicial practices, no doubt has allowed the reduced use of death sentences and executions in recent years. Nevertheless, this dialectic might be proved rather weak if the party-state decides to swing back in the direction of "heavy penaltyism."

In chapter 6, Zhigang Yu carefully reviews China's domestic debate over abolition of the death penalty. Discussing the impact of this debate at three different levels (normative values, criminal justice practices, and judicial decision making in individual cases), Yu points out that death penalty abolition as a desired normative value has gradually faded over time as Chinese scholars have reached a consensus with regard to the role of the death penalty in criminal justice practice (i.e., abolition is a long-term goal, but retention is necessary at this stage). Rather, it is in individual cases that the use of the death penalty has been challenged the most in recent years. Yu argues that the key to China's practice in the future is how to combine theory and criminal justice practice and to further engage the public.

In chapter 7, Xingliang Chen examines China's guiding case system, a reform measure adopted in 2010 to standardize judicial sentencing. Chen details two homicide decisions issued by the SPC and one kidnapping decision issued by the SPP and discusses their potential impact on judicial death sentencing. As he points out, given its nascent history, the role of the guiding case system is still rather limited. Moreover, principles generated from these three published guiding cases mostly repeat existing laws and judicial interpretations without creating new rules. The real effect of this reform measure remains to be seen.

In chapter 8, Moulin Xiong conducts an empirical analysis of China's death penalty based on data (2005–2012) collected from eight courts in five provinces. Data analyses show that China's use of the death penalty was mainly limited to violent crimes (e.g., murder, assault, robbery, kidnapping) and drug offenses (e.g., selling, trafficking, manufacturing) in practice, although many other offenses are death eligible by law. Data on the numbers of death sentences with immediate execution and those of death sentences with suspension show a declining trend for the use of the former but an increasing trend for the latter, confirming the impact of the new policy of "balancing leniency and severity" in the new century.

In chapter 9, Shanhe Jiang focuses on survey studies of public opinion on China's death penalty, critically analyzes results of past studies, and discusses potential implications. Among other findings, Jiang's review shows that the majority of Chinese citizens support the death penalty (often at a higher level than people from Western industrialized nations), and deterrence is the strongest predictor of the attitudes of Chinese citizens toward capital punishment. To many Chinese, capital punishment is only an issue of penal policy, not an issue of human rights. Because the Chinese government often cites such public support to favor its retention of the death penalty, there is still much work to do to help accelerate China's progress toward abolishing the death penalty.

In chapter 10, Hualing Fu examines the relationship among media, public opinion, and death penalty judicial decisions in China. Fu shows that unlike the experiences of Western democracies, China's penal populism (expressions of public emotions about the criminal justice establishment) as exhibited in death penalty cases often targets judicial decision making in individual cases rather than legislative changes. Given the vulnerable status of Chinese courts (e.g., lack of judicial independence, intervention by the party-state), Chinese judges often struggle in responding to public outcries typified by challenges from the victims, and they try to find a proper balance between upholding the law (e.g., limiting unnecessary executions) and meeting the victims' needs (e.g., through the practice of "cash for clemency"). This judicial struggle is likely to continue in the future because the public has limited channels to voice their legitimate concerns in China.

In chapter 11, David T. Johnson and Michelle Miao take a comparative perspective and contrast China's current practice of the death penalty with capital punishment in the Chinese past, with the practice of other Chinese societies (Hong Kong, Taiwan, and Singapore), and with the practice of other Communist nations (Vietnam and North Korea). Such comparisons, they argue, highlight not only distinctive features of China's practice and unique challenges for the abolition of China's death penalty but also (interestingly) some potentials for accomplishing this mission.

Finally, in chapter 12, Hong Lu and I first turn to two more high-profile cases in recent years to highlight major problems and challenges of the existing death penalty system in China. Second, we examine significant gaps between China's current practices and international standards. Last, we project future death penalty reforms with a particular emphasis on the legislature and the judiciary and aim for full compliance with international standards.

NOTES

1. For more information on Zhang's case, see Zhang (2008:129) and Y. Chen (1993).
2. See, e.g., a report by the *China's Human Rights Bi-weekly*, retrieved August 29, 2014, from http://shuangzhoukan.hrichina.org/article/554.
3. For studies of the strike-hard campaigns, see Liang (2005); Tanner (1999); and Trevaskes (2002, 2003, 2007).
4. For a full version of the decision, see "Decree on Severely Punishing Criminals Who Threaten Public Security," retrieved July 21, 2015, from http://www.law-lib.com/law/law_view.asp?id=2686 (in Chinese).

5   Some sources online (a minority opinion) indicated that Zhu was convicted of rape, which is normally subject to 3 to 10 years of imprisonment but is possibly subject to harsher punishment (up to the death penalty) if the circumstances of the crime are "extremely severe" (Criminal Law, Article 139). Unfortunately, the official record is not available to ascertain Zhu's convicted offense.
6   See a detailed report in "The Case of Two Wang Brothers," Bbs.tiexue.net, retrieved August 29, 2014, from http://bbs.tiexue.net/post_5192460_1.html.
7   There are many reports on Du's wrongful conviction case. For instance, see a summary retrieved August 25, 2014, from http://wenku.baidu.com/view/4664c6778e9951e79b89271d.html.
8   Sun was charged and convicted of the murder of his girlfriend, Chen Xinghui, in 1996 and was twice sentenced to death by the Zhaotong Intermediate People's Court in Yunnan Province. In 2003, the Yunnan High People's Procuratorate initiated a reinvestigation procedure and petitioned for a retrial on the grounds of insufficient and problematic evidence produced in previous trials. In 2004, the Yunnan High People's Court finally declared Sun's innocence. Sun was awarded 160,000 yuan of state compensation. See a special report by the *People's Daily* (*Renmin ribao*), April 14, 2004.
9   In October 1997, a villager, Zhao Zuohai, got into a fight with another villager, Zhao Zhentang, who went missing afterward. In May 1998, a dead body was found and was believed to be that of the missing Zhao Zhentang. Zhao Zuohai was arrested as the primary suspect, was found guilty of murder by the Shanqiu Intermediate People's Court in Henan Province in December 2002, and was sentenced to death with a two-year suspension. In April 2010, the missing Zhao Zhentang returned alive, and Zhao Zuohai was pronounced innocent in May by the Henan High People's Court. Zhao was awarded 650,000 yuan of state compensation. See "Zhao Zuohai," Baike, retrieved September 5, 2004, from http://www.baike.com/wiki/%E8%B5%B5%E4%BD%9C%E6%B5%B7. See also Lewis (2011).
10 In April 1994, a female body was found and was believed to be that of the missing wife of She Xianglin. She was arrested and convicted of murder and sentenced to death in October 1994. The Hubei High People's Court sent the case back to the trial court for a retrial in 1995 on the grounds of insufficient evidence. In June 1998, She was found guilty again after the retrial and sentenced to 15 years' imprisonment. In March 2005, She's missing wife reappeared alive. She was pronounced innocent in May 2005 and was awarded 700,000 yuan of state compensation. See "Wrongful Conviction of Killing His Wife in Hubei," *Sina News*, retrieved September 5, 2014, from http://news.sina.com.cn/z/hbshaqi/.
11 For a more detailed discussion of Dong's case, see Lu and Miethe (2007:100–103).
12 See, e.g., reports by the *Chinese Business Daily* (*Huashang bao*) (September 6, 2002), and the *Nanfang Daily* (*Nanfang dushi bao*) (September 8, 2002).
13 For the full regulation, see the *Legal Daily* (*Fazhi ribao*) (December 25, 2008).
14 See a report in the *Guangming Daily* (*Guangming ribao*) (May 29, 2014).
15 See reports in the *Chengdu Business Daily* (*Chengdu shangbao*) (July 17, 2013).

16 See discussion in "What's Wrong with the Execution of Zeng Chengja," jcrb.com, retrieved September 12, 2014, from http://thinklaw.fyfz.cn/b/759441 and Liu (2013:249–252).
17 Figures reported by Amnesty International, retrieved September 7, 2014, from http://www.amnesty.org/en/death-penalty/numbers.
18 See data collected and reported by Amnesty International, retrieved September 7, 2014, from http://www.amnesty.org/en/death-penalty/executions-of-child-offenders-since-1990.
19 This hearing was widely reported by the media. See, e.g., "The Supreme People's Court First Retrial of the Death Penalty Case: Experts Say It Is Improvement of the Legal System," *Xinhua News*, retrieved September 7, 2014, from http://news.xinhuanet.com/legal/2013-06/19/c_116209617.htm.
20 See reports in the *Legal Daily* (July 2, 2013) and the *People's Daily* (July 3, 2013).
21 It was reported that by the end of 2010, 57 people had been sentenced to the death penalty in Chongqing (*Chongqing Morning Post [Chongqing chenbao]*, January 21, 2014). For notorious cases in which criminal defense lawyers were penalized for their criminal defense work on behalf of their clients, see Congressional-Executive Commission on China (2003); and Li (2010).
22 "The Voluntary Nature of Organ Donation by Executed Offenders." *Sina News*. Retrieved September 7, 2014, from http://news.sina.com.cn/c/2006-04-10/11589579328.shtml.
23 News reported in the *Beijing News* (*Xinjing bao*) (March 26, 2012).

REFERENCES

Amnesty International. (1997). Annual report on China. Retrieved from http://www.amnesty.org.

Amnesty International. (2013). Death sentences and executions 2013. Retrieved from http://www.amnestyusa.org/research/reports/death-sentences-and-executions-2013?page=2.

Baard, E., & Cooney, R. (2001, May 1). China's Execution, Inc.: The People's Republic has long been suspected of selling organs from prisoners. *Village Voice*. Retrieved from http://www.villagevoice.com/2001-05-01/news/china-s-execution-inc/full/.

Bakken, B. (Ed.). (2005). *Crime, Punishment, and Policing in China*. Lanham, MD: Rowman & Littlefield.

Brook, T., Bourgon, J., & Blue, G. (2008). *Death by a Thousand Cuts*. Cambridge, MA: Harvard University Press.

Cao, L., Sun, I., & Hebenton, B. (2014). *The Routledge Handbook of Chinese Criminology*. New York: Routledge.

Chen, W., & Spronken, T. (Eds.). (2012). *Three Approaches to Combating Torture in China*. Antwerp, Belgium: Intersentia.

Chen, X. (2006). Destiny of the death penalty in China in the contemporary era. *Frontier Law China, 1,* 53–71.

Chen, Y. (1993). *Yifen xue xie de baogao* [A Report Written in Blood]. Shenzhen: Haitian Publishing House.

Congressional-Executive Commission on China. (2003). Defense lawyers turned defendants: Zhang Jianzhong and the criminal prosecution of defense lawyers in China. Retrieved from http://www.cecc.gov/publications/issue-papers/defense-lawyers-turned-defendants-zhang-jianzhong-and-the-criminal.

Gittings, J. (2001, May 22). Guilty—And you have 15 minutes to live. *Guardian.* Retrieved from http://www.theguardian.com/world/2001/may/22/china.johngittings.

Hood, R., & Hoyle, C. (2008). *The Death Penalty: A Worldwide Perspective* (4th ed.). New York: Oxford University Press.

Jiang, N. (2013). A comparison of wrongful convictions in death penalty cases between China and the United States. *International Journal of Law, Crime and Justice, 41*(2), 144–166.

Johnson, D. T., & Zimring, F. E. (2009). *The Next Frontier: National Development, Political Change, and the Death Penalty in Asia.* New York: Oxford University Press.

Lewis, M. K. (2011). Controlling abuse to maintain control: The exclusionary rule in China. *NYU Journal of International Law and Politics, 43,* 629–697.

Li, E. (2010). The Li Zhuang case: Examining the challenges facing criminal defense lawyers in China. *Columbia Journal of Asian Law, 24*(1), 129–169.

Liang, B. (2005). Severe strike campaign in transitional China. *Journal of Criminal Justice, 33,* 387–399.

Liu, R. (2013). *Sixing de quanqiu shiye* [A global vision of the death penalty and the Chinese context]. Zhongguo shehui kexue chubanshe [China Social Science].

Lu, H., & Miethe, T. (2007). *China's Death Penalty: History, Law, and Contemporary Practices.* New York: Routledge.

Lubman, S. (2014, July 10). Power shift: Hopeful signs in China's legal reform plan. *China Real Time.* Retrieved from http://blogs.wsj.com/chinarealtime/2014/07/10/power-shift-hopeful-signs-in-chinas-legal-reform-plan/.

Miao, M. (2013). The politics of China's death penalty reform in the context of global abolitionism. *British Journal of Criminology, 53*(3), 500–519.

Owen, A. K. (1995). Death row inmates or organ donors: China's source of body organs for medical transplantation. *Indiana International and Comparative Law Review*, *5*(2), 495–517.

Sarat, A., & Boulanger, C. (Eds.). (2005). *The Cultural Lives of Capital Punishment: Comparative Perspectives*. Stanford, CA: Stanford University Press.

Tanner, H. (1999). *Strike Hard!: Anti-crime Campaigns and Chinese Criminal Justice 1979–1989*. New York: East Asian Program, Cornell University.

Trevaskes, S. (2002). Courts on the campaign path in China: Criminal court work in China's "Yanda 2001" anti-crime campaign. *Asian Survey*, *42*(5), 673–693.

Trevaskes, S. (2003). Yanda 2001: Form and strategy in a Chinese anti-crime campaign. *Australian and New Zealand Journal of Criminology*, *36*, 272–292.

Trevaskes, S. (2007). Severe and swift justice in China. *British Journal of Criminology*, *47*, 23–41.

Trevaskes S. (2012). *The Death Penalty in Contemporary China*. New York: Palgrave Macmillan.

Yu, Z. (2009). Abolition or retention: Rethinking the death penalty in China. *Social Sciences in China*, *30*(2), 178–190.

Zhang, N. (2008). The political origins of death penalty exceptionalism: Mao Zedong and the practice of capital punishment in contemporary China. *Punishment and Society*, *10*, 117–136.

2

The Criminal Justice System and the Death Penalty

▸ HONG LU, YUDU LI, *and* CHARLOTTE HU

THIS CHAPTER PROVIDES AN OVERVIEW of the substantive and procedural laws regarding the death penalty in China. It starts with a description of death-eligible offenses stipulated in the revised 2011 Criminal Law (CL) and various judicial sentencing guidelines for death penalty cases. It then describes the general criminal procedure and highlights the particular procedural provisions for death penalty cases in the revised 2012 Criminal Procedure Law (CPL). Last, the chapter uses a recent death penalty case to illustrate how death penalty laws are translated into practice.

CRIME AND PUNISHMENT IN THE CRIMINAL LAW

After the establishment of the People's Republic of China (PRC) in 1949, there was no CL until 1979, when China was at the dawn of embarking on economic reforms. Since then, the CL has been revised in 1997 and subsequently amended eight times (December 25, 1999; August 31, 2001; December 29, 2001; December 28, 2002; February 28, 2005; June 29, 2006; February 28, 2009; and February 25, 2011).[1] All major crimes and punishments are stipulated in this legal document.

Crime Rates by Type and Over Time

The *Law Yearbook of China* publishes the main official crime data in China, including crimes such as murder, rape, robbery, and assault.[2] This makes it possible to assess the overall crime pattern over time and by category. As

TABLE 2.1 Criminal Cases Filed by the Police 1981–2012

YEAR	MURDER	ASSAULT	ROBBERY	RAPE	THEFT	TOTAL	CRIME RATE (PER 10,000)
2012	11,286	163,620	180,159	33,835	4,284,670	6,551,440	484
2011	12,013	165,098	202,647	33,336	4,259,428	6,005,037	446
2010	13,410	174,990	237,258	33,696	4,228,369	5,969,892	445
2005	20,770	155,056	332,196	33,710	3,158,763	4,648,401	356
2000	28,429	120,778	309,818	35,819	2,373,696	3,637,307	287
1995	27,356	72,259	164,478	41,823	1,132,789	1,690,407	140
1990	21,214	45,200	82,361	47,782	1,860,793	2,216,997	201
1985	10,440	15,586	8,801	37,712	431,323	542,005	52
1981	9,576	21,499	22,266	30,808	744,374	890,281	89

Source: Law Yearbook of China (1987–2013).

table 2.1 shows, the overall crime rate was 89 per 10,000 people in 1981 and increased to 484 per 10,000 people in 2012—a more than fivefold increase in 32 years (*Law Yearbook of China,* 1987–2013). This was primarily due to the economic reforms that transformed China from a state-planned economy to a market economy, and the accompanying social changes, which included increases in crime.

The impact of the economic reforms on crime is not evenly distributed among different crime types. While violent crimes increased gradually (e.g., the murder rate increased by 18%), property and economic crime types grew exponentially (e.g., theft increased 476%) during the same period (see table 2.1).

Conviction and Sentencing

Table 2.2 shows the total number of defendants processed and convicted by year and by the three sentence types. As shown in table 2.2, from 2002 to 2011, the total number of defendants processed by the courts increased from 706,707 to 1,051,638, a nearly 49% increase in 10 years. However, those who were sentenced to more than five years of imprisonment, life imprisonment,

TABLE 2.2 Criminal Cases Tried at First Instance and Defendants Convicted

YEAR	TOTAL NUMBER OF CASES TRIED AT FIRST INSTANCE	TOTAL NUMBER OF DEFENDANTS TRIED	CONVICTED (%)	SENTENCED TO FIVE YEARS OR MORE OR DEATH SENTENCE (%)	SENTENCED TO FIXED-TERM IMPRISONMENT UNDER FIVE YEARS (%)	SENTENCED TO CUSTODY AND PROBATION (%)
2002	628,549	706,707	99.6	22.7	48.9	28.4
2003	634,953	747,096	99.6	21.4	48.2	30.4
2004	644,248	767,951	99.9	19.1	47.4	33.5
2005	683,997	844,717	99.9	17.9	46.9	35.2
2006	701,379	890,755	99.9	17.2	46.1	36.7
2007	720,666	933,156	99.9	16.2	46.2	37.6
2008	768,130	1,008,677	99.9	15.8	46.0	38.2
2009	766,746	997,872	99.9	16.3	46.1	37.6
2010	779,641	1,007,419	99.9	15.8	45.9	38.3
2011	839,973	1,051,638	99.9	14.2	43.8	42.0

Note: Because the *Law Yearbook of China* started to report criminal sentences by categories in 2002, table 2.2 contains data only from 2002 to 2011. However, to provide a reference point, the total number of criminal cases tried at first instance was 298,291 in 1986, when the *Law Yearbook of China* first published systematic national crime data in China. In 1995, the number increased to 496,082.

or the death penalty decreased from 160,422 in 2002 to 147,230 in 2011. Similar patterns of steady decline occurred among those who were sentenced to a fixed criminal sentence of less than five years. In contrast, the proportion of those who were given a light sentence, such as custody and probation, showed a consistent increase over the same time period, from 28.4% in 2002 to 42% in 2011.

The data, however, do not make it easier to assess the pattern of death penalty sentences. This is because a wide range of sentence categories were collapsed into one (e.g., more than five years of imprisonment, life imprisonment, or a death sentence in the same category), and the number of death penalty cases was extremely small in comparison with other types of sentences in the same category (e.g., life sentences or fixed sentences of more than five years).

Offenses and Offenders Eligible for the Death Penalty

The current CL makes a total of 55 offenses eligible for the death penalty in China. These offenses range from violent crimes, such as murder and robbery, to nonviolent, nonlethal crimes, such as theft and bribe taking. As table 2.3 shows, the number of death-eligible crimes is not evenly distributed among the crime categories. For example, while the crime category of violating the duties of military servicemen has 12 such crimes, the category of encroaching on property has only 1 death-eligible offense.

TABLE 2.3 THE CURRENT 55 DEATH-ELIGIBLE OFFENSES

Crimes endangering national security (7 death-eligible offenses)

1. Plotting to jeopardize the sovereignty, territorial integrity, and security of the country
2. Instigating to split the country
3. Organizing, plotting, or carrying out armed rebellions or armed riots
4. Organizing, plotting, or acting to subvert the political power of the state
5. Espionage
6. Stealing, secretly gathering, purchasing by bribery, or illegally providing national secrets or intelligence to foreign institutions
7. Providing the enemy with armed equipment or military materials

Crimes endangering public security (14 death-eligible offenses)

8. Arson
9. Breaching dikes
10. Causing explosions
11. Poisoning
12. Threatening public security with dangerous methods
13. Sabotaging transportation instruments
14. Sabotaging transportation infrastructures
15. Sabotaging electric power
16. Sabotaging inflammable or explosive facilities
17. Hijacking an aircraft
18. Illegally manufacturing, trading, transporting, and mailing guns, ammunition, or explosives
19. Illegally trading or transporting nuclear materials
20. Stealing guns, ammunition, or explosive materials
21. Forcibly seizing guns, ammunition, or explosive materials

Crimes undermining the socialist market economic order (7 death-eligible offenses)

22. Producing or distributing bogus medicines
23. Producing or distributing poisonous or harmful foods
24. Smuggling weapons and ammunition
25. Smuggling nuclear materials
26. Smuggling counterfeit currencies
27. Counterfeiting currency
28. Financial frauds

Crimes infringing on the rights of people and their democratic rights (5 death-eligible offenses)

29. Murder
30. Rape
31. Statutory rape
32. Kidnapping
33. Abducting women and children

Crimes encroaching on property (1 death-eligible offense)

34. Robbery

Crimes disrupting the order of social administration (4 death-eligible offenses)

35. Organizing a jail break
36. Prison riots using weapons

37. Smuggling, trafficking, transporting, or manufacturing narcotics
38. Organizing other people to engage in prostitution
39. Forcing another person into prostitution

Crimes endangering the national defense interest (2 death-eligible offenses)

40. Sabotaging military weapons, military installations, or military communications
41. Knowingly providing unqualified weapons or military installations to the armed forces

Crimes of graft and bribery (2 death-eligible offenses)

42. Graft
43. Bribe taking

Crimes of violating duties of military servicemen (12 death-eligible offenses)

44. Refusing to carry out an order in wartime
45. Deliberately concealing military intelligence, furnishing falsified intelligence
46. Refusing to disseminate military orders or falsely disseminating military orders
47. Surrendering to the enemy
48. Deserting on the eve of a battle
49. Obstructing commanding officers or on-duty servicemen from carrying out their duties
50. Defecting to a foreign country
51. Illegally obtaining military secrets
52. Fabricating rumors to mislead people during wartime
53. Stealing or robbing weapons or military materials
54. Unlawfully selling or transferring military weaponry
55. Injuring or killing innocent residents or looting property from innocent residents during wartime

Source: The 2011 Criminal Law, http://wenku.baidu.com/link?url=l-XDaKSeK1jYNLuPgEZAQvY 3DwGKRIkMIgd4BrWhhwEOMpuBBUwazkEjMwQ6TREYpupfP9pNZh5K2bv45i4hPsZ5m0J 1BiEUg5XPf9K-pIu (retrieved August 2014).

In addition, not all individuals who commit death-eligible offenses may be subject to the death penalty. The current CL excludes three types of defendants: (1) minors under 18 years of age at the time of crime commission; (2) criminal defendants 75 years of age or older unless they used especially cruel methods; and (3) female defendants who are pregnant at the time of the sentence (Article 49).

Estimates of Death Sentences and Executions

Previous studies of China's death penalty have cited various sources to estimate the number of death sentences and executions over time. Table 2.4 presents estimates based on sources such as Amnesty International (1980–2008), Death Penalty Worldwide (2009–2013), and Teng and Liang (2012).

As table 2.4 reveals, the number of death sentences and executions fluctuated greatly over the 33 years, exhibiting no clear upward or downward trends. Perhaps the only exceptions were the estimates provided by the Dui Hua Foundation (e.g., starting from 2002, the number of executions steadily declined each year from the initial 12,000 executions in 2002 to 3,000 executions in 2013) and by Death Penalty Worldwide (e.g., its estimate of the number of executions decreased from 5,000 in 2009 to 3,000 in 2013).

Sentencing Guidelines for Death Penalty Cases

Besides reducing the scope of death-eligible offenses in the CL, recent reform initiatives also have attempted to standardize and reduce punishments and make them proportionate to the crime, including death-eligible cases. For example, a 1999 decree issued by the Supreme People's Court (SPC), Stabilizing Criminal Trials in Rural Areas for Courts at All Levels, required that homicides caused by marriage, neighbor, or family disputes be viewed differently from cold-blooded murders that pose serious public safety threats. In particular, if the victim was found at fault or had aggravated the circumstances, or if mitigating factors were present, the death penalty with immediate execution should not be meted out (Martinez, Vertino, & Lu 2014).

The Guiding Opinions on Sentencing for the People's Courts implemented in 2012 attempted to reduce judges' discretion and make punishment proportionate to the crime (Wang & Liu 2012). Even though this document is not specifically designed to address death sentences, it helps judges put criminal sentencing in context by prescribing a baseline and a formula for factoring in relevant aggravating or mitigating factors. For example, the baseline for rape is 3 to 5 years of imprisonment; for rape involving especially grave circumstances, such as raping a minor, public rape, and gang rape, the baseline is raised to 10 to 12 years of imprisonment. From there,

TABLE 2.4 Estimated Number of Death Sentences and Executions 1980–2013

YEAR	NUMBER OF DEATH SENTENCES	NUMBER OF EXECUTIONS
2013	—	2,400[a]/3,000[b]
2012	—	3,000[b]/3,000[c]
2011	—	4,000[b]/4,000[c]
2010	—	5,000[b]/5,000[a]
2009	—	5,000[b]/5,000[a]
2008	7,003	1,718/5,000[a]
2007	1,860	470/6,500[a]
2006	7,500–8,000	2,010[c]/7,000[a]
2005	5,186	2,148/8,000[a]
2004	7,395	3,797/10,000[a]
2003	2,756	1,146/10,000[a]
2002	3,248	1,526/12,000[a]
2001	5,265	3,048
2000	3,058	1,457
1999	3,857	1,813
1998	3,899	2,258
1997	3,707	2,607
1996	7,101	4,272
1995	4,165	3,276
1994	4,032	2,331

the judge can calculate the final sentence by taking additional aggravating or mitigating factors into account.[3] Therefore, even though rape is subject to the death penalty in China's CL (Article 236), a judge shall not sentence a rapist to death unless the crime involves extreme circumstances. The extreme circumstances that deserve the death penalty seem to be changing over time and certainly need to be tested in judicial practice (e.g., see the Tang Hui case in chapter 12).

Within this context, the guiding case system recently set up by the SPC and the Supreme People's Procuratorate (SPP) is particularly useful. Through cases, abstract terms can be clarified or quantified (for a detailed description of the guiding case system, see chapter 7).

YEAR	NUMBER OF DEATH SENTENCES	NUMBER OF EXECUTIONS
1993	3,760	1,831
1992	2,697	1,708
1991	2,703	2,086
1990	2,005	2,029
1989	2,826	2,229
1988	1,240	1,903
1987	1,185	796
1986	1,272	743
1985	1,435	1,125
1984	2,068	1,513
1983	1,160	1,399
1982	1,435	1,609
1981	3,209	3,278
1980	1,295	1,229

[a] Dui Hua Foundation, http://duihua.org/wp/?page_id=136 and http://duihua.org/wp/?page_id=9270.
[b] Death Penalty Worldwide, http://www.deathpenaltyworldwide.org/country-search-post.cfm?country=China.
[c] China Against the Death Penalty (2012).
Source: All data are from Amnesty International unless otherwise noted.

CRIMINAL PROCEDURE ON THE DEATH PENALTY

The PRC did not have a criminal procedure law until 1979. The law passed in that year was substantially revised in 1996 with added safeguards for defendants' rights. On March 14, 2012, the CPL was amended again. The discussion of the general criminal procedure in this chapter follows the 2012 CPL.[4] We will first describe the general process of a death penalty case, with statutory time limits for major decisions at each stage. We will then specifically describe levels of jurisdiction, criminal investigation by police, procuratorate charging and supervision, defense rights, trials, special procedures for death penalty cases, and the postsentencing phase.

Generally speaking, a death penalty case is processed similarly to other major criminal cases in the Chinese criminal justice system, with a few exceptions (e.g., mandatory legal representation and the final review and approval phase). The typical process for a death penalty case involves the following phases: custody, arrest, charging, trial of first instance, trial of second instance (appellate review), the final review and approval process, and the posttrial phase, including execution. We will describe the procedural requirements and safeguards for the rights of the accused in each of these major phases.

Levels and Divisions of Jurisdiction

Before we turn to the specifics regarding criminal procedure, it is important to note the division of power among the three players in the criminal justice system and jurisdictional issues regarding various types of cases, including death penalty cases.

Article 3 of the 2012 CPL states: "The public security organs are responsible for the investigation, detention, performing arrests, and preliminary inquiry. The people's procuratorates are responsible for reviewing, approving arrest, investigating cases directly accepted by the procuratorates, and initiating public prosecutions. The people's courts are responsible for trials. Unless the law specially provides, other organs, groups, or individuals have no right to perform these powers."

This stipulation is important, given the longtime nonseparation of executive and judicial power and the intertwined roles and functions of the police, procuratorates, and courts in China. For example, China's courts had long assumed the function of conducting criminal investigations. The 2012 CPL clearly states that the court's responsibility is to try the case, suggesting a shift toward a clearer separation of power and role.

The clearer division of labor presumably makes each institution accountable for its own decisions. This is crucial, particularly for death penalty cases. For example, an error made by police during the criminal investigation stage would be more likely to be detected and corrected by the court under the current system of the separation of power since there would be less institutional or personal attachment to the erroneous decision.

The Chinese court system has three provincial levels: basic, intermediate, and high courts. At the national level, there is the SPC. Chinese courts follow a two-tiered trial system. The basic court has jurisdiction over the first-instance trial of ordinary cases. The intermediate court has jurisdiction over the second-instance trial and review. The ruling of the court of second-instance trial and review is typically final.

Death penalty crimes and some other types of major noncapital crimes (e.g., cases of endangering national security or terrorist activity) are handled differently. Intermediate courts have jurisdiction over the first-instance trial of these major cases, whereas the provincial high court has jurisdiction over the second-instance trial and review (Article 20). For cases resulting in a death sentence with immediate execution, the final review and approval authority rests with the SPC.

Criminal Investigation by Police

The Chinese police force is highly centralized, with a clear chain of command from the central government to the provincial and local governments. Restructuring of the Chinese criminal justice system has occurred to correct imbalanced authority tilted heavily in favor of the police, the prosecutor, and the court by instituting a relatively more balanced authority shared between the state (represented by the police, the prosecutor, and the court) and the defendant (represented by his or her defense lawyers). However, police in China remain very powerful social control agents (Dai 2008). Two of the main responsibilities of the Chinese police are criminal investigation and apprehension.

In handling criminal cases, the police are subject to relevant clauses in the CPL in regard to interrogation and searches and seizures. The 2012 CPL made several improvements in these areas to ensure fairer and more transparent handling of criminal cases in the beginning stages of the criminal justice process.

The 2012 CPL stipulates the following requirements on issues of police custody:

- Summons and custodial summons shall not exceed 12 hours; in complicated cases, when custody and arrest are needed, summons and custodial summons may not exceed 24 hours (Article 117).
- The person shall be delivered to the detention center within 24 hours (Article 83).

- Family members must be contacted within 24 hours (Article 83).
- A criminal suspect shall not be put under residential surveillance for more than 6 months (Article 77).
- A criminal suspect shall not be placed on bail for more than 12 months (Article 77).
- Interrogation shall be done by at least two interrogators (Article 116).
- The first interrogation shall be done within 24 hours while the individual is in custody (Article 84).
- Police shall submit an arrest request to the procuratorate within 3 days of custody; an extension may be granted (for up to 34 days) for major crimes (Article 89).
- The procuratorate shall issue a decision on whether to approve an arrest within 7 days (Article 89).

The law stipulates the following legal requirements for an arrest:

- Police shall deliver the suspect to the detention center, notify family members, and interrogate the suspect within 24 hours of an arrest (Articles 91 and 92).
- The procuratorate shall investigate the necessity of an arrest of a suspect or defendant and shall suggest release or change of the coercive measure when an arrest is deemed unnecessary. The respective organ shall inform the procuratorate of its response within 10 days (Article 93).
- Interrogators shall first ask whether the criminal suspect has committed the crime, allow the suspect to describe criminal circumstances or explain that there is no crime, and then ask questions; the criminal suspect shall answer the questions truthfully but shall have the right to refuse to answer questions unrelated to the crime (Article 118).
- The suspect shall be informed of the leniency policy for truthfully describing his or her own criminal activities (Article 118).
- For suspects who might be sentenced to life in prison or death, or in other major criminal cases, an audio or video recording of the entire session shall be made (Article 121).
- A search warrant must be presented to the subject of the search, except in an emergency (Article 136); however, the search warrant is issued by the police (if the search is to be made by the police) or the procuratorate (if the search is to be made by the procuratorate), not by the court.

- An arrest must be approved by the procuratorate or the court and must be carried out by the police (Article 78).
- Postarrest investigative detention of suspects shall not exceed two months; in special circumstances, an incremental extension of one month, two months, or unlimited extension may be requested (Articles 154, 155, and 156).

Two observations can be made about this summary of the investigative stage of the criminal justice process. First, law enforcement and procuratorate agencies responsible for criminal investigation remain powerful in China. These agencies share, if not exclusively possess (e.g., military and prison police forces have the authority to approve a search or arrest warrant within their jurisdictions), the power of approving a search or arrest warrant. The lack of supervision by a relatively independent third party on important decisions, such as examining and issuing an arrest or search warrant, puts the suspect in a disadvantageous position early in the criminal justice process. This early investigative phase is the most critical phase in the entire criminal justice process because once a person is charged with a crime, a conviction is almost guaranteed in China. Despite the fact that defense lawyers now have the right to be present during the first interrogation session, which may minimize potential abuse of state power and provide the suspect the needed support, whether and to what extent suspects understand this new right and actually use it remains questionable.[5] Nevertheless, the 2012 CPL provides an important safeguard for individuals' rights in this beginning phase by shortening and specifying the time it requires for custody and arrest decisions.

The second observation concerns confession evidence. There are several developments regarding confession in the 2012 CPL. The first deals with the self-incrimination clause. The current law makes it clear that no one shall be coerced to incriminate oneself in a crime. For example, Article 50 stipulates that extortion of confessions by torture and other illegal evidence-gathering methods, such as enticement and trickery, is strictly prohibited; no person may be forced to prove his or her own guilt. However, this does not mean that criminal suspects or defendants have the right to remain silent. For example, Article 118 further states that suspects shall truthfully answer investigators' questions and shall be informed of the leniency policy for truthfully describing their own offense. In addition, other parts of the law, such as Article 170, stipulate that when investigating the case, the procuratorate shall interrogate the criminal suspect, and Article 186 states that the judge may interrogate the defendant during a trial. In these areas, the law does not specify whether suspects or defendants are required to answer their questions or what the legal consequence will be if they refuse to answer or do not answer truthfully. Thus, although the law makes one step forward by recognizing the importance of preventing forced self-incrimination, it does not provide an operable way for suspects or defendants to avoid violating the law while protecting their own rights. This is particularly important in death penalty cases because offenders could potentially put themselves in grave danger by truthfully answering the interrogators' questions. Thus, unless offenders can be persuaded otherwise (e.g., leniency in exchange for a truthful confession), a truthful and voluntary confession is unlikely to occur, at least under rational choice theory.

The second aspect regarding confession evidence is the requirement of complete, unedited audio or video recording of suspect interrogations for those who face serious penalties, such as the death sentence or life imprisonment (2012 CPL, Article 121). The impetus for adopting this change in the law was the traditional emphasis of the Chinese police on obtaining a confession from a criminal suspect, no matter the cost, to clear a case. This new stipulation represents an important development in the Chinese CPL. With strict enforcement of this rule along with other evidentiary requirements (e.g., the exclusionary rule), the potential abuse of power by the investigative agencies could be curbed.

In addition, the 2012 CPL further stipulates in Article 53 that a guilty verdict may be reached on the basis of credible and sufficient evidence even if there is no confession from the defendant; in contrast, a guilty verdict may not be reached if there is only confession evidence. In this regard, the law provides incentives for good police work by emphasizing investigation and research rather than exclusive reliance on confession.

Taken as a whole, the 2012 CPL represents one of the boldest legal reforms with regard to protecting the criminal suspect or defendant's rights during the precharging phase. Although scholars of both China and the West have warned that there is a major discrepancy between the law in books and the law in practice (Clarke & Feinerman 1995), there are hopeful signs that the police investigative power may be curbed to the extent that corruption and abuse of power will be less evident in major crimes, particularly in death penalty cases.

Charging and Supervision by the Procuratorate

As in other countries, the procuratorate in China is primarily responsible for deciding whether to charge a suspect and for indicting the defendant before the respective court for a trial. Whether or not a defendant receives a death sentence largely depends on the severity of the crime and related circumstances. Regarding the procedural requirements of charging, the 2012 CPL stipulates that the procuratorate shall make the charging decision within a month of receiving a case from the police; in special circumstances, it may request a half-month extension (Article 169). The police may also request up to one month to conduct a supplemental investigation. A maximum of two supplemental investigations may be requested (Article 171).

In addition to having the authority to bring a criminal charge against a defendant, the procuratorate plays a supervisory role for the police. For example, the procuratorate approves arrest and search warrants and continuously reviews the necessity of an arrest (Article 93). The procuratorate also plays a supervisory and advisory role for the court, especially in death penalty cases, because the SPP may advise the SPC during the final review and approval process of a death penalty case.

Moreover, the procuratorate has the separate responsibility of conducting criminal investigations of offenses committed by government officials and agencies, including crimes of embezzlement and bribery (both are death-eligible offenses), violations of a citizen's personal rights (e.g., illegal detention), extortion of confessions by torture, and illegal searches and seizures (CPL, Article 18). This unique organizational structure allows the procuratorate, not the police, to investigate party members and governmental functionaries.

Overall, the procuratorate is an extremely powerful agency, with the authority to initiate criminal investigation of government officials, review criminal cases, supervise public security organs, and advise the court. In addition, its decision to charge a criminal defendant literally convicts him or her because the conviction rate has been nearly 100% in China throughout the past 20 years, as reported in the *Law Yearbook of China*.

Although the 2012 CPL has made several improvements (e.g., earlier intervention of defense lawyers and setting time limits on various decisions, such as custody, arrest, and charging decisions), it does not establish sufficient mechanisms to curb potential abuses of power. For instance, it does not authorize the court to review search or arrest warrant requests or specify the conditions under which a search or arrest warrant shall be issued. In addition, even though the procuratorate is accountable to the Standing Committee of the National People's Congress (SCNPC) in law, because of the limited supervisory capacity and sanctioning power of the SCNPC, the procuratorate's power is rarely checked in practice (Chen 2006). Because of the unique fact-finding process in China, it is assumed that the facts of cases have already been ascertained once they reach the court (Fu 1998). For example, the standards for initiating public prosecution are that the facts of a criminal suspect's crime have been ascertained, that the evidence is reliable and sufficient, and that criminal responsibility should be investigated according to law. This pretrial-investigation-focused criminal justice system restricts the courts' role in supervising the investigative behaviors of police and the procuratorate. Even though the newly amended CPL allows judges to ban evidence gathered through illegal means, the courts' supervisory power over the unlawful and deleterious investigative activities of police and prosecutors remains limited. What courts can do is restricted to "the scrutiny of law and facts on the record prepared by the police and procurators" (Fu 1998:41).

Defense Rights

The 2012 CPL made some important improvements with regard to defense rights. First, under the 2012 CPL, criminal suspects can now retain defense counsel. This is crucial, given that most evidence is collected during initial police interrogations and the criminal proceeding's precharging stage. In addition, the 2012 CPL expanded the scope of state-appointed defense counsel beyond capital cases to include cases involving the possibility of a life sentence. This suggests an enhanced role of criminal defense in the criminal justice process. Moreover, the law requires the prompt arrangement of attorney-client meetings within 48 hours of defense lawyers' requests (Article 37), and surveillance of these meetings is not permitted.

Second, the 2012 CPL was the first to add the attorney-client privilege (Article 46). However, defense lawyers are required to report immediately to judicial organs on the planned or ongoing criminal activities of their clients. To further ensure that defense counsel can perform their duties without obstructions from the three agencies of the criminal justice system, the law affords defense counsel the right to appeal or protest to the procuratorate or the procuratorate at the higher level, should their duties be hindered (Article 47).

This dramatic legislative move can be traced back to the 1996 CPL. To change the longtime police practice of obtaining convictions based on suspects' confessions, the 1996 CPL made it clear that without the corroboration of other forensic evidence, statements from suspects alone cannot result in a conviction. In June 2010, two rules were established that formed the basis for the 2012 stipulation: Rules on Certain Issues Concerning Examination and Judgment of Evidence in Death Penalty Cases and Rules on Certain Issues Concerning the Exclusion of Illegal Evidence in Criminal Cases. Their purpose was to restrict evidence used in criminal cases by excluding illegally obtained evidence, specifically confessions extracted through torture and testimony of questionable origin, especially in death penalty cases (Martinez, Vertino, & Lu 2014).

Overall, in death penalty cases, the 2012 CPL provides much earlier, broader and more professional legal representation to criminal suspects and defendants, even though defense lawyers' new rights and authorities remain subordinate to national security and public safety concerns and are subject to supervision and approval of the investigating agencies (e.g., the police and the procuratorate). In addition, defense lawyers are subject to disbarment and criminal penalties if they engage in professional misconduct or conduct outlawed by the Criminal Law (e.g., fabrication of evidence).[6] Nevertheless, these new stipulations provide additional procedural safeguards for the accused.

Trials of First and Second Instance

Most death penalty cases are first tried in the intermediate court and then in the high court at the provincial level and last are reviewed and approved by the SPC. The following is a summary of key new stipulations regarding the trial of first instance for death penalty cases in related CPL articles.

- The trial is presided over by a collegial panel of three adjudicators (Article 178).
- When a case is complicated (e.g., a death penalty case), the collegial panel may request that the president of the court make a decision to ask the adjudicative committee to discuss and make a judicial ruling (Article 180).

- All trials must be public unless state or commercial secrets or personal privacy issues are announced and explained in the court (Article 183).
- During the opening statement, the court should inform the defendant of his or her right to defense counsel (Article 185).
- The procuratorate may interrogate the defendant; victim and defense lawyers, upon the approval of the court, may ask the defendant questions; the adjudicator may interrogate the defendant (Article 186).
- When deemed necessary by the court, expert witnesses must appear for validation of their evaluation results in court (Article 187).
- Witnesses may be forced to appear in court, except the defendant's spouse, parents, or children (Article 188).
- The defendant has the right to make the final statement (Article 193).
- The court shall rule on the basis of the totality of circumstances and proof beyond reasonable doubt (Article 53).
- Available verdicts include guilty or not guilty (Article 195).
- The trial shall conclude in two months (Article 202) (in the 1996 CPL, it was one month); in complicated cases, extensions can be made incrementally for three months (a maximum of two times) or upon the approval of the SPC (Article 202).
- The defendant may appeal and the procuratorate may protest the decision within 10 days of the sentencing ruling (Articles 217 and 219).

Three conclusions can be drawn from this summary of the court proceedings. First, even though the current CPL strengthens the defendant's right to confront his or her accusers by requiring crucial and disputed witnesses to appear in court, not all witnesses are required to appear in court for cross-examination. Documents and written testimony are permitted in Chinese courts. This may deprive the defense of the opportunity to cross-examine witnesses.

Second, the procuratorate and the judge may question the defendant; thus, the defendant does not have the right to remain silent. In the United States, being compelled to testify during an investigation or in court about one's own crime is regarded as a violation of constitutional rights. These constitutional protections are based on the presumption of innocence and the right to due process. However, under the civil law system in China, the primary function of the crime-control model is truth finding and crime prevention. Under this framework, defendants do not enjoy the (special) right to remain silent. Instead, they are expected to cooperate with law enforcement agencies to help solve the crime, just like other witnesses.

Third, the adjudicative body that hears the case may not be the one that metes out the sentence. Instead, sentencing decisions can be made by the adjudicative committee, which is chaired by the president of the people's court. The committee does not hold public hearings and only reviews the case on paper. This practice may be particularly disadvantageous to the defense because the defense counsel has little direct access to the committee. In contrast, the procuratorate may have more influence on the case outcome because of its supervisory role over the court. In addition, the adjudicative committee members consist of the court's president and high-ranking officers and judges of the court. Although these members have more trial expertise, they tend also to have closer ties with the Communist Party and are influenced by the local government (e.g., the president is typically nominated by the personnel department of the respective party apparatus and approved by the Standing Committing of the People's Congress in the respective jurisdiction). Thus, the decision on major crimes is inevitably influenced by professional judgment, as well as political factors (X. He 2012).

Nevertheless, the 2012 CPL shows some promising features. For example, it establishes the standard of proof beyond reasonable doubt and extends the trial length from one month to two months, presumably to allow more time for cross-examination and debate among courtroom players. Because the prosecution-dominated trial is replaced by a more balanced representation of both prosecution and defense, defense lawyers no longer have the burden of proof but can concentrate on challenging the prosecution's case.[7]

The trial of second instance (appellate review) for death penalty cases shall be open to the public (Article 223, item 2), and the scope of the investigation shall not be limited to contested areas (Article 222). As for the time requirement, the 2012 CPL stipulates that upon receiving an appeal or protest, the court of second instance shall notify and allow the procuratorate to review the case file within one month (Article 224). The law however, does not specify how long defense lawyers have to review the case file. The second-instance trial shall conclude in two months (Article 232), and an extension may be granted in complicated cases (Article 232). The court can sustain or modify the lower court's ruling or return the case to the original trial court for retrial (Article 225). In addition, procedural violations (e.g., the trial was not made public; violation of the defendant's due process rights) now may constitute grounds for a retrial (Article 227).

As these legal stipulations show, the scope of the second-instance trial is to evaluate all facts and evidence and determine whether the law has been applied appropriately. In reality, as some studies have found, the majority of appeals have been no more than a review of the files and interviews with the relevant parties, and when the appeal courts find errors in the case, most cases are remanded; they are rarely invalidated or dismissed (Qi 2007; Zhou 2006).

Although there has been concern that local protectionism and personal connections in China interfere with adjudication, the second-instance trial court may not fully address this concern, given its proximity in physical location and administrative relationship to the first-instance trial court. However, for death penalty cases, this issue is somewhat addressed by an additional review and approval process conducted by the SPC.

Special Procedures for Death Penalty Cases

To reduce arbitrariness in death penalty decisions, the United States separates the trial and sentencing phases, whereas in China, the last phase involves reaffirmation of the final review and approval authority of the SPC. Articles 235–240 of the CPL contain major requirements for this process:

- The SPC has final review and approval authority for all death sentences with immediate execution; the provincial high court has the final review and approval authority for death sentences with a two-year suspension (Articles 235, 236, and 237).
- The review is automatic (Article 236).
- The review shall be done by a three-person collegial panel (Article 238).
- The SPC shall interrogate the defendant (Article 240).
- If the defense lawyer requests, the SPC shall listen to the opinion of the defense lawyer (Article 240).
- The SPC's decision shall be approval or disapproval of the death sentence; for a disapproved death sentence, the SPC may send the case back to the lower court for retrial or change the sentence (Article 239).

- The SPP may advise the SPC of its opinion. The SPC shall report the result of the review to the SPP (Article 240).

Under the CPL, the final review and approval process is automatically activated regardless of whether the evidence and facts are clear. Since 2007, the SPC has had five criminal courts to review death penalty cases.[8] When it is reviewing death penalty cases, the SPC forms a three-judge collegial panel. The process involves a review of written documents, as well as an interrogation of the defendant. Members of the collegial panel first review the case by going over the case files. If the panel is inclined to agree with the verdict of the lower court, it will interrogate the defendant. If the panel has questions about the case, it will conduct further investigations. During the review, defense attorneys may present defending opinions for their clients.

Because of the nature of the offense and the gravity of the punishment, a death penalty case is likely to attract more attention and controversy than any other criminal sentence. As a result, the SPC's decision is likely to be affected by both internal and external factors, including judicial reform (e.g., the recent reform effort to restrict the use of death sentences for particular types of crimes, such as murder of a family member) and public opinion (e.g., "public indignation" is a commonly cited justification for judicial rulings). The 2008 Party Plan suggesting the removal of the Political Legal Affairs Committee's (part of the Communist Party's apparatus) direct interference in individual judicial cases represents a move toward a more independent judiciary in China (Trevaskes 2011).

One distinctive feature of the SPC's final review is the supervisory role performed by the SPP. This structural feature reflects the crime-control model at its core because the legal system is designed to prevent and control crime. The improved legal protection of individual rights, as stipulated in the 2012 CPL, is primarily intended to improve the fairness and accuracy of the overall justice system so as to reduce conviction errors, rather than to protect defendants' fundamental rights.

In contrast, the role that the defense counsel plays in the SPC's final review and approval decision is not entirely clear. For example, the law is not clear on how the judging panel of the SPC interrogates the defendant—face-to-face, via electronic device, interrogation by a third party, or via written responses. Given that death row inmates require maximum security, and that many are in remote provinces, such as Qinghai or Yunnan, transporting them to Beijing, where the SPC is located, will be not only costly but also risky. Even though the SPC has increasingly relied on video conferences in interrogating death row inmates since the 2000s, it seems that a clear stipulation of the way and the means of interrogation of the defendant during the final review may have a bearing on the final decision. A related issue involves defense lawyers' opinions. It seems crucial how their opinions are passed on to the SPC's judging panel, whether via face-to-face meetings or in writing. The law, however, does not address this issue.

The Postsentencing Phase

After the SPC's final review and approval, if a death sentence with immediate execution is affirmed, the decision is final. The execution must be carried out within seven days (Article 251).

However, during this brief window, an execution may be stopped in two ways. One is through the adjudication supervision procedure (Articles 242–246), under which the case may be retried and execution may be stopped. The other is action by the executioner. If errors in the ruling are detected, or the defendant performed meritorious services, the executioner shall stop the execution procedure and inform the SPC (Article 251).

Although these additional safeguards are reassuring, it may be difficult to challenge the final decision in practice, given the short time between execution order and actual execution and the fact that the execution is ordered by the SPC, which has the highest authority in adjudication. In particular, as an advisory and supervisory authority of the SPC, the SPP is not an independent, third party but a state agency, which makes it even more difficult to have a final death sentence decision overturned.

A DEATH PENALTY CASE AS AN EXAMPLE

A high-profile case, the Nian Bin poisoning case, illustrates some of the key issues involving criminal procedure and legal reforms in China. Defendant Nian was convicted of fatally poisoning two children and was sentenced to death four times in eight years. In 2014, Nian was finally exonerated and set free after serving seven years behind bars on death row. This case has been hailed as setting a new benchmark for judicial reforms in China and is expected to have a long-lasting impact on criminal investigation and sentencing. The following is a summary of the timeline and key events of this case.[9]

On the night of July 27, 2006, two families neighboring Nian (Nian rented a shop selling groceries next to these families) suffered food poisoning after dinner. Six were sent to the hospital, and two of them died. Both were children (10 and 8 years of age). In the early morning of July 28, upon receiving the report of the case, the Pingtan County police searched the crime scene and collected over 150 pieces of evidence but filed only 5 pieces of evidence.[10] On August 7, the police detained Nian for custodial investigation (*juliu shencha*). On August 8, the police issued a custodial summons (*juliu chuanxun*) to Nian. The same afternoon, Nian admitted that he had placed poison in the water pot. On August 9, the police detained Nian, accusing him of lacing the victims' dinner with sodium fluoroacetate, which is used to kill mice, to take vengeance on one of the victims, Mrs. Ding, for stealing business away from his grocery store.

On August 18, the Pingtan County Procuratorate approved an arrest warrant. On October 11, the police transferred the case, labeled as murder, to the county procuratorate. On November 6, the county procuratorate transferred the case to the Fuzhou Municipal Procuratorate but changed the charge to poisoning. The municipal procuratorate returned the case for supplemental investigation once. On January 8, 2007, the county procuratorate transferred the case again to the municipal procuratorate. The chief procurator of the municipal procuratorate extended the normal investigation processing time allowed under law by 15 days. On February 6, the municipal procuratorate indicted Nian and charged him with "placing dangerous materials" (poisoning) (*toufang weixian wupin zui*).

Approximately one year later, on February 1, 2008, the Fuzhou Intermediate Court sentenced Nian to death with immediate execution. Nian appealed. On December 18, the Fujian High Court returned the case for retrial, citing unclear facts and insufficient evidence. On June 8, 2009, the intermediate court sentenced Nian to death a second time with no new evidence. Nian appealed again. On April 7, 2010, the high court sustained the death sentence. The automatic review and approval process by the SPC was activated. On October 28, the SPC did not approve the death sentence, citing unclear facts and insufficient evidence, and sent the case back for retrial. On May 5, 2011, the high court withdrew its ruling and sent the case back to the intermediate court for retrial, again citing unclear facts and insufficient evidence. On September 7, the intermediate court sentenced Nian to death a third time (with the death sentence given by the high court, a total of four times) without new or additional evidence. Nian again appealed. The high court decided to postpone the trial this time, stating that the case was "very complicated" (Boehler 2013).

On August 22, 2014, the high court acquitted Nian of all charges, vacated the death sentence that had hung over him since 2008, and immediately released him. The spokesperson of the Fujian High Court stated that besides Nian's own confession, the evidence used to convict Nian was not sufficient and could not be corroborated (e.g., the method used by Nian to place the poison was not clearly established, and sources of the poison were not clearly identified). The court thus deemed that the standard of proof beyond a reasonable doubt had not been reached on the basis of the totality of the evidence and decided to acquit Nian (Cheng 2014).

Several issues in this case caught the attention of legal practitioners and academics, as well as the general public. The first issue was the confession evidence obtained through torture, because the entire case was built on this evidence. Nian's case was not unique. It is estimated that 95% of wrongful convictions have been due to coerced confession (Cheng 2014) in China in the past three decades. Still, two aspects of the police torture and confession evidence in this case are worth noting. The first was the brutality of the physical and psychological torture. Nian claimed that he had suffered unbearable physical torture and threats by the police. The police beat him by placing books on him and then pounding them with hammers, inserted bamboo slivers between his ribs, and threatened to arrest his wife if he refused to cooperate. He attempted to kill himself by biting into his tongue (although the police acknowledged the suicidal incident, it denied its responsibility for the incident). At the time of Nian's first custodial summons in 2006, the CPL did not require police to inform a criminal suspect of his or her right to an attorney. Thus, it is not difficult to see why an average criminal suspect, without the presence of an attorney and experiencing brutal physical torture and psychological threat, would gave in to police demands. The second aspect involved institutional tolerance of the police abuse. Although Nian's interrogation session in which the confession was made was video recorded, at least an hour of the video footage was missing. The Fujian Public Security Bureau nevertheless certified its authenticity, the Fuzhou

Procuratorate used it as key evidence to charge Nian, and the Fuzhou Intermediate Court and the Fujian High Court (except in the last sentence ruling) both accepted the tape as authentic and rejected Nian's claim of a coerced confession in court (Han 2013). Even after Nian's acquittal, there has been little effort directed at addressing and preventing future similar police abuses.

Second, although numerous factors can lead to abuse by police, one of these factors involves the institutional goal of public security that focuses on solving crimes. For example, during the strike-hard campaigns, police work was guided by slogans such as "Cracking the case by the deadline" (*xianqi po'an*) and "Crimes involving deaths must be cracked" (*ming'an bipo*) (Cheng 2014). In 2004, during a wave of a strike-hard campaign, the Ministry of Public Security issued a directive that all "murder cases must be solved." This order resulted in a dramatic increase in the number of murder cases "solved" in the following year (Cheng 2014). This crime-fighting approach was also exemplified in the Nian case. The Nian case was listed as one of the 10 major criminal cases in Fujian Province in 2006, and it was jointly investigated by the Fuzhou Municipal and County Public Security Offices, with special supervision by the Fujian Provincial Public Security Bureau (Wang 2014). In addition, police departments at all levels use clearance rates, particularly those of major violent crimes, such as murder, robbery, and public explosion, as one critical criterion in awarding promotions and raises. Major personnel involved in "solving" Nian's case were given cash awards and promoted to a higher rank in a public ceremony sponsored by the Pingtan County Party Committee and government on August 23, 2006, right after an arrest warrant was issued and before the case was even moved to the trial stage (Han 2013). These institutional factors, along with the potential lack of adequate training and resources for the police and an underestimation of the complexity of some criminal cases, may provide a breeding ground for police abuse.

Third, the courtroom has a unique dynamic within the Chinese context. The police, the procuratorate, and the court routinely work together on major criminal cases. This makes sense to some extent because it promotes resource conservation and information sharing. However, it weakens necessary institutional oversight and results in an imbalance of power. These drawbacks were manifested in the Nian case. For example, although the police work in the Nian case was shoddy (e.g., mismatched timelines, missing parts of the video recording, inconsistent or contradictory evidence and statements), no court seemed willing to challenge the police and procuratorate's case and order the case dismissed. This was partly due to a weak judiciary in China that can withstand neither political interference by the party[11] nor institutional pressure from the police and procuratorate. If the party's priority is to suppress crime and maintain order, and the police and procuratorate follow through by "cracking" a major case, the court may feel compelled to play along. The conviction rate of over 99% in 2002–2011 is a testament to this institutional setup. Within the adjudicative structure, even though a higher court has a supervisory role over a lower court, because of jurisdictional issues, local politics, public exposure, and personnel reasons (e.g., a high ratio of overturned cases may affect annual bonuses, raises, and promotions), higher courts are generally reluctant to overturn a legal ruling of a lower court, let alone dismiss the case.[12] In the Nian case, his lawyer, Zhang (2014), stated that the Fujian High Court was "courageous" in returning the case to the Fuzhou Intermediate Court for retrial because a returned case is typically perceived as a slap in the face to the original trial court and may result in potential political and professional embarrassment. In addition, by passing the baton to another party (even though it meant the same party involved in the messy case), the high court could potentially avoid being held accountable for the legal decision. This passiveness and indecision are likely to lead to a lengthy delay, particularly in major, complicated cases, such as the Nian case.

Fourth, criminal defense lawyers played a critical role in this case. Defense lawyer Zhang, along with other high-profile defense lawyers who later joined the defense, provided critical support in this case. She reduced and waived the attorney fee, withstood physical threats made by the victims' family members and pressure from the police and procuratorate, and strategically used the media to generate public and legal scholars' support for this case. To be sure, defense lawyer Zhang was an insider in the Chinese criminal justice system. Before starting her own law firm in 1994, Zhang served as a judge for over a decade. But it was her persistence and resolve (*sike pai*) that sustained her and her defense team throughout the seven-year ordeal. In the absence of nongovernmental organizations in China, Nian's family had little financial and emotional support to pursue the case. In a sense, their defense team provided that support (Han 2013).

If the Nian case serves as a timely reminder that the current criminal justice system is not error proof, it also sheds light on areas of the law and policies that could be improved to potentially enhance the system's capability of error detection and correction. These areas include establishing an effective system of checks and balances among the police, the procuratorate, and the court; adopting the principle of presumptive innocence; and creating a mechanism that encourages early detection and correction of errors.

Granted, the Nian case has already prompted, or maybe is the result of, a series of new initiatives aimed at addressing these problem areas. For example, a 2013 SPC opinion specifically prohibited courts from being involved in joint criminal investigations with the police and the procuratorate (T. Yang 2014; Cheng 2014). In 2014, the SPC unveiled its Fourth Five-Year Reform Plan to create a "more professional model for the judiciary" to improve its independence and professionalism (Tiezzi 2014).[13]

* * *

In some respects, Nian was lucky despite his seven-year ordeal of life-and-death decisions. Had he not received four death sentences with immediate execution, his case would not have reached the SPC, and Nian would most likely still be in prison serving a long sentence (T. Yang 2014).

Nian was also lucky because his case progressed along with the development of the judicial reform. For example, when Nian was arrested in 2007, the SPC took back its final review and approval power of all death penalty cases; when Nian was sentenced to death with immediate execution in 2010, the SPC announced the new requirement to exclude evidence gathered illegally; when Nian was sentenced to death the fourth time and the case was sent to the high court for review the third time in 2011, the CPL was amended by a new stipulation that mandates that the second-instance trial court make an adjudicative decision instead of sending a case back for retrial again after receiving a retried case from a lower court. In addition, the revised CPL required that when the method of evidence gathering is legally questionable, the relevant police officers shall appear in court to testify, and witnesses shall appear in court to be cross-examined in order for their witness testimony to be admitted as evidence (Articles 57, 58, 59). In fact, it was in open court that police officers admitted fabricating evidence and their shoddy police work; this ultimately cemented the acquittal decision for Nian

(Luo 2013). Thus, without these recent improvements in the CPL, it is unlikely that Nian would have been set free (Lin Li 2014; Zhang 2014).

Despite Nian's dramatic fate, Nian's defense lawyer, Zhang, said that such cases were really common in China because when involving shoddy detective work, wrongful convictions are likely to ensue (Mudie 2014). For this reason, Zhang said that the Nian case sets a new benchmark for judicial reforms, and its impact will last for a long time (Lin Li 2014). Given the progress made in the past several decades in the CL and the CPL, we are hopeful that judicial reforms in China will serve as a catalyst for the formalization and professionalization of the legal system, particularly regarding the death penalty.

NOTES

1. "Criminal Law of the People's Republic of China—Chinese and English Versions," Baidu Wenku, retrieved September 13, 2014, from http://wenku.baidu.com/link?url =BkRDWomd1bM_MRfJVykSTu7_Ppe4mj1Zauxfmb9_gvCFPohUpa59m -IbEq2DWGLmchUbonw6D8HxM3DOVK_veLqANzzryJaYoT8f-Hj9sBO.
2. The inaugural issue of the *Law Yearbook of China* appeared in 1987. Although crime data are no longer regarded as a state secret, the reporting rate and the method of recording and classification of crimes by public security departments across China remain unclear; therefore, the reliability of these official crime data is questionable.
3. "The Collection of the Guiding Cases Issued by the Supreme People's Court," Baidu Wenku, retrieved August 6, 2014, from http://wenku.baidu.com/link?url =NLeAsktoYBGsG_49Pig5AROSX3VPTNsE7cJukoBgjBGM10RxvxTczvU _UvqzF1SNgehVLK_OR6htzk9Qf9uRv6B69Ej-y676DNwMZy3LrM7.
4. Criminal Procedure Law (2012), China Law Translate, retrieved July 22, 2014, from http://chinalawtranslate.com/en/criminal-procedure-law/.
5. Ma's (2003) study shows that there is a gap between the law in books and the law in reality, particularly regarding the power of the police and the rights of criminal suspects.
6. See Fu (1998) for details of obstacles defense lawyers routinely encounter during the course of their work (e.g., reviewing case documents, raising questions in court).
7. Article 12, 1996 CPL: "No person shall be found guilty without being judged as such by a People's Court according to law." http://chinalawtranslate.com/en/criminal -procedure-law/.
8. Information retrieved from the SPC website (http://www.court.gov.cn/jgsz/) on July 18, 2014.
9. The timeline is constructed from several reports (Han 2013; Limin Li 2014; Lin Li 2014; Wang 2014; T. Yang 2014; You 2014; Zhang 2014).
10. The recorded pieces of evidence included the vomited substance in the victims' mother Ding's bedroom, a metal pot on Ding's stove, a pressure cooker by Ding's stove, a water

pot, and the handle on the door from Nian's grocery store to Ding's store, according to information from Baidu Baike on the Poisoning Case of Nian Bin, retrieved August 30, 2014, from http://baike.baidu.com/view/10434875.htm?from_id=15440664&type =syn&fromtitle=念斌案&fr=aladdin (retrieved August 30, 2014).

11 It was also argued that crime control and order maintenance are directly tied to the political agenda of establishing a harmonious society under the Hu Jintao administration. Thus, by appeasing the public and projecting an image of a safe and harmonious society, the Communist Party gains its legitimacy (H. He 2014).

12 For a more detailed analysis of judicial independence in China, see Fu (2003).

13 The new reform plan attempts to increase judicial independence through a more centralized judicial appointment system at the provincial level so as to reduce local protectionism and corruption. It also attempts to empower judges to rule on cases after hearing them instead of relying on the adjudicative committee (Tiezzi 2014).

REFERENCES

Amnesty International. (1980–2008). amnestyusa.org.

Boehler, P. (2013, May 25). Deadline for death sentence in Fujian murder case extended. South China Morning Post. Retrieved December 1, 2014, from http://www.scmp.com/news/china/article/1245885/deadline-death-sentence-fujian-murder-case-extended.

Chen, R. H. (2006). Shuilai jiandu jianduzhe? [Who will supervise the supervisor?] Retrieved August 30, 2014, from http://article.chinalawinfo.com/ArticleFullText.aspx?ArticleId=34869.

Cheng, G. (2014, August 25). Dui shensu buzhi de anjie yiding yao chongxing shengcha [Cases with repeat petitions shall be reinvestigated]. Retrieved August 30, 2014, from http://www.sn.xinhuanet.com/2014-08/25/c_1112212556.htm.

Clarke, D. C., & Feinerman, J. V. (1995). Antagonistic contradictions: Criminal law and human rights in China. *China Quarterly, 141*, 135–154.

Dai, M. (2008). Policing in the People's Republic of China: A review of recent literature. *Crime Law Social Change, 50*, 211–227.

Death Penalty Worldwide. (2009–2013). Annual number of reported executions. Retrieved September 18, 2014, from http://www.deathpenaltyworldwide.org/.

Dui Hua Foundation. Criminal justice: Death penalty reform. Retrieved September 13, 2014, from http://duihua.org/wp/?page_id=136.

Fu, H. (1998). Criminal defense in China: The possible impact of the 1996 criminal procedural law reform. *China Quarterly, 153*, 31–48.

Fu, H. (2003). Putting China's judiciary into perspective: Is it independent, competent, and fair? In E. G. Jensen & T. C. Heller (Eds.), *Beyond Common*

Knowledge: Empirical Approaches to the Rule of Law (pp. 193–219). Stanford, CA: Stanford University Press.

Han, Y. (2013, July 26). Nibin an beihou de lajuzhan [Behind the yo-yo cycle of the Nian Bin case]. Retrieved July 30, 2014, from http://www.nbweekly.com/news/special/201307/33894.aspx.

He, H. (2014, September 3). Death sentence reversed in China, but justice left wanting. *Epoch Times.* Retrieved September 7, 2014, from http://www.theepochtimes.com.n3/930954-death-sentence-reversed-in-china-but-justice-left-wanting.

He, X. (2012). Black hole of responsibility: The adjudication committee's role in a Chinese court. *Law and Society Review, 46*(4), 681–712.

Law Yearbook of China. 1987–2013. Beijing: Law Yearbook of China.

Li, L. (2014, August 22). Nianbin toudu an, you duoshao xuanyi dengdai puojie? [How many questions need to be answered in the Nianbin poison case?] Retrieved September 18, 2014, from http://www.legalweekly.cn/index.php/Index/article/id/721.

Li, L. (2014, August 25). Nianbin an lvshi: zhuoguo yuanan duo nan jiuzheng yin fayuan zhicuo bugai [Erroneous cases due to court's refusal to reverse the mistake]. Retrieved August 30, 2014, from http://news.china.com/domestic/945/20140825/18733108_1.html.

Luo, J. (2013, July 9). Nianbin an disanci ersheng jingcha chengren weifa quzheng [The police admitted gathering evidence illegally in the Nian case]. Retrieved September 18, 2014, from http://china.caixin.com/2013-07-09/100553529.html.

Ma, Y. (2003). The powers of the police and the rights of suspects under the amended criminal procedure law of China. *Policing: An International Journal of Police Strategies and Management, 26*(3), 490–510.

Martinez, V., Vertino, T., & Lu, H. (2014). The death penalty in China. In L. Cao, I. Sun, & B. Hebenton (Eds.), *The Routledge Handbook of Chinese Criminology* (pp. 130–145). London: Routledge.

Mudie, L. (2014, August 22). After eight years on death row, Chinese man found not guilty of murder. Retrieved September 19, 2014, from http://www.rfa.org/english/news/china/murder-08222014140431.html.

Qi, M. (2007). Lun woguo de xingshi chongshen fahui zhidu [On the system of remanding a case to the original court for a retrial]. Master's thesis. Retrieved August 1, 2014, from http://cdmd.cnki.com.cn/Article/CDMD-10459-2007122608.htm.

Teng, B. & Liang, X. (2012). China against the death penalty—Report 2012. Retrieved September 18, 2014, from http://www.worldcoalition.org/media/resourcecenter/CADP2012report-EN.pdf.

Tiezzi, S. (2014, July 12). Beijing's blueprint for judicial reform—The Supreme People's Court outlined reforms to increase judicial professionalism and independence. Retrieved September 19, 2014, from http://thediplomat.com/2014/07/beijings-blueprint-for-judicial-reform/.

Trevaskes, S. (2011). Political ideology, the party, and politicking: Justice system reform in China. *Modern China, 37*(3), 315–344.

Wang, H. (2014, August 25). Nianbin an yizui congwu buneng zhiyu biaoyang faguan [NianBin case cannot be stopped at praising the judge]. Retrieved August 30, 2014, from http://guancha.gmw.cn/2014-08/24/content_12739172.htm.

Wang, Z., & Liu, G. (2012). The sentencing standardization reform in China. Retrieved August 1, 2014, from http://works.bepress.com/cgi/viewcontent.cgi?article=1000&context=zhiyuan_wang.

Yang, T. (2014, August 25). Fangzhi "Nianbin an" zaixian, haixu geng wanshan de zhidu sheji [To prevent Nian Bin case from reemerging, system improvement is a must]. Retrieved August 30, 2014, from http://news.ynet.com/3.1/1408/25/9318714.html.

You, W. (2014, August 25). Nianbin an cong sixin dao wuzui de fansi [Reflection on the conversion from death sentence to acquittal in Nian Bin case]. Retrieved August 30, 2014, from http://xmwb.xinmin.cn/html/2014-08/25/content_2_1.htm.

Zhang, Y. (2014, August 25). Nianbin an lvshi Zhang yansheng: gongan buduan cangni zhengju zeren zhongda [The Public Security Bureau shall bear major responsibility for hiding evidence in this case]. Retrieved September 18, 2014, from http://news.sina.com.cn/c/2014-08-25/184230740660.shtml.

Zhou, X. (2006). Xingshi fahui chongshen zhidu yanjiu [A study on the system of sending back the case for retrial]. Master's thesis. Retrieved July 5, 2014, from http://cdmd.cnki.com.cn/Article/CDMD-10652-2006145101.htm.

3

Crimes of Counterrevolution and Politicized Use of the Death Penalty During the Mao Era

▸ NING ZHANG

THE CHINESE TERM *counterrevolutionary* in its legal sense is an invention of the twentieth century, a product of two revolutions, the Nationalist revolution in 1911 and the Communist revolution in 1949. Although the official use of this concept had already begun during the Republican regime, it expanded dramatically during the Communist period. The purpose of this chapter is to study judicial and extrajudicial practices relating to counterrevolutionaries during the Maoist period and, more specifically, the use of the death penalty as punishment for this category of crimes.

I wish to illustrate the specific importance of the campaign to suppress counterrevolutionaries during the 1950s in the crystallization of what can be considered a specifically Maoist theory and practice of the death penalty. This political movement occurred from 1951 to 1953 because of a remarkably rapid process of institutionalization. It has contributed to stabilizing and systematizing practices that unquestionably existed previously. Although one must regard with caution the role of the individual in the historical process, we are obliged to recognize the decisive nature of the personal intervention of Mao Zedong in this particular case, intervention that occurred repeatedly and in opposition to a certain reluctance from his entourage. Because sources that provide direct information about judicial practices are rare and difficult to access, this episode remains insufficiently documented. Our knowledge of the political context of these practices has been greatly advanced by the recent publication of numerous documents of this period.

In order to draw a provisional picture of this complex situation, this chapter is divided into two parts. The first part narrates the sequence of events and concludes with an analysis of three cases judged in Shanghai in 1951 that provide concrete examples of these developments. The second part analyzes some of the basic characteristics of this specific regime of the death penalty. In regard to both general features (such as politicization that became characteristic of judicial practices) and particular institutional innovations (such as the application of quotas or the establishment of the suspended death penalty), the redefinition of the penal culture during the campaign to suppress counterrevolutionaries affected the entire Maoist period. It represents a heritage that is still perceptible in the conceptions and the practices regarding capital punishment in China today.

Before examining in detail the campaign at the beginning of the 1950s, it is appropriate to recall very briefly the origin of the regulations governing the crime of counterrevolution, as well as the series of principal laws on the subject from the Republican era to the post-Maoist period in twentieth-century China.

CRIMES OF COUNTERREVOLUTION

The first piece of law specifically dealing with crimes of counterrevolution dated back to 1927. Titled the Regulations on Counterrevolutionary Crimes and promulgated by the Nationalist government led by Wang Jingwei, the law ultimately failed to be implemented. A year later, on March 9, 1928, the Chiang Kai-shek government in Nanjing promulgated the Provisional Law on the Punishment of Counterrevolutionary Crimes. Out of six counterrevolutionary crimes, five were subject to the death penalty. In 1931, this law was renamed the Emergency Law to Punish Individuals Who Undermine the Security of the Nationalist State and was aimed primarily at the Communists.[1] Meanwhile, the Communist Party also established parallel legislation directed against its former allies. In Jiangxi Province, the Communists established an autonomous government and set up a similar penal system to eliminate Nationalist "bandits" and their supporters among the local elites. In 1934, the Regulations of the Chinese Soviet Republic on Punishing Counterrevolutionaries was enacted to carry out purges within the party itself and legitimize a considerable number of executions. Out of 28 counterrevolutionary crimes stipulated in these regulations, 27 were subject to the death penalty. The total number of victims of these purges remains unknown.

After the Communist takeover of the central government in 1949, the Chinese judicial system functioned without a penal code until 1979. However, the Regulations on the Punishment of Counterrevolutionaries in the People's Republic of China (PRC), issued in 1951 (the 1951 Regulations hereafter), served as the major guide in identifying and punishing "counterrevolutionaries." Suffice it to say that the 1951 Regulations functioned as the Maoist main criminal law, with a power that went beyond that of various constitutions adopted and revised during the Mao era (in 1949, 1954, and 1975). By allowing qualification of many behaviors as "counterrevolutionary," the 1951 Regulations made possible their particularly severe repression, with frequent resort to the death penalty. It was not until 1996 that a major revision of the 1979 Criminal Law replaced the crime of counterrevolution with that of "endangering state security."

REVOLUTIONARY JUDICIAL PRACTICES: THE CAMPAIGN TO SUPPRESS COUNTERREVOLUTIONARIES (1950-1953)

Although it coincided with the participation of the Volunteers of the Chinese People in the Korean War, the campaign to suppress counterrevolutionaries launched in 1950 can first be considered as marking the transition from Maoist practices of repression in times of war to those that applied in times of peace. In the words of Mao, it was a question of moving from the fight against "enemies with guns" to the struggle against "enemies without guns" (Mao 1961:364). The military revolution had to give way to the construction of "revolutionary legality." This campaign exhibited many characteristics of the application of the death penalty in the Mao era. Moreover, it was during this campaign that Mao spoke most frequently on the subject of the death penalty. His personal influence on the process can thus be better perceived here than at other times.

The campaign had three major stages. The first stage (October 1950–October 1951) was marked by the direct intervention of Mao in its launching through the mobilization of the masses in the cities and the enactment of the 1951 Regulations. The second stage (November 1951–November 1952) involved strengthening law enforcement after a conference on national public security was held in Beijing in September 1951. The third stage (December 1952–1953) was aimed at "reactionary sects and secret societies" and the counterrevolutionaries who traveled or hid in boats (Wan 2006:491–492). The first two stages will be the focus of the discussions in this chapter because of their crucial roles in the institutionalization of these practices and the greater accessibility of archives concerning them.

Launching of the Campaign: A Decision by Mao

From the autumn of 1948, the Communist army began to take control of the country from the northeast. Within two years, most areas were under Communist military authority. However, this new power was confronted everywhere by limited but often violent resistance, whether in rural or urban areas and in newly conquered regions or those already under control. Under these circumstances, the Central Committee of the party, then headed by Liu Shaoqi, promulgated the Directive on the Repression of the Activities of Counterrevolutionaries on March 18, 1950 (Central Archives of the Chinese Communist Party [CCP] 1991:358–360). On June 8, some provincial party committees asked the Central Committee for permission to launch a severe crackdown at the regional level. This prompted the central government to reissue the same directive on July 21 on behalf of the Council of State Affairs and the Supreme People's Court. However, this directive existed only on paper because Mao was still hesitating: such repression launched in the cities could arouse too many enemies and endanger the newly installed Communist government (Mao 1991:1:397–400). It was not until October 10, 1950, two days after the order given by Mao to send Chinese troops into Korea, that the Central Committee of the CCP, this time under the leadership of Mao himself, reiterated the same instructions. The campaign then began with this directive, now called the October 10 Directive.

The timing of this decision was carefully thought out. Mao clearly explained to Luo Ruiqing, then the minister of public security, "Before, it was not the ideal time to launch a major crackdown against counterrevolutionaries because at that time we had not yet settled our financial problems and our relationship with some capitalists was still too tense. Now the situation is quite different. Our financial problem is under control and the war in Korea has just broken out. This is an opportunity not to be missed. It may be the only opportunity for us to suppress counterrevolutionaries. It is valuable for us. You must take this opportunity not only to eliminate the counterrevolutionaries, but above all to mobilize the masses" (Yang 2006:41). Liu Shaoqi confirmed this view:

> What has allowed us to organize the repression against counterrevolutionaries on a large scale? It is the war in Korea! This war has been very beneficial to us and has allowed us to successfully conduct a lot of business (for example, the extension of agrarian reform, the conclusion of the Sino-Soviet Pact, the launching of campaigns to increase production and to repress counterrevolutionaries). The response to this war has been so strong that agrarian reform and the repression of counterrevolutionaries make little noise. This has made it easier for us. Without the commotion surrounding this war, these actions would have been severely criticized. Here and there landowners have been put to death: these actions could have aroused opposition everywhere, which could have prevented us from successfully carrying out our operations.[2]

However, the responses from the provinces to this decision varied. At first, few of them reacted. The October 10 Directive required regional leaders to send the Central Committee a "project" for local repression before November 10, 1951, but it was only toward the end of the month that the Central Committee received a few projects from the Administrative Committees of the Southwest and the North Administrative Regions and from the municipality of Beijing. Among these projects, Mao particularly appreciated that of the Administrative Committee of the Southwest, which suggested specific penalties to punish counterrevolutionaries: the death penalty for perpetrators of the most heinous crimes, imprisonment for those guilty of serious offenses, and the imposition of surveillance on other offenders (Mao 1991, 1:664). The proposal of the Beijing Municipal Party Committee also pleased him because it suggested organizing repression in three stages, first aimed at Nationalist agents and then at reactionary parties and groups before attacking the various reactionary forces in society. In Mao's view, these accurate and robust methods deserved to be promoted throughout the country (ibid.:675–676). Mao's encouragement greatly accelerated repression in these regions where local officials were already very enthusiastic. Such was the case in Sichuan. A recent study based on statistics stored in the local archives showed a significant change in the number of counterrevolutionaries killed before and after October 10, 1950, in two areas. For instance, in one of these two areas (in the west of Sichuan), 1,349 people were put to death over a period of ten months before that date; however, 2,130 people were executed within two months afterward (Yang 2006:42).

Nevertheless, in some regions, leaders reacted in a more prudent manner. This was the case with the Committee of the Administrative Region of Eastern China. On December 28, 1950, Yao Shushi, head of this regional committee, sent a report to the Central Committee that presented an analysis of repression activities. According to the report, between January and October 1950, 2,911 Nationalist agents, counterrevolutionaries, and bandits had been executed, 13,093 people had been imprisoned, and 101,636 members of various parties or "reactionary" groups had been inscribed in a special register by the police.[3] Worried about possibly excessive repression, Yao still seemed reluctant to engage in the campaign newly launched by Mao. The CCP Central Committee also showed its understanding in its reply: "If a large number of counterrevolutionaries have already been killed in a region, the intensity of repression should be reduced somewhat, depending on circumstances, which is to say by leaving intervals between each collective execution of criminals, and reducing social tensions. There must not be too much news published about the death sentences. Thus, one can make public only the executions of the main culprits, but not those of the secondary culprits."[4] Mao, however, saw things differently.

Mao's Fight Against Big Cities

On January 17, 1951, a report submitted by the Committee of the South Central Region reached Mao. It reported that within a few months, the 27th Army had eliminated more than 4,600 bandit leaders, Nationalist agents, and local tyrants in 21 districts of Western Hunan and was also preparing another crackdown for the year ahead (Mao 1991, 2:36–37). This result fully satisfied Mao, who subsequently established it as a national model. By contrast, the action in Henan was considered inadequate. There, executions halted after reaching the figure of 3,000 people. Equally timid seemed to be the attitude of several provinces in the Eastern Region, where, despite high population densities, the total number of death sentences amounted to 2,911. In Mao's view, too few people in the newly liberated areas had been eliminated in the course of land reform, so these areas could become gathering places for the forces of reaction. "Major projects of serial executions" must be applied in these areas, "particularly in places where bandits, local tyrants and Nationalist agents gather" (ibid.).

Four days later, in a telegram to the Committee of the Municipality of Shanghai, Mao gave precise instructions:

> In a big city like Shanghai, it would probably be necessary to execute 1,000 or 2,000 people during the course of this year in order to address the problem [of counterrevolutionaries]. It is absolutely necessary to kill 300 to 500 people in the spring, in order to curb the arrogance of the enemy and raise the morale of the people. As for Nanjing, I ask you to direct the municipal committee of the city to organize investigation, arrest and interrogation operations, and kill 100 to 200 important counterrevolutionary elements during this spring. (ibid.:47)

A few months later, he sent a further directive to the heads of committees of the municipality of Shanghai and Nanjing, giving the exact number of death sentences he had planned:

> Shanghai is a big city with a population of six million. You have already arrested some 20,000 people but only 200 of them have been sentenced to death. Considering this situation, I think you should kill at least another 3,000 bandit leaders, professional bandits, local tyrants, Nationalist agents and heads of superstitious sects during the year 1951. In other words, at least 1,500 people will have to be executed during the first six months. You can gauge whether this figure is appropriate. In a telegram dated February 3, sent by Ke Qingshi to Yao Shushi, it was reported that 72 people have been executed and 150 others will be put to death in Nanjing. This figure is far from adequate. Nanjing is a city of five million inhabitants and it is the capital of the Kuomintang. Reactionary elements deserving of death cannot be limited to those 200 people. There are too few killings in Nanjing, we must kill many more of them.[5]

On the same day, Mao sent another telegram to the leaders of the Guangdong Committee: "You have already killed more than 3,700 people, and that is very good! You can kill 300 or 400 more," and "This year's objective can be set at 8,000 or 9,000 people" (Mao 1991:2:51).

Mao's direct intervention in the launching of the repression quickly met with a strong response from local leaders, who took the initiative of proposing execution figures for their own constituencies. However, without any reference figure at the national level, locally determined numbers varied greatly, and the majority of those proposed by local authorities did not seem to meet Mao's demands. In this situation, Mao began to calculate the proper proportion between the number of death sentences and regional population figures before asking the CCP Central Committee to deliberate his proposal. This proposal was embodied in a telegram dated April 20, 1951: "It was decided to put to death a thousandth of the total population. First, half this number should be killed, and then a decision be taken according to the circumstances."[6] In order to legalize this project of repression, a "law" was created.

Emergence of the "Law" on Repression of Counterrevolutionaries

On February 21, 1951, Mao, as chairman of the Central People's Government, issued an order to publish the 1951 Regulations in the *People's Daily*. As the first piece of law of a penal nature, the 1951 Regulations played a fundamental role in the gradual formation of the penal system and of the spirit of judicial practice during his era. These regulations were also decisive in the definition of major crimes punishable by the death penalty throughout the reign of Mao. They therefore warrant a detailed analysis.

Composed of 21 items, the 1951 Regulations stipulated in Article 2 that "all acts which are carried out with the aim of overthrowing the People's democratic regime and sabotaging the democratic People's cause are counterrevolutionary crimes." Despite the lack of precise definitions, one can identify a hierarchy of penalties: the death penalty, life imprisonment, and four degrees of incarceration, as well as rules for the reduction of penalties, exemption from punishment, confiscation of property, and deprivation of political rights. The 1951 Regulations also stipulated that all culprits accused of counterrevolutionary crimes must be tried by a military court during the period of military control. What is particularly important for the subject of this chapter is the number of counterrevolutionary crimes carrying the death penalty, as stipulated by these regulations. Of the 17 counterrevolutionary crimes defined, 13 were subject to this extreme penalty, including high treason, incitement to defection, armed rebellion, espionage, spreading of counterrevolutionary ideas, illegal border crossing, organization or use of superstitious sects and secret societies for counterrevolutionary purposes, and other more common crimes, such as arson and looting.

Available sources do not yet allow us to ascertain the context and the process of development of these regulations. Nevertheless, the promulgation of these regulations now made it possible to legitimize the determination of the supreme leader of the party to suppress his enemies, real or imaginary, under legal and governmental forms, in big cities that had hitherto benefited from a prudent policy on the part of the Communists.

In reality, there were still variations in the application of the CCP's policy of repression, depending on whether it concerned provinces still at war or those already under Communist control, rural or urban areas, or small towns or large cities. In some provinces, military operations were still ongoing. This was the case in Guangxi. A report dated January 16, 1951, sent by the secretary of the CCP committee of the province, stated that between September and December 1950, more than 3,000 bandit leaders and professional bandits had been executed and more than 90,000 "Nationalist bandits exterminated" (Mao 1991, 2:62–63). The same situation was to be found in the provinces of Sichuan, Guizhou, and Hunan, where battles between the Communists and the Nationalists were not yet over. However, in large cities, we find that the Communists remained cautious despite repeated intervention from Mao. The publication of the 1951 Regulations allowed city leaders to include those elites who had remained outside the CCP in order to mobilize citizens to participate in the repression in the name of the government.

Great Repression in Action

Major cities whose leaders were the first to respond to the project of repression were Beijing and Tianjin. In fact, well before the publication of the 1951 Regulations, 675 people were arrested in Beijing on the night of February 17, 1951, under the direction of Luo Ruiqing, then head of the Public Security Bureau, and 58 counterrevolutionaries were publicly executed the next day. But the extent of the repression was to be different after the promulgation of the 1951 Regulations.

PROJECTS FOR REPRESSION

On February 22, 1951, the day after the promulgation of the 1951 Regulations, a new project of repression of the CCP Committee of Beijing Municipality was sent to the Central Committee and to the administrative region in the north. Attached was a summary of the crackdown in the city since the "liberation": 224 bandits, agents, and local tyrants had been executed, about 6,000 people had been imprisoned, 10,322 were under surveillance, and 47,500 members of parties and leagues, as well as special agents, had been classified in a special police register. In the new project, it was proposed "to execute at intervals and in groups, in different locations, approximately 1,300 criminals who meet the conditions requiring the application of the death penalty (if we add those already executed, the total number rises to 1,500. . . . [Specifically,] an initial group of 350 people will be executed before March 15, 1951; a second group of 750 people will be executed between late March and mid-April. . . . [Further,] on each occasion, at the appointed time, we will convene representatives from different levels of the People's Assembly and representatives of large factories, universities, democratic parties and people's organizations to inform them of counterrevolutionary activities and make known the crimes and the evidence gathered in order to arouse their hatred. These criminals will then be executed in groups. Among those we have already arrested but not yet tried, and among the key suspects we are currently investigating but who have not yet been arrested, there is still a large number of individuals deserving of death (according to the information we currently have, they number about 300). We intend to review this situation and deal with it in an upcoming project" (Archives of the Municipality of Beijing and the Research Institute on the History of the Chinese Communist Party Attached to the CCP Committee of the Municipality of Beijing 2001:101–102).

Three days later, the CCP Central Committee responded with the following instructions: "In all major cities with the exception of the Northeast region, the repression against counterrevolutionaries has not yet been conducted sufficiently widely and rigorously. We must now launch it without delay. These cities are principally Beijing, Tianjin, Qingdao, Shanghai, Nanjing, Canton, Hankou, Chongqing, and other provincial capitals, which are the main hideout of counterrevolutionary organizations. We must organize to conduct investigations and arrests and then serially execute those counterrevolutionaries guilty of the most heinous crimes and against whom we have irrefutable evidence" (ibid.:100).

What deserves attention in this first project of repression in Beijing is its concrete proposals on the strategy to be followed in the organization of trials: it was above all a question of mobilizing the urban population.

This proposal subsequently became a general strategy applied in large cities.

Comprehensive data are not available on the project in Tianjin. However, Mao's reply to the new project proposed by Huang Jing, then mayor of Tianjin, makes it possible to form a partial idea. According to this project, the municipal committee intended to execute 1,500 people in 1951. Apart from the 150 people already executed, 500 more executions were planned by the end of April. Mao appreciated the positive response of Chongqing without specifying the content of the project. He also asked Shanghai, Nanjing, Qingdao, Guangzhou, Wuhan, and other cities to develop concrete projects of repression for a few months until the end of the year (Mao 1991, 2:168–169).

The Shanghai leaders proposed two projects. The first was proposed on January 1, 1951, before the promulgation of the 1951 Regulations. Yao Shushi, then secretary general of the Committee of the East Administrative Region, and Chen Yi, mayor of the municipality, declared their intention to prepare a rigorous attack against counterrevolutionary elements in January, in response to repeated requests by Mao. A month later, in a report to Mao on February 2, they criticized themselves for their slow response and offered to kill a large number of those who deserved to die in the coming months. Statistics showed that during this period, 14 people were executed in two groups in January, 34 people were put to death in six groups in February, and 5 others were killed in late March. A second project that aimed at mass mobilization against counterrevolutionaries took shape on March 15 despite local opposition. The goal was to arrest about 10,000 people, to execute 3,000, to imprison 4,000, and to put 3,000 more under surveillance.[7]

In a reply dated April 13 to a report on the repression of counterrevolutionaries carried out on April 1 in Jinan, Shandong Province, Mao indicated that to date he had received reports on the launching of repression in six cities (Beijing, Tianjin, Qingdao, Jinan, Chongqing, and Lanzhou) and projects in Shanghai, Nanjing, and Hangzhou. He called on all medium and large cities to send a report on their work of repression (Mao 1991, 2:235).

LARGE-SCALE ARRESTS

On March 7, 1951, Beijing launched large-scale arrests of 1,050 people. On March 13 and 23, 2,007 people were arrested at home by a force of more than 10,000 police officers, soldiers, militia, and mobilized cadres (Guo 2001:33,

423). In Chongqing, on March 14, more than 4,000 people were arrested, according to Kuang Kaowen, who took part in the arrest (Shen 2009). At Qingdao in Shandong Province, more than 1,000 people were arrested during April 1951 (Local Records Office of Qingdao 1998:31).

In Shanghai, after the Decision on the Rigorous Repression of Counterrevolutionaries was passed by the assembly representing various circles in the municipality of Shanghai, a general roundup of counterrevolutionaries was launched on April 21. During the day, in the district of Huangpu alone, 1,535 people were mobilized and 289 people were arrested. This operation marked the general launch of the campaign in Shanghai (Local Records Office of the Municipality of Shanghai, chapter 26). A week later, a second operation was launched in all the districts of Shanghai with the formation of 4,445 groups composed of 35,889 members of the military, police, workers, cadres, and students. A total of 8,359 people were denounced and arrested under the five categories of counterrevolutionaries, including bandits, bullies, spies, heads of reactionary parties and leagues, and heads of the secret society Huidaomen (N. Zhang 2010). On May 5, there were 651 arrests in a third operation. In total, 9,010 people were arrested during the last two operations, according to figures from the *Annals of Public Security* (Bureau of Shanghai Public Security 1997:105). On the other hand, a speech by the chief of the municipal police, published in the daily *Wenhuibao* on May 1, 1951, gave the figure of 24,000 people arrested.

MASS TRIALS HELD IN CITIES

After the arrests, there were plans to hold mass trials. On March 15, 1951, the Beijing Municipality summoned an expanded convention composed of members of the municipal consultative conference and representatives of various circles of the city to prepare a rally denouncing the crimes of counterrevolutionaries on a municipal scale (Mao 1977:34–38). On March 24, a gathering of 5,000 people was held in the concert hall of Sun Yat-sen Park. It began with speeches by Peng Zhen, then mayor of Beijing, and Luo Ruiqing, chief of the Central Police. Victims were asked to publicly denounce 14 defendants. During these denunciations, slogans echoed in waves around the room: "Shoot the spies!" "Shoot the bandit leaders, shoot the professional bandits!" "Shoot the local tyrants!" "Shoot the heads of secret reactionary societies!" The meeting ended with a significant statement by Wang Beiran, head of the Bureau of Military Justice of the Military Control Committee of the Municipality of Beijing and chairman of the Municipal People's Court:

> From the moment these heinous counterrevolutionaries were transferred from the Bureau of Municipal Public Security to the Bureau of Military Justice, we have accelerated the process. Our review shows that the evidence of the crimes committed by them is irrefutable. Why then have we not tried them before? Because it is an important matter, we wish to discuss it with you. This is why we submit the case to you now. Today, everyone asks unanimously that they be severely repressed. The whole country says they deserve death. Our office can no longer hesitate. After this meeting, we will work all night to complete the formalities required so that we can execute them tomorrow. ("Beijing" 1951; *The People of Beijing and Tianjin Suppress Counterrevolutionaries on a Large Scale* 1951:1)

The course of this meeting was broadcast by radio in the capital and around the country. The next day, 199 people accused of counterrevolutionary crimes were led under escort around the city and paraded in particular in places where they had committed their "crimes" (Archives of the Municipality of Beijing and Research Institute on the History of the Chinese Communist Party Attached to the CCP Committee of the Municipality of Beijing CCP 2001:293). The nature of these crimes was displayed. The defendants were then executed "under the supervision of the masses" ("Counterrevolution Crackdown" 1951).

This same model was reproduced in Tianjin on March 31, 1951, with 193 sentences carried out (*The People of Beijing and Tianjin Suppress Counterrevolutionaries on a Large Scale* 1951:83–91). It was then promoted in all provinces. During its propagation, caution and hesitation expressed by local leaders gave way to "enthusiasm" for large-scale repression, following the example of Hunan celebrated by Mao. Under pressure from Mao, Shanghai eventually held the same type of trial (until then considered by Yao Shushi to be unthinkable in a large metropolis). The "Beijing experiences" and "denunciation meetings" were therefore introduced in Shanghai. The day after the large-scale arrest of April 27, 1951, the main local newspaper *Liberation* published two editorials to launch the campaign ("Rise up" 1951; "Rise up together" 1951). On April 29, the Municipal Committee of the CCP organized a meeting with more than 10,000 representatives of the city. Pan Hannian, then deputy mayor of Shanghai, and Yang Fan, chief of police, began with a report on the results of the operation on April 27 before appealing for a general mobilization to denounce counterrevolutionaries in Shanghai society. This session was followed by a meeting of denunciation against nine people accused of "heinous crimes, with blood on their hands and hated by the people." They were shot at the end of the meeting. This session was heard live on radio by 3 million people in the city and in the southern region of Jiangsu. On April 30, 285 people judged as "having to die to calm the outrage of the people" were executed in three separate locations. Thousands of people attended, showing "great anger and emotion" (Bureau of Shanghai Public Security 1997:105–106; Centre for Studies in the History of the Shanghai Municipal Committee of the CCP 2004:48).

CASES FROM SHANGHAI (APRIL–MAY 1951)

Three death penalty cases at the initial stage of Shanghai's crackdown on counterrevolution crimes are discussed here to provide a glimpse of the campaign, although they cannot fully represent the national crackdown (Archives of the Municipality of Shanghai. B1/2/1059/1412/26–31, B2/2/2/94).

Case 1: Wan Keqin's Robbery Case

On April 27, 1951, the then-incumbent president of Shanghai's People's Court, Han Shuzhi, and vice president Ye Fangyan presented a motion to the Shanghai Military Control Council: "This court accepted the robbery case by Wan Keqing et al. (1951 Criminal case No. 2573). As convicted by prior adjudication, defendant Wan Keqin has committed heinous crimes. However, the previous sentence was too light. According to Article 3 of the Decisions on Implementing the 1951 Regulations issued by the Eastern China's Military Political Council, this court proposes to repeal the previous sentence and resentence him to the death penalty. Please advise if this is feasible."

On a piece of unsigned paper written on May 23, 1951, there was an inscription that read, "Denouncing meeting initiated by the Military Control Council may not be necessary," and it appeared to be the prosecutors' opinion. Two days later, the Shanghai Military Control Council instructed: "In Wan Keqin's counterrevolutionary robbery case, he is proposed to be resentenced to death. This is to be granted. The two accomplices, Wen Yaomin and Cai Jiguang, were only sentenced to two-year imprisonment and one-year imprisonment respectively in the first instance. This is slightly light and should be resentenced."

Case 2: Gang Leader Zhang Wentian's Death Penalty Case

Zhang Wentian's case involved another motion from the Shanghai People's Court, on May 10, 1951, which reads as follows: "Gang leader Zhang Wentian's case has been adjudicated. This court deems that Zhang should be sentenced to death. According to the 1951 Regulations, this court hereby submits the drafted verdict with complete files of this case for the verification of the Shanghai Military Control Council."

On the next day, the procuratorate instructed in red ink: "The death sentence is to be granted. Please contact the district government to see if they can mobilize fisherman in the Rihui harbor area." Five days later, on May 16, the procuratorate proposed a more detailed plan: "(1) Zhang Wentian, the leader of a gang group, has committed bloody crimes in both northern Jiangsu Province and Shanghai. The death sentence is granted. (2) This procuratorate deems it appropriate to contact the district government to mobilize the general public. The court is instructed to hold a denouncing meeting before execution."

Prosecutor Wang Fang signed this proposal on May 22. Three days later, Mayor Chen Yi approved the proposal, and the Shanghai Military Control Council instructed the court: "Zhang Wentian's case has been adjudicated and he is sentenced to death. This Council grants the death sentence. Zhang's gang group has taken Rihui Harbor as their turf and bullied local fishermen for years. He has committed multiple bloody crimes in both northern Jiangsu Province and Shanghai. A denouncing meeting may be held to raise people's political awareness and increase people's enthusiasm toward the counterrevolution campaign. The court is expected to contact the police department, which is charge of waterway safety and local government, to make corresponding arrangements."

Case 3: Jin Xing's Case

Jin Xing was sentenced to one year of imprisonment by the Shanghai People's Court for illegal gun possession and spreading words of counterrevolution on August 26, 1950. On April 19, 1951, the procuratorate deemed the original sentence too lenient, recommended a retrial, and clearly stated,

"According to sections 3 and 4 of Article 17 and sections 1 and 2 of Article 10 of the 1951 Regulations, he is sentenced to death."

On May 23, 1951, the following verdict was handed down by the Military Control Council: "The original sentence is repealed. Before the founding of the PRC, Jin Xin was a leader of Secret Services of Kuomintang. After the founding of the PRC, he spread counterrevolutionary words, estranged employees from employers, and concealed weaponry. He is sentenced to death."

These three cases share common features. First, they are among the first death sentence cases during the crackdown on counterrevolution in the first half of 1951. Second, all these cases were sentenced more harshly at retrial, in which the original sentence was repealed and the death sentence was imposed according to the 1951 Regulations. Third, the procuratorate played a special role in all cases.

In addition, they all reflect some features of trials at that time. The first feature is the uncertain definition of counterrevolutionary crimes and how its application was broadened in reality. Strictly speaking, the defendants in the first and second cases were not counterrevolutionaries because they were not directly engaged in "overthrowing the people's democratic regime and sabotaging the democratic people's cause." However, because these crimes were capable of enraging the general public, they were deemed suitable for mobilizing people. The procuratorate therefore recommended a denouncing meeting. "Public outrage" apparently played a key role in the harsher sentences in these two cases, and it had been used to promote an anger-pacification judicial model in big cities featuring denouncing meetings. It is interesting to note that the procuratorate's attitude was not as clear and firm in the first case. The note was not signed, and it emphasized, "Denouncing meeting initiated by the Military Control Council may not be necessary." It seems to show that at the earlier stage of the movement, Shanghai's legal authorities were hesitant about organizing denouncing meetings.

The second feature is that the 1951 Regulations was very abstract in terms of sentencing criteria, offered too much discretion, and opened the possibility for harsher sentencing. For example, in the third case, the antigovernment behaviors of the accused consisted only of some words and speeches. In addition, the accused was already in custody and would pose no further direct social political harms. The same defendant had originally been sentenced to one year of imprisonment but was sentenced to death at retrial.

The third feature is that the 1951 Regulations was retroactive. It stipulated that "counterrevolution crimes committed prior to the enactment of this regulation are also subject to the rules of this regulation" (Article 18). Therefore, 432 cases that occurred before the April 27, 1951, massive arrests in Shanghai were retried (many were treason cases that had been closed, and 108 of the cases involved gang crimes and robbery). Over 200 people were resentenced to death, more than 10 received the death penalty with suspension, over 20 received life imprisonment, and more than 80 received fixed-term imprisonment ("Report" 1951:1).

My discussions so far have tried to reconstruct the process through which new penal practices involving the death penalty were established during the campaign to suppress counterrevolutionaries. It is now time to approach this phenomenon in a more analytical way in order to emphasize some of its essential characteristics.

CHARACTERISTICS OF THE MAOIST REGIME OF CAPITAL PUNISHMENT

A decisive aspect of the campaign to suppress counterrevolutionaries is its profound impact on official practices with regard to the death penalty in China. I single out a few of these practices, which became institutionalized and were to leave their mark on the entire Maoist and even post-Maoist periods.

Politicization of the Legal System: Implementation

First, one observes a politicization of the legal system. In this politicization, party directives play a decisive part, in contrast with previous situations where a certain amount of autonomy could be conceded to judicial organs. Politicization, however, is a relative concept, and a comparison will be made with the situation prevailing under the rule of the Nationalist Party in order to better perceive the specifics of the Maoist case.

The launching of the campaign to suppress counterrevolutionaries makes possible precise observation of how a penal policy was decided at the top of the party. The personal intervention of Mao was decisive. Because of his intervention, between March 18, 1950, and February 21, 1951, a directive of the party became a state "law." The 1951 Regulations remained in force until 1980, and some of its articles were incorporated into the Criminal Law of 1979. In general, in the verdicts to which I have been able to gain access, all the indications are that the 1951 Regulations served as the only explicit reference in the first three decades of Communist rule, even in the judgment of crimes that were relatively minor, such as theft. The 1951 Regulations was regularly invoked in cases of behaviors punishable by the death sentence.

The case of Shanghai enables us to observe the tensions that existed during this political transformation. In this city, the establishment of the supremacy of the party's ideology collided directly with a concern for legality stemming from efforts of half a century toward modernization of the legal system.

Two factors need to be considered here. One is the existence of a policy specially prepared by the Communists to seize control of Shanghai before the capture of the city by the People's Liberation Army. To overcome this metropolis, considered the "last obstacle to the Communist revolution" (Archives of the Municipality of Shanghai 1989:68), the Communist Party identified three areas of intervention. The first, which had to be "left intact," concerned production, trade, transport, and communications. The second, which had to be "gradually reformed," was that of education, culture, and the press. The third, which had to be "completely destroyed," concerned the state apparatus, the Nationalist Party, the army, and the police (Archives of the Municipality of Shanghai 1989:70–82). As part of the third category, all courts, prosecutors, and prisons were taken over by the Political Affairs Section. In contrast, the police system, which also belonged to the last category, was placed under the control of the Ministry of Public Security (ibid.:105–115). That ministry was founded in Beijing on July 6, 1949, under the direction of the Military Committee of the Central Committee of the CCP (Z. Wang 2008). This heralded the central position of the police in the organization of the legal system of the PRC.

The other factor is the transition period between the abolition by the Central Committee of the Party of all laws promulgated by the former regime in February 1949 (J. Zhang 2001:158) and the publication of the 1951 Regulations. For two years, there was a gap in legal regulation The lack of legal references in forming judgments created problems for those working in the system of justice.

At the end of 1949, in order to adapt to this situation, the People's Court of Shanghai Municipality, where some legal professionals had kept their positions, sought to standardize certain rules in order to avoid arbitrariness in the application of penalties. A project titled the Criteria for the Application of Penalties was submitted for review by the national Supreme Court. In this project, the principle of the application of penalties depending on the severity of the crime was maintained, and crimes carrying the death penalty were restricted to those involving homicide or crimes that threatened the security of the state. Under the category of crimes of a political nature, the death sentence could be passed only on the leaders of armed gatherings (Article 10) and on those who committed specific acts in order to hinder the revolution, sabotage the "People's democratic dictatorship," or subvert the government of the PRC "in collusion with imperialist armies, or using their military aid." Any accused person who was guilty only of "intention," "conspiracy," or "preparation" of such acts would systematically receive a reduced sentence and be sentenced to imprisonment for 3 to 7 years. Mere accomplices to such activities were to be punished with imprisonment for a term of 7 to 15 years. Those guilty of espionage, in the most serious cases, would be sentenced to life imprisonment (Archives of the Municipality of Shanghai, B1/2/308). However, the People's Supreme Court quickly rejected the project.

Shen Junru (1875–1963), who had been a famous lawyer under the Republic and had become the first president of the People's Supreme Court, stated the reasons for the rejection of the project in a letter to the court of the Municipality of Shanghai. In his opinion, the project "does not sufficiently express the position of the People's dictatorship and the need to consolidate the revolutionary order." For example, he stated,

> In Chapter II on the crime of endangering the security of the State, Article 9 states that all those who attempt to obstruct and commit acts of sabotage against the People's democratic dictatorship, and subvert the Government of the PRC, regardless of how serious the circumstances, will be punishable by a maximum imprisonment of seven years. Those who are guilty of collusion with the enemy will be punishable by a maximum imprisonment of fifteen years, and even in the most serious cases, the penalty will be limited to imprisonment for life. Article 12, on espionage, provides only life imprisonment as the maximum penalty. According to Article 36 of Chapter VI, con-

cerning crimes of counterfeiting notes of the People's Bank, the maximum penalty is ten years imprisonment. Among all these crimes, not one is liable to the death penalty. (ibid.:21)

Comparison with the Practice of the Nationalist Government

In order to better understand these controversies, it is useful to compare the 1951 Regulations with its counterparts in the 1920s and 1930s, which had been promulgated by the Nationalist government in Nanking. Although both governments defined counterrevolutionary crimes according to political principles, the differences between the two are worth noting.

First, the 1928 provisional law provided for degrees of punishment in accordance with the penal code of the era, including the death penalty, life imprisonment, four degrees of temporary imprisonment, detention, fines, and deprivation of civil rights. On the contrary, the 1951 Regulations prescribed penalties without reference to any legal code.

The second difference lies in the strict distinctions made between committed crime and attempted crime and between main culprits and accomplices, in particular as regards the application of the death penalty. Under the Communist 1951 Regulations, these traditional legal concepts were eliminated, and vague notions were put forward, such as "serious circumstances," "guilty of the most heinous plans," "causing great popular indignation," and "having been involved in a blood debt." On the contrary, the Nationalist law strictly respected these distinctions.

The third difference concerns the question of retroactivity. In the 1951 Regulations, Article 18 stipulated that the provisions were applicable to all counterrevolutionary crimes committed before the promulgation of the regulations, while Article 13 of the Nationalist law stated that only criminals who had not yet been tried before the publication of the law could be judged by it.

The fourth important difference is the principle of analogy used in the Communist 1951 Regulations. Article 16 stressed that crimes not covered by these regulations were to be judged by analogy according to their provisions. In contrast, Article 8 of the Nationalist law referred the punishment of certain crimes to the requirements of the criminal code.

The fifth difference concerns the nature of the court. Although there was no specific provision in the Nationalist law, it is known that the Nanjing

Nationalist government drew up several regulations in this regard; for instance, counterrevolutionary cases were handled by special tribunals, which were different from both ordinary and military courts (National History Archives, Taiwan, microfilm 150:793–806, 839–840, 1246; microfilm 314:2047). In contrast, Article 20 of the 1951 Regulations stipulated that counterrevolutionary crimes must be tried by a military court during the period of military control.

Finally, there is a difference in the number of crimes subject to the death penalty prescribed by these two laws. As mentioned earlier, the Nationalist law identified only 6 counterrevolutionary crimes, of which 5 carried the death penalty. The 1951 Regulations defined 17 counterrevolutionary crimes, of which 13 were punishable by the death penalty. Crimes of this nature covered wider areas, and the number of crimes punishable by death was much higher in the latter than in the former.

We do not have overall figures for the implementation of the 1928 Nationalist law, in particular concerning the number of death sentences. Fragmentary information provides us with some idea. Before this law was put into force, the cleanup of Communists, which began at dawn on April 12, 1927, had already claimed several thousand victims (Chevrier 1983:73). The municipal police reported that 140 Communist leaders and 500 workers lost their lives during this cleanup, led by Chiang Kai-shek in Shanghai. Another report stated that there were about 700 victims (Isaacs 1961:177). According to Dick Wilson, in the weeks following this semimilitary operation, between 5,000 and 10,000 people were eliminated in Shanghai (Wilson 1991:17). In Fuzhou, dozens of Communists were arrested and executed (Fairbank 1983:629). Jonathan Fenby gives the following figures: 34,000 dead, 40,000 wounded, and 25,000 arrested (Fenby 2008:148). Within these statistics, it is difficult to make the essential difference between the victims of massacres in the streets and those who were tried and executed.

Another study addresses some legislative and judicial aspects of the purge of Communist elements carried out by the Nationalist authorities. It appears that, beginning on April 12, 1927, over 1,000 Communists were arrested in Canton. In November of the same year, in order to treat these cases, classified as "counterrevolutionary" activities or "local despots and evil gentry," the Guangdong government promulgated the Regulations on the Establishment of Special Criminal Courts in Canton. However, the jurisdiction of such courts was limited to cases liable to temporary imprisonment (Liu 2008:265–266). This study informs us of the existence of a special report of the Central Committee of the Kuomintang dated November 22, 1927. According to this report, "Many reactionary Communist elements and local despots and evil gentry" had been denounced and held in prison throughout China since the establishment by the Kuomintang of judicial bodies charged with purging the Communists. In Nanking, the capital, "several hundred Communist suspects are being held in prison or in military organizations, and the majority of these prisoners have not been tried." However, in this report, the central government was concerned that the burgeoning arrests could be the result of unjustified accusations, and it criticized the abusive and unauthorized creation of courts by the bodies in charge of the purge. It decided in March 1929 to maintain special criminal courts at two levels (central and local) to deal with cases of counterrevolution and to close the other courts. From that date, all cases had to be judged according to the 1928 provisional law. A procedural law was also enacted in July 1928. It stipulated that cases carrying the death penalty must be submitted for approval before execution. At the same time, a law on the composition of juries for counterrevolutionary cases was implemented. This law provided that a jury had to be composed of six members of the Nationalist Party, who must be local residents and aged at least 25 (ibid.:264–269).

We do not have a record of these political convictions under the Kuomintang, particularly those carrying the death penalty. But it is clear that the degree of politicization of the legal system was less advanced than that under Mao.

Criminalization of Social Behaviors

It is not difficult to see that crimes of a political nature were henceforth at the center of the Maoist legal system, and that the death penalty served as a major means of repression. Although the charge of "counterrevolutionary crime" was created by the Nationalists, the Communist regulations further accentuated the political nature of offenses deemed to deserve capital punishment. In fact, the Communist campaign to suppress counterrevolutionaries probably represented a period in Chinese history when the use of the death penalty to punish political crimes was most intense. According to an official report dated January 1954, between December 1950 and mid-1952, about 2.62 million people were arrested for counterrevolutionary crimes. Of these, 712,000 were sentenced to death, 129,000 were imprisoned, and 1.2 million were "placed under the supervision of the masses."[8] The accusation of counterrevolutionary activities was to remain thereafter the leading category of crimes, particularly those punishable by death.

Until 1996, when the revised Criminal Law abolished this type of offense, crimes of counterrevolution constituted "the most serious and the most dangerous crimes" over 47 years of Communist legal practice (Centre for Research on the Criminal Code and the Code of Criminal Procedure, the Central Staff School in Political Science and Law 1981:1). They were also a convenient pretext for multiplying campaigns of political repression. The last campaign of mass repression under Mao took place on January 31, 1970, when thousands of counterrevolutionaries, as redefined by the Directive on the Offensive against Counterrevolutionary Activities, were tried and executed.[9] This Maoist legacy was continued by President Hua Guofeng in 1977 and later marked the era of Deng Xiaoping, although in a very different spirit and with very different methods.

A Quota System of Political Repression

A quota system of repression was invented by Mao during the 1950s campaign and was subsequently adopted on a regular basis in all the political campaigns during his rule. This doctrine was contained in a report by Luo Ruiqing, presented at the Third National Conference on Public Security (held from May 10 to May 15, 1951). This report, prepared according to Mao's directives, became the Decision of the Third Conference on Public Security and was adopted on May 15 and sent to the provincial and regional party committees. According to this decision, "The number of counterrevolutionaries sentenced to death should be limited to a certain percentage [of the population]" (Mao 1977:40). In rural areas, it should generally not exceed one-thousandth of the total population; in cities, it was advisable to aim at only 0.5 of one-thousandth (Pang & Chongji 2003:199). "As for counterrevolutionaries deserving death who had been identified within the organs of the party, the government, and the military or in industrial, commercial, or religious circles, as well as in other democratic parties and people's organizations, one must generally execute one or two out of ten" (*Chronicle of Important Events in Contemporary China* 1993:227).

This method of calculation was then applied in campaigns of repression, such as the Three Antis and the Five Antis in 1951–1952, the Purge of Counterrevolutionaries in 1956, the Anti-Rightist movement in 1957, and the Strike Against Counterrevolutionaries in 1970. A similar logic could still be seen in various campaigns against crime in the 1980s and 1990s, including the strike-hard campaigns. Another method of identifying targets of repression developed by Mao during this campaign was to distinguish three levels of counterrevolutionaries: those who were hidden in society, those who concealed themselves within government and military organizations, and those who acted within the Communist Party. This distinction was to serve as a key criterion to differentiate the use of the death penalty from that of the death sentence with a two-year suspension.

Decentralization of Power to Impose the Death Penalty

A form of regionalization or even decentralization of the imposition and review of the death penalty was deliberately encouraged during the 1950s campaign. Thus, in a telegram dated January 22, 1951, Mao gave the following orders to administrative officials of the South Central Region:

> In all cases involving bandit leaders and local tyrants or important secret agents encountered during the extermination of (military) banditry, the death penalty may be applied by a regional or subdivisional military court. As for major counterrevolutionaries without any direct link with the extermination of banditry, the death penalty may be imposed by a local court or by the Bureau of Military Justice, under the direction of the Military Control Committee. Tyrants and rural landowners who do not submit to the law will be delivered to the peasants who will be responsible for organizing the trial and surveillance and for forming a People's Court for judgment. Such a division of labor on three levels will allow us to carry out our work quickly and in an appropriate manner. (Mao 1991, 2:51)

The real effects of this directive were difficult to assess, but the 1951 Regulations set a precedent by decentralizing the power to review cases punishable by death. According to the October 10 Directive of 1950, "All cases carrying the death penalty and long-term imprisonment shall be heard and decided by the court, before being approved by the Governor of the province for the execution of the sentence" (J. Zhang 2001:171). The abuse of repression can already be seen in a directive of Mao enacted in May 1951, more than a month after the first operation in Beijing:

> In order to guard against "leftist" deviations which are developing in the crackdown on counterrevolutionaries, we have decided that, from June 1, all over the country... the power of arrest will be recovered without exception by the Party Committee and the government at prefecture level. As for the power to kill, it will be recovered without exception by the government at provincial level. In areas far from the capital of a province, the provincial government must send representatives. No locality can be allowed to modify this decision. (Mao 1977:40)

The fact that the (officially recognized) "democratic parties" were morally involved and the masses were actually mobilized according to the Beijing model gave the signal at the national level that a broader initiative was allowed in the business of repression. Although in large cities this mass mobilization generally remained under control, in the countryside or at the district level in some regions, it turned into personal revenge and killings for purely local reasons. A report dated May 17, 1951, sent by Ye Jianying, then head of the Southern Bureau, outlined the situation as follows:

> The Guangxi Committee and its Bureau of Public Security made a self-criticism recognizing that among those executed, about 30% did not deserve death. Forty people sentenced to death in Longzhou and Leiping were judged without their files containing any criminal act, class origin, curriculum vitae, or even date of birth. At the district or sub-prefecture level there have been executions decided by individuals on their own initiative. For example, the head of the organization department of the CCP Committee of Yongning district personally gave permission to kill 126 people. In the sub-prefecture of Cangwu 14 people were killed before government approval was received from a higher level. In another sub-prefecture, 24 people were put to death under the same conditions. The killing of 52 people was allowed in the district of Yishan, and in the district of Guixian, eight people were secretly shot in the night. In some places, people were killed with sticks, and people went so far as to tear off their ears or tear out their hearts, and there were calls for an increase in the proportion of death sentences.[10]

Even in major cities, the application of this directive was closely monitored by Mao himself. This was the case in Shanghai. In fact, on May 11, 1951, after a series of repressions, Yao Shushi sent a report calling for the reassumption of the powers of arrest and execution, which had been delegated for a month to local governments and to the masses in the cities of the Eastern Region. Mao replied that Yao should allow the delegation of these powers to continue for another few months (Mao 1991, 2:337).

Alternating centralization and decentralization of the power to review sentences involving the death penalty was to become a regular practice under Mao. One effort at recentralization was expressed in the Decision Regarding the Approval and Final Judgment by the Supreme Court of Cases Subject to the Death Penalty (ibid., 2:196), enacted in 1957 by the National People's Congress. Its objective was to standardize the criteria for death sentences, which had been applied differently in different provinces. This was another corrective to the perverse consequences of the provincialization of that power. However, less than two months later, new instructions were issued, no longer emanating from the government, but from the Central Committee of the party. This was the Directive Concerning Measures on the Judgment and Approval of Cases Punishable by the Death Penalty (September 10, 1957). According to this directive,

> Cases carrying the death penalty processed by the People's Courts of a province, an autonomous region or a municipality shall be submitted to higher courts for review and approval before being referred to the People's Supreme Court. In cases which require the approval of the Party Committee of a province, municipality or autonomous region, superior courts must submit them to the Committee of the Party concerned for approval, before sending them to the Supreme Court for execution. For capital cases to be executed immediately after the judgment, the High Court may send a report in conjunction with the Party Committee of a province, municipality or autonomous region to the Party Central Committee, to the State Council and to the Supreme Court, and the latter can verify and approve them quickly by telegram. (J. Zhang 2001:197)

However, the meaning of this directive cannot be fully grasped without reference to another document of the same year, the *Report of the Meeting on the Work of the Judiciary and the Fight Against Rightists in the People's Supreme Court*, dated December 14, 1957. This report proposed that "henceforth, on condition that the regulations are not broken, the orders and policies of the Party, and the political and judicial organs are under the leadership of the Party Committee and 'People's Committees' at the level of the provinces, municipalities and autonomous regions; and all activities related to trials must categorically obey the direction and supervision of the Party. Local Party Committees have the right to intervene in all court cases. All ideas and actions which favor judicial independence and the rejection of the Party's powers of supervision are errors which must absolutely be corrected" (ibid.:197–198). There were clearly tensions at the time among different decision-making bodies in the party and the government. In order to shed light on these texts, one would no doubt have to factor in the infighting between supporters of a more moderate and legalistic line and those who backed Mao Zedong's radical line.

Without precise data, it is difficult to get an idea of the degree of real implementation of these decisions and directives. In any case, it is clear that with the outbreak of the Cultural Revolution in 1966, any desire to maintain centralized powers of review in cases punishable by death was overcome. The slogan "Crush public security, the prosecutor, and the court," launched on August 7, 1967, by the minister of public security, Xie Fuzhi, symbolized a decade characterized by the suspension of normal legality and the installation of organs of an exceptional type. In this chaotic situation, it is not surprising to see, for example, the setting up in Guangxi Province of Poor Peasants' Supreme Courts to suppress the "four types of enemies" (landlords, rich peasants, counterrevolutionaries, and undesirable elements) (ibid.:212). Dozens of cases carrying the death penalty for political reasons were published on the occasion of the rehabilitation of the executed in the early 1980s, once again for political reasons. These examples showed clearly that the power of review did not reach up to the Supreme Court. In spite of an attempt at recentralization of this power in 1979 with the promulgation of the Criminal Procedure Law, there was further provincialization in 1983 with the launch of the strike-hard campaign against economic crimes. It was not until 2007 that this power was recovered by the Supreme Court, partially because of the efforts of a new generation of Chinese jurists who are more attentive to human rights and to international standards of the rule of law.

Mass Trials and Social Terror

The institutionalization and wider use of mass trials is another characteristic of the practice of the death penalty developed after the 1950s campaign. This type of trial dated back to the Stalinist-style purge carried out in the Soviet Republic of Jiangxi in 1929–1931, but its systematization and institutionalization in the cities began with the campaign to suppress counterrevolutionaries, first launched in Beijing and Tianjin before it spread to other provinces.

A mass trial usually consisted of three stages: a rally denouncing the accused attended by thousands of citizens in a symbolic place in the city center, public exhibition of the condemned in the streets, and finally, execution in a field in the suburbs. It was also characterized by a summary procedure that made it impossible to distinguish an ordinary criminal trial from a military trial. From then on, until the 1980s, the execution of condemned prisoners under Mao and his successors took place roughly in this way. Today, certain practices, such as collective execution of the condemned or public exhibition of the guilty, although prohibited by the Supreme Court, still reappear from time to time in some provinces, particularly during the strike-hard campaigns, which presented opportunities for demonstrating the repressive power of the state at the regional level (Qu 2003).

Death Sentence with Reprieve

The "death sentence with a two-year suspension" was Mao's invention (X. Zhang 1998:360). Its aim was to reduce the execution rate. This practice was aimed at "eight or nine of the ten percent of counterrevolutionaries who exist within the Party, in political and military circles, in the world of education and the economy and within the Communist Youth League" (Mao 1977:44). A particular target was "those who, though deserving of death for the serious damage they cause to the State, have not created a debt of blood or caused popular outrage" (ibid.:43).

Once again, Mao saw this measure from a utilitarian perspective. It was "conservative" and "right" because "it can avoid errors, elicit approval from society, divide the counterrevolutionary forces in order to exterminate them completely, and keep a large workforce for the construction of the country" (ibid.:42). The same spirit was reflected at that time by the creation of two other typically Maoist repressive practices: reeducation through labor (*laogai*) and rehabilitation "under the supervision of the masses," which thus became widespread in society. According to Mao, "Methods applied to counterrevolutionaries are to kill them, lock them up, control them or release them. Where killing is concerned, everyone knows what that is. Locking up means imprisonment with forced labor. Control is re-education under the supervision of the masses within society" (ibid.:280–281).

These three Maoist methods, applied simultaneously during the campaign, became widespread. Reeducation under the supervision of the masses became a system with the enactment of An Interim Measure for the Control of Counterrevolutionary Elements on July 17, 1953 (J. Zhang 2001:180). Reeducation through labor was institutionalized on September 7, 1954, by the publication of the Regulations on Re-Education Through Labor in the PRC (ibid.:184). The practice of the death sentence with a two-year suspension was officially formulated on May 8, 1951, by the Decision of the CCP Central Committee on the Policy of Application of the Death Sentence with a Two-Year Suspension to the Majority of Counterrevolutionaries. Initially this was aimed only at counterrevolutionaries, but it was increasingly applied to other types of crimes. This was the case, for example, in 1952, with "corrupt elements" during the Three Antis campaign. It subsequently appeared in the Project of the Guiding Principles of Criminal Law of the PRC in 1954 before being incorporated as an officially recognized punishment in the 1979 Criminal Law (Z. Zhang 2004:12–15).

In reality, this procedure gradually acquired a new dimension. Indeed, since 1957, the review procedure of a death sentence with a two-year suspension has been separated from that concerning an immediate death sentence. The former can thus be considered de facto a separate sentence (ibid.:126–129). Since 1979, there have been practical concerns regarding the imposition of suspended death sentences. Under the provisions of the Criminal Procedure Law of 1979 and the subsequent revisions (e.g., 1996, 2012), a suspended death sentence, once imposed by an intermediate court, must be reviewed and approved by a provincial high court regardless of whether there is an appeal. However, because the Criminal Procedure Law does not specify that the criminal sentence shall not be increased as a result of a defendant's appeal, an appeal involves a risk of receiving a heavier sentence. Z. Zhang's study shows that only about 25% of the 188 cases that received suspended death sentences during the 1990s and the early years of the twenty-first century resulted in an appeal. Among them, 3 cases received heavier sentences and 4 more lenient sentences (Z. Zhang 2004:158–319).

Although the direct intervention of Mao Zedong in the application of the death penalty became less visible after the campaigns of the 1950s, his temperament and his personal vision, encouraged by the cult of personality, contributed greatly to the formation of distinctive traits in judicial practices related to the death penalty.

•   •   •

A judicial regime deeply marked by Mao's personality still profoundly influences legal practices in today's China, in particular those concerning the death penalty. This is evident in three ways:

1. Political decisions still intervene directly in legal judgments. The death sentences passed on corrupt officials are often an example of this feature. The role of the Central Committee for Disciplinary Inspection of the CCP is much more important than that of the court in a trial. Despite certain legal formalities, this is evident in the case, in 2012–2013, of Wang Lijun (former police chief of Chongqing), Bo Xilai, and his wife, Gu Kailai.
2. The type of political campaign developed during the crackdown on counterrevolutionaries continued in the strike-hard campaigns initiated in 1983, which put to death 24,000 people in one year[11] and were transformed in the years after 2000 into campaigns aimed at "cleaning up the Mafia." The latter, which sought to eliminate by summary means those violating public order or responsible for "economic crimes," were based on special regulations that made it possible to expedite legal procedures and increase the number of cases punishable by death (N. Zhang 2005:9; Zhao 2005). Suffice it to mention as examples the methods used during the cleanup of mafias in Chongqing, carried out by Bo Xilai in 2009–2010, such as absence of public trials, swift executions, systematic use of torture, obstacles aiming at blocking effective legal assistance, and incitement to "public outrage." In such actions, one can easily recognize practices similar to those used in the campaign of repression of counterrevolutionaries in 1951.
3. In particular, the system of the death sentence with a two-year suspension has so far remained untouched, and although the legal definition of its twin system of reeducation through labor was officially abolished in 2001, its institutional function, structure, and habitus have not substantively

changed. Paradoxically, the system of the death sentence with a two-year suspension is taken today by many jurists as a good way to limit the number of executions.

NOTES

1. This law stated that "all attempts to subvert the Chinese Nationalist Party and the Nationalist government or to sabotage the Three Principles of the People" were considered counterrevolutionary crimes. "Cases involving the Communist Party should be treated as counterrevolutionary offenses," said the Judicial Yuan of the Kuomintang. Human Rights Watch/Asia, 1997, Chapter 6.
2. "Report by Liu Shaoqi to the First National Conference on Propaganda Work," May 7, 1951, quoted by Yang (2006:41).
3. "Report of the Office of the CCP Eastern Region of China on the Problem of Repression of Counterrevolutionaries," December 28, 1950, quoted by Yang, (2006:42).
4. "Instructions of the CCP Central Committee on the Report of the Committee of CCP in the Eastern Region of China on the Problem of Suppressing Counterrevolutionaries," January 8, 1951, quoted by Yang (2006:42).
5. Mao, "Instructions for the Crackdown on Counterrevolutionaries in Shanghai and Nanjing," February 12, 1951, quoted by Yang (2006:48–49).
6. "Telegram from Mao Zedong to Deng Xiaoping, Yao Shushi, Deng Zihui, Ye Jianying, Xu Zhongxun and Informing Bo Yibo and Gao Gan," April 20, 1951, quoted by Yang (2006:48).
7. "Project of the Municipality of Shanghai to Suppress Counterrevolutionaries," April 20, 1951, quoted by Yang (2006:55).
8. "Statistics of Some Key Figures Concerning the Repression of Counterrevolutionaries," April 20, 1951, quoted by Yang (2006:76).
9. According to statistics, between February and November 1970, over 18.4 million traitors, spies, and counterrevolutionary elements were unmasked. More than 284,800 people were arrested, and thousands of them were executed (N. Wang 1988:333).
10. "Report by Ye Jianying on the Repression of Counterrevolutionaries in the South," May 17, 1951, quoted by Yang (2006:66).
11. See "Report by CCP Central Committee of Politics and Law on the Achievement of the First Campaign of the 'Strike Hard' and the Launching of the Second One," October 31 1987, quoted by Huang (2007:112).

REFERENCES

Archives of the Municipality of Shanghai. B1/2/308.
Archives of the Municipality of Shanghai. B1/2/1059/1412/26–31, B2/2/2/94.

Archives of the Municipality of Shanghai (Ed.). *Shanghai jiefang* [Shanghai's Liberation], Beijing: Beijing Archives.

Beijing shiqu gejie renmin daibiao kuoda lianxi hui taolun zhenya fangemin wenti jingguo -1951 nian 3 yue 24 ri [Beijing holds an enlarged meeting of representatives from all works on counterrevolution crackdown experience, 1951, March 24]. (1951, March 25). *People's Daily*, p. 1.

Beijing shi zhongyao wenxian xuanbian [Selected Important Documents on the Municipality of Beijing] (vol. 1951). Beijing: China Archives.

Chevrier, Y. (1983). *La Chine moderne.* Paris: Presses Universitaires de France.

Dangdai zhongguo zhongda shijian shilu [Chronicle of Important Events in Contemporary China]. (1993). Beijing: Hualing.

Fairbank, J. K. (1983). *The Cambridge History of China* (vol. 12), *Republican China, 1912–1949.* London: Cambridge University Press.

Fenby, J. (2008). *The Penguin History of Modern China: The Fall and Rise of a Great Power, 1850–2008.* London: Allen Lane.

Guo, F. (Ed.). (2001). *Tianjin tongzhi: Gong'anzhi* [The Annals of Public Security of Tianjin]. Tianjin: Tianjin People's Publishing House.

Huang, W. (2007). *Sihuan zhidu de dangdai jiazhi* [The Contemporary Value of the Sihuan System]. Beijing: Kexue chubanshe.

Human Rights Watch/Asia. (1997). The use of counterrevolution: A cautionary tale. *Human Rights in China*, 9(4), 26–27. Retrieved July 5, 2012, from http://hrichina.org/content/4694.

Isaacs, H. R. (1961). *The Chinese Revolution.* Stanford, CA: Stanford University Press.

Jingjin renmin dazhangqigu zhenya fangeming [The People of Beijing and Tianjin Suppress Counterrevolutionaries on a Large Scale). (1951). Beijing: People's Publishing House.

Liu, H. (2008). Geming/fangeming-Nanjing minguo zhengfu shiqi guomindang de falü lunshu [Revolution and counterrevolution: The judicial discourses of Kuomintang during the period of Nanjing government]. In Wang, P. (Ed.), *2008 falü sixiang yu shehui bianqian* [2008: Judicial Thought and Social Changes] (pp. 255–304). Taipei: Institute for Studies on Law, Academia Sinica.

Mao, Z. (1961). *Selected Works of Mao Tse-tung* (vol. 4). Beijing: Foreign Languages Press.

Mao, Z. (1977). *Mao Zedong quanji* [Selected Works of Mao Zedong] (vol. 5). Beijing: People's Publishing House.

Mao, Z. (1991). *Jianguo yilai Mao Zedong wengao* [Mao Zedong's Manuscripts since the Founding of the PRC]. Beijing: Central Literary Contributions Publishing House.

National History Archives, Taiwan. (n.d.). Guomin zhengfu dang'an [Archives of the Nationalist Government]. Microfilms 150 and 314.

Pang, X., & Chongji, J. (2003). *Mao Zedong zhuan: 1949–1976* [A Biography of Mao Zedong: 1949–1976]. Beijing: Central Literary Contributions.

Qingdao shizhi: Gong'an sifa zhi [Local Records Office of Qingdao: The Annals of Public Security of Qingdao]. (1998). Beijing: Xinhua.

Qu, X. (2003). Yanda de xingshi zhengce fenxi [An analysis of the criminal politics of the "Strike Hard"]. In Chen Xingliang (Ed.), *Fazhi de shiming* [The Mission of the Rule of Law] (pp. 197–205). Beijing: Law Press.

Quan Shanghai, quan Huadong yiqi qilai, kongsu he jianju fangeming fenzi [Rise up together, all people of Shanghai and East China, to denounce and report counterrevolutionaries]. (1951, April 29). *Liberation*, p. 1.

Quan Shanghai renmin xingdong qilai, yansuzhenya fangeming fenzi [Rise up, all people of Shanghai, and forcefully suppress counterrevolutionaries]. (1951, April 28). *Liberation*, p. 1.

Shanghai gong'anzhi [Bureau of Shanghai Public Security]. (1997). Shanghai: Academy of Social Sciences Press.

Shanghai shi difangzhi bangongshi [Local Records Office of the Municipality of Shanghai]. (n.d.). *Zhenya fangeming* [Suppress counterrevolutionaries]. In *Huangpu quzhi* [The Annals of Huangpu District] (chapter 26). Retrieved April 25, 2008, from http://www.shtong.gov.cn/node2/node4/node2249/huangpu/node35610/node35619/no.

Shen, B. (2009). Jinwan xingdong kouling : Zhenfan-zhuanfang yuan xinan junzheng weiyuanhui gong'an bu ganshi [Password tonight: Suppress the counterrevolutionaries—Interview with a former executive of the Public Security Bureau of the Committee of Military Control of the Southwest]. Retrieved July 5, 2012, from http://news163com/09/0801/15/5FL15TF500013HTH.html.

Shi jianchashu guanyu 432 ming fangeming fenzi chongpan baogao [Report of the Municipal Prosecutor's Office about the 432 re-trial counterrevolutionaries cases]. (1951, June 15). *Liberation*, p. 1.

Shi junguanhui jieshou renmin yaoqiu, chujue fangeming shou'e 285 ming [The Military Control Committee of the Municipality of Shanghai put to death 285 counterrevolutionairy culprits according to people's demand]. (1951, May 1). *Wenhui bao*, p. 1.

Wan, C. (Ed.). (2006). *Zhongguo jingzheng shi* [History of Police in China]. Beijing: Zhonghua.

Wang, N. (1988). *Dadongluan de niandai* [Years of Turmoil]. Zhengzhou: Henan People's Publishing House.

Wang, Z. (2008). Gong'anbu shi zenme chengli de [How the Ministry of Public Security was founded]. In *Gong'an shihua* [The History of Public Security]. Retrieved March 14, 2008, from http://www.mps.gov.cn/cenweb/brjlCenweb/jsp/policehistory/article.jsp?infoid=ABC.

Wilson, D. (1991). *China's Revolutionary War*. London: Weidenfeld & Nicolson.

Yang, K. (2006). Mao Zedong yu zhenya fangeming yundong [Mao Zedong and the campaign to suppress counterrevolutionaries]. In Chen Y. (Ed.), *Liang'an fentu: lengzhan chuqi de zhengjing fazhan* [Different Roads Between Mainland China and Taiwan: Political and Economic Development] (pp. 31–76). Taipei: Institute of Modern History, Academia Sinica.

Zhang, J. (2001). *Zhongguo bainian fazhi dashi zhonglan* [A Survey of Memorabilia of the Chinese Legal System in a Century]. Beijing: Law Press.

Zhang, N. (2005). The debate over the death penalty in today's China. *Chinese Perspectives, 9*, 1–10.

Zhang, N. (2010). 1951–9152: Shanghai sifa shijian de zhengzhihua guidian [A political turning point in judicial practice in Shanghai: 1951–1952]. *Leaders, 32*, 92–108; *33*, 90–108.

Zhang, X. (1998). *Zhonghua renmin gongheguo xingfashi* [History of Criminal Law in the People's Republic of China]. Beijing: People's Public Security University Press.

Zhang, Z. (2004). *Sixing xianzhi lun* [Theory and Practice of the Death Sentence Reprieve]. Wuhan: Wuhan University Press.

Zhao, Z. (2005). Sixing de sifa xianzhuang jiqi zhanwang [The legal status of the death penalty and its prospects]. Retrieved March 17, 2005, from http://beizhen.com/article_show.asp ?ArticleID=969.

Zhenya fangeming bixu dazhang qigu [Counterrevolution crackdown needs a wide publicity]. (1951, April 3). *People's Daily*, p. 1.

Zhonggong Shanghaishi weidangshi yanjiushi [Center for Studies in the History of the Shanghai Municipal Committee of the CCP]. *Zhonggong shanghai lishi shilu: 1949–2004* [Annals of the Chinese Communist Party in Shanghai: 1949–2004]. Shanghai: Shanghai Education).

Zhonggong zhongyang wenxian yanjiushi [Central Archives of the Chinese Communist Party]. (1991). *Gongheguo zouguo de lu, Jianguo yilai zhongyao wenxian zhuanti xuanji* [The Road of the Republic: Selected Important Documents: 1949–1952]. Beijing: Central Literary Contribution.

Zhongyang Zhengfa ganbu xuexiao xingfa, xingshi susongfa jiaoyanshi [Center for Research on the Criminal Code and the Code of Criminal Procedure, Central Staff School in Political Sciences and Law]. (1981). *Zhonghua renmin gongheguo xingfa fenze jiangyi* [Lectures on the Criminal Code of the People's Republic of China]. Beijing: Masses Press.

China's Death Penalty in a State-Power-Based Society

▸ YUNHAI WANG

STUDIES OF THE DEATH penalty typically regard it as a result of a pure legal system. That is, the death penalty is usually a legal reaction to a crime prescribed by law, and a death sentence is usually meted out by a state-sanctioned judiciary through a legal procedure. The death penalty as an object of study has been commonly viewed as a constant whose meaning or function does not vary by time or place.

These assumptions are not an accurate depiction of the function of the death penalty in a society, both historically and culturally. In fact, the so-called death penalty can have different meanings and carry varied functions in different societies or even in the same society at different times. Some forms of the death penalty should properly be called "political death penalty" or "cultural death penalty." For example, the death penalty in contemporary Japan should be deemed a cultural death penalty. Japan has used the death penalty so rarely that people doubt whether its death penalty system has had any significant meaning. The average number of executions conducted in Japan from 1980 to 2013 was just 2.2 persons every year even after Japan's criminal policy became more punitive in the late 1990s.[1] On the other hand, Japan has never tried to abolish the death penalty and has shown a strong will to continue it. This current situation of Japan's death penalty practice originates from Japanese culture, under which the relationships between the state and the citizens are usually defined on the basis of paternalism. Acting as the "parent" of Japanese citizens, the state (the Japanese government) cannot apply the death penalty to its "children" capriciously; at the same time, the state cannot give up the death penalty as the final tool to show its authority as a parent (Wang 2012:6).

Although death penalty scholars take into account some political or cultural factors when they discuss the death penalty abolition movement in some countries, it is important to underscore the polysemy of the death penalty, as shown in the example of Japan's death penalty. In order to understand and predict the course of the death penalty in China, it is necessary first to discuss what the death penalty in China means and what it encompasses within China's social, cultural, and historical backgrounds. In other words, what is the nature of China's death penalty?

Some scholars turn to a socialist system approach when they study the death penalty in China. Under this approach, they mainly attribute the numerous death sentences and executions imposed in the era of the People's Republic of China (PRC) to Communism (Zhang 2008:117). Some of them argue that in Chinese history there were fewer death sentences, executions, and less preference for the death penalty than the present day (Johnson & Zimring 2009:226, 248). However, the death penalty, both as a term and as a legal punishment, has deep roots in Chinese history and has been frequently used to suppress criminal activities and especially to punish political rebels throughout China's various dynasties and the brief Republic era.

Chinese rulers in history usually employed two means to rule Chinese society: "rule by virtue" ("Dezhi") and "rule by law" ("Fazhi"). Although these two ways of ruling are often explained as contradictory to each other, they are not. Rather, they are two edges of the same sword. Rulers choose which edge to use mainly on the basis of their judgment on the social conditions that they are facing and the necessity for their ruling. The argument that there were fewer death sentences and executions and less preference for the death penalty in Chinese history pays attention only to rule by virtue without considering the other edge, rule by law. For example, some Western scholars have called the short-term halt of execution during the Tang dynasty (747–759) an "abolition" and have taken it as proof that there was less preference for the death penalty (Benn 2002:209; Johnson & Zimring 2009:246). However, there is great doubt whether the Tang dynasty officially abolished all its death penalty without any reservation against its political rebels and really forbade many executions from being conducted without following the legal procedure outside the courts in this period. Actually, in the Tang dynasty's legal system, criminal offenses usually were categorized into two completely different types. One was normal offenses, such as murder, theft, and robbery, that took place among civilians, and the other encompassed offenses that were deemed absolutely unpardonable. Ten offenses, including rebellion against the dynasty, disloyalty to the emperor, and disrespect to parents, were designated such absolutely unpardonable crimes (*shi e bu she* in Chinese). In any case of such crimes, the offender must be punished by the death penalty with no exception and without necessity to follow legal procedures. These crimes were not only unpardonable but also exceptional from the legal perspective in the official legal system and the courts. In the whole period of the Tang synasty, these ten unpardonable and exceptional offenses were never invalidated (Hu 2008:232; Niida 1980:235; Zhou 1985:260).

In contrast, another view explains the prevalence of the death penalty in China by turning to Chinese history and culture (Lu & Miethe 2007:27). But this historical-cultural approach faces the same problem, that is, it usually pays attention to the edge of rule by law without giving enough consideration to the other edge of rule by virtue. It tends to take rule by law as the norm and rule by virtue as an exception, although the real relationship between them is parallel and simultaneous. Moreover, culture is a very vague concept. The cultural approach has often assumed that the functions of a culture always stay the same in any society or at any time. In actuality, the functions of a culture are most likely to be different in different societies or at different times.

In order to understand the death penalty in China, we need a new perspective that can overcome the limitations of both the socialist system approach and the historical-cultural approach and can show the key factors that influence the nature and extent of the death penalty in China.[2]

CHINA AS A STATE-POWER-BASED SOCIETY AND THE NATURE OF THE DEATH PENALTY

The theory of a state-power-based society is derived from my analysis of the social core (Wang 2008a:140). Every society has a fundamental core, which I call a *social character*. A social character identified for a society as its core should have had the strongest impact on all other characters of that society as a whole, and permeated most, if not all, aspects of social lives.

As I have argued previously, three elements are essential to form the core of a society: (1) state power, (2) law, and (3) culture (Wang 1995:72; 2008a:140). State power is a physical coercive force that is legitimized politically. Law is a judicial, professional, and formal state force. Culture is an informal spiritual force that exists in every person and every private group and forms social moral values and social customs of a particular society.

However, these three elements do not have the same impact on the core of a society. For Chinese society, state power is the absolute dominating force and determines the content of law and culture in many regards. I thus label state power a social character of China and, correspondingly, China a state-power-based society (Wang 1995, 2005, 2008a).

My argument that China is a state-power-based society is based on the following grounds (Wang 1995:73). First, in Chinese society, the most important social force is nothing but state power. State power is the fundamental core of Chinese society. Individuals' social position, human rights, and individual success or failure basically depend on the state power. The social order is mainly created and maintained by the state power. The state power is universal and is also the final social standard of Chinese society. It can be argued that whether China can continue with its current political identity hinges on whether there will be a strong and stable state power. In essence, China is a political concept and is defined by the scope of its state power. The identity of China is foremost based on state power (Wittfogel 1957).

Second, from ancient China to the present, there has been a legal principle called *Fazhi*, which is similar to the Western legal term *rule of law* as a concept. However, the contents of law in *Fazhi* are punitive rules, and this *Fazhi* principle did not constitute a legal order or the rule of law (Unger 1976); rather, it simply served as a means for the emperors and their officials to impose punishment and was always subordinate to the state power. The state power had the full authority to determine when and how to enforce *Fazhi*. To this day, this nature of *Fazhi* in China has not changed fundamentally. Hence, law cannot be regarded as the original core of Chinese society and remains a subordinate force in contemporary Chinese society.

Third, there has been a culture in Chinese society. However, Chinese culture is not only subjected to the influence of the state power but also actively seeks the intervention of the state power, for it lacks stable and autonomous bases to operate and survive independently. As a result, it cannot truly be considered real culture independent from the state power but rather is subsumed by the state power. For example, from ancient China to the present, there has been a cultural principle called *Dezhi*, which means "rule by virtue of Confucianism." Although Confucianism has been described as China's most prominent religion (Cohen 1984), close scrutiny of its content and function suggests that this statement may not be apt. In fact, the contents of Confucianism are sermons about how people should obey the state power, and its main function is to interweave state-power relations into society's cultural norms. Confucianism focused heavily on how people should make themselves adaptable to the state power. It served as an instrument by which the state power ruled over people's spiritual beliefs and practices. The example of Confucianism shows that culture cannot be the original core of Chinese society.

In a state-power-based society like China, the essence or nature of the death penalty is nothing but political. This political nature means that the death penalty must be considered first and foremost from a political perspective and understood as a political tool for ruling society by political leaders, rather than from a legal perspective, that is, as a legal punishment of a specific crime by legal professionals. In a society like China's, the relationship between the state political powers and the practice of the death penalty has always been too close to sever. The death penalty has always shown a strong and deep subordination to the state political power and therefore the legal professional has not had independent power to apply it as a criminal punishment. As a result, what kind of death penalty system should be set up and how to use the death penalty are mainly determined not by legal or criminal principles but by political ideologies or policies (Wang 2008b:197). Political motivation, function, and mechanisms are the key points in understanding the death penalty in China. It is this political essence that has caused the prevalence of the death penalty in China from ancient times to the present. The death penalty in China should be defined as a political death penalty. This nature has never changed even though Chinese rulers in history sometimes professed a preference for rule by virtue and at other times advocated rule by law.

A STATE-POWER-BASED SOCIETY AND ITS DEATH PENALTY POLICY IN THE PRC ERA

The political essence of China's death penalty has remained the same in contemporary China, including the current era of the PRC. However, even though the PRC's political leaders still claim that China follows socialism in its political and social structures, its socialist system has changed over time.

The doctrine and the ideals of socialism were originally advocated by Westerners, such as Karl Marx and Friedrich Engels. The doctrine espoused by Marx and Engels was founded on their analysis of Western societies, such as Germany, France, and England. Why was a doctrine or an ideal of socialism that was born in the West imported to a Far Eastern country, where it has been accepted and practiced for several decades? The common answer, proposed by the Chinese Communist Party (CCP), is that the doctrine of socialism can change Chinese society fundamentally, and the CCP has changed Chinese society through practicing the doctrine of socialism. However, my observation is that the doctrine of socialism can justify the traditional Chinese social character of being a state-power-based society (Wang 2005:174). In this sense, it can be argued that the doctrine of socialism is naturally suited to Chinese society. In addition, Chinese socialism has never truly followed Marx's original socialism; rather, Chinese socialism is colored by the traditional social character of the state-power-based society. In other words, it is not socialism that determines the Chinese social character of the state-power-based society; rather, it is the state-power-based society that determines the nature of Chinese socialism.

Since the foundation of the PRC in 1949, China has persistently declared itself a socialist country. Yet the concrete contents and the real practices of Chinese socialism have varied greatly, depending on who the leader of the state is and what political ideology or political policy he advocates. Consequently, general policy on the death penalty in China has also varied, as detailed here (Wang 2008a:142).

Mao's "Political China" and Its Death Penalty Policy

It should be pointed out that Mao's era lasted from 1949 to 1978 although Mao died in 1976 (but his policies continued). Mao's era is referred to as the era of a "political China" where the state power dealt with everything in a completely political manner. During this era, a political ideology called the *class-struggle theory* was held as the supreme principle of the Chinese social system. Under this ideology, Chinese society and the Chinese people were divided into either the exploiting class (the enemy) or the working class (the people). This division was based on whether citizens were property owners, and the relationship between them was defined as one of life or death, to kill or to be killed.

The new state power of China (the CCP and its government) and the new Chinese law existed as the power and law of the working class only. Therefore, their greatest mission was to eliminate all private ownership and eradicate the exploiting class. In order to achieve this goal, the Chinese state power entered a political mode and encouraged all of Chinese society and the Chinese people to take part in the political struggles against the enemy. This was done through the launching of countless political mass movements on a daily basis. Consequently, in Mao's political China, all social events, social values, and social relationships were dealt with as political matters, and the whole society and people were politicized.

Since the political ideology of the class-struggle theory was held as the supreme principle, it politicized the whole Chinese society. Crimes, criminal justice, and punishments were also defined as political actions. Not only counterrevolutionary crimes but also some serious nonpolitical crimes were held to be attacks by the enemy, exploiting class on the working class or the revolutionary government (Wang 2005:183). This means that these crimes were deemed "crimes against the socialist system" (the most serious crimes).

According to the class-struggle theory, the relationship between the exploiting class and the working class is to kill or to be killed. In order to avoid being killed by the enemy (the exploiting class), it is logical and necessary for the working class and the revolutionary government to sentence the enemy to death and kill them. This served as the most important justification for the use of the death penalty in Mao's era.

Moreover, from the standpoint of the class-struggle theory, the legal system and the criminal law were merely political tools for the class struggle. The state power might turn to them if it considered them useful and convenient; otherwise, it would be unnecessary for the state power to adopt and follow a legal system and a criminal law. In fact, capital offenses were limited in Mao's political China as a result of legal action, and the capital cases processed formally by the Chinese courts were also few. Outside the legal system and the courts, however, many executions occurred as a result or in the name of political class struggle.

In Mao's era, the social character of the state-power-based society and the political essence of the death penalty exhibited complete and clear consistency. The most important function of the death penalty in Mao's era was the political concept of "revolution or counterrevolution." This was reflected in the 1979 Criminal Law, which was passed at a time when the CCP and its government started to change Mao's political ideology and policy.

In the 1979 Criminal Law, there were 28 offenses (in 15 provisions) punishable by the death penalty. Many of them concentrated on political crimes and were based on political concepts such as "counterrevolution" or "state's political benefit." For example, at least 14 offenses (50% of all offenses) and 9 provisions (60% of all provisions) were directly connected with counterrevolution or the state's political benefit. In other words, political consideration for the state alone underlay significantly the death offenses in the 1979 Criminal Code.

Deng's "Economic China" and Its Death Penalty Policy

Mao's class struggle eventually led China to the brink of collapse. After Mao's death, Deng Xiaoping became the supreme leader of China and began to change Mao's policy. On the one hand, Deng declared that China had to remain a socialist country and allow socialism to endure. On the other hand, he formally threw out the class-struggle theory. To replace it, Deng advocated a new basic principle of the Chinese socialist system, encapsulated as "doing one's all to develop the economy and enrich the people." Under this new principle, economic development and individual wealth became the most important tenets of the Chinese social system. A policy known as "Reform and Openness" was promoted and enforced. Furthermore, the CCP and its government not only recognized individual private ownership and the market economy but also encouraged both. Personal fortune was advanced as a glorious goal. In consequence, under Deng's economic China, all social events, values, and relationships were dealt with as economic matters. As a result, the entire society and its people were basically economicized or monetarized. Although this economicization or monetarization of Chinese society looks like an economic phenomenon, it actually is not. Rather, it is a political phenomenon because the rise and expansion of private ownership and the market economy in China since the 1980s are not outcomes of natural economic development, as seen in some typical capitalist countries, but artificial. They are the political result that the Chinese state power (represented by the CCP) advocated and pushed for as a political matter, using its political authority.

The general policy of the death penalty in Deng's era was not an exception. Unlike in Mao's era, the death penalty in Deng's era was prescribed as a legal punishment in the formal criminal law and was imposed by formal courts (e.g., no use of the death penalty was allowed without going through formal criminal procedures and formal courts). On the other hand, the prescriptions of the death penalty in the criminal law and the practice of the death penalty by courts were promoted largely from an economic or monetary perspective. As a result, the focus of the death penalty policy in Deng's China shifted from counterrevolution to the economy and money because many economic and monetary crimes or nonviolent crimes were now prescribed as offenses punishable by death, and a high number of death sentences and executions were carried out because of connections with economic order, property, or money.

As described earlier, the number of offenses punishable by death was 28 in the 1979 Criminal Law, but it was increased to 82 before the 1997 Criminal Law was passed (Z. Zhao 2003:2). Most of the new death-eligible offenses were related to economic order, property, or money. For example, on March 8, 1982, the National People's Congress (NPC) passed a single bill called the Decree on Severely Punishing Criminals Who Disturb National Economic Order, in which smuggling, speculating in economic or monetary affairs, theft, habitual theft, stealing or exporting precious cultural relics, selling drugs, and taking bribes were prescribed as offenses punishable by death for the first time.

The 1997 Criminal Law was passed at a time when the CCP and its new leaders had started to adjust Deng's economics-oriented policy and recognize the importance of the rule of law. One of the purposes of this new criminal law was to rearrange the existing offenses punishable by death and reduce the number of death offenses (Z. Zhao 2001:174). Nevertheless, 68 offenses punishable by death were still retained in the new law (Chen 2003:6).

The 1997 Criminal Law consists of two parts. Part I deals with general provisions, whereas Part II contains specific provisions on crime. There are

10 chapters under Part II, and each chapter addresses a specific crime category.

Compared with the 1979 Criminal Law, the 1997 Criminal Law shows three main characteristics. The first is that almost half of the offenses punishable by death concentrate on economic or monetary crimes and are based on economic or monetary concepts, such as economic order, monetary benefit, or property. Chapter 3 primarily deals with death offenses (under Part II, specific provisions): "Crimes of Undermining the Socialist Economic Order." Among the 68 death offenses (in 49 provisions), at least 32 offenses (47% of all death offenses), and 24 provisions (49% of all death provisions) are related directly or indirectly to economic order, monetary benefit, or property.

The second characteristic is that among all capital offenses, the percentage of nonviolent crimes is very high. Specially, among 68 offenses punishable by death, about 58 offenses (85% of all capital offenses) can be categorized as nonviolent crimes, and many of them should be deemed crimes merely aimed at monetary benefit or property and economic order. In contrast, only 10 offenses (14% of all capital offenses) are violent crimes.

The third characteristic is that the number of death offenses increased from 28 in the 1979 Criminal Law to 68 in the 1997 Criminal Law; moreover, the number of death provisions more than tripled, from 15 to 49. The increase is mainly due to the addition of offenses that are related to economic order, economic benefit, or property.

Jiang, Hu, and Xi's "Legal China"

From the mid-1990s, Jiang Zemin, Hu Jintao, and Xi Jinping held the position of the supreme leadership of China. In this new era, Jiang, Hu, and Xi began to be aware of the importance of law and legal systems. Consequently, they recognized the necessity of following the principle of rule by law, perhaps even the rule of law. In 1997, the CCP formally declared that it would try to build a "socialist legal China" that relies on rule by law as one important political direction for the future. With great expectations, this chapter deems Jiang, Hu, and Xi's current China an era of "legal China,"

However, it can be argued that Jiang, Hu, and Xi's era is basically the succession of Mao and Deng's China. The Chinese government has insistently declared that China is a socialist country, and many measures have been taken to promulgate the supreme principle of Chinese socialism, one-party rule by the CCP, as before. Meanwhile, thorough and strong policies and measures have been enforced to expand and extend the Chinese market economy and encourage all of Chinese society and the Chinese people to focus their energies on the development of the market economy and attaining personal riches. Principles of the market economy and monetary values have become universally accepted standards in a way previously unimaginable. As a result, China has become an increasingly complex and diverse society.

Accordingly, the situation surrounding the death penalty in China has also become more complex and diverse. The state power has advocated policies and measures aimed at encouraging individual private ownership and expanding the market economy more intensely than in Deng's era. Monetary or economic social values still dominate Chinese society and people's lives. As a result, crimes of destroying economic policies and measures are still linked with the death penalty.

On the other hand, the world has entered a new era since the 1990s that can be called the *globalization and information era*. This change has had a very strong impact on Chinese socialism and the Chinese state power. The principle of one-party rule has been challenged both inside and outside China with greater intensity than in earlier times because the election system in China is so inadequate. In order to avoid such challenges and promote the legitimacy of one-party rule, the Chinese state power has tried to grasp and represent the will and benefits of the general people as much as possible (Wang 2012:12). In so doing, the CCP has become more sensitive to the will and general welfare of the people. Unfortunately, most Chinese people not only support the death penalty but also demand that it be used more often (Qu 2005:10). This has served to a great degree as justification for the use of the death penalty in today's China.

At the same time, as mentioned earlier, under the legal China of Jiang, Hu, and Xi, an awareness of the rule of law has emerged. With changes among the Chinese leadership and the CCP, Chinese law and the Chinese legal system have been able to achieve some independence and autonomy as a legal profession. With such independence and autonomy, it has become possible for the NPC courts, and other judicial professional agencies to take on more cautious policies toward the death penalty and to improve its use from a legal professional perspective to the extent that politics allow. In particular, two events have had a very direct and important impact on the death penalty policy and system in China so far. One is a new policy called "Building a Harmonious Society," which was advocated formally by the CCP and its top leader Hu in 2006. Shortly after, in order to respond to the call of "Building a Harmonious Society," a new concrete criminal policy called Balancing the Leniency and Severity of Punishment was adopted and promoted by the Chinese courts and other judicial agencies. The other event is a formal policy by the CCP and its leader Xi to limit or reduce the use of the death penalty, signaled by the issuance of the CCP Central Committee's Decision to Deepen the Policy of Reform and Openness in November 2013. According to this document, it is necessary for all Chinese courts and other judiciary agencies to adopt a more cautious death penalty policy and to limit or reduce both death sentences and executions in the near future.

In sum, the legal China of Jiang, Hu, and Xi has been an era where nonchanges and changes have existed simultaneously. China is still fundamentally a state-power-based society, but the state power has started to change its way of ruling. The nature of the death penalty in China is still political, but its contents have changed. Many improvements to death penalty policies and the death penalty system have become possible and have actually been practiced under Jiang, Hu, and Xi's legal China, although the system is still heavily influenced by Mao's political China and Deng's economic China.

The Nonchanges: Application of the Death Penalty in a State-Power-Based Society

The nonchanges mentioned earlier have concentrated on the style of criminal law enforcement and concrete application of the death penalty in the new era. Given its character as a state-power-based society, China is still meting out a special criminal policy and carrying out a unique style of law enforcement for death sentences and executions in China.

Because China is a state-power-based society, the state power in China is the dominant force of the society and is responsible for carrying out almost all social functions in creating and maintaining social order. By nature, the social order in China is a minority's social order, that is, a social order created and maintained only by the police force and other public officials, in contrast to a majority's or mass social order, which is created and maintained by most (if not all) members of Chinese society (Wang 2008a:145).

Although the social order in China is primarily a minority's social order, a problem of limited capability in creating and maintaining social order usually occurs. That is, when the social order is usually created and maintained only by the police force and other public officials mainly through physical, coercive methods (such as restriction and deprivation of people's physical mobility and freedom), and because the number of police and government officials in China is limited, the state power cannot make all (or even the majority) of the people become members of the police force or government officials. Police and other officials, as a group of limited number, therefore, can create and maintain effectively only part of the social order, not all of it. In order to solve this problem of limited capability, the state power has adopted a special criminal policy that this study terms a *narrow but heavy* policy (Wang 2008a:145). This means that the scope of crime prescribed in the criminal law is very narrow, but the punishment for it is very severe. As a result, only part of all criminal actions that are considered "significant" to the state power's ruling are chosen and prescribed as "crimes." Instead of prescribing more crimes, the state power usually condemns the chosen crimes through harsher punishment. The state power is always trying to achieve a large radial effect in deterring crimes by focusing on such carefully chosen crimes and sentencing violators to harsher punishment than is necessary. As the most serious punishment, the death penalty has always been expected to carry a fuller and stronger radial effect in deterring crimes than any other punishment.

Moreover, in order to produce more and more radial effect, the manner or style of enforcing the criminal law and dealing with crimes is uniquely termed a *campaign style* for enforcing the criminal law, a style that has been used both in traditional China and in contemporary China. The infamous strike-hard campaign (*yanda*) that has dominated in the past two and half decades in China is just one kind of such campaigns (Liang 2005; Trevaskes 2007). The main contents or characteristics of such campaigns are as follows: The state power and its political leaders, on the basis of their political consideration of the social condition (especially the public security situation), usually choose some "typical" or "significant" crimes as targets and launch a campaign aimed at cracking down on such crimes more speedily and strictly during a specified term. During this campaign, the political leaders mobilize legislators, the police, prosecutors, judges, and other people concerned (even the whole society) and ask them to cooperate with one another and to concentrate their efforts on the target crimes. As a result of such a campaign, application of the criminal law becomes stricter; criminal procedure from investigation to execution is shortened and simplified, and therefore, cases can be handled faster; and sentences become harsher. In a nutshell, the enforcement of the criminal law and the countermeasures against crimes in such campaigns are changed from a legal and professional action to a political and mass movement. The death penalty in contemporary China is mostly influenced by such campaigns, and more and more death sentences and executions will be meted and carried out as long as such campaigns are launched and continued.

In fact, the death sentences and executions meted out in Chinese courts so far have concentrated mainly on four kinds of crimes, although there are many offenses punishable by death prescribed in the Chinese Criminal Law. The four kinds of crimes the Chinese courts are focusing on include serious violent crimes, such as murder, rape, robbery, and arson; drug crimes; economic or monetary crimes; and public official crimes (e.g., bribery and embezzlement). Why do death sentences and executions concentrate mainly on these four kinds of crimes? The primary reason is the political component of the death penalty in China.

With respect to serious violent crimes, it is normal for any society where the death penalty is still retained to stress the violent characteristics of such crimes as a reason for practicing the death penalty. China is no exception. However, there are some other political reasons for the CCP and its government to insist on death sentences and executions for serious violent crimes. As described earlier, in a state-power-based society like China, its social order, public security in particular, is created and maintained mainly by the state power. It is regarded as both the privilege and the obligation of the state power to create and maintain social order. An orderly society can enhance the political legitimacy of the state power, especially under one-party rule. In contrast, a chaotic and lawless society may jeopardize the very foundation of the political power of the CCP and the government (Zhongyangdangxiao 2001:32). Because serious violent crimes cause direct and grave harm to individuals and society and instill fear of crime and a sense of insecurity in individuals, communities, and even society at large, these crimes (e.g., murder, robbery, aggravated assault, rape, kidnapping of children or woman, arson) have a special meaning in the CCP's assessment of social order in Chinese society. In order to demonstrate its capability to maintain social order, to appease the public, and to enhance its political legitimacy to rule Chinese society, the Chinese state power has never been hesitant to take the toughest attitude and measures toward serious violent crimes, including the use of death sentences and executions.

The frequent use of death sentences and executions for drug-related offenses is due to China's official political ideology, based on the modern history of China and the CCP. According to that ideology, the modern history of China has been a disgraceful and painful history full of foreign invasions and colonization. This period began in 1840 when the United Kingdom defeated China in the Opium War. As a result, China lost its sovereignty and territory and gradually became a semicolonial country after the United Kingdom and other Western imperial nations (Japan in particular) began to conquer China on a large scale after the Opium War. Western imperial nations and Japan used two weapons in their invasions and colonization: guns and opium. Foreign guns destroyed the Chinese people physically, and opium mentally. It was the CCP that led the Chinese people to fight against the imperial nations, won both the physical gun war and the mental opium war, and finally built a new China. In this historical context, drug offenses, including opium offenses, have been deemed not only crimes (as defined in the criminal law) that potentially cause harm to the individual, the family, and society but also serious political behaviors that can destroy the Chinese nation and the state. Meanwhile, it is deemed a great achievement and a source of legitimacy of the CCP through its one-party rule to be able to resist the expansion of opium and other drugs and make the Chinese people safe from them. Therefore, given the political context of China, it is necessary for the CCP and its government to take very harsh countermeasures against drug crimes, including death sentences and executions.

With respect to economic or monetary crimes, it was in 1982 that China started to impose death sentences and carry out executions on such offenders. Since the 1978 Reform and Openness policy, the CCP and its government, as their main political policy and with their strong authority, have enforced many new measures to establish private ownership and introduce a capitalist system of a market economy to replace the traditional socialist public ownership and the planned economic system in China. Although the economic reforms have succeeded in changing the state-planned economy to the market economy, there have also been unexpected changes in

Chinese society. One of these unintended consequences is the rapid increase in economic or monetary crimes. Facing increased economic or monetary crimes, the top leader, Deng, stressed that such crimes seriously challenged the Reform and Openness policy, corroded the organizational body of the CCP and its government, and severely destroyed the government's image and authority. Deng suggested a new countermeasure called the Two Hands Principle and asked the CCP and its government to conduct two efforts simultaneously (Xiao 1996:18): to enforce the Reform and Openness policy thoroughly and to crack down on economic or monetary crimes harshly. On the basis of Deng's proposal, the NPC passed a single criminal law, the Decree on Severely Punishing Criminals Who Disturb National Economic Order, on March 8, 1982, which made the death penalty available for economic or monetary crimes for the first time in contemporary China. This process shows that two factors should be understood as reasons for China's use of the death penalty for economic or monetary crimes. First, the emergence and expansion of individual private ownership and the market economy in the past three decades in China have not been an outcome of natural economic development but an artificial result enforced by the CCP and its government because of its political ideology, policy, and authority. For the CCP and its government, economic or monetary crimes, which disturb the emergence and expansion of individual private ownership and the market economy, are deemed not only regular crimes but also serious challenges to its political ideology, its policy, and its authority in particular. In other words, economic or monetary crimes in China have been endowed with some characteristics of political crimes. Second, economic or monetary crimes in China today are still viewed in light of the traditional moral standards based on Confucianism espoused by the CCP and its government even though the standards have become contradictory with its new policy of Reform and Openness. Under the traditional moral standards influenced by Confucianism, money and property are often viewed as the greatest evil to corrode public officials, and the state should do everything to keep its public officials away from property and money at any cost.

With respect to public official crimes (e.g., bribery and embezzlement), it is also possible to find in the political context the reason for China's practice of death sentences and executions (Wang 2013:134). One-party rule has been the most fundamental principle in contemporary China. The CCP and its government have always adhered to this principle without any hesitation and have justified their adamant adherence to it with the following rationale: As a historical fact, it is the CCP that made the most sacrifices and led all of China and the Chinese people to resist Western imperial nations and Japan's invasion and colonization, and finally built a new China. Today it is also the CCP and its government that have managed to keep the new China independent, peaceful, and developing as a great country in the world. This fact has automatically proved, according to the rationale, that it is the CCP that sacrificed first for the Chinese nation and the Chinese people and has been seeking the greatest benefits for the Chinese nation and the Chinese people without considering any self-interest and privileges. Therefore, it is logical for the CCP to rule China. However, this legitimacy is seriously injured and challenged when some members of the CCP and some officials of its government take bribes or embezzle public money or property, because such crimes show that those members of the CCP and officials of its government have sought self-interest and privileges rather than the general happiness and welfare of the whole Chinese nation and the Chinese people. In this political context, public official crimes in today's China are not viewed merely as ordinary crimes but as political crimes that can destroy the legitimacy of the CCP's one-party rule. In order to recover the legitimacy damaged by public official crimes and to show its unchanged will to sacrifice for the whole nation and the Chinese people, it is necessary for the CCP and its government to punish corrupt officials harshly, even by the death penalty.

The Changes: Improvements in Death Penalty Practice in Contemporary China

As discussed earlier, the legal China of Jiang, Hu, and Xi has been an era where the nonchanges and the changes have been conducted simultaneously. As part of the changes, many improvements in death penalty practice have been implemented, although China still remains a state-power-based society, and the nature of the death penalty is still largely political.

Reducing the Number of Death Offenses

On February 25, 2011, the NPC passed an act to revise the 1997 Criminal Law and thereby withdraw the use of the death penalty from 13 offenses previously punishable by death. This movement should be valued positively, although these removed offenses were primarily nonviolent and nonlethal in nature and had been rarely punished by the death penalty before (Wang 2011:123).

Restricting and Reducing Death Sentences and Executions

In order to practice the CCP's political Building a Harmonious Society policy and the criminal Balancing the Leniency and Severity of Punishment policy, Xiao Yang, then chief judge and president of the Chinese Supreme People's Court (SPC), declared a new standard regarding death sentences on November 8, 2006. Xiao demanded that Chinese judges not issue a death sentence in circumstances where the defendant does not have to be sentenced to death even though he or she could be sentenced to death according to the criminal law. Xiao's declaration has been seen as a significant change to China's existing death penalty policies. It is also hoped that this change will reduce the number of death sentences in China. In fact, before this declaration, the SPC had begun to set a higher and more stringent standard for death sentences by issuing new judicial interpretations. After Xiao's declaration, this movement became more active and effective. For example, on January 15, 2007, the SPC issued an interpretation called Opinions on Providing Judicial Protections to Building a Socialist Harmonious Society and asked Chinese local courts to avoid sentencing murder offenders to death with immediate execution in cases where the murder occurred because of disputes among family members, lovers, or neighbors, or in cases where one or more mitigating circumstance existed. In such cases, it is necessary for a court to prove special aggravating circumstances if it insists on sentencing the murderer to immediate death. This new standard is much stricter than before.

Moreover, in today's China, a new, surprising, and very controversial practice, called *cash for clemency*, has been adopted and implemented more widely among Chinese courts as a measure to reduce death sentences. This standard has been established via several interpretations of the SPC. According to this standard, Chinese courts can sentence an offender to other forms of punishment rather than immediate execution if the offender has shown a willingness to pay economic or monetary compensation to the victim (or the victim's family), and the latter has agreed to accept it and give up his or her demand for immediate execution in return for the compensation (Feng 2012:98).

At the same time, Chinese courts have been trying to reduce the number of executions. There are two kinds of death sentences in the Chinese criminal system: the death penalty with immediate execution and the death penalty with a two-year suspension. Under the former, the offender is executed about one week after all the legal procedures have ended and an order of execution has been handed down. In contrast, under the death penalty with a two-year suspension, when a court sentences an offender to death, it also declares at the same time and in the same judgment that the execution will be suspended for two years. After all trial procedures end, the offender will be sent to a prison to serve his or her time. If the offender has not committed any intentional crime during the two-year suspension, the death sentence will be commuted to either an unfixed term of imprisonment with labor or a fixed term of imprisonment (25 years) with labor. This will occur simultaneously with the expiration of the two-year suspension. If the offender has committed a serious intentional crime during the suspension, however, the execution will be carried out about one week after a court hearing is completed and an order of execution is handed down.

The preceding discussion indicates that the crucial point in determining whether death-eligible offenders actually live or die is the kind of death sentence to which they are condemned. What is the standard by which Chinese courts determine the sentence? There is a very abstract provision regarding death sentences in the 1997 Criminal Law (Article 48): "In the case of an offender who should be sentenced to death, if immediate execution is not essential, a two-year suspension of the execution may be announced." It is very clear that this provision cannot work as a practical standard for Chinese courts in their daily operation, and, therefore, a more concrete and practical standard is necessary, but there is no such definite standard to which Chinese courts can refer. Rather, courts may refer to and rely on local precedents, knowledge, and experience, all of which are rather vague. In fact, the decision of a Chinese court whether a death-sentenced offender actually lives or dies remains discretionary. The actual number of executions may change from time to time depending on how Chinese courts use this discretionary power. From 2003, Chinese courts have become more active than ever in handing down more suspended death sentences, especially after the previously mentioned declaration of policy changes made by Xiao Yang in 2006. Xiao also stressed that Chinese courts would issue more and more suspended death sentences. On February 8, 2010, the SPC issued another judicial interpretation titled Opinion on Certain Issues Concerning Implementing the Criminal Justice Policy of Balancing Leniency and Severity, in which it asked the local courts to consider using the death penalty with a two-year suspension as the benchmark and the norm in death penalty cases and the death penalty with immediate execution as the exception. As the result, since 2007 the number of the suspended death sentences issued by Chinese courts has exceeded that of the immediate sentences (Liu 2013:102).

A CHINESE ENHANCED DUE PROCESS FOR CAPITAL CASES

Normal criminal procedures in China can be divided into four stages: investigation, prosecution, first trial, and appeal. Every stage is deemed separate from the others and is conducted independently. Moreover, the Chinese Criminal Procedure Law contains important provisions specifying the statute of limitations that every stage should follow when the suspect or defendant has been arrested and kept in detention. These provisions indicate that in a normal case, the investigation has to be completed in two months, the prosecution in one month, the first trial in two months, and the appeal trial in two months. China has a "two-trial finality system" (Criminal Procedure Law, Article 10), which mandates that the decision of the appeal (i.e., the second instance) will be final. Therefore, the result of a criminal case may be decided within a relatively short period (the maximum time is seven months in a normal case, although in some special cases extensions are permissible). In contrast, because there is no provision about the minimum number of days in which a case can be handled, it is never a problem if the police, the public prosecutor, and the judge deal too quickly with a case. With respect to the time limits at every stage, one can say that the weight of Chinese criminal procedure is placed on the pretrial stages.

This process is only for cases that do not involve the death penalty, however. For death penalty cases, there are many special provisions in the Criminal Procedure Law. Chinese courts are divided into four levels: local courts, intermediate courts, (provincial) high courts, and the national SPC.

Local courts have no authority to hold a death penalty trial. Moreover, in a death penalty case, a court cannot begin a trial without the presence of a defense attorney. Furthermore, when the defendant has not retained a particular attorney, the court has to appoint a defense attorney who will be paid by the state. The most important special provision for death penalty cases is that there are three additional safeguard procedures after the normal procedures are completed. In cases that do not involve the death penalty, the decision of the appellate court will be final instantly. In death cases, however, after the completion of the appeal procedure, a death review procedure by a provincial high court will start automatically. Then, a death confirmation and approval procedure by the SPC will commence. Eventually, after completing its review and approval, the SPC will conduct an execution order procedure and issue an order of execution. The offender will be executed within seven days after the execution order is issued. There is no time limit for these three additional procedures. Until June 2006, all appeal trials, including cases involving death sentences, reviewed only the dossier of the trial of first instance, and it was therefore not necessary for the appellate court to hold an open trial. Since July 1, 2006, however, all appeal trials involving death sentences have been required to be open, in the same manner as in the first trial. Traditionally, both the death review procedure and the death confirmation and approval procedure were merely symbolic. Since 2006, however, the scope of the review has been expanded, and substantive review has begun.

The most significant improvement took place on January 1, 2007. In the 1980s, the death review and approval authority was delegated to the provincial high courts for cases of serious crimes, such as murder, robbery, and rape, even though the Criminal Procedure Law required that the procedure be conducted by the SPC. However, on October 31, 2006, the NPC made a decision that from January 1, 2007, the death review and approval procedure in all death cases would be conducted only by the SPC. This change means that the death review and approval procedure will potentially become more substantive and more unified with better quality. It is reported that every year, the SPC has denied about 15% of death sentences by lower courts through this procedure since 2007 (B. Zhao 2014:151).

On May 30, 2010, the SPC and other central judicial agencies published two interpretational documents: Rules on Certain Issues Concerning Examination and Judgment of Evidence in Death Penalty Cases and Rules on

Certain Issues Concerning the Exclusion of Illegal Evidence in Criminal Cases. These two documents further established special rules and procedures for death penalty cases. In a death penalty trial, it now becomes absolutely necessary for the judge to examine the evidence that claims the defendant's guilt or aggravating circumstances under higher criteria than those in normal criminal cases, and to make sure that the proof that leads to a guilty verdict and to a death sentence for the defendant is absolutely beyond reasonable doubt, and that the conclusion of guilt and the death sentence is absolute. Meanwhile, all judicial agencies, including the courts, are now obliged to exclude evidence illegally collected in criminal procedures, especially in death penalty cases, where the judge must confirm the legality of all evidence and make sure that no illegal oral evidence or testimony will be allowed to prove the defendant's guilt and to be used as evidence for imposition of the death sentence. All illegal evidence connected with guilt and the death sentence has to be excluded without exception.

On March 14, 2012, the NPC passed an act to revise the 1996 Criminal Procedure Law. In this revision, it became obligatory for the police and other judicial agencies to make an audio or video recording when they conduct interrogation of the suspect or the defendant in death penalty cases (and in cases where the punishment may be life imprisonment).

With the adoption of these special procedures and new changes, the Chinese criminal procedure in death penalty cases, in contrast to that of nondeath cases, has begun to become more stringent and oriented to due process, and its weight has been moved from the pretrial stage to the trial stage, a shift toward a Chinese enhanced due process, in my judgment.

THE FUTURE OF CHINA'S DEATH PENALTY IN A STATE-POWER-BASED SOCIETY

As argued in this chapter, the nature of the death penalty in China is political since China is a state-power-based society, and this political component means that there has been a close connection between the state political power and the practice of the death penalty. The prevalence of the death penalty and its changes in China have mainly depended on changes in the state power's political ideologies or policies. This nature has not changed fundamentally, although there have been many substantive improvements to the death penalty system under Jiang, Hu, and Xi's legal China.

Facing this conclusion, some scholars may claim that democratization in China should become the key point for the future of China's death penalty, and democratization can lead China to improve or even abolish its death penalty. This claim is only half correct in my assessment.

Unlike a system of rule of law, where the fundamental principle is legality and its essence is rule of human rights, the fundamental principle of democracy is majority determination, and its essence is the rule of numerical majority power. Democratization is a double-edged sword for the problem of the death penalty (Wang 2008a:150). Past experience of death penalty practices in the world indicates that what democratization can do is to take the death penalty away from the state political power's hand and allow the death penalty system to be considered as a legal professional problem handled through the rule of law or a criminal policy without direct intervention by the state political power. However, at the same time, democratization can also make the death penalty a subject of election politics or even mass politics and force it to be dependent on the so-called will of the majority, especially in today's world, when globalization and information technology have been making an important impact, and so-called public opinion or the will of the majority is shaped quickly and easily (Wang 2012:12). What the history of improving or abolishing the death penalty in the world tells us is that there has been no country so far whose death penalty was improved or abolished through the leadership of public opinion or the will of the majority. Therefore, democratization itself does not lead naturally to improving or abolishing the death penalty. It is as necessary to withdraw the death penalty from the hands of public opinion or the will of the majority as it is to keep the death penalty out of the hands of the state political power.

The future of the death penalty (e.g., the movement to abolish the death penalty) in China will depend on keeping the death penalty away from both the state political power and the mass public, developing the independence of the rule of law and the judicial system, and making the death penalty a pure legal or criminal problem.

NOTES

1 This estimate is calculated by the author from information in the following documents: Hogaku Seminar Special Issue (Nihonhyouronsha, Tokyo), December 1990, p. 271.

Annual Report of Statistics on Correction (Tokyo: Ministry of Justice of Japan); 1995, 1:37; 1999, 1:81; 2003, 1:81; 2007, 1:81; 2013, 1:81.

2   In my view, for scholars who study China, it is necessary to distinguish between doctrines or thoughts created or advocated by academic or professional thinkers or scholars, such as Confucius, and customs and traditions that laypeople hold and follow in their daily life (in this chapter, I define the later as *culture* or *social culture*). Chinese history or social phenomena in China should be explained on the basis not only of the doctrines or thoughts of great thinkers but also of the laypeople's culture. At the same time, it is necessary to balance the empirical statistical data and the whole condition of society in order to analyze social phenomena in China rationally. This is more important when one is narrating Chinese history (including the history of the death penalty in China).

REFERENCES

Benn, C. (2002). *Daily Life in in Traditional China.* Westport, CT: Greenwood.

Chen, X. (2003). *Zhongguo sixing tantao* [A Study on China's Death Penalty]. Beijing: Chinese Procurator.

Cohen, P. A. (1984). *Discovering History in China: American Historical Writing on the Recent Chinese Past.* New York: Columbia University Press.

Feng, C. (2012). Qianxi woguo sixing liangxing tixi zhong de jingji peichang de helixing yu juxiangxing [Analysis about the rationality and limitation of compensation in Chinese death penalty sentencing system]. *Law Science Magazine* (Beijing), *5*, 98–103.

Hogaku Seminar Special Issue. (1990). Nihonhyouronsha, Tokyo.

Hu, D. (2008). *Zhongguo gudai sixing zhidushi* [A Study of the Death Penalty System in Ancient China]. Beijing: Law Press.

Johnson, D. T., & Zimring, F. E. (2009). *The Next Frontier: National Development, Political Change, and the Death Penalty in Asia.* New York: Oxford University Press.

Liang, B. (2005). Severe strike campaign in transitional China. *Journal of Criminal Justice, 33,* 387–399.

Liu, R. (2013). *Sixing de quanqiu shiye: Zhongguo yuejing* [A Global Vision of the Death Penalty and the Chinese Context]. Beijing: Chinese Social Science.

Lu, H., & Miethe, T. D. (2007). *China's Death Penalty: History, Law, and Contemporary Practices.* New York: Routledge.

Ministry of Justice of Japan. *Homusho: kyousei toukei nennpou* [Annual report of statistics on corrections) for 1995, 1999, 2003, 2007, 2013. Tokyo.

Niida, N. (1980). *Chuugoku houseishi: keihou* [A Study of Chinese Legal History: Criminal Law]. Tokyo: Press of the University of Tokyo.

Qu, X. (2005). Zhongguo sixing de duoyuanhua yu yitihua yanjiu [Research on diversity and conformity of Chinese death penalty culture]. In Z. Chen (Ed.), *Sixing: Zhongwai guanzhu de jiaodian* [Death Penalty: The Global Focus) (pp. 3–16). Beijing: Press of Zhongguo Renmin Gongan University.

Trevaskes, S. (2007). Severe and swift justice in China. *British Journal of Criminology, 47*, 23–41.

Unger, R. M. (1976). *Law in Modern Society: Toward a Criticism of Social Theory*. New York: Free Press.

Wang, Y. (1995). Three social models in a comparative study of criminal law: China as a "power society," America as a "law society," Japan as a "culture society." *Hitotsubashi Journal of Law and Politics, 23*, 71–81.

Wang, Y. (2005). *Shikeino hikakukenkyuu-chuugoku, beikoku, nihonn* [A Comparative Study on the Death Penalty in China, Japan, and U.S.A.]. Tokyo: Seibundou.

Wang, Y. (2008a). The death penalty and society in contemporary China. *Punishment and Society, 10*, 137–151.

Wang, Y. (2008b). *Nihonnokeibastu wa omoika karuika?* [Is the Punishment in Japanese Heavy or Light?]. Tokyo: Shueisha.

Wang, Y. (2011). Chuugokuno keihoukaisei to shikeiseidono henkou [The revision of the Chinese Criminal Law and the changes of its death penalty system]. *Houritujihou, 83*(4), 118–123.

Wang, Y. (2012). The death penalty and society in East Asia—How to understand and compare the death penalty in China, Japan and South Korea. *Hitotsubashi Journal of Law and Politics, 40*, 1–14.

Wang, Y. (2013). *Wairo wa naze chuugokude shizainanoka?* [When Does China Sentence a Bribery Offender to Death?]. Tokyo: Kokusai Shoin.

Wittfogel, K. A. (1957). *Oriental Despotism: A Comparative Study of Total Power*. New Haven, CT: Yale University Press.

Xiao, Y. (1996). *Zhongguo xingshi zhengce he celue wenti* [The Problems of Criminal Policy and Strategy in China). Beijing: Law Press.

Zhang, N. (2008). The political origins of death penalty exceptionalism: Mao Zedong and the practice of capital punishment in contemporary China. *Punishment and Society, 10*, 117–136.

Zhao, B. (2014). Dangdai zhongguo sixing gaige zhengyi wenti lunyao [Some issues on the death penalty reform in current China]. *Legal Science, 1*, 146–154.

Zhao, Z. (2001). *Sixing xianzhi lun* [On Limiting the Death Penalty]. Wuhan: Wuhan University Press.

Zhao, Z. (2003). *Sixing zuiming tonglun* [On the Offences Punishable by Death in China]. Zhengzhou: Zhengzhou University Press.

Zhongyangdangxiao (2001). *Yanda douzheng yu shehui zhian ganbu duben* [Officials' Book on Yanda and Social security]. Beijing: Zhongyang dangxiao.

Zhou, M. (1985). *Zhongguo xingfa shi* [The History of Chinese Criminal Law]. Beijing: Qunzhong.

5

From "Killing Many" to "Killing Fewer"

▸ SUSAN TREVASKES

IN MANY PARTS OF THE WORLD, recent historical experience of the death penalty debate has been centered on the binary of retention versus abolition. In China, however, in the death penalty debate and in the larger story of its operation over decades, abolition has not been part of the political conversation. Here the binary is severity and leniency, which articulate the death-sentencing spectrum in ideology and operation.

The dialectic of severe and lenient death sentencing is central to application of the death penalty within the Criminal Law itself since China has in effect two death sentences. One, *immediate execution (sixing liji zhixing)*, is the expression of relative severity. The other, the *death sentence with a two-year reprieve (sixing huanqi zhixing*, abbreviated as *sihuan)*, is an expression of relative leniency.

From the 1950s to the present, Chinese death penalty practice has centered on a way of thinking about whom, what, and how to punish that is closely tied to Maoist "utilitarian dialectics" (Keith 1994:154). The severity-leniency dialectic reflects a Maoist understanding of political action as the *unity-of-opposites (duili tongyi)*.[1] Judicial decision making has been guided by a dominant political principle that favors severe punishment for a minority of the worst offenders and relative leniency for a majority of offenders. The proportion of the minority relative to the majority has been expanded or reduced over time in line with shifts in the dominant ideas about the importance of protecting social and political stability and capital punishment's relative utility in that task.

In all criminal justice systems, judges make decisions about the severity of punishment for serious crimes in the context of pushes and pulls of national politics. In China, the Criminal Law remains explicitly a vehicle for criminal justice policy, which has infused capital punishment with a distinctly political purpose based on China's national modernization agenda. This has been particularly so since 1979, when this agenda has placed utmost importance on upholding social stability as a precondition for the success of the nation's economic reforms. For the next quarter century, while Chinese authorities asserted that severe punishment serves as a crime deterrent, the strike-hard (*yanda*) criminal justice policy favored the capacious use of the death penalty. The years between 1983 and 2003 were dominated by this policy. Party officials launched three generic strike-hard anticrime campaigns in 1983–1986, 1996, and 2001–2003, along with many dozens of specialized campaigns targeting one crime type in particular, such as drug crimes, terrorism, or robbery. In the first and "bloodiest" (M. S. Tanner 2000:93) campaign in 1983, 24,000 people were executed in the space of eight months ("1984 10 yue 31 ri" 1984). The punitive strategy in these campaigns was to mete out "severe and swift punishment" (Trevaskes 2007a:106), which was enabled by changes in the Criminal Law, the Criminal Procedure Law, and the Organic Law of the People's Courts. One notable legislative change was to delegate authority to review and approve most death sentences to the provinces. This encouraged provincial authorities to "kill many."

After roughly 25 years during which an ethos of severity dominated punishment through the strike-hard criminal justice policy, a historic shift saw impressive reform in the first decade of the twenty-first century as strategic legal developments in late 2006 and early 2007 altered the politico-legal landscape of capital punishment in China. The Supreme People's Court (SPC) was handed back the exclusive authority to review and approve all "immediate execution" sentences on January 1, 2007. This reform ushered in a new criminal justice policy called Balancing Leniency and Severity and a new era of what politico-legal authorities call "killing fewer, killing cautiously" (*shaosha shensha*). According to the SPC, the number of executions decreased by around 30% in 2007 compared with the previous year ("China sees" 2008). A rapid and major reduction in the scale of criminal executions has been made possible largely through the use of sihuan, that is, the suspended death sentence, to replace the use of the death penalty with immediate execution. Sihuan is the main conduit through which the party-state has achieved a relatively more lenient death-sentencing regime that kills far fewer than in the 1980s, the 1990s, and the early years of the twenty-first century (Liu 2007). However, the status and use of sihuan are by design ambiguous within the Chinese Criminal Law, which complicates its role in the "kill fewer" reform. This study examines the role of sihuan as the death sentence that has enabled the Criminal Law, the judiciary, and the party-state—therefore, the Chinese nation and its criminal justice system—to progress along the path of the "kill fewer" reform since 2007.

The first part of this chapter considers the legal environment of the death penalty in the pre-2007 era. Here I explore difficulties and uncertainties around use of the death penalty, particularly locating vital dividing lines—between a custodial and a death sentence and between severe death sentencing (i.e., execution) and leniency (i.e., sihuan). I also explore reformers' strategies to overcome some legal barriers or at least blunt their negative impact through using sihuan to "leave some leeway," including the pre-2007 experience of using sihuan as a safety valve in cases marked by uncertainty in facts or evidence and enlarging the scope of sihuan's application to expand the repertoire of mitigating factors in sentencing.

The second part looks at the politico-legal environment of sihuan in the crossover period from "killing many" to "killing fewer" from around 2005 to 2006. Here I examine the role of political and politico-legal rhetoric in broadening sihuan's leniency function. I focus on judicial reform rather than on legislative change. Of particular interest here is the formalization of the new criminal justice policy, Balancing Leniency and Severity, which largely replaced the discredited strike-hard policy, through the vehicle of various SPC provisions, including an SPC judicial opinion in 2010 that outlines the policy in detail. The balancing policy now guides judges in deciding how to distinguish between those who deserve immediate execution and those whose lives can be spared.

The third part rounds off this study by outlining some of the post-2007 scholarly debates about possible amendments to the Criminal Law that might further the "kill fewer" cause.

THE CRIMINAL LAW'S AMBIGUITY ON THE DEATH PENALTY AND SIHUAN

The PRC's first Criminal Law in 1979 (CL79) has been a tool to protect more than the interests of Chinese society and citizens right from the start. It was designed to act as a vehicle through which politico-legal authorities could regulate social relations in a way that also—and, when necessary, foremost—would protect party-state interests (Trevaskes 2010a, 2012). Since such a high priority was placed on social stability as a precondition for successful modernization, and since lawmakers understood severe punishment as an effective means to achieve this precondition, CL79 by design privileged harsh justice.

Within three years of introducing CL79, the party under Deng Xiaoping developed a criminal justice policy to "strike hard" against serious crime in response to a perception that the incidence of crime was escalating, destabilizing society and so impeding the party's national economic reforms (H. Tanner 1999; M. S. Tanner 2000; Trevaskes 2007a, 2010a). After the disastrous Cultural Revolution, CL79 was intended to provide a degree of normalization for the application of criminal punishment in China and to put an end to the widespread use of arbitrary punishment as experienced in the Mao era. By 1983, a moral panic within the ranks of senior party officials, including Deng Xiaoping, put into play a series of changes to the Criminal Law that allowed for the return of swift, harsh, and arbitrary punishment through the strike-hard policy. To legally legitimize the implementation of that policy, in early September 1983, the National People's Congress (NPC) amended CL79 and the 1979 Criminal Procedure Law. These changes allowed for punishment beyond the existing maximum punishment in the Criminal Law. They extended the death penalty to include offenders targeted in the campaign and shortened the time that it would normally take to prosecute targeted crimes. Crucially, they lowered the level of the court of authorization for review and approval of death sentences from the SPC to the provincial level (H. Tanner 1999; M. S. Tanner 2000; Trevaskes 2007a). The rationale for these changes given by the party was that criminal justice agencies had failed to adequately deal severe blows to serious crimes. These agencies were criticized for valuing procedural accuracy to the point where punishment was becoming ineffective in deterring crime (Guo 2003:534).

Authorities mounted the first strike-hard anticrime campaign in August 1983, and state executions in the garb of "striking hard" took off at a dramatic pace. Local court judges supported or complied with expansive use of execution in local courts under the Communist party-state's instructions from Beijing. "Severe and swift" (*congzhong congkuai*) punishment was effected through both generic campaigns and relentless national "specialized struggles" against specific crime targets throughout the 1990s and well into the first years of the twenty-first century (Trevaskes 2010a:2). Severity within the strategy of severe and swift punishment translated into handing down the most severe punishments within the options set down by the law, while swiftness meant accelerating and simplifying criminal procedure to deal with targeted criminals (Trevaskes 2007b).

An intimate connection exists between the Criminal Law and criminal justice policy in China. How is the Criminal Law affected directly through criminal justice policy? At base, it is through the large interpretive space that invites ambiguity, which forces judges to rely heavily on criminal justice policy to inform their interpretation of this ambiguous law. Ambiguity crafted strategically into China's Criminal Law through slippery wording and silences provides law and judges with interpretive flexibility to accommodate ideological shifts or other political influence as favored by the party-state through policy (X. Chen 2009). Strongly encouraging judges to refer to criminal justice policy for guidance thus ensures that the party's standing preferences on sentencing are achieved through the Criminal Law via judicial discretion. Although this ambiguity conveniently accommodates political atmospherics for the party, it also makes interpreting the Criminal Law difficult for the judiciary, especially if criminal justice policy does not provide needed guidance. How have judges identified a case deserving the severest punishment—the death sentence—and whether sentencing should be lenient or severe death sentencing? How do they decide between (1) a custodial and a death sentence and (2) immediate execution or sihuan?

Locating the Dividing Line Between a Custodial and a Death Sentence

In the general provisions of CL79, Article 43 was the sole reference to death penalty decision making. It set out the general conditions under which the death sentence could be applied, stating simply, "The death penalty shall be applied only to criminals who have committed the most heinous crimes." In the 1997 amended code, the content of Article 43 was effectively shifted into Article 48, and although some of the wording was altered, still no elaboration was provided in the general provisions. The implication here is that ambiguity of law creates the quasi-politico-legal space in law for judicial discretion informed by policy.

Specific provisions of the 1997 Criminal Law (CL97) also do not specify the actual conditions or circumstances of a crime that should attract a death sentence rather than a custodial sentence, other than stating that the offense in question must be "particularly serious" or that the amount of property involved must be "especially huge" (W. Huang 2007:140–144). Indeed, the amorphous "extremely serious crime" was the sole criterion for applying the death penalty to the 68 capital offenses that the amended Criminal Law in 1997 identified. "Extremely serious crime" remains today the exclusive, ambiguous foothold to identify application of the death penalty. This ambiguity on what identifies a crime deserving the death sentence makes it difficult for judges to locate the dividing line between a custodial and a death sentence.

Under the Article 48 proviso, offenders who have not been convicted of an "extremely serious crime" cannot be handed a death sentence. Without detail clarifying "extremely" or "serious," how are judges to determine what distinguishes a capital case from a custodial sentence? Judges must use their discretion, which the paucity of detail in Article 48 makes into an expansive part of the interpretive space in sentencing, where judges turn largely to criminal justice policy to inform themselves. The Criminal Law was amended in 2011 to identify 55 capital offenses, down from 68 in 1997. In practice, the vast majority of death penalty sentences are for only a handful of offense types. These are primarily (1) intentional homicide and felony murders such as kidnapping, robbery, and rape resulting in the death of the victim, assault resulting in death or serious injury to the victim, robbery involving violence, and arson and bombing crimes that result in death or injuries; and (2) serious drug offenses of four kinds: trafficking, transporting, smuggling, or manufacturing narcotics (Trevaskes 2012). Since the annual numbers of those executed are a state secret, researchers cannot know the statistical breakdown of offense types given the death penalty. However, published scholarly studies revealing the limited figures for various jurisdictions point to intentional homicide, serious assault resulting in death, and aggravated robbery (Nie 2011) as the leading capital offenses in the vast majority of courts in the pre-2007 period, with the exception of major drug provinces such as Yunnan, where serious drug crimes lead.

Homicide is commonly the number one offense that draws the death penalty in most of the roughly 360 courts that try capital cases in China. Death penalty scholars Zhao Bingzhi and Yin Jianfeng note in their study of capital case sentencing that in all provinces, intentional homicide accounts for between 30% and 60% of all executions and in some provinces as high as 70% to 80% (Zhao & Yin 2011:162). In a court where researcher Qi Jianjian conducted her study of lawyers' and judges' experiences with the death penalty, the vast majority of capital cases from 1979 to 2002 were for murder (most) and robbery (second most): 52% of executions were for homicide, 5% for serious assault resulting in death, 5% for rape with violence, 36% for robbery with violence (including robbery resulting in death), and 2% for arson (Qi 2007:199). In another jurisdiction, provincial appellate judge Chen Huajie noted that overall, a handful of crime types, including intentional homicide, intentional assault resulting in death, robbery, rape, and bombing and kidnapping resulting in death made up over 80% of all death penalty cases in Guangdong Province in the late 1990s and the early years of the twenty-first century (H. Chen 2005:287). In the major drug provinces, such as Yunnan, the majority of offenders given the death penalty are executed for drug-related offenses or homicide (Li 2011; H. Zhang 2011).

These data on categories of crime in cases that drew the death penalty indicate that judges sentence in accordance with the capital offenses that the Criminal Law obliquely identifies. Comparative numbers of executions and death sentences handed down over time can suggest the influence of criminal justice policy on judges' discretion when they are interpreting this purposively ambiguous law and deciding on the severity of sentencing. Data cannot, however, reveal the difficulty for judges in locating the dividing line between a custodial and a death sentence in cases where the nature and circumstances of a crime do not fit neatly with the capital offenses identified only by type in the Criminal Law. Similar difficulties apply in distinguishing between lenient and severe death sentencing.

Locating the Dividing Line Between Lenient and Severe Death Sentencing

For the vast majority of capital offenses identified in CL97, the death penalty is not a mandatory sentence. Most capital offenses entail discretionary sentencing where options include a 10- to 15-year custodial sentence, a life sentence (up to 25 years for some who have been sentenced to sihuan) and the death sentence. But once an offender has been convicted of an extremely serious crime, which automatically attracts the death penalty, judges have the binary choice to hand down a death sentence with a two-year suspension or an immediate execution. Article 48(1) states, "The death penalty shall be applied only to criminals who have committed extremely serious crimes," followed by the qualifier that "if the immediate execution of a criminal punishable by death is not deemed necessary, a two-year suspension of execution may be pronounced simultaneously with the imposition of the death sentence."

Here too, the ambiguity of the law gives broad scope to judicial discretion in the interpretive space of capital case sentencing. Again, this can present difficulty for judges in locating a dividing line, in this context to distinguish between lenient (a suspended death sentence) and severe (immediate execution) death sentencing. The ambiguity here is not just in the cryptic identification of criminals who have committed "extremely serious crimes," as noted earlier. Vitally, it is in the article's reference to the death sentence with a two-year suspension.

A suspended death sentence is in effect a life sentence since in the vast majority of cases, offenders are resentenced to a life sentence of between 18 and 23 years after the two-year probation period. Yet no detail is provided in CL97 to identify which criminal circumstances deserve immediate execution and which deserve a suspended death sentence; the law gives no indication of how to deem whether immediate execution is "necessary." Since both types of death sentence belong to the same category of punishment in law, they are not regarded in law as separate categories of sentencing. They are merely two different means of carrying out the same punishment: the death penalty (W. Huang 2007). In practice, the crucial difference, of course, is that one outcome involves the death of the offender, and the other allows his or her life to be spared.

Leading criminal law expert Zhao Bingzhi interprets the reference to sihuan in Article 48 as an expression of the principle of leniency (*congkuan*); a case must contain legal or discretionary mitigating circumstances for judges to consider sihuan. Hence, for Zhao, the demarcation line between sihuan and immediate execution hinges on a judge's (or judicial committee's) interpretation of what is considered a "most extremely serious" crime. Zhao notes that Article 48 provides two basic conditions for the use of sihuan: that the criminal deserves to be executed, and that the execution does not need to be immediate; that is, sihuan is for those whose crimes fit the label "extremely serious" but are not as serious as crimes of those who must be executed immediately. By this logic, those who must be executed immediately include those whose crimes caused grave social harm, where the offender poses a grave risk to society, and where grave malicious intent was present in the mind of the offender (B. Zhao 2006:313–314). Other leading Chinese death penalty scholars, such as Chen Xingliang, join Zhao Bingzhi in claiming that the factor that counts more than any other in determining the seriousness of a crime is the social harm it has caused, that is, the gravity and breadth of the consequences of the crime (X. Chen 2009; B. Zhao 2006). Yet some scholars argue that disproportionate stress is given to the main "objective" sentencing factor (social harm) over other subjective factors, such as the offender's state of mind and degree of malice (Trevaskes 2012:91–93).

From 1979 until around 2005–2006, when China's harsh justice policy began to be tempered by a more lenient approach to achieve "balance," most people convicted of homicide were executed rather than given a suspended death sentence. This observation is supported by a study of 500 randomly selected homicide cases across China from 1979 to 2005. Scholars Gao Weijian and Jia Guofang found that most defendants convicted of homicide were executed rather than given sihuan (2007:181). Of the 754 defendants in the 500 cases, they found that 59.7% (450 offenders) were given the death sentence with immediate execution; 13.5% (102 offenders) were given the death sentence with a two-year reprieve; 106 (14.1%) were given a life sentence; and 96 (12.7%) were given a term of imprisonment.

Most of those in the 500 cases in Gao and Jia's homicide study who were given a suspended death sentence were convicted of homicide relating to domestic or economic disputes (about unpaid loans or unpaid wages and the like). Gao and Jia suggest that the suspended death sentence was given in these cases probably as a buffer zone between a custodial and a death sentence. Here judges were perhaps reluctant to give a custodial sentence, but they were also reluctant to give these types of offenders the same death sentence as they would give to more socially dangerous offenders, such as violent robbers or rapists. Unlike cases of violent robbery and rape, where offenders tend to be habitual, in partner homicide, offenders are not usually considered such a grave risk to social stability (Gao & Jia 2007:184). Indeed, it appears that sihuan has long served as a buffer zone for judges who have struggled to locate dividing lines between custodial and death sentencing and between severe and lenient death sentencing.

Leaving Some Leeway for Uncertainty

The very nature of sihuan—allowing life rather than forcing death—positions it as an extremely useful option for sentencing when a case fulfills the requirements for the death penalty, but the judge has reason not to be completely certain that the offender meets the requirements for immediate execution. After all, execution is a finality; a human life cannot be resuscitated if an error in sentencing, evidence, or some other aspect of the case is subsequently uncovered. That is why for decades sihuan has served as a buffer zone when there is uncertainty in a capital case. Capital case judges and scholars claim that this buffer zone function is a common part of death sentencing in Chinese courts (H. Chen 2005:287; Gao & Jia 2007:184; Z. Zhang 2004:31). Sihuan enables judges to "leave some leeway" (*liuyou yudi*) where circumstances are uncertain.

Uncertainty can arise from multiple sources. One is from the law itself. First, as we have already seen, the Criminal Law is deliberately packed with ambiguity so that it does not provide detail to guide judges' legal interpretation. For example, Article 48 instructs judges to apply sihuan when immediate execution "is not deemed necessary," but since this article then provides no detail about "necessary," the legal landscape of sihuan is in many ways a land of uncertainty. Second, since the ambiguity of the law forces on judges considerable judicial discretion that policy is to inform, judges may be uncertain about interpreting the precise tenor of policy suitable for a judgment.

Other sources of uncertainty relate to the nature of specific criminal cases, where circumstances cannot be identified as clear cut because of the absence of information. As is true for any country, in some capital cases in China, evidence is incomplete or facts are unclear. In these instances, a court's judgment notice will often rationalize the use of sihuan obliquely by stating that sihuan was given "on the basis of specific circumstances of the case" (*genju benan juti qingkuang*) (Z. Zhang 2004:245).

One common uncertainty arises in cases involving a group crime where one or more offenders are yet to be apprehended. The degree of culpability to be apportioned to the offenders who have been apprehended and have been convicted of a capital offense often can be determined only when the criminal responsibility of the other offender(s) is clear. This is common for cases where the main principal offender flees and is not apprehended. In some cases, judges favor "leaving some leeway" to allow for a future possible contingency, that is, for the possible eventual capture of a principal offender who would most likely be executed while his or her (convicted) co-offenders would be serving a life sentence through sihuan (Z. Zhang 2004:245). The following is an example of this type of case:

On February 11, 1996, Luo, Wang, Sun, Hou, and Huang robbed a number of trucks on a stretch of highway. Luo was the main organizer who planned the robberies and was therefore considered a principal offender. In this case of multiple robberies resulting in the death of a victim, Luo was given a suspended death sentence in the absence of necessary evidence. The rationale for the sentence in the judgment notice was that the sentence was determined "on the basis of specific circumstances of the case." Luo had been responsible for organizing a number of previous robberies, so it would not have been unusual for a judge to sentence Luo to immediate execution. However, the alleged killer, Hou, who was one of the drivers, had fled and was never captured. Luo argued consistently that he had not been present at the exact moment at which Hou had stabbed the victim because he had then been engaged in assaulting another passenger. The court accepted the facts as described by the offenders and was unwilling to hand down an immediate death sentence to the robbery organizer, Luo. He was given a suspended death sentence on the basis of "leaving some leeway" to sentence the alleged main offender, Hou, to immediate execution at some time in the future if he was ever captured (Z. Zhang 2004:228).

Leaving Some Leeway for Other Sentencing Factors

The sentencing rationale of leaving some leeway through sihuan may also be applied to circumstances other than uncertainty. Appellate judge Chen Huajie, writing about his experience in reviewing lower-court death sentences in the early years of the twenty-first century, identified 15 key types of considerations that influenced sihuan sentencing decisions in judicial practice in the province where he worked in before 2007 (H. Chen 2005:41–49). These considerations illustrate how tenuous the dividing line is between life and death in capital cases. The descriptions that follow of the application of sihuan in common practice in Chen's jurisdiction validate the assertion widespread in the field that judges choosing between sihuan and execution have relied almost entirely on judicial discretion rather than on detailed statutory rules. The 15 key types are presented here on the basis of the key considerations influencing judicial decision making.

Situation 1: Societal interests: A high degree of social harm caused by a serious crime is the main rationale for applying the death penalty. In some cases, though, a court will recognize that although the social impact of the crime is substantial, the case may not attract a great deal of public indignation, or the community may even show some degree of sympathy for the offender.

Situation 2: Political pressure: When anticrime campaigns are prevalent, the death penalty with immediate execution is routinely applied as a deterrence and retribution mechanism. Conversely, when the social order is deemed to be stabilized as a result of the campaign, judges are encouraged to pull back from using immediate execution and to apply sihuan on a more regular basis than would be the case during campaign periods.

Situation 3: Victim's involvement in the initial conflict: Courts can take into consideration any obvious fault that the victim may have had in relation to the initial conflict that led to a homicide.

Situation 4: Legally prescribed mitigating circumstance: The most common circumstance is where an offender has surrendered voluntarily in accordance with Article 67 of CL97.

Situation 5: Erring on the side of caution when not all facts can be fully substantiated: In this type of case, the general facts of the case are clear and the overall evidence is compelling, but either there are some minor details of evidence that police are unable to substantiate or, in the case of group crime, the court cannot determine the exact degree of criminal responsibility of each defendant.

Situation 6: Group crime: In capital cases involving a group crime, the major principal offender is usually given the death penalty with immediate execution, while other principal offenders often are given the death penalty with a two-year reprieve.

Situation 7: The defendant has knowledge that is important in another criminal case: A defendant's life may be spared so he or she can appear as a prosecution witness in another criminal case.

Situation 8: Cultural or similar considerations: These include cases that have evolved into violent conflict in both Han and ethnic minority border areas, especially relating to border issues that concern forest areas and trees, feeding pastures, water sources, and building foundations, and cases that escalated from clan disputes.

Situation 9: Lack of malicious intent and of premeditation: This rationalization involves cases of intentional homicide and assault resulting in death that have escalated from domestic, neighborhood, or civil disputes.

Situation 10: The defendant's age: Crimes in this category involve elderly defendants who are aged 70 years or older, where the crime is extremely serious, but where the community reaction to the crime is not as strong as it would otherwise have been if the offender was younger.

Situation 11: Many defendants are from the same family: This typically involves drug cases where there are multiple defendants who are all principal offenders and are from the same family, and it is therefore deemed inappropriate to execute all principal offenders.

Situation 12: The defendant's family's circumstances: Mothers in capital cases who have dependent children under 12 years old will often be given a two-year reprieve even when the offense is regarded as a major crime.

Situation 13: The defendant's ethnic or religious background: Offenders who are community leaders of ethnic minorities or religious groups, overseas Chinese, or (returned) overseas Chinese with PRC residence permits are often given a suspended death sentence if there is some expectation that there will be negative community reaction to their execution.

Situation 14: Potential international reaction: Depending on the precise nature of the crime, some cases that have had international exposure may provoke negative international reaction if immediate execution is imposed.

Situation 15: The defendant's show of remorse in a tangible way. This situation applies to homicides that are extremely serious but where the offender either came to the immediate aid of the victim in a bid to save his or her life or offered financial compensation to the victim's family.

This summary of considerations that influenced judicial assessment of the need for sihuan signals various types of relationships with the law. One is the judiciary's. Here we see that by enabling leeway, sihuan has effectively provided a form of legal cover for judges should they be found to have erred in sentencing or should circumstances that informed their sentencing subsequently shift to reveal that a different finding and sentencing need to be made. Immediate execution cannot provide judges with these opportunities. Simultaneously, too, sihuan has enabled judges to demonstrate that their sentencing fulfills the requirements for severity of punishment—sihuan is a death sentence—while also satisfying other urgings, whether personal or policy, toward lenience.

The summary of influential considerations also suggests the utility of sihuan for sending messages to society at large. Some of these are about people's relationship to the law, such as compliance with law and deterrence of crime. But others are about people's relationship to society, including respect for society at large by not causing social harm and respect for the elderly, for family, and for maternal responsibilities, and expressing tangible remorse after offending. Others are messages not to be sent to the domestic or international communities. But perhaps one of the most vital relationships evident here, one that for subtle reasons Judge Chen has not stated directly, is the relationship of politics to the law. Here we see signs of the direct influence of policy on judicial interpretation and sentencing, particularly in leanings toward severity through a death sentence. We also see the political utility of sihuan as the death penalty ostensibly in name only. In the next part I examine how because of this dual identity, sihuan has also been useful for "killing fewer" to achieve the more tempered, balanced approach in the criminal justice policy that replaced the severity of the strike-hard policy in 2006.

ENHANCING SIHUAN'S LENIENCY ROLE

Rhetorical Moves from "Killing Many" to "Killing Fewer"

The two distinctive templates that developed in the era of mass campaigns in the 1950s have also dominated the ethos of death sentencing in the post-Mao era. The concern is primarily with the scale of killing. What some legal commentators have called "kill many" (*duosha* or *duoyong sixing*) (W. Huang 2007:42; Lu 2011) is an understanding of punishment informed by crime-control ideologies and enabled by the substantive and procedural vagueness of law manifest in immediate execution as a prescribed punishment (X. Chen 2005:36–37). The party's call to "strike hard" at serious offenders exemplifies this mind-set of killing many. Kill fewer—the second and current template—is predicated on the Maoist dictum from the 1950s to "kill fewer, kill cautiously" (*shaosha shensha*) (Lu & Guo 2006).

This was a call by Mao to urge officials to apply caution and restraint after he came to realize that his "kill many" urgings produced overkill in the few months of the campaign to suppress counterrevolutionaries in 1950, during which over 500,000 people were executed. In the Mao and post-Mao eras, the "kill fewer" catchphrase has encouraged suspended death sentencing as an alternative to immediate execution (Trevaskes 2012).

Strike hard was introduced as a policy and as a type of anticrime campaign in 1983 and dominated death sentence decision making for decades until around 2005–2006. Its replacement policy, Balancing Leniency and Severity (*kuanyan xiangji*), was endorsed by both the party's central Politico-Legal Commission and the SPC and is now China's leading national criminal justice policy. Inspired by reformers within the SPC, it encourages judges to err on the side of relative leniency when sentencing all but the most egregious criminals (X. Chen 2006; Lu 2011; Tian & Si 2008; B. Zhao 2012). In the atmosphere of the Hu Jintao era of a harmonious society in the twenty-first century, emphasis gradually shifted to the idea that "when there is a choice to kill or not to kill, always choose not to kill" (*kesha kebusha, yilu busha*) (Dong 2007; Fan 2008:150). This catchphrase is the antithesis of thinking encouraged by Deng Xiaoping, that in striking hard against crime, "when there is a choice to kill or not to kill, choose to kill" (*kesha kebusha, sha*) (L. Zhao 2007).

"Kill many" and "kill fewer" are politically useful not just as policy templates. They are also rhetorical gestures given concrete expression through policy and are used to achieve policy legitimacy. The strike-hard policy exhorted judges to punish a wide gambit of crime "severely and swiftly," thus beefing up the rhetorical call to "kill many." The more recent Balancing Leniency and Severity policy promotes the idea that the vast majority of offenders deserves and can be given less harsh punishment, and it encourages judges to reserve harsh punishment for only a small minority of society's most heinous criminals.

Not all judges and police favored the intensity of the strike-hard position on extensive use of the death penalty to kill offenders. Even in the 1990s, a number of senior politico-legal authorities were highly critical of the expansive latitude given to strike hard (M. S. Tanner 2005; Trevaskes 2010a). Reformers seeking to reduce the scope of strike hard's extensive use across a wide gamut of violent offenses and drug crimes needed to devise an alternative to immediate execution that would sit relatively comfortably with the existing punitive culture. Discussion among experts and judges about contracting strike hard and expanding sihuan's role in greater leniency had in fact begun when reformist judge Xiao Yang took over the presidency of the SPC in 1998, years before policy was eventually changed in around 2005–2006. Xiao Yang and other senior judges within the SPC attempted to reform sentencing conventions in 1999 in a particular category of homicide sentencing—homicides that had escalated from domestic or neighborhood disputes. The SPC issued a sentencing guidance document titled Minutes of Criminal Trial Work Symposium on Maintaining Stability in Rural Areas, which outlined the reformers' intentions to encourage the use of sihuan in cases of domestic or neighborhood disputes where the victim was in some obvious way at fault or was directly responsible for the conflict that led to the attack, or where statutory mitigating circumstances were present (SPC Minutes 1999). However, with the launch of a new two-year strike-hard campaign in 2001, the idea of focusing lenient death sentencing on the chosen type of homicide crimes was shelved until around 2005–2006, when generic strike-hard campaigns were discontinued.

With crime rates not falling and Chinese society increasingly brutalized (Bakken 2011:43), strike hard's political popularity had waned. The political virility of the large-scale generic campaign format was knocked out with the end of the final campaign in late 2003. Luo Gan, the party's head of politico-legal affairs, declared that strike hard would be "routinized" into everyday practice rather than operating through large-scale crackdowns, and that greater emphasis would now be given to preventing crime and stabilizing the mass public protests that were manifestly on the rise (Trevaskes 2010a, 2010b).

Expanding the Criteria for What Is Considered Lenient Death Sentencing

Immediate execution was (and remains) the preferred sentencing option for violent crimes, such as rape, robbery, and kidnapping that end in the death of the victim. In Gao and Jia's study mentioned earlier, for those convicted of robbery-related felony murders, 69.4% were sentenced to immediate execution, and 12.1% received a suspended death sentence. In all, 81.5% of those offenders were given the death penalty (including the suspended death sentence) (Gao & Jia 2007:183). Kidnapping resulting in murder (79.3% of kidnappings), rape resulting in the death of the victim (89.5% of rapes), neighbor disputes (73.1% of such disputes), and robbery resulting in murder (69.3% of robberies) accounted for the greatest percentages of offenders sentenced to death with immediate execution. In comparison, only 58.1% of offenders whose motive was a relationship issue were executed (Gao & Jia 2007:181–183). A gradual shift toward applying greater leniency in death sentences began around 2005–2006, but it did not apply to all categories of violent crime and certainly not to homicides in the commission of rape, kidnapping, and robbery. Legal experts and judges began discussing sentencing reform for crimes for which judges traditionally had been more inclined to hand down relatively lenient sentences. These are crimes such as homicide cases where the motive involved partner or other family relationship issues, especially where the victim was to some degree at fault; and domestic disputes and murder triggered by trivial incidents, especially where the offender had no history of violence (X. Chen 2005).

The advent of a reform-minded SPC president with some reform-minded judges around him provided the necessary fuel for reform moves. In around 2005–2006, reform-minded legal experts and judges began debating how sihuan's leniency role might be expanded as a way to limit the use of immediate execution. The discussion involved sharing information about how sihuan was commonly used at the time. "Leaving some leeway" was clearly a primary reason for judges to use sihuan until 2005–2006. SPC reformers identified that a space had opened to move seriously on reforming the death penalty. Here reform did not involve an amendment to the Criminal Law to expand the statutory circumstances that allow lenient sentencing. It could not; legal reformers in the SPC were responsible for implementing the law, not making the law, which is the responsibility of politicians. They recognized that working from behind to amend the law through the political system was virtually impossible, given inevitable resistance from strike-hard political hard-liners. They thus chose to work through the judicial system, where they had responsibility. They concentrated on amending the mind-set of judges in their conduct of judicial discretion while sentencing by standardizing the use of key discretionary circumstances not covered in the law as reasons for lenient death sentencing, that is, sihuan, in homicide cases. These circumstances relate mainly to the state of mind of the offender and the victim, including the degree of malicious intent displayed in the act, the offender's background, and the role of the victim in disputes that led to homicide (H. Chen 2011; X. Chen 2005:40; W. Huang 2007:137, 154; Liu 2007:36).

As part of the debate and discussion, various judges and experts put forward criteria lists as examples of guidelines for lenient death sentencing. Zhao Bingzhi offered seven criteria concerning offender and victim as typical of the internal criteria standards that many courts in the pre-2007 period were already using:

That the offender

- surrendered to police and admitted guilt (showing remorse) or performed a major act of meritorious service;
- showed remorse and gave police information, which was recognized as meritorious behavior;
- has a good reputation in the community, and the crime did not involve a significant degree of malicious intent by the offender, who carried out the crime as a random or one-off event that resulted in the most serious type of crime;
- is considered a principal offender in a group, but is not considered the ringleader; or
- is of low intelligence but is still classed as legally responsible for his or her actions;

or that the victim

- was to some degree partially at fault for events that led to the crime, and the defendant therefore did not hold sole criminal responsibility for the crime; or
- was obviously at fault for the dispute or incident that led to the crime (e.g., the crime resulted from a minor incident or accident), and the criminal act was totally spontaneous in nature. (B. Zhao 2006:313–314)

SPC Moves to Instill a "Kill Fewer" Regime

SPC reformers' moves to restructure the regime of punishment that for decades had inclined toward "heavy penaltyism" through the strike-hard criminal justice policy were, and had to be, handled with political savvy. The moves were launched in the context of a new political atmosphere of greater tolerance and harmony building, which emerged through the party's Harmonious Society governance agenda in 2004. National generic strike-hard campaigns had been discontinued, but specialized campaigns remained in force, and striking hard, particularly through severe and swift punishment, remained an official policy toward serious offenders. After the party's 2006 Resolution of the CCP Central Committee on Major Issues Concerning the Building of a Socialist Harmonious Society, results of two major reform moves became evident.

One was a significant shift in the death penalty debate to the question of whom to strike hard, with agreement to restrict the most severe punishment to a smaller cohort of the most serious criminals (Trevaskes 2012). The other move was an institutional shift with even greater ramifications for use of the death penalty. The exclusive authority to review and approve all immediate execution sentences was to be returned to the SPC effective January 1, 2007, after more than two and a half decades in the hands of provincial courts. Around the time of the handing back of authority, the SPC issued a number of judicial opinions and other directives (Dong 2007).

Three days before the handing back, the SPC announced an important opinion that was to usher in a new era in lenient death sentencing. It concerned new provisions related to application of the death penalty in the new period from January 1, 2007, when the SPC resumed its review authority, namely, that the SPC would expect lower courts to sentence offenders in capital cases in the spirit of what the SPC now called the country's "foundational" criminal justice policy: Balancing Leniency and Severity (SPC Decision 2006). The intention of this opinion was not to dismiss the strike-hard policy outright but to downplay its importance. The opinion did not discuss whether to use the death penalty but which death penalty to use. It identified the circumstances under which offenders should not be sentenced to immediate execution: offenders in capital cases who surrendered to authorities or who provided important evidence in a criminal case and, in all but the most exceptional circumstances, nonprincipal offenders in capital cases. For murder cases that had escalated from domestic or neighborhood disputes, or in cases where the perpetrator immediately confessed to a crime and provided financial compensation to the victim's family, courts should not consider immediate execution as the first option in sentencing. The document reserved strike-hard severity for only the most serious criminals.

Two weeks after the handing back of authority, the SPC issued further explanations on applying the policy of Balancing Leniency and Severity, reaffirming and clarifying the previous opinion's exceptions to immediate execution. This opinion stressed that although strike hard still held for national security terrorist crime and mafia-style syndicate crime, courts should hand down a sihuan sentence in homicide cases that had escalated from a domestic or neighborhood dispute, that involved provocation or where the victim was to some degree at fault, or where the defendant was extremely remorseful and provided immediate compensation to the victim's family (SPC Opinion 2007).

Both of these provisions stressed the importance of using existing statutory conditions for mitigated punishment, making it crystal clear to lower courts that the SPC fully intended to use its authority to reject all applications for execution where facts were insufficiently clear and the evidence was not compelling. It would reject these applications and return the case to the provincial court for retrial or resentencing (SPC Decision 2007). Rebalancing punishment culture on this scale required support not only from the SPC but also from three other politico-legal bodies, the Supreme People's Procuratorate (SPP), the Ministry of Public Security (MPS), and the Ministry of Justice (MJ). On March 9, 2007, the SPC, the SPP, the MPS, and the MJ provided this affirmation, announcing the Joint Opinion containing 52 detailed articles, which was a significant pronouncement of the new interpretation of death penalty procedures. Judges were urged to continue to implement the strike-hard policy, but crucially, only toward an exceptionally small minority (*ji shao*) of offenders whose crimes were exceptionally serious (*ji yanzhong*). They were to sentence these criminals to death in accordance with the dictates of building a harmonious society and "killing fewer, killing cautiously." Article 7 declared that the Balancing Leniency and Severity policy should be applied to all cases with mitigating circumstances, such as voluntary surrender and confession (Joint Opinion 2007).

The "kill many" mind-set held by many police, prosecutors, and judges over decades was being progressively eroded through policy exhortations to "kill fewer" (X. Huang 2011; Huang & Zhou 2011). Within this environment, a groundswell of debate and discussion began in scholarly and legal circles. This did not happen in a political or policy vacuum. It required political support from the highest echelons. Two years before the historic handing back of authority to the SPC, in a statement by China's president, Hu Jintao, at a Politburo meeting in May 2005, he linked his Harmonious Society reform agenda to death penalty reform, stating that "we need to give more attention to improving the quality of death sentencing" (L. Zhao

2012). The imprimatur of President Hu encouraging reform of the death penalty regime to more tightly control the use of death penalty opened possibilities for courts to promote the standardization or institutionalization of a "kill fewer" mind-set. But this shift required more than discussion of good ideas about how to broaden sentencing criteria for sihuan and how to narrow criteria for immediate execution. It had to be captured in a new criminal justice policy that would need to be endorsed by the party. SPC directives around the time of the handing back of authority to review the death penalty were positive steps in the direction of more lenient sentencing and killing fewer, but they did not make it sufficiently clear how judges were to know precisely where to draw the dividing line. They did not specify with absolute precision which crime circumstances the SPC expected judges to continue to punish severely with immediate execution and which precise crime circumstances judges were expected to punish relatively leniently with sihuan.

THE NEW SEVERITY AND LENIENCY DIALECTIC IN A NEW POLICY

The Balancing Leniency and Severity policy was first formally recognized by China's central party authorities in 2006, rhetorically at least, as a means to help build a harmonious society (X. Chen 2006). Strike hard had fallen from political grace as rapid police interrogations led to widespread torture, and hasty judgments by courts led to unjust punishments for innocent parties and to penalties harsher than those offenders deserved under law (Ni, Wu, & Zhang 2007). As the preceding discussion suggests, the SPC reformers were instrumental in working from within the politicolegal field to generate this policy shift. They recognized at the time a political climate where they could judiciously flag President Hu Jintao's rhetorical badge of a harmonious society to help vital political supporters maneuver the shift through the complexities and resistances of policy making (Trevaskes 2012).

The new policy seeks to reconcile the severity-leniency dialectic in its title through the term *balancing* or *tempering* severity with greater leniency. Essentially, the policy stresses the importance of individuating sentencing decisions, that is, dealing with each individual case by taking into account its particular circumstances, rather than applying the same or similar across-the-board light or heavy sentences for particular crime categories. In doing so, it encourages judges to look more closely at both the subjective (state of mind) and objective elements of the crime, including a wider range of mitigating circumstances than was allowed in past (strike-hard) times. *Balancing* means applying, when appropriate, relatively light punishment even in cases of serious and violent crimes if the circumstances of a case demand it and applying relatively harsher punishment to minor crimes when the circumstances call for greater punishment (Trevaskes 2010b). Like its strike-hard predecessor, it focuses on the issue of how much severity and how much leniency are required of China's punishment regime to control crime and prevent social instability. Strike hard favored the idea that a large proportion of the "minority" of offenders deserving the death penalty be executed immediately. The balancing policy favors the reverse: that a smaller proportion of this minority be executed immediately, and that the rest (the majority) of this minority be given a more lenient death sentence or even a custodial sentence.

The balancing policy thus retains "severe punishment" through immediate execution for a small range of circumstances and offenders. Most important, it provides detail to enable judges to rationalize greater leniency in sentences for a wider range of crime circumstances in both minor and serious crimes. This step accentuates the concept of mitigating and aggravating circumstances that already exists as a principle in the Criminal Law by providing judges with the information they need to identify these circumstances. It also addresses the lack of judicial discretion for many serious violent crimes, as well as the overly expansive use of judicial discretion for other crimes.

Formalizing the Balancing Leniency and Severity Policy

With the more lenient balancing policy in place, the politico-legal ground was ready for the SPC to help embed the ethos of more lenient sentencing in everyday judicial decision making. On February 8, 2010, the SPC issued a major policy interpretation document on how courts across the nation are to implement the Balancing Leniency and Severity policy. This 45-article judicial opinion explains to the courts that in implementing the new policy, they are to work on a case-by-case basis, dealing with each case individually by taking into account its particular circumstances rather than by simply applying the same or similar across-the-board light or heavy sentences that hitherto were applied to particular crime categories (SPC Opinion 2010).

Providing guidance on interpreting the severity of a crime, the opinion advises that the new policy encourages judges to mete out severe punishments by

- handing down the most severe custodial punishment or the death penalty only for cases where the social dangerousness of the criminal act is extremely severe and for extremely serious crimes that would normally attract a heavy custodial punishment or the death penalty; or
- punishing with relative severity (but not necessarily with the death penalty or the most severe custodial punishment) crimes in which the criminal offense is serious; or
- punishing with relative severity in cases to which aggravated circumstances described in the Criminal Law can be attributed to crimes that demonstrate malicious intent, and for crimes that can be considered dangerous to the person. (SPC Opinion 2010, Article 6)

Providing guidance on interpreting the circumstances of a crime, the opinion advises that offenses that remain the specific target of "severe punishment" are

- crimes that seriously endanger state authority or public order, including crimes that endanger national security, crimes committed by terrorist groups, crimes organized by superstitious sects, crimes committed by mafia-style organized crime groups, crimes committed by criminal gangs, and individual crimes that seriously harm public safety (e.g., spreading poisons in dams);
- serious violent crimes and crimes that "seriously affect the masses' sense of security," including intentional homicide, intentional assault resulting in death (manslaughter), rape, kidnapping, trafficking in women and children, armed robbery, serious cases of bag snatching (i.e., resulting in violence or attempted violence), and serious cases of theft; and
- crimes involving smuggling, trafficking, or transporting and manufacturing illicit drugs, and crimes that endanger public health. (SPC Opinion 2010, Article 7)

The Balancing Policy at Work in Sentencing Guidelines

From 2007 onward, a number of provincial high courts began developing new sihuan guidelines for their provinces to further formalize the balancing policy in judicial practice (Trevaskes 2012:137–139). The Tianjin High Court, for instance, based its standardized sentencing recommendations on the dictum that "when there is a choice to kill or not to kill, without exception always choose not to kill" (*kesha kebusha, yilu busha*). This dictum can be put into practice in any of the following three circumstances where it is not necessary to execute immediately:

1 When the victim is in some way at fault for the original conflict leading to the crime.
2 In economic crimes, regardless of the amount of money or property involved. If the vast majority of stolen funds or property has been recovered, in all circumstances do not execute immediately. If the amounts involved are huge (*juda*) or if the social impact of the crime is great but the actual monetary amount is not great, do not execute immediately.
3 In cases where the defendant has confessed to the basic facts of the crime or to the majority of the facts of the crime in the pretrial stage, then once convicted, the offender should not be executed immediately in any circumstances. After the defendant has been formally charged, if he or she has also given additional information about the case, and if he or she confesses to a similar crime, the offender should not be executed immediately. For example, if a defendant is detained and charged with 1 count of rape and during the course of interrogation admits to 10 other counts of rape, he should not be given immediate execution. (Fan 2008:151)

A number of judges and legal experts have advocated that the SPC devise national sentencing guidelines on the application of sihuan to guide judges in deciding the kinds of cases in which they can "choose not to kill." The SPC has produced national sentencing guidelines for a number of minor crimes but has not produced authoritative guidelines for capital sentencing. This is possibly because of the political sensitivity of serious crime in high-crime provinces or because certain crimes, such as serious drug offenses, are highly prevalent in some jurisdictions, such as Yunnan, but relatively uncommon in other provinces.

The effect of the new policy, along with the handing back of exclusive authority to the SPC to review and approve immediate execution sentences, is readily visible. For the first time in PRC history, in 2007, suspended death sentences outnumbered executions ("Suspended death sentences" 2007). Death penalty figures are a state secret, but estimates by legal experts put the figure these days at around 3,000 to 4,000, down from over 10,000 early in the twenty-first century. During an anticrime campaign in the mid-1990s, the figure was around 15,000 in a one-year period, but even this was down from the eight-month period from late 1983 to mid-1984 in strike hard's infancy, when the figure reported in the *People's Daily* was 24,000.[2] Because data on state executions are a state secret, precise numbers of the fall in executions since the balancing policy was put into effect cannot be known publicly. Indications discussed by death penalty scholars suggest that balancing has served to give life to "kill fewer" as the practice of Chinese courts and as the ethos of Chinese criminal justice today.

THE FUTURE: AMENDING THE CRIMINAL LAW

Since 2007, a number of changes have been made across the legislative landscape toward a more effective and more just criminal justice system. These include removing 13 nonviolent offenses from the list of capital offenses in the Criminal Law in 2011 and introducing new rules relating to examining and judging evidence in death penalty cases and excluding illegal evidence in criminal cases to improve procedural justice in the 2012 Criminal Procedure Law.[3] Changes to both laws aim to correct long-standing issues around applying and interpreting evidence in criminal cases and in particular types of capital cases. However, Article 48, the key death penalty provision in CL97, which allows the death penalty to be applied to serious offenders who are convicted of an "extremely serious crime," has yet to be amended. A number of death penalty scholars argue that the NPC should now amend the Criminal Law to clarify Article 48 since it is the principal reference for death penalty decision making (X. Chen 2009; Lu 2011; Zhao 2012).

Yet to keep the Criminal Law consistent with criminal justice policy so that the Criminal Law can most effectively enable implementation of the balancing policy—and vice versa—Article 61 in the CL97, the key provision relating to sentencing criteria, needs significant expansion. Scholars and legal experts in China have long held that a judge needs to take into account three concerns in considering giving a death sentence. First, the "objective" consequences of the crime, that is, the social harm it has caused to society, must be considered extremely grave. Second, the offender must be considered a grave risk or danger to society. Third, the offender must have demonstrated "subjective" malice in the brutal method of the crime (Ma 2009).

Yet overwhelmingly, for decades the first criterion, social harm, has been the main (and in many instances the sole) focus of death sentencing rationales (X. Chen 2005; B. Zhao 2006:386). A number of criminal law experts have argued that there is danger in overemphasizing social harm since doing so has the potential to discount the importance of a wide range of other factors, such as the offender's malicious intent or the offender's risk to society (X. Chen 2009; B. Zhao 2006:386). This is because what judges regard in sentencing as "extremely" harmful to society is highly dependent on prevailing political policy about the importance of maintaining social stability.

Article 61 of China's Criminal Law states in very general terms that the basis of considerations informing sentencing discretion should include "the facts of a crime, the nature of a crime, the circumstances of a crime, and the degree of social harm the crime has caused." Absent here are the subjective, state-of-mind aspects to help explain the offender's behavior that led to or inspired the harm that the crime caused and that should be factored into the sentencing equation. Some leading criminal justice scholars argue that discretionary sentencing should be based not only on the objective deed but also on the personal character of the criminal. Zhao Bingzhi and Peng Xinlin call for an amendment to Article 61 to address shortcomings of the existing law. Sentencing discretion should be based on information identifying the degree of social harm and other circumstances that may be favorable or unfavorable to the criminal. This includes consideration of information about (1) the normal behavior of the criminal; (2) the criminal's motive in committing the crime; (3) the purpose of the crime; (4) the nature and extent of the victim's fault, if any; (5) the degree of malice of the criminal's state of mind; (6) the means of committing the crime; (7) the time and location of the crime; (8) the harm and effects of the crime; (9) the relationship between the criminal and the victim; (10) the object of the crime; (11) the repentance of the criminal; (12) the remedies taken by the criminal to relieve the damage; and (13) the financial compensation the criminal offered to the victim (Zhao & Peng 2011:4).

Zhao, Peng, and others believe that in addition to amending general provisions in CL97, such as Article 61, at this stage in China's development it is entirely feasible to eliminate all nonviolent crimes from the list of possible capital offenses and to leave in CL97 only crimes that gravely endanger national security or public security and violent crimes resulting in death. The scholars recommend that to achieve this, the death penalty with immediate execution can be entirely abolished for property crimes by moving the capital punishment option for aggravated robbery from CL97's section on property crimes to its section on intentional homicide. They also opine that the sentencing of drug and robbery cases needs to be vastly improved to move away from discretion relying on consequences of the crime—the amounts of property stolen or drugs transported—as the main (and in many cases the sole) sentencing rationale.

Reformers in China, both judges and scholars, are continuing their efforts to instill a mind-set of "kill fewer, kill cautiously" in death sentencing. While those interested in death penalty reforms have been waiting for legislators to catch up, impressive judicial reforms led by the SPC have advanced the "kill fewer" cause. Impressive as these efforts and achievements are, however, they are insufficient alone to ensure that policies such as strike hard are not resuscitated to dominate death penalty practices in the future.

Indeed, strike hard is not yet a relic of history. For example, it is still encouraged to control drug crime and is still part of the punishment repertoire in China's ongoing war on drugs (Zhao & Yin 2013). In the *National Narcotics Control Commission Annual Report* for 2012, the Ministry of Public Security continued to exhort police to maintain the "high pressure of striking hard" (*yanda gaoya*) on drug criminals (NNCC 2012). Strike hard also still holds for the nonviolent crime of drug transporting. Drug mules, who are usually poor farmworkers hired by criminal syndicates, can be executed for transporting over 50 grams of heroin. More drug mules are executed than traffickers, manufacturers, and smugglers (H. Zhang 2011). Strike hard has also been returned to the punishment repertoire in China's ongoing war on terrorism. In May 2014, authorities announced a yearlong antiterrorism strike-hard campaign immediately after a series of bombing and violent attacks. Continuing the strike-hard policy against serious drug crime and so-called terrorism in the restive province of Xinjiang suggests there is still a long road to travel between killing many and killing fewer in both the philosophy and the implementation of China's criminal justice policy. Indeed, the dialectic between "kill many" and "kill fewer" lives on even while balancing suggests that the harshness of earlier severe punishment that killed many has ended. Strike hard, we see, can be given life at any place and time at the hand of the party-state as a reason to kill many.

· · ·

A dialectic of "severe" and "lenient" death sentencing dominates the death penalty saga in contemporary China. Expressed in the concepts of "killing many" and "killing fewer" and cast in the Criminal Law's sentencing options as "immediate execution" and "suspended death sentence," notions of severity and leniency have provided the conceptual positioning on which the party-state has determined its approach to capital punishment as articulated in criminal justice policy. Since criminal justice policy informs sentencing decisions in practice, a dialectical shift has positioned sihuan—the suspended death sentence—in a distinctive place to express both severity and leniency. Simultaneously, it is a death sentence rhetorically and a life sentence (almost always) in practice.

For over two decades, from the early 1980s to the mid-2000s, the party-state maintained a harsh justice regime to promote social stability for the economic success of Deng Xiaoping's economic reform agenda. The Criminal Law's purposive lack of a clear demarcation between severe punishment and less severe punishment compelled the expansive use of judicial discretion in deciding capital punishment. Influenced heavily by the party's preferred criminal justice policy, judges were compelled to "strike hard" at a wide range of serious offenders rather than sentencing offenders on a case-by-case basis. As the taste for across-the-board severity waned, the issue of which categories of crime would continue to deserve swift and severe punishment began to distill to the more fundamental question of what constitutes the most serious crime (i.e., prioritizing the interests of whom or what). Providing less discretionary space to the influence of the strike hard policy's ethos and more to interpreting the law through considering mitigating circumstances, this served as the means for limiting execution to fewer categories of offenders and to a much smaller range of crimes that were without mitigating factors. This was a canny practical way for reformers to dismantle the culture of strike hard by changing not the Criminal Law itself but judicial interpretation of it.

Through their influence on judicial discretion, both strike hard and the reformist Balancing Leniency and Severity criminal justice policy have served to place "kill many" and "kill fewer," respectively, as the conceptual ground on which sentencing decisions are made. The former has favored death sentencing through immediate execution to kill many; the latter has drawn use of the death sentence toward much greater use of sihuan to kill fewer.

NOTES

1   For an examination of the unity of opposites and Maoist thought, see Knight (1980).
2   Figures of around 15,000 in the mid-1990s and 8,000 to 10,000 in the early years of the twenty-first century are estimates from various published Western sources. Johnson and Zimring estimated the figure to be around 6,000 per annum in 2006 and 2007 and around 15,000 during the 1990s, when anticrime campaigns were prevalent. Chinese experts whom the author interviewed in Beijing put the figure today at around 3,000. For an insightful discussion of estimates of the number of executions, see Johnson and Zimring (2009:231–242). For the 1983–1984 figure, see "1984 10 yue 31 ri" (1984).
3   For an insightful study of the exclusionary rule, see Lewis (2011).

REFERENCES

Bakken, B. (2011). China, a punitive society? *Asian Journal of Criminology, 6*, 33–50.

Chen, H. (2005). *Lun sixing shiyong de biaozhun* [Criterion for Application of the Death Penalty]. Beijing: Renmin chubanshe.

Chen, H. (2011). Bawo sixing shiyong biaozhun de ruogan sikao [Reflections on the standards for application of the death penalty]. In B. Zhao (Ed.), *Sixing shiyong biaozhun yanjiu* [Research on Standards for Application of the Death Penalty] (pp. 84–94). Beijing: Zhongguo fazhi chubanshe.

Chen, X. (2005). An examination of the death penalty in China. *Contemporary Chinese Thought, 36*, 35–52.

Chen, X. (2006). Kuanyan xiangji xingshi zhengce yanjiu [A study of the criminal justice policy of balancing leniency and severity]. *Faxue zazhi* [Journal of Law Science], *1*, 17–25.

Chen, X. (2009). A study of the death penalty as applied to those engaged in the transportation of drugs. *Chinese Sociology and Anthropology, 41*, 48–65.

China sees 30% drop in death penalty. (2008, May 5). *Xinhua News*. Retrieved June 13, 2014, from http://www.chinadaily.com.cn/china/2008-05/10/content_6675006.htm.

Dong, R. (2007, February 6). Zhuanfang zuigao fayuan yuanzhang xiao yang: Wei hexie shehui tigong sifa baozheng [Exclusive interview with SPC president Xiao Yang on providing legal guarantees for the building of a harmonious society]. Retrieved February 6, 2007, from http://www.chinacourt.org.

Fan, C. (2008). Shilun sixing anjian de sifa kongzhi [Debates on judicial constraints in death penalty cases]. In J. Cohen and B. Zhao (Eds.), *Sixing sifa kongzhilun jiqi cuoshe* [The Death Penalty: Judicial Control and Alternative Punishments] (pp. 149–155). Beijing: Falu chubanshe.

Gao, W., & Jia, G. (2007). Guyi sharen anjian, sixing shiyong de shizhang fenxi [A positivist analysis of the application of the death penalty in intentional homicide cases]. In W. Gao et al. (Eds.), *Zhongguo sixing wenti de shehuixue yanjiu* [Social Science Research on Issues of the Death Penalty in China] (pp. 169–197). Beijing: Zhongguo renmin gongan daxue chubanshe.

Guo, X. (Ed.). (2003). *Jianguo yilai gongan gongzuo dashi yaolan* [An Outline of the Chronicles of Public Security Work since Liberation]. Beijing: Qunzhong chubanshe.

Huang, W. (2007). *Sihuan zhidu de dangdai jiazhi* [The Contemporary Value of the Sihuan System]. Beijing: Kexue chubanshe.

Huang, X. (2011). Fanzui jinghe qingxingxia sixing shiyong wenti [Determining appropriate criminal charges and the application of the death penalty]. In B. Zhao (Ed.), *Sixing gean shizheng yanjiu* [Empirical Study of Death Penalty Cases] (pp. 168–178). Beijing: Zhongguo fazhi chubanshe.

Huang, X., & Zhou, Q. (2011). Lun sixing shiyong de shenzhongxing wenti [On the cautious application of the death penalty]. *Faxue zazhi* [Journal of Law Science], *12*, 74–77.

Johnson, D., & Zimring, F. (2009). *The Next Frontier: National Development, Political Change, and the Death Penalty in Asia*. New York: Oxford University Press.

Joint Opinion. (2007, March 9). Zuigao renmin fayuan zuigao renmin jianchayuan gonganbu sifabu guanyu jinyibu yange yifa ban'an, quebao sixing anjian zhiliang de yijian [Joint opinion from the Supreme People's Court, the Supreme People's Procuratorate, the Ministry of Pubic Security, and the Ministry of Justice on further measures to strictly apply the law in case work and to ensure the quality of decision making in capital cases].

Keith, R. (1994). *China's Struggle for the Rule of Law*. London: St. Martin's.

Knight, N. (1980). Mao Zedong's "On Contradiction" and "On Practice": Pre-liberation texts. *China Quarterly, 84*, 641–668.

Lewis, M. K. (2011). Controlling abuse to maintain control: The exclusionary rule in China. *International Law and Politics, 43*, 629–697.

Li, S. (2011). *Dupin fanzui xingfa wenti yanjiu* [Research on Issues Relating to Drug Crime in the Criminal Law]. Beijing: Zhongguo jiancha chubanshe.

Liu, S. (2007). *Sixing pianlun: Sixing fuhequan shouhui zhiji de sikao* [Key Aspects of the Death Penalty: Reflections on the Return of the Authority to Review Death Sentences to the SPC]. Beijing: Renmin fayuan chubanshe.

Lu, J. (2011). *Xingshi zhengce yu xingfa yanbian* [The Evolution of Criminal Justice Policy and Criminal Law]. Beijing: Zhongguo renmin gongan daxue chubanshe.

Lu, J., & Guo, L. (2006). Kuanyan xiangji de lishi shuoyuan yu xiandai qishi [The historical roots and some contemporary revelations about balancing leniency and severity]. In J. Lu (Ed.), *Xingshi zhengce pinglun* [Commentaries on Criminal Justice Policy] (vol. 1, pp. 45–67). Beijing: Zhongguo fengzheng chubanshe.

Ma, X. (2009). Case of Dong Wei committing crime of intentional homicide. Retrieved May 24, 2014, from http://www.criminallawbnu.cn/criminal/info/showpage.asp?showhead=S&pkid=24634.

Ni, S., Wu, C., & Zhang, M. (2007, May 14). China rejects "strike hard" anti-crime policy for more balanced approach. Retrieved June 20, 2014, from http://news.xinhuanet.com/english/2007-03/14/content_5846317.htm.

Nie, L. (2011). Woguo qiangjie zui sixing shiyong biaozhun de tantao [Investigation into judicial controls on the application of the death penalty for robbery crimes in China]. In B. Zhao (Ed.), *Sixing shiyong biaozhun yanjiu* [Research on Standards for Application of the Death Penalty] (pp. 194–200). Beijing: Zhongguo fazhi chubanshe.

1984 10 yue 31 ri: yanda diyizhanyi chengguo xianzhu [October 31, 1984: The fruits of yanda's first offensive are outstanding]. (1984). *Renminwang ziliao* [People's Daily resources online]. Retrieved June 20, 2014, from http://www.people.com.cn/GB/historic/1031/3642.html.

NNCC. (2012). *National Narcotics Control Commission Annual Counternarcotics Report*. Retrieved September 5, 2013, from www.jhak.com/jdzy/zgjdzy/20120710/7327.html.

Qi, J. (2007). Sixing wenti diaocha baogao [Investigative report on death penalty issues]. In W. Gao et al. (Eds.), *Zhongguo sixing wenti de shehuixue yanjiu* [Social Science Research on Issues of the Death Penalty in China] (pp. 198–222). Beijing: Zhongguo renmin gongan daxue chubanshe.

SPC Decision. (2006, 28 December). *Zuigao renmin fayuan guanyu tongyishi sixing anjian hezhunquan youguan wenti de jueding* [SPC decision on certain issues relating the unification of application of authority to approve death sentences].

SPC Decision. (2007, February 27). *Zuigao renmin fayuan guanyu fuhe sixing anjian ruogan wenti de guiding* [SPC directive on issues relating to approval of death sentences].

SPC Minutes. (1999, October 27). *Quanguo fayuan weihu nongcun wending xingshi shenpan gongzuo zuotanhui jiya* [SPC minutes of the national meeting of criminal trial work on maintaining stability in rural areas].

SPC Opinion. (2007, January 15). *Zuigao renmin fayuan guanyu goujian shehuizhuyi hexie shehui tigong sifa baozheng de ruogan yijian* [SPC opinion concerning the provision of legal guarantees for the building of a socialist harmonious society].

SPC Opinion. (2010, February 8). *Zuigao renmin fayuan guanyu guanche kuanyan xiangji xingshi zhengce de ruogan yijian* [SPC opinion on certain issues concerning implementing the criminal justice policy of balancing leniency and severity].

Suspended death sentences exceed immediate executions for 1st time. (2007, November 23). *Xinhua News*. Retrieved June 15, 2014, from http://english.cri.cn/2946/2007/11/23/195@297492.htm.

Tanner, H. (1999). *Strike Hard! Anti-crime Campaigns and Chinese Criminal Justice, 1979–1985*. Ithaca, NY: Cornell University East Asia Program.

Tanner, M. S. (2000). State coercion and the balance of awe: The 1983–1986 "stern blows" anti-crime campaign. *China Journal, 44*, 93–125.

Tanner, M. S. (2005). Campaign-style policing in China and its critics. In B. Bakken (Ed.), *Crime, Punishment, and Policing in China* (pp. 171–188). Lanham, MD: Rowman & Littlefield.

Tian, L., & Si, J. (2008). Sixing de sifa kongzhi [Judicial controls on the death penalty]. In J. Cohen & B. Zhao (Eds.), *Sixing sifa kongzhilun jiqi cuoshe* [The Death Penalty: Judicial Control and Alternative Punishments] (pp. 192–199). Beijing: Falu chubanshe.

Trevaskes, S. (2007a). *Courts and Criminal Justice in Contemporary China*. Lanham, MD: Lexington.

Trevaskes, S. (2007b). Severe and swift justice in China. *British Journal of Criminology, 47*, 23–41.

Trevaskes, S. (2010a). *Policing Serious Crime in China: From "Strike Hard" to "Kill Fewer."* London: Routledge.

Trevaskes, S. (2010b). The shifting sands of punishment in China in the era of harmonious society. *Law and Policy, 32*, 322–361.

Trevaskes, S. (2012). *The Death Penalty in Contemporary China*. New York: Palgrave Macmillan.

Zhang, H. (2011). *Dupin fanzui zhengyi wenti* [Study on the Contesting Issues Relating to Drug Cases]. Beijing: Falu chubanshe.

Zhang, Z. (2004). *Zhongguo sihuan zhidu lilun yu shijian* [Theory and Practice of the Suspended Death Sentence system in China]. Wuhan: Wuhan daxue chubanshe

Zhao, B. (2006). *Sixing gaige tansuo* [Explorations in Death Penalty Reform]. Beijing: Falu chuabanshe.

Zhao, B. (2012). Guanyu zhongguo xianjieduan shenyong sixing de sikao [Reflections on the cautious use of the death penalty in contemporary times]. *Zhongguo faxue* (Legal Science in China], *6*, 5–22.

Zhao, B., & Peng, X. (2011). Lun zhuoding liangxing qingjie zai xianzhi sixing shiyongzhong de zuoyong [On the function of using discretionary sentencing circumstances in limiting the application of the death penalty]. *Zhongguo xingshifa zazhi* [Journal of Criminal Law in China], *2*, 3–9.

Zhao, B., & Yin, J. (2011). Guyi sharen zui sixing sifa kongzhi lungang [Outline of judicial controls relating to intentional homicide in death penalty cases]. In B. Zhao (Ed.), *Sixing shiyong biaozhun yanjiu* [Research on Standards for Application of the Death Penalty] (pp. 161–172). Beijing: Zhongguo fazhi chubanshe.

Zhao, B., & Yin, J. (2013). Lun zhongguo dupin fanzui sixing de zhubu feizhi [Discussion on the gradual path to abolition of the death penalty for drug crimes in China]. *Faxue zazhi* [Journal of Criminal Law Science], *5*, 1–12.

Zhao, L. (2007, January 4). Zhongguo sifa kaiqi shaosha shidai: Congzhong congkuai chengwei lishi henji [Chinese justice enters a new era of fewer executions: "Severe and swift" punishment becomes a vestige of history]. *Nanfang ribao* [Southern Daily].

Zhao, L. (2012, July 6). Xiao Yang wenji chuban guanjianci gaige xianfa fazhi: gaige youzhang kexun, dixian jiu shi xianfa [Xiao Yang's collected works published, his keywords being "reform," "the constitution," and "the rule of law": Arguing that there actually are rules in existence that should be used as a reference point, the bottom line being the Constitution]. *Nanfang zhoumo* [Southern Weekend]. Retrieved June 15, 2014, from http://www.infzm.com/content/78155.

6

The Abolitionist and Retentionist Debate

▸ ZHIGANG YU (TRANSLATED BY CHARLOTTE HU)

SOCIOLEGAL SCHOLARS HAVE BEEN FASCINATED with the death penalty for centuries because of its embodiment of the issue of an inherent right to life and its interconnection with politics, economy, society, and culture. This chapter reviews the multifaceted debate involving the death penalty in China and explores major determinants of death penalty policies in contemporary China.

THE EVOLUTION OF THE DEATH PENALTY DEBATE IN CHINA

Compared with European countries where the death penalty abolition movement originated, the debate over whether to abolish or retain the death penalty emerged relatively late in China. The debate in China started approximately 100 years ago, gained some momentum, lapsed into a long silence, and finally reemerged in the 1990s.

The Burgeoning Stage (from the Qing's Penal Code to the Early Republic of China)

At the end of the eighteenth century, as the death penalty debate started to gain momentum in Europe, the Qing dynasty regarded the death penalty as an indispensable tool for safeguarding the sanctity of the royal powers, maintaining the rigid feudal hierarchy, and protecting traditional values. In the second half of the nineteenth century, however, using military action, European countries turned China into a semicolony. To maintain the country's independence, some Chinese elites sought to emulate the West by reforming the nation's political system, as well as the legal system. The New Penal Code of the Qing dynasty—created by jurist Shen Jiaben and his colleagues at the end of the Qing dynasty—marked both China's departure from a feudal penal code and the beginning of China's modern criminal law.

When he was writing the New Penal Code of the Qing dynasty, Shen Jiaben translated and consulted criminal laws from other countries. Shen was also a firm believer in the Western abolition movement, deeming it an act of "benevolent governance" (J. Liu 2009:113). Within this context, it was the first time that Chinese scholars considered the possibility of abolishing the death penalty in China. However, for the following reasons, the majority of Chinese citizens at that time supported retaining the death penalty.

First, from the perspective of jurisprudence, criminal sanctions were viewed as medicine, and crime was seen as the disease to be cured. In determining the best course of treating a disease, a doctor considers both the disease and the potency of the medicine to determine its effectiveness. In some cases, amputating a body part to save a life might be necessary. Similarly, the death penalty was viewed as being necessary for eradicating crime. Second, from a historical perspective, the death penalty had been an important tool to punish those who violated the fundamental rules of the monarchy and the patriarchy. Third, from the perspective of social impact, it was argued that abruptly abolishing the death penalty could result in more (and more dangerous) criminal behavior and thus threaten public safety (Y. Zhang 1996).

As a result, the death penalty was retained in the New Penal Code. However, some progress was made. The debate resulted in reducing the number of death-eligible offenses, improving the procedure for applying the death penalty, and making execution methods more humane. For China, which had been using the feudal penal code for thousands of years, these changes were groundbreaking.

The New Penal Code had not yet been implemented in its entirety when the Qing dynasty ended, although some of its ideas had been put into practice. For example, when the Provisional New Penal Code of the Republic of China was being legislated in the initial stage of the Republic of China, the death penalty debate was brought up once again. Ju Zheng, a famous jurist of the Republic era, argued that the death penalty system had major flaws. Specifically, he argued that the death penalty failed to rehabilitate and instead excluded offenders. He also described it as the most vicious and cruel punishment, especially in light of potentially irrevocable errors in its administration. In addition, he noted that no evidence suggested that the death penalty deterred crime. Therefore, Ju maintained that abolishing the death penalty was "not only in line with the call of providence and the will of the people, but also beneficial to the development of a country ruled by law" (Liang & He 1999:21).

Although complete abolition did not have majority support during the Republic era, in comparison with the Qing Penal Code, the number of death-eligible crimes was further reduced—there were only 19 eligible crimes in the Republic penal code (J. Liu 2009). The motivation for discussing the abolitionist movement in China at that time was the desire of reformers to modernize China's feudal legal system. However, without broad-based support in culture and society, this Western idea of abolition quickly faded and was replaced by the mainstream discourse on the scope and application of the death penalty.

The Silent Stage (from the Early Republic Era to the 1990s)

Although the notion of abolishing the death penalty had some influence on the enactment of the Qing penal code and the subsequent Republic penal code, it was destined to fade into the background because of the lack of popular support in China. For example, the Law on the Punishment of Thieves and Bandits in the Republic era reversed the abolitionist position in the Republic penal code by adding a large number of death-eligible crimes to suppress crime and maintain order (J. Liu 2009), indicating that although the abolitionist idea was good in theory, it did not reflect social conditions in China at the time. The marginalization of the abolitionist view was also reflected in the enactment and revision of the Criminal Law of the Republic of China in 1928 and 1935 and the subsequent 1948 Emergency Sentencing Regulations Against Crimes Endangering the Country During Wartime.

In 1949, upon the establishment of the People's Republic of China (PRC), the principle of "retaining the death penalty while executing fewer and with caution" was adopted (Gao 1981:74). The retentionist view thus dominated criminal justice policies. There was little debate about retention or abolition of the death penalty; instead, the majority of Chinese scholars focused on criticizing the Western abolitionist movement.

For instance, in contrast to the international community's opinion during the late 1970s and early 1980s that the death penalty went against human rights (Michelle 1962), Chinese scholars Ge Ping and Wang Honggu argued: "It is exactly the death sentence of an extremely few outrageous criminals that safeguarded the human rights of the general population, which fully embodies the revolutionary humanitarianism" (Ge & Wang 1980:29). Chinese scholar Cheng Guanghai also pointed out: "It is counterrevolutionary for countries with dictatorship of the exploiting class to retain the death penalty against the fight of the working class, whereas it is necessary for countries with the people's democratic dictatorship to retain the death penalty for a few extremely outrageous criminals. Therefore, when commenting on the death penalty abolition in some capitalist nations, we should acknowledge its historic progress, but at the same time be wary of its class limitation and deceptive nature" (Cheng 1986:29). Scholar Guo Xi claimed that "death penalty abolition is by no means what the capitalist/bourgeoisie class can do. Death penalty abolition is only reasonable when class is eliminated and class struggle is gone.... To build socialism and finally realize socialism, we should not abolish the death penalty but rather retain it and make use of it." He further suggested, "Stick with the death penalty and never abolish it" (X. Guo 1980:26–27).

There are two reasons that help explain why the majority of Chinese citizens favored the retentionist view at that time. First, from the early days of the Republic era to the early days of the PRC, China experienced a series of wars among warlords—the war against the Japanese invasion and the liberation war. Under these conditions, judicial and extrajudicial killings were deemed not only necessary but also critical to maintain a stable regime.

Second, although the war ended after the founding of the PRC, the political climate at the time (e.g., the Cold War), coupled with Mao's ideology of class struggle and the fight between the enemy and the people, precipitated the retention of the death penalty to fight against "the enemy from the reactionary class." In addition, because of the remaining problems of the civil war and the tensions in the international arena, the Chinese government was not optimistic about its national security. Crimes of splitting the state, subverting the state power, and espionage were still rampant and reaffirmed the need to retain the death penalty. Therefore, within the context of the official confirmation of the retentionist view and against the backdrop of the international and domestic political and economic situation, the dissenting opinion in this debate disappeared and remained silent for a long time.

The Rise of the Debate (from the 1990s to the Present)

In the 1990s, with China's rapid economic development, the attitude of the general public began to change. The international abolition movement again caught the attention of policy makers and legal scholars in China. Currently, the retentionist and the abolitionist camps are debating in the academic and policy arenas, as well as in the public arena (e.g., on the Internet over high-profile cases).

The reemergence of the debate surrounding abolition of China's death penalty started with recognition of the overinclusiveness of its capital offenses (Cheng 1985; Ge & Wang 1980; Ma 1980; Wan 1986; Xue 1989). Although mainstream scholarship has long argued for stringent restrictions on the application of the death penalty, it was not until the 1990s that a large-scale reduction of death-eligible offenses was called for. For example, Professor Zhao Bingzhi (1996) stated in 1996 that death penalty crimes should be restricted to crimes of endangering national security, endangering public security, and endangering and infringing on the rights of persons. In 1997, Professor Gao Minxuan called for the reduction of the death penalty, limiting the number of crimes subject to it to 10 (Gao & Zhao 1998). At this point, many scholars had not argued for complete abolition of the death penalty but had instead expressed certain doubts about its validity and effectiveness. At the initial stage of the abolitionist movement, Chinese scholars were rather conservative and cautious. For example, Hu Yunteng stated that it would take a century for China to abolish the death penalty (Hu 1995).

Since then, the abolitionist debate has revolved around several issues. The first involves the philosophical argument. For example, Professor Qiu Xinglong held that capital punishment is inhuman because it deprives a person of his or her right to life (Hu, Zhang, & Qiu 1998). Similarly, Professor Hu Tengyun pointed out, "The inhumanity of the death penalty does not lie only in the deprivation of the right of life itself, but also in the fact that it contradicts the central theme of 'treating human beings as human beings,' and deprived the other rights associated with the right to life" (Hu, Zhang, & Qiu 1998:36). The second point deals with the utilitarian aspect of the death penalty. For example, Professor Jia Yu argued that there is no evidence suggesting that the death penalty deters crime (Jia 2003). Third, abolitionists have also explored ways to abolish the death penalty completely. Professor Qu Xinjiu suggested three ways to achieve abolition in China: (1) to publicize abolition and make it more widely accepted and supported; (2) to educate politicians through results of empirical studies; and (3) to cultivate a culture of humanitarianism among the general public through continuous education and open public debates (Qu 2003).

There is no doubt that the abolitionist arguments have gained ground in China since the 1990s. However, it is the pragmatic view that seems to dominate the current legal field. For example, Professor Chen Xingliang said, "From a theoretical perspective, I am an abolitionist, but from a practical perspective, I am a retentionist" (Chen 2003:42). This was perhaps because many scholars and legal practitioners realized that under the current conditions in China, complete abolition is not realistic. In contrast, retentionists are firm believers that the death penalty has a real, positive effect on crime prevention and justice (Feng 2005; M. Liu 2004; Xie 2005).

Both external and internal forces drove the reemergence of this debate. One of the major external forces was the international abolitionist movement. With regard to foreign debate over the death penalty, the attitude of Chinese scholars underwent a change. As discussed earlier, in the beginning period of the debate, foreign opinion was introduced into China as an advanced legal concept. During the silence period of the debate, from the early days of the Republic of China till the founding of the PRC, this debate was largely neglected because it did not concern China's many urgent problems. After the founding of the PRC, although the debate was heightened again in the international community, Chinese scholars overwhelmingly criticized the debate in capitalist countries; they argued that the retentionist view was repressive and the abolitionist view was deceptive (Zhou & Ouyang 1982). Nevertheless, concern over the debate in the international community enables Chinese scholars to critically assess these opposing arguments. With the rise of the international abolition movement, relevant foreign theories and empirical data have become important sources to inform the Chinese debate (Jia 2003).

Internal forces include China's socioeconomic development and the accompanying transformation of public opinion and values. Although most Chinese citizens currently do not endorse complete abolition, they generally support safeguarding the human rights of criminals and ensuring the humanity of punishment. This could become the public foundation for the abolition movement in China. As public opinion changes in China, the general public will be more likely to accept abolition of the death penalty formally in legislation and in practice. The lesson of past reforms is that any major reform initiatives in China must have grassroots support and not simply be prompted by a few elites.

THE THREE CONFLICTS: VALUE, CRIMINAL POLICY, AND INDIVIDUAL CASE CHOICE

After decades of argument, the debate over the death penalty in China has gradually focused on three perspectives: abstract values regarding abolishing the death penalty, criminal policy on abolishing the death penalty, and the application of the death penalty in individual criminal cases.

The Value Debate

Beccaria argued that it is unreasonable for a government representing the public will to enact laws depriving an individual of life (Beccaria 2006). Since then there has been much debate over values regarding abolishing the death penalty. Is the death penalty in line with the concept of human rights? Is the death penalty moral? Is a nation entitled to carry out the death penalty? These questions have a common theme, and China's death penalty debate is first and foremost a conflict about the abstract values of the death penalty. This leads to the direct question whether the death penalty should be abolished.

To some extent, the debate over values regarding abolishing the death penalty in China is based on research in Western countries. Common points of view include the opinion that the death penalty is an infringement on the value of life (Chen 2004:69), that it is not justified in terms of morality (Qiu 2002), and that it runs counter to the concept of human rights (Sunstein & Vermeule 2005). Retentionists raise counterarguments on these issues. For example, Professor Qiu Xinglong argues, "The death penalty is not only morally permissible, but also morally required. To be specific, the death penalty is morally required, not because of punishment, but to prevent innocent people from being victimized" (Qiu 2002:51). On the relationship between the death penalty and human rights, Professor Zhang Yuanhuang holds, "The death penalty comes from the natural desire of humanity," and one "cannot ignore the fact that it accords with human nature" (Y. Zhang 2008:82). Professor Feng Jun further argues that the death penalty should be applied only to heinous criminals who should be deprived of rights (Feng 2005).

When one views the death penalty debate from the morality perspective, it seems that the majority of Chinese legal scholars are now in favor of abolishing the death penalty. For instance, in a 2002 seminar in Hunan Province, China, among dozens of Chinese criminal law scholars who were discussing the question whether to abolish or retain the death penalty, very few insisted on retaining the death penalty. The overwhelming advantage and predominant position of death penalty abolitionists has persisted for over 10 years (Tian 2005).

The Criminal Justice Policy Debate

The second aspect of the debate lies in the policy arena and can be summarized in three areas.

THE DEATH PENALTY AS DETERRENCE

It has long been thought that the death penalty deters crime. Early Chinese textbooks widely endorsed this view, and some scholars maintain that policy makers in China also wholeheartedly believe in the policy's deterrent value (Jia 2006). However, concerns have been raised that its deterrent effect may be exaggerated (Y. Zhang 2008). Scholars, citing the law of diminishing marginal utility, have argued that when the severity of criminal punishment reaches a certain level, its deterrent effect can be expected to decline (Sun 2011). Available empirical evidence from Western research also provides contradictory evidence about the deterrence effect. Chinese scholars, depending on their perspective in the abolitionist debate, sporadically cite these research findings to advance their position. For example, abolitionists cite the U.S.-specific research finding that rates of serious crimes did not increase but in fact decreased after a state abolished the death penalty (Cooter & Ulen 1988). In contrast, retentionists cite American studies to prove that the death penalty inhibits serious crimes. For example, one study found that "on average, every execution of capital punishment could prevent

18 murder cases from happening"; this was widely cited to support the retentionist view (Y. Liu 2013; Sunstein & Vermeule 2011). It remains questionable whether and to what extent Western ideas and experiences will truly have an impact on domestic policies in China, particularly regarding death penalty issues.

THE DEATH PENALTY AS RETRIBUTION

The death penalty is also highly retributive. Retentionists argue that in the current social context, punishing the most heinous criminals with the death penalty is an embodiment of social justice, thus justifying its retributive function (Xiao & Wang 2011). For example, Professor Wang Shizhou maintains that the primary function of the death penalty is retribution, whereas other lighter punishments serve the purpose of crime prevention (S. Wang 2003). In contrast, abolitionists view the retributive function as barbaric and unjustified because modern criminal law no longer endorses the cruel and inhumane punishment philosophy of "a tooth for a tooth, an eye for an eye." For instance, Professor Yin Jianfeng claims, "Life for a life is no more than an intuitive manifestation of revenge/retaliation of human race, an outdated notion of retribution of equal harm" (Yin 2008). Similarly, Yang Tongjin and Liu Hanqin (2009) hold that retribution as a justification for the death penalty is a serious contradiction of modern philosophies regarding human rights.

Nevertheless, in meting out criminal sentences (particularly in death penalty cases), judges seem to rely overwhelmingly on retributive principles (e.g., making the punishment fit the crime) rather than other factors. For example, Wang Shengjun, president of China's Supreme People's Court, points out that there are three considerations in deliberating death sentences: (1) the provisions of the laws, (2) the overall condition of public safety, and (3) social and public opinion (Lan 2008). In addition, public indignation has been cited as a justification for imposing the death sentence in many regions of China (Zhai 2011).

WRONGFUL EXECUTIONS

Because of the irreversible nature unique to the death penalty, it must be meted out with extreme caution. In recent years, the Chinese media and the judicial system have exposed a series of wrongful convictions in death penalty cases. Representative cases include the Teng Xingshan case, the She

Xianglin case, the Zhao Zuohai case, the Li Jiumin case, the uncle-and-nephew case in Zhejiang Province, and the Zhang Zhenfeng case (for detailed description and analysis of these cases, see D. Han 2013). These cases triggered nationwide attention and prompted death penalty debates among legal scholars and practitioners.

In response to the inherent risk associated with the death penalty, some retentionist scholars argue that from the victim's perspective, innocent lives are taken away without any remedies either (Zhao 2011). "We cannot attribute all blames to the death penalty," "The death penalty in itself is not the reason for wrongful convictions," and "We are capable of keeping wrongful convictions in death penalty cases at the lowest possible level by strengthening the regulation and implementation of criminal procedure law and enhancing judicial supervision. We cannot stop using the death penalty just because of concerns over wrongful convictions" (Y. Wang 2012:131).

The Chinese leadership in the political and legal system has paid increasing attention to wrongful convictions. Consequently, they have implemented a range of mechanisms and measures to curb the problem. However, whether and to what extent these measures will have an impact on death penalty policies remains to be seen. Meanwhile, the debate will continue.

The Debate Over Individual Cases

In many instances, theoretical differences can be clarified only when they are applied in specific, individual cases. This is particularly true in death penalty cases. For example, in recent high-profile cases debated in the public in China, it was neither the abolitionists nor the retentionists but the general public who tended to drive the debate and who often dictated the judicial rulings.

Although it is difficult for the general public to participate in scholarly and policy debate, with the aid of the Internet, the general public's opinion on the death penalty can easily influence individual cases. With the deepening of judicial reforms, human rights consciousness and legal awareness have gradually taken root in China. Breaking the barriers of the retentionist/abolitionist divide, the public seems to have formulated its own perspectives regarding justice in the death penalty debate. However, although its perspectives are easily overlooked in the academic and policy debate, public opinion has the potential to erupt quickly, gather support, and change directions of judicial rulings in certain high-profile cases. The Liu Yong case is one where China's legal elites and the general public confronted each other fiercely. Liu Yong, a defendant, charged with organizing a criminal gang and intentional assault, was convicted and sentenced to death with immediate execution by the first trial court in 2002. Immediately after the first ruling, 14 famous jurists jointly drafted expert opinions on Liu Yong's gang-involvement case in Shenyang. They pointed out the evidentiary issues and the possibility of coerced confession and called for a reduced sentence. The review court, citing the possibly coerced confession by the police, changed the original ruling to a suspended death sentence. However, the revised verdict aroused much resentment among the public. The public not only disapproved of the revision of the sentence but also criticized the expert opinions. Specifically, people accused the experts of being arbitrary, interfering with judicial authority, and serving the rich and the powerful. The media also cautioned the jurists about the danger of obstructing justice. In reaction to the turbulent public opinion, the Supreme People's Court initiated a rarely utilized procedure (the judicial supervision procedure) and resentenced Liu to the death penalty with immediate execution to appease the public in 2003 (Supreme People's Court, 2003, Criminal Case no. 5; for detailed analyses of the Liu Yong case, see also L. Li 2003; Lin 2004; and Song 2003).

AN ANALYSIS OF THE THREE CONFLICTS

The debate over retention or abolition of the death penalty does not seem to contribute to death penalty policy decisions either in the short run or in the long run. The lack of interaction among the three key areas of the debate, namely, the theory, judicial practice, and the public, is problematic if the debate is to influence policy making.

The Useless Value Debate

The theoretical basis of the death penalty debate can be traced back to the philosophical debate about morality, the value of life, and human rights. However, consensus has not been reached on how to define and interpret these concepts. Meanwhile, different interpretations of the same concept serve as grounds for both parties of the debate. For example, on whether the death penalty respects life, it seems that any interpretation is valid. "The death penalty embodies the respect for the victim's life, saves the lives of potential victims, and resonates with the right to life, but at the same time, the death penalty runs against the sublime value of the right to life, as it ignores the life of the offender, abuses state power, neglects unfair factors in the procedures, misplaces social responsibilities, and indulges the primitive vengeance mentality of mankind" (Shi 2012:75). Some scholars argue that the starting point of the death penalty debate is very often the same; however, "from the same starting point, completely different claims are derived: some believe the death penalty should be retained; others believe it should be abolished" (M. Zhang 2011:475). If we dwell on the debate at this level, we may never get an answer.

In addition, there seems to exist an inherent contradiction among academics who also act as policy makers. Many scholars are abolitionists at heart but retentionists in action. For these reasons, the value debate has little utility.

The Assimilating Policy Debate

Although there is a huge gap between the goal of the abolitionists and retentionists, they currently agree on one thing: given current social conditions, it will be difficult to achieve complete abolition. Instead, judicial restrictions on the death penalty seem to be the ideal choice.

PARTIAL ACKNOWLEDGMENT OF CHINA'S CURRENT CRIMINAL LAW POLICIES

It should be noted that there are radical scholars in the death penalty debate; some scholars argue that China should completely abolish the death penalty as soon as possible: "The sooner the better, hopefully tomorrow" (Qu 2005:557), or "Give me an enlightened politician and I will abolish [the] death penalty in China in one day" (Qiu 2004:214). However, most death penalty abolitionists do not endorse a shock therapy sort of criminal policy but rather dedicate themselves to the study of long-term strategies that would progressively reform death penalty abolition (Y. Wang 2012). Some scholars propose to abolish the death penalty over an interim period of three or four decades: "By the middle of this century, when China becomes a developed country, it could consider abolishing the death penalty comprehensively" (B. Zhao 2005:99). Some scholars even believe that it will take almost a century for China to achieve this (Tian 2005). Of course, regarding the timeline for death penalty policy reforms, abolitionists and retentionists disagree with each other. Abolitionists believe in maintaining the current criminal policy to ensure a peaceful transition to death penalty abolition and presenting a timetable or itinerary for future death penalty abolition. Retentionists, in contrast, believe that the current criminal policy is reasonable in itself; they say that policy makers should worry about adjusting death penalty policies only when the social environment changes in the future, without giving a timetable for China's death penalty abolition.

INCREASING AGREEMENT IN INDIVIDUAL CASES IN JUDICIAL APPLICATIONS

China's death penalty abolitionists generally call for the gradual reduction of death penalty crimes and stringent restrictions on the application of the death penalty in order to secure a gradual transition to abolishing the death penalty. Judicial restriction on the application of the death penalty is deemed an important means to abolish it. For instance, some scholars suggest that without changing criminal legislation, China could impose more suspended death sentences to render China a de facto death penalty abolition state. As Zhang and Huang (2004) point out, currently China can choose to make the death penalty with a two-year suspension a mandatory procedure for the death penalty to achieve the effect of immediate death penalty abolition. Some scholars argue that although the current death penalty policies are unreasonable, they cannot be phased out in a short time (Lu 2004). Instead, China should expand its application of the death penalty with suspension to pave the way for full-scale abolition of the death penalty. Death penalty retentionists also argue for stringent judicial restrictions on the application of the death penalty. It can be concluded that even most retentionists agree with the abstract value of abolishing the death penalty and thus endorse the restriction and reduction of the death penalty. On the other hand, even abolitionists agree with China's present death penalty policy and merely want further perfection of the policies.

The death penalty policies of the PRC date back to Mao Zedong's speech "On the Problems of the Party's Present Policies" in January 1948, in which he said, "We must kill less and forbid reckless killing. It is wrong to kill more and kill recklessly, because it will alienate our Party from the public and lose the citizens' compassion for us." Subsequently, the 1979 Criminal Law stipulated that "the death penalty is applicable only to those extremely heinous criminals." The 1997 Criminal Law provided that "the death penalty shall be applied only to criminals who committed the most heinous crimes." Both laws are in line with the spirit of "kill less and kill with caution." In 2007, the Supreme People's Court, the Supreme People's Procuratorate, the Ministry of Public Security, and the Department of Justice jointly promulgated the Opinion on Further Strictly Enforcing the Law to Ensure the Quality of Death Penalty Cases, which further clarified the criminal policy of "retaining the death penalty and strictly restricting the use of the death penalty." The PRC's criminal policies regarding the death penalty have been consistent, but, of course, the choice of which criminals are labeled those who "have committed heinous crimes and shall be sentenced to death" and the choice "to kill or not to kill" remain in the hands of jurists. There have been differences in the application of the death penalty at different times and in different regions. For example, during the strike-hard campaigns in the 1980s, death penalty application standards were relaxed, but we cannot say that China changed its overall policies on the death penalty.

It is worth noting that "to kill less" and "to kill with caution" have different meanings in China's death penalty policies. "To kill with caution" embodies judicial deliberation—the death penalty shall not be applied recklessly. "To kill less" points to a gradual reduction in future applications of the death penalty. Specifically, since the Eighth Amendment to the Criminal Law (2011) and the Decisions on Key Issues in Furthering the Reform of the CPC's 18th National People's Congress Third Plenary Session (2013) put forward the recommendation for a "gradual reduction of the application of death penalty," "to kill less" has increasingly signified both the judicial reduction of the application of the death penalty and the legislative reduction of eligible crimes. China's death penalty retentionists and abolitionists both are highly supportive of "to kill less" and "to kill with caution." Therefore, although the debate over the death penalty is more controversial in theory, in the more practical areas of death penalty legislation and judicial application, the difference is not obvious.

The Muted Legal Community in Debates on Individual Cases

The Liu Yong case is a microcosm of the conflict between public opinion and the legal elites in an individual death penalty case. Legal scholars paid much more attention to the legal doctrines and the reform goals of killing less and with caution; the public saw legal scholars as a powerful interest group manipulating experts' opinions to serve their interests.

Li Changkui's case is a classic example in which the abolitionists compromised. In this case, the second-instance court changed the original sentence of death with immediate execution to a suspended death sentence, causing widespread public dissatisfaction (Q. Wang 2012). The adjudicating court responded to public opinion, saying, "Death penalty abolition is an overall trend. Ten years from now, upon retrospect, many people will have a different opinion.... Now we are faced with tremendous pressure, but this case will be a landmark, a textbook example 10 years from now" (Liu & Du 2011:A23). This is clearly a judicial effort to restrict the scope of the death penalty while also serving as an example of law as social engineering. Specifically, the court sought to change public perceptions to pave the way for further reforms.

However, the revised ruling of the second-instance court did not receive wide support. Some scholars did offer support of this decision by stating that "in this case, the defendant turned himself in, and the case belongs to intentional homicide cases involving marriage and family disputes. It is because of these circumstances that the second-instance court meted out the suspended death sentence. The ruling reflects the policy to strictly restrict the death penalty" (Chen 2013:6). But other scholars thought that the decision went too far (Zhao 2011), and others thought that that "the stride is a little too huge and borders on radicalism" (Fu 2013:18).

In several high-profile cases, the public demanded the death sentence with immediate execution, and the provincial high court yielded to the public's demand and changed the lower court's sentence to the death sentence. This phenomenon merits consideration. In many serious criminal cases, the general public (out of concern for its own safety and compassion for the victims) calls for the death sentence, even in countries where the death penalty has already been abolished. For example, in the 1976 Patrick Henry kidnapping and homicide case, the French public was outraged by the cold-blooded criminal, who kidnapped and killed an eight-year-old boy (Badinter 2008). Therefore, the public started a campaign to reinstate the death penalty. The outlet for public opinion is present in many nations. Legal elites would benefit from careful handling of public opinion, refraining both from criticizing the public too strongly and from following public opinion blindly.

In China, however, judicial sentencing decisions have seemed to be hijacked by public opinion, particularly in high-profile death penalty cases. That pattern was repeated in cases such as those of Li Changkui, Yao Jiaxin (discussed below), Liu Yong, and Dong Wei (discussed in chapter 1).

THE KEY TO THE DEATH PENALTY DEBATE: A COMBINATION OF THEORY, JUDICIAL PRACTICE, AND PUBLIC AWARENESS

Overall, decades of death penalty debate have had positive effects. The legal community has a more systematic and rational understanding of the value and purpose of criminal punishment, as well as the strengths and limitations of criminal policies. The debate has also promoted the study of criminal legal theory. However, in regard to China's future death penalty choices, no consensus has been reached in the legal community. More importantly, the theoretical debate of legal elites has grown further apart from judicial practice and public awareness, forming a huge gap between scholarship and policy. To change this, the criminal law circle must be more policy oriented, ensuring that theory matches China's death penalty judicial status quo and facing the public's perception of the death penalty up front.

Judicial Application Standards for the Death Penalty

As discussed earlier, there are discrepancies between theory and practice in the death penalty debate. Outside the academic debate, there are hardly any rules that can be used to distinguish a death penalty sentence with immediate execution from a death penalty sentence with a suspension. Because the judiciary is the most direct link to the death penalty, the judicial application standard of the death penalty is one of the key issues that merit attention.

Although their starting points differ, retentionists have a higher expectation than abolitionists for judicial application of the death penalty. Specifically, they hope to restrict the application of the death penalty with immediate execution and to clarify the application standard. One expects that the application standards proposed by both sides will be different, especially for intentional homicide cases. However, the attention of the theoretical community prevents the debate from going any further. Neither abolitionists nor retentionists have come up with any specific judicial application requirements for the death penalty with immediate execution. This has also prevented scholars on both sides from presenting systematic proposals on judicial practice and individual cases and thus from obtaining approval and support from adjudicating agents. Retentionists and abolitionists must come up with their respective judicial application standards for the death penalty with immediate execution, justify their validity, and allow jurists to make choices in order to make progress in the debate over death penalty abolition.

In China's current judicial practice, jurists are in urgent need of theoretical support on how to determine and quantify the application standard for the death penalty. At present, aside from certain statutory mitigating circumstances (such as voluntary surrender, performing a meritorious service, being an accessory to the crime, attempted offense), jurists rely on the Opinion on Certain Issues Concerning Implementing the Criminal Justice Policy of Balancing Leniency and Severity issued by the Supreme People's Court in 2010. This opinion stipulates that leniency can be granted for several circumstances, such as civil disputes, the victim's fault, active compensation, sincere remorse, and forgiveness from the victim and his or her family. There are no other systematic rules that guide the practice of death penalty sentencing. In addition, the rules established in the SPC's 2010 opinion are controversial. For example, it stipulates, "Defendants who turned themselves in, apart from those who committed extremely severe crimes, showed serious malicious intent, posed great threat to security or used voluntary surrender maliciously to circumvent criminal punishments, shall generally be punished with leniency in accordance with the law." In other words, lenient punishments are not applicable to defendants who "have committed heinous crimes," while committing extremely severe crimes is a mandatory requirement for a death sentence. According to this judicial interpretation, voluntary surrender does not guarantee lenient treatment in death penalty cases, so the sentence outcome is less predictable both for the defendant and the judge.

Significantly, although China labels both the death penalty with immediate execution and the death penalty with a two-year suspension the death penalty and states that this death penalty standard shall apply to both penalties, the two types of death penalties actually are markedly different. The latter cannot be deemed a true death sentence. It should be pointed out that it is problematic in Chinese legislation to include both types of death penalties without differentiating them in the specific provisions of the criminal law. In the statutory provisions, both the death penalty with immediate execution and the death penalty with a two-year suspension are labeled the death penalty and do not seem to be vastly different, but for criminals, there is a life-and-death difference. However, the present judicial interpretation contains almost no instructions for choosing between the death penalty with immediate execution and the death penalty with a two-year suspension. Because of the lack of standardized criteria, the criteria adopted to distinguish the death penalty from life imprisonment are also used to distinguish the two types of death penalties from each other. This can lead to confusion. For example, in some cases in which the court meted out the death penalty with suspension on the basis of mitigating circumstances, the court took "good confession attitude" and "truthfully confessed to one's crimes" as mitigating circumstances. However, without truthfully confessing one's crimes, how can one be deemed to have a "good confession attitude"? Therefore, "good confession attitude" should incorporate "truthfully confessed one's crimes." The court ruling was redundant because it cited both as two mitigating circumstances. Some scholars have shrewdly pointed out that "the choice between suspended death sentence and immediate execution is, in essence, not a legal matter, but rather a policy matter, or merely a moral judgment matter" (Bai 2006:144). Some Chinese scholars also consider the application standard for a suspended death sentence unclear and difficult to operationalize. For instance, Ye (2012) states that when an offender is granted the victim's forgiveness, the suspended death sentence shall apply, excluding circumstances where the conscience of the human race is stricken hard. The circumstances where "the conscience of human race is stricken hard" are as nonspecific as the term *extremely heinous crimes* (Ye 2012:94). It is because specific criteria are lacking that confusion exists in the application standard of the death penalty with immediate execution.

Therefore, the most significant and urgent matter in China's death penalty judicial practice is the differentiation of application standards for the death penalty with immediate execution and those for the death penalty with suspension. In China, where the death penalty will not be eliminated by legislation anytime soon, the judicial application standard of the death penalty with immediate execution is at the heart of the death penalty debate.

Both retentionists and abolitionists should come up with criteria in line with their own beliefs, and the criteria should be in accordance with China's judicial practice so that they can be accepted and assimilated by judicial organs. The party who can successfully sell its standard to judicial organs will obviously have a huge advantage in the death penalty debate. Meanwhile, potential impact of such a standard on the abolition of the death penalty will far outweigh the purely theoretical debate.

Fight for the Support of Public Opinion

Both retentionists and abolitionists should learn that, since the popularization of the Internet, public opinion matters and sometimes may be decisive in a legal ruling.

DECISIVE IMPACT OF PUBLIC OPINION

A wide range of factors determine China's future death penalty policy choices, including international and domestic pressures, the authorities' political considerations, and public opinion. However, it seems that public opinion will play a more decisive role in the future of China's death penalty.

First, international pressure can be only an external factor and cannot be decisive. China's death penalty practice has been under international pressure for decades. Now, with China's rising international status, it is in a better position to confront international pressure. Therefore, this pressure will have a diminished impact on China's criminal policies.

Second, domestic pressure is primarily dominated by the public's attitude toward the death penalty. This is true particularly when public opinion is inconsistent with state policy on death penalty issues. The political leadership is required to listen to the public, carefully guide public opinion, and incorporate public opinion into its policy initiatives.

Similarly, legal scholars have increasingly paid attention to public opinion on important issues, such as the death penalty. For example, in 1995, the Legal Research Institute of the Chinese Academy of Social Sciences and the National Statistics Bureau jointly conducted a public opinion poll on support for the death penalty. Out of a total of 4,983 people surveyed, fewer than 5% of the respondents supported abolition. In 2003, 163.com conducted surveys of 16,612 Internet users on the issue of the death penalty. Results showed that over 83% were against abolishing the death penalty, while fewer than 16% were supportive of the abolitionist movement. In April 2008, sina.com conducted surveys on its website on the issue of the death penalty. Again, the majority (67.2%) of those surveyed were against abolishing the death penalty, some (21.8%) supported restricting the use of the death penalty, and only a small percentage of respondents (11%) favored complete abolition (M. Yang 2010). One scholar surveyed a sample of 1,873 college undergraduate students on the same issue. The results were consistent with other findings: 75.4% were against abolishing the death penalty, 21.7% were supportive of it, while 2.9% remained undecided (Jia 2005). These survey results indicate that the vast majority of the Chinese population is not supportive of abolishing the death penalty.

There are generally two different attitudes toward public opinion. One group of policy makers embraces public opinion and incorporates it into public policy. For example, some scholars claim that "the restriction and reduction of the death penalty has become the consensus of China's leadership, legal professionals, and the general public" (Zhao 2014:146). The other group of policy makers ignores public opinion polls, insisting that abolition does not require a consensus among the general populace (Wang & Li 2012).

Abolitionists might point out that when the death penalty was abolished in many countries, the public did not overwhelmingly support the decision (Liang 2004). However, it should be noted that even when the public does not support abolishing the death penalty, it is not likely to think of abolition as an intolerable political behavior because the government has discussed the potential for abolition for long periods.

In China, if the Chinese leadership has the political will to abolish the death penalty, abolition could occur in a short period of time. However, such abolition may be short-lived because even if the Chinese leadership can handle the initial public resistance to abrupt abolition, in the long run (and whenever severe crimes occur) criminal justice policy will be questioned. The potential recurring tension between the citizens and the government would be detrimental to the political leadership, particularly for the Communist Party, whose legitimacy is founded on public support (for a detailed discussion of how major high-profile cases have challenged criminal justice policies, see Gu 2008; W. Zhang 2008; and Zhou 2010).

Importantly, the balance of legislation, judicial practice, and public expectation is of special significance in China. China has already adopted the rule of law as the basic national strategy and is at a critical turning point.

Now what stands in the way of China's drive for rule by law is not only the judicial and administrative organs' adherence to the principle but also the public's legal consciousness and internalization of this idea of the rule of law. China's legalization process is still in its infancy. The general public has yet to develop trust and confidence in the judiciary, and the judiciary has yet to establish authority and legitimacy. Every time there is a discrepancy between judicial rulings and public expectations (e.g., the Hu Bin case, the Peng Yu case, the Xu Ting case), public confidence in the judiciary is tested.[1] On whether to abolish or to retain the death penalty, which concerns the draconian sanctions against severe crimes most capable of provoking strong sentiments from the general public, the public's perception of the death penalty should be respected.

TWO FACTORS INFLUENCING PUBLIC OPINION

With respect to the impact of public opinion on individual death penalty cases, Chinese legal scholars have mixed views. Some believe that public opinion should not interfere with judicial decisions. The intrusion of public opinion places judicial organs under unnecessary pressure (which is a violation of judicial independence) and is becoming an important source of judicial partiality (Jia 2006). Other scholars claim that public opinion should be allowed to affect justice because the general public's attitudes toward crimes can be considered social consequences of crime (Sun 2009). Interestingly, although the issue is in essence one of judicial independence (as opposed to being an issue of abolishing or retaining the death penalty), many abolitionists are inclined to believe that public opinion should not influence death penalty sentencing (Zhao 2014). Retentionists, in contrast, maintain that it may be that "public opinion kills people" (Jia 2006). It seems, however, that although Chinese citizens do not approve of full-scale abolition of the death penalty, that does not mean that they would choose the death penalty in every case. Chinese public opinion is affected by two factors in each death penalty case. No matter whether one is a retentionist or an abolitionist, scholars in both camps should have a better understanding of public opinion.

First, it is clear that public opinion is against abolishing the death penalty. Because of economic and social development and cultural tradition, Chinese citizens generally do not endorse full-scale abolition of the death penalty. The reason for this lack of support may be that ordinary citizens believe that the death penalty must be meted out to criminals who have committed extremely heinous crimes. Only in this way can justice be served (in the public's opinion). The death penalty may also satisfy the public's need for safety. For example, in recent years, China has been contending with grave terrorist threats. For terrorist attacks that cause a great number of casualties, Chinese citizens are adamant in their desire for imposition of the death penalty with immediate execution (Dai & Hu 2014). Failure to execute these criminals will not only frustrate citizens' sense of justice but will also reduce the public's expectation for judicial justice. Significantly, the public does not commonly argue that jurists "must impose the death penalty"; such calls center only on serious and lethal violent crimes. For nonviolent crimes eligible for the death penalty (as stipulated by the Criminal Law), such as drug offenses, the call for the imposition of death penalty with immediate execution is not that loud. People can accept suspended death sentences and life imprisonment.

Second, the public's lack of confidence in judicial justice must be considered. The term *justice of law* has many connotations, and for the general public, the most obvious one is judicial justice. A closer examination of public opinion in death penalty cases indicates that the confrontation between the general public and judicial organs is very often not due to the judicial organ's reluctance to impose the death penalty, but rather because citizens doubt the impartiality of the rulings. For instance, in the aforementioned Liu Yong case, the criticism of the second-instance revised sentence revolved around whether "the revised sentence [was] impacted by Liu Yong's wealth and social status." Likewise, in the Li Changkui case, the public did not accept the ruling because compared with the similarly high-profile Yao Jiaxin case, Yao was sentenced to death for murdering one person during his reckless driving, while Li, in contrast, raped one person and killed two (one of whom was a child). The dangerousness of Li apparently outweighs that of Yao (hence the nickname "rival of Jiaxin"), but the court sentenced him to the death penalty with a two-year suspension. Therefore, in many circumstances, it is unbiased judicial justice, not the death penalty, that the general public is after (Lu 2011).

Therefore, Chinese criminal law scholars should take note of public opinion. In serious violent crimes involving multiple deaths, the public's call for the death penalty with immediate execution is not to be compromised. For other serious criminal offenses, however, including intentional homicides that lead to one person's death, it is likely that the general public would accept not imposing the death penalty with immediate execution. A look at

China's death penalty judicial practice shows that there are cases where a suspended death penalty was meted out for two counts of murder. Of course, the premise that this kind of ruling is to be accepted is that the public felt that the rulings were fair and impartial. Therefore, a uniform judicial standard and public identification with the death penalty are closely associated.

POLICY INCORPORATING PUBLIC OPINION

Public opinion on the death penalty not only influences judicial practice but also affects legislative choices with regard to the death penalty. Legislators base criminal policies on citizens' expectations and demands (Nishihara 2004). As a result of the Decisions on Key Issues in Furthering the Reform of the CPC's 18th National People's Congress Third Plenary Session, policy makers have proposed a gradual reduction in the number of crimes eligible for the death penalty. However, the legislative choices in cutting back death penalty crimes should take public opinion into consideration. That said, public opinion will need some level of guidance, and China's death penalty issue cannot be solved simply by referendum.

The public's perception of the death penalty not only affects the judicial application of the death penalty but also is related to legislative choices in reducing death penalty crimes—it is a core element in China's death penalty choices. Therefore, another key area of the death penalty debate is the support of public opinion. Both retentionists and abolitionists should consider how to make themselves acceptable to mainstream public opinion.

For a long time, Chinese abolitionists have avoided the topic of Chinese public opinion. On the contrary, they prefer to cite international trends in abolition as evidence (Y. Guo 2005; Liang 2004; R. Wang 2005; X. Zhang 2007). Apart from the issue of the validity of drawing conclusions about China based on international policies, the reasoning itself is erroneous (Yu 2009). It is absurd for Chinese abolitionists to consider international trends while ignoring China's mainstream public opinion. Therefore, Chinese abolitionists should change their attitude and consider their theoretical proposal in light of Chinese public opinion. For instance, many abolitionists suggest that the next step is to abolish the death penalty for corruption and bribery crimes (Zhou 2006). However, if one considers the Chinese public's deep dissatisfaction with the corruption issue and the severe overall anticorruption situation, abolishing the death penalty for embezzlement and bribe-taking crimes now may send a signal that the nation has relaxed its sanctions on corruption-related crimes; such a signal will certainly trigger a strong public opinion uproar. Therefore, "at present and in a relatively long period of time from now, retaining [the] death penalty for such crimes is an objective estimation" (W. Li 2012:183). When abolitionists are making future legislative proposals for reducing death penalty crimes, they should also consider the social context and public opinion, among other factors. Therefore, it is advisable to reduce other death penalty crimes first and supplement such restrictions with other measures (e.g., judicial restrictions) to guide public opinion.

Meanwhile, Chinese retentionists are expected to come up with their own proposals while taking public opinion into consideration. Chinese retentionists widely believe that they have the support of mainstream public opinion, but they have neglected analysis and guidance of public perceptions. Public opinion is constantly changing, and public support for retentionists is not necessarily eternal. There have already been many cases where the public has not endorsed the judicial organ's imposition of the death penalty (Deng 2013). More important, in the general trend of death penalty restriction and reduction, death penalty retentionists should come up with legislative reduction and judicial restriction measures in line with their theory to avoid being marginalized in the overall trend.

FULL-SCALE DISCLOSURE OF CHINA'S DEATH PENALTY RULINGS

There have been mixed opinions on whether China's death penalty rulings should be fully disclosed. Proponents argue that disclosure will enhance judicial transparency and judicial supervision (R. Liu 2013), while opponents claim that full disclosure of death penalty rulings may conflict with the national interest (S. Wang 2004). It is noteworthy that China is now undergoing full-scale judicial reform. The Regulations on the Internet Posting of People's Court Rulings promulgated by the SPC in 2013 stipulates that "People's Court rulings that came into effect shall be disclosed on the Internet, with the following exceptions: rulings that involve national secrets or personal privacy; the defendant being a minor; cases concluded by mediation; other circumstances that are not appropriate to be disclosed." This presents an opportunity for full disclosure of Chinese death penalty rulings, but the regulation has a clause for "other circumstances" that leads to uncertainties about the disclosure. The Implementing Regulations on Internet Posting of Provincial Court's Rulings (Pilot) issued by the High Court of Sichuan Province (2014) even stipulates that cases "where the defendants are sentenced to the death penalty with immediate execution" may not be disclosed.

There are several benefits associated with publishing court documents. The most pressing issue involving death penalty reform is the standardization of sentencing practices for the death penalty with immediate execution and the death penalty with suspension in China. Full disclosure will provide empirical evidence for the study of death sentence patterns and help construct sentencing guidelines feasible in judicial practice (Y. Yang 2008). It will also help facilitate an empirical and policy-based death penalty debate rather than one based only on theory. Meanwhile, the disclosure of court rulings will help enhance judicial transparency and allow public oversight of the adjudicative process. Since public opinion could be a decisive factor in shaping public policy with regard to the death penalty, the full disclosure of death penalty rulings might reduce misperceptions and enhance the public's confidence in and understanding of China's judiciary.

NOTE

1   The Hu Bin case: On May 7, 2009, when driving at a high speed in Hangzhou City, Hu Bin hit and killed a passenger who was crossing the road. Hu's case drew a lot of public attention and sparked a heated discussion about traffic safety. The police initially estimated his driving speed at 70 km/h, which was widely doubted. Hu was sentenced to three years in prison.

    The Peng Yu case: On November 20, 2006, 65-year-old Xu slipped and injured herself at a bus stop. The 26-year-old Peng Yu helped her and sent her to the hospital at Xu's request. Later, Xu claimed that she was hit by Peng, which Peng strongly denied. Xu filed a lawsuit against Peng. The Gulou District Court in Nanjing City (the court of first instance) held Peng liable and argued that "The more realist thing for Peng Yu to do is to capture the person who hit the plaintiff, instead of kindly helping her get up." This ruling caused a public outcry. During the trial of second instance, Peng and Xu reached a mediation agreement.

    The Xu Ting case: On April 21, 2006, Xu Ting and his friend Guo Anshan withdrew a significant amount of money from a malfunctioned ATM. Xu withdrew RMB 175,000 (USD 28,595) and Guo withdrew RMB 18,000 (USD 2,941). Later, Guo turned himself in and was sentenced to one year in prison. Xu absconded and remained at large for one year until he was captured. In December 2007, the court of first instance sentenced him to life imprisonment, which was widely deemed too harsh. On February 22, 2008, the case was remanded to the original trial court where Xu was resentenced to five-year imprisonment.

All three cases revealed the public's lack of trust in the Chinese judiciary.

REFERENCES

Badinter, R. (2008). *Abolition: One Man's Battle Against the Death Penalty*. Lebanon, NH: University Press of New England.

Bai, J. (2006). Sixing shiyong shizheng yanjiu [Empirical study on death penalty application]. *China Social Science, 5*, 135–145.

Beccaria, C. (2006). *An Essay on Crimes and Punishments*. Clark, NJ: The Lawbook Exchange, Ltd.

Chen, X. (2003). Sixing cuifei zhi yingran yu shiran [The necessity and reality of death penalty abolition and retention]. *Legal Science, 4*, 39–42.

Chen, X. (2004). Guanyu sixing de tongxin [Correspondence on the death penalty]. In X. Chen & Y. Hu (Eds.), *Zhongguo xingfaxue nianhui wenji* [Article Collections of the Annual Chinese Criminal Law Conference] (pp. 67–84). Beijing: China University of Political Science and Law Press.

Chen, X. (2013). Sixing zhengce zhi fali jiedu [A jurisprudence interpretation of death penalty policies]. *Journal of Renmin University of China, 6*, 2–9.

Cheng, G. (1985). Dangqian kuoda sixing shiyong fanwei shishu biyao [It is necessary to expand the application of death penalty at present]. *Modern Legal Studies, 1*, 86–91.

Cheng, G. (1986). *Shiping ziben zhuyi guojia feichu sixing* [On the death penalty abolition in capitalist countries]. *Legal Studies, 2*, 29.

Cooter, R., & Ulen, T. (1988). *Law and Economics*. Glenview, IL: Scott, Foresman.

Dai, L., & Hu, R. (2014, May 3). Binjian xiang baokong fenzi chuji! [Shoulder to shoulder, fight against the violent terrorists!]. *People's Daily*, p. 2.

Deng, H. (2013, September 26). Xia Junfeng zhihou de qingli jiujiu [The entanglement of sense and sensibility in the aftermath of the Xia Junfeng case]. *Xi'an Daily*, p. 12.

Feng, J. (2005). Sixing fanzuiren yu diren [The death penalty, criminals and enemies]. *Chinese and Foreign Legal Studies, 5*, 608–615.

Fu, L. (2013). Sixing anjian caipan guocheng zhong de ruangubin jiqi qichu [The judicial rickets in death penalty case sentencing and its remedy]. *Legal Science, 10*, 16–23.

Gao, M. (1981). *Xinzhongguo xinfa de yunyu he dansheng* [The Incubation and Creation of PRC's Criminal Law]. Beijing: Law Press.

Gao, M., & Zhao, B. (1998). *Xinzhongguo xingfa wenxian ziliao zonglan* [Collections of Materials on PRC's Criminal Law]. Beijing: People's Public Security University of China Press.

Ge, P., & Wang, H. (1980). Tan sixing [On the death penalty]. *Legal Studies, 1*, 29–44.

Gu, P. (2008). Gongzhuong panyi de fali jiexi—dui Xu Ting an de yansheng sikao [A jurisprudence interpretation of public opinion sentencing—Extended thoughts on the Xu Ting case]. *Chinese Legal Science, 4*, 167–178.

Guo, X. (1980). Tan sixing [On the death penalty]. *Journal of Beijing University of Political Science and Law, 2*, 24–28.

Guo, Y. (2005). Sixing jiazhi fenxi [An analysis of the value of the death penalty]. *Jiangxi Police Institute, 1*, 25–28.

Han, D. (2013). Sixing yuancuoan de xianfa kongzhi—yi shige sixing yuancuoan de fenxi wei shijiao [The constitutional control of wrongful convictions in death penalty cases—From the analysis of ten wrongful convictions in death penalty cases]. *Journal of Renmin University of China, 6*, 10–18.

Hu, Y. (1995). *Sixing tonglun* [A General Discussion of the Death Penalty]. Beijing: China University of Political Science and Law Press.

Hu, Y., Zhang, J., & Qiu, X. (1998). Sixing wenti sanrentan zhi san—shengmin de huhuan sixing rendao jie? [Three persons' talk on the death penalty III—The call for life: Is death penalty humane?] *Chinese Lawyers, 12*, 34–37.

Jia, Y. (2003). Zhongguo sixing bijiang zouxiang feizhi [China's death penalty will surely come to an end]. *Legal Science, 4*, 45–53.

Jia, Y. (2005). Sixing shizheng yanjiu zhi sixingguan de diaocha baogao [Death penalty views among college students in China: An empirical study]. *Legal Science Review, 3*, 20–33.

Jia, Y. (2006). *Sixing yanjiu* [Death Penalty Study]. Beijing: Law Press.

Lan, C. (2008, April 12). Zuigao fayuan yuanzhang: qunzhong ganjue ying zuowei pan sixing yiju [President of the Supreme People's Court: Sentiments of citizens should be the basis of death penalty sentencing]. *Youth Times*, p. A2.

Li, L. (2003, November 9). Falv zhuanjia lunzheng ganrao sifa gongzheng jixing zhidu chansheng guaitai [Legal expert opinions obstruct judicial justice—Deformed system yields freak]. *Southern Metropolitan News*, p, 11.

Li, W. (2012). Tanwu huilu fanzui sixing zhidu zhengyi wenti yanjiu [Controversial issues in the death penalty system for corruption offenses]. *Hebei Legal Study, 6,* 179–183.

Liang, G. (2004). Gongzhong rentong zhengzhi jueze yu sixing kongzhi [Public identification, political choice, and death penalty control]. *Legal Studies, 14,* 15–27.

Liang, G., & He, H. (1999). Ershi shiji de zhongguo xinfaxue [China's criminal law studies in the 21st century]. *Chinese and Foreign Legal Science, 2,* 17–29.

Lin, D. (2004). Liuyong an zheshe chu fajuejia de beiai [The sadness of jurists reflected from the Liu Yong case]. *Prosecutorial Review, 2,* 10–11.

Liu, J. (2009). Qingmo zhi minguo shiqi sixing guannian biange qiantan [A brief analysis of the changes in death penalty perceptions from the end of the Qing dynasty to the early Republic]. *Legal Science Journal, 6,* 111–114.

Liu, M. (2004). Riben sixing zhidu de xianzhuang yu woguo sixing zhidu de zhanwang [The current status of Japan's death penalty system and the prospect of China's death penalty system]. *Jianghai Journal, 5,* 104–110.

Liu, R. (2013). Sixing de xianfa weidu [The constitutional dimension of the death penalty]. *Journal of the National Prosecutors Academy, 4,* 18–19.

Liu, Y. (2013). Sixing weisheli zhengbian de shuli ji jiexi [The combing and analysis of the debate over death penalty's deterrence effect]. *Crime Studies, 2,* 17–23.

Liu, Z., & Du, L. (2011, July 13). Wo qihunanxia, dan shi shihou gaibian le [I am torn on the issue, but it is time to change the death penalty]. *New Express,* p. A23.

Lu, J. (2004). Sihuan zhidu de xingshi zhengce yiyi jiqi kuozhang [The criminal policy significance of the death penalty with suspension and its expansion]. *Jurists, 5,* 137–141.

Lu, J. (2011, July 8). Yunan "sai Jiaxin" sihuan panjue huo jiangbian [The suspended death sentence ruling of the Yunnan Province "Rival of Jiaxin" case may change]. *Yunnan Political Consultation News,* p. 4.

Ma, K. (1980). Woguo xingfa zhongde xising [On the death penalty in Chinese criminal law]. *Legal Studies Material, 3,* 10–14.

Michelle, B. (1962). Lun feichu sixing [On death penalty abolition] (Q. Zhang, Trans.). *Modern Foreign Philosophy Social Science Digest,* (6), 24–27.

Nishibara, H. (2004). *Xingfa de gengji he zhexue* [The Root and Philosophy of the Criminal Law] (X. Gu, Trans.). Beijing: Law Press.

Qiu, X. (2002). Sixing de dexing [The morality of the death penalty]. *Political Science and the Law, 2,* 51–54.

Qiu, X. (2004). Sixing de jiazhi fenxi [An analysis on the value of the death penalty]. *East China Criminal Justice Review, 2*, 211–240.

Qu, X. (2003). Tuidong feichu sixing—xingfa xuezhe de zeren [Promoting death penalty abolition—The responsibilities of criminal law scholars]. *Legal Science, 4*, 43–44.

Qu, X. (2005). Lun jinzhi liyong sixingfan de shiti shiti qiguan—sixingfan anpai shenghoushi de guifan fenxi [Prohibiting the use of bodies and organs of death row inmates—An analysis of the regulation on the affairs of death row inmates after they are gone]. *Chinese and Foreign Legal Science, 5*, 557–572.

Shi, C. (2012). Sixing yu shengminquan de hezhi yu beili [The death penalty and the right to life—Consistence and departure]. *Hebei Legal Study, 7*, 75–81.

Song, Y. (2003). Cong Liuyong anjian gaipan yingqi de shehui fanxiang kan gongkai caipan liyou de biyaoxing [The necessity of publicizing sentencing grounds judging from the impact of the resentencing of the Liu Yong case]. *Political and Legal Forum, 5*, 174–175.

Sun, G. (2009). Sixing feichu yu minyi guanxi zhi shenshi [Review of the death penalty and public opinion]. *Journal of East China University of Political Science and Law, 2*, 94–99.

Sun, G. (2011). Sixing weisheli de jingjixue fenxi [An economic analysis of the deterrence effect of the death penalty]. *Journal of Yellow River Technology University, 3*, 116–119.

Sunstein, C. R., & Vermeule, A. (2005). Is capital punishment morally required? Act, omission and life-life tradeoffs. *Stanford Law Review, 58*(3), 703–750.

Tian, H. (2005). Lun sixing cunfei de tiaojian [The requirements of death penalty abolition and retention]. *Legal Studies, 2*, 66–74.

Wan, C. (1986). Jianyi dui zhapianzui zengjai sixing de guiding [Suggestions on increasing the death penalty for fraud]. *Legal Science, 3*, 20.

Wang, Q. (2012). Falv shijieguan wenluan shidai de sifa minyi he zhengzhi—yi Li Changkui an wei zhongxin [Judiciary, public opinion, and politics in a chaotic legal worldview era—Centering around the Li Changkui case]. *Jurists, 3*, 1.

Wang, R. (2005). Sixing xianzhi lun [On death penalty control]. *Liaoning Normal University Journal, 1*, 31–33.

Wang, S. (2003). Xiandai xingfa mudi lilun yu zhongguo de xuanze [The purpose theory of modern criminal sanction and China's choice]. *Chinese Legal Science, 3*, 107–131.

Wang, S. (2004). Guangyu zhongguo sixing zhidu de fansi [Reflection on China's death penalty system]. *Peking University Journal, 3*, 89–97.

Wang, W., & Li, Y. (2012). Duanqi nei feizhi sixing de zhengdangxing fenxi [The justification of abolishing the death penalty in a short term]. *People's Forum, 4*, 74–75.

Wang, Y. (2012). Zhongguo sixing yanjiu de sange wuqu yu lujing tiaozheng [Three mistaken areas of death penalty research and its adjustment]. *Social Science Journal of Jilin University, 5*, 129–136.

Xiao, Z., & Wang, H. (2011). Dui sixing de zhuiwen—sixing weishenme yingdang cunzai? [Inquiry into the death penalty—Why should the death penalty exist?]. *Jianghuai Forum, 1*, 78–85.

Xie, W. (2005). Sixing youxian cunzai lun [The limited existence of the death penalty]. *Chinese and Foreign Legal Science, 5*, 598–607.

Xue, R. (1989). Guanyu wanshan woguo xingfa zhong sixing shiyong fanwei de sikao [On the perfection of death penalty application scope in China]. *Chinese Legal Science, 4*, 80–88.

Yang, M. (2010). Sixing de shehui taidu [Societal attitude toward the death penalty]. *Oriental Outlook Weekly, 46*, 4.

Yang, T., & Liu, H. (2009). Yingyong lunlixue shiye zhizhong de sixing cunfei zhizheng [The death penalty debate from the applied ethics perspective]. *Journal of Renmin University of China, 3*, 97–104.

Yang, Y. (2008). Sixing anjian gongkai shenpan yanjiu [Study on the public trial of death penalty cases]. *Chinese Legal Science, 4*, 27–36.

Ye, L. (2012). Sihuan shiyong zhi shizhi biaozhun xintan [A new probe into the substantive criteria of suspended death penalty application]. *Studies in Law and Business, 5*, 94–102.

Yin, J. (2008). Guyi shangrenzui sixing sifa kongzhi lungang [Judicial control of the death penalty in intentional homicides]. *Politics and Law, 11*, 13–20.

Yu, Z. (2009). Feizhi sixing guojia de shuliang tongji jielun zhi fansi [Reflections on the statistics of death penalty abolitionist countries]. *Legal Science, 1*, 89–98.

Zhai, C. (2011, August 26). Jiuwei yi—"busha buzuyi pingminfen" [Long time no see—"Public indignation could not be appeased without executing the defendant"]. *Strait Herald*, p. A2.

Zhang, M. (2011). *Xingfa xue* [Science of Criminal Law]. Beijing: Law Press.

Zhang, W. (2008). Sifa gongzheng de falv jishu yu zhengce—dui Peng Yu an de chengxufa sikao [Law, technology and policy of judicial justice—Thoughts on the procedure law of the Peng Yu case]. *Jurists, 8*, 138–152.

Zhang, W., & Huang, W. (2004). Sihuan yingdan chengwei sixing zhixing de bijin chengxu [Death penalty with suspension should be made the mandatory procedure of execution]. *Modern Legal Science, 4*, 75–79.

Zhang, X. (2007). Fuchu sixing de lilun yuqi yu baoliu sixing de xianshi biran—lun woguo sixing de xianshi biran [The theoretical expectation of death penalty abolition and the realistic necessity of death penalty retention—On the realistic necessity of China's death penalty]. *Social Sciences Study, 1*, 81–86.

Zhang, Y. (1996). *Daqing xin xinlv zongze quanji* [The Full Collection of the New Penal Code General Provisions of the Qing Dynasty]. Beijing: Zhang Yongxin.

Zhang, Y. (2008). Sixing weisheli de fanzuixue fenxi [A criminological analysis on the deterrence effect of the death penalty]. *Chinese Legal Science, 1*, 75–82.

Zhao, B. (1996). Xingfa gaige wenti yanjiu [Study on the Reform of the Criminal Law]. Beijing: China Legal Publishing House.

Zhao, B. (2005). Lun zhongguo feibaoli fanzui sixing de zhubu feizhi [The gradual abolition of the death penalty for China's nonviolent crimes]. *Political Science and Law Forum, 1*, 93–99.

Zhao, B. (2009). *Xingfa xin jiaocheng* [New Textbook on Criminal Law]. Beijing: Renmin University of China Press.

Zhao, B. (2011). Guanyu zhongguo xianjieduan shenyong sixing sikao [Thoughts on approaching the death penalty with caution in current China]. *Chinese Legal Science, 6*, 5–22.

Zhao, B. (2014). Dangdai zhongguo sixing gaige zhengyi wenti lunyao [Controversial issues in contemporary China's death penalty reform]. *Law Science, 1*, 146–154.

Zhao, B., & Miao, M. (2013). Lun guoji renquanfa guifan dui dangdai zhongguo sixing gaige de cujin zuoyong [On the positive impact of international human rights laws and regulations on China's death penalty reform]. *Journal of Social Science of Jinlin University*, (4), 5–18.

Zhou, Y. (2006). Weifan tanhui yingchu tanmozui sixing [To fight against corruption, the death penalty for corruption offenses should be abolished]. *Legal Science, 5*, 43–45.

Zhou, Y. (2010). Wangluo xin yaoyan yanjiu—yi Hu Bin tishen shuo weili [Study of new rumors in the cyberspace—Taking the "stand-in" of Hu Bin as an example]. *Journal of Shenzhen University (Humanities and Social Sciences Edition), 4*, 142–143.

Zhou, Y., & Ouyang, T. (1982). Tantan zichan jieji guojia de sixing [On the death penalty in capitalist countries]. *Foreign Legal Science, 2*, 1–7.

Guiding Cases for China's Death Penalty

ANALYSIS AND REFLECTION

▸ XINGLIANG CHEN (TRANSLATED BY CHARLOTTE HU)

ON JULY 9 and November 26, 2010, the Supreme People's Procuratorate (SPP) and the Supreme People's Court (SPC) of China passed and promulgated, respectively, the Regulations on Guiding Cases (Guanyu anli zhidao gongzuo de guiding, hereafter the Regulations), signifying the formal establishment of China's guiding case system. The cases issued through the guiding case system, known as guiding cases, are cases that shall be taken as references when judicial organs at various levels handle similar cases. Therefore, guiding cases are different from regular cases, and in some sense they are legal precedents in civil law countries but are different from case laws in common law countries.

I refer to the guiding case system as a legal precedent system with Chinese characteristics. Since the implementation of the guiding case system, the SPC and the SPP have promulgated a number of guiding cases,[1] three of which are death penalty cases: Wang Zhicai's homicide case (SPC case no. 4), Li Fei's homicide case (SPC case no. 12), and Xin Yuanlong's kidnapping case (SPP case no. 2). These death penalty guiding cases could potentially have a significant impact on China's death penalty practice.

A BRIEF INTRODUCTION TO CHINA'S GUIDING CASE SYSTEM

At present, China's legal system is characterized by the civil law legal tradition. There are three basic laws in the criminal law area: the Criminal Law, the Criminal Procedure Law, and the Prison Law. The Criminal Law was first promulgated in 1979 and then underwent a major revision in 1997, followed by eight amendments with partial revisions. The Criminal Law is one of China's most important laws and the main source of legal regulations in the criminal justice system.

Other than the Criminal Law, China has a unique judicial interpretation system. The Standing Committee of the National People's Congress passed the Decision on Strengthening Judicial Interpretation (Guanyu jiaqiang sifa jieshi gongzuo de jueyi) on June 10, 1981. This decision granted the SPC and the SPP the right of judicial interpretation and was deemed the official origin of that right. Judicial interpretations appear in the form of normative documents. The judicial interpretations of the SPC may be taken as grounds of judicial rulings and shall be cited in judicial documents. The judicial interpretations of the SPP are the legal grounds of official investigation and prosecution. In addition, the SPC and the SPP often jointly issue judicial interpretations. Therefore, judicial interpretations are legally binding on judicial activities and are China's quasi-laws.

Both laws and judicial interpretations appear in the form of written laws, which are typically abstract and general. Because written laws are abstract and general and often allow judicial discretion, the application of laws and judicial interpretations may lead to differential judicial decisions for similar cases. Viewed as a form of judicial unfairness, this practice has become one of the issues to be addressed by Chinese judicial reform.

Of course, there are many other reasons for differential judicial rulings, including, for instance, external intervention of administrative organs in judicial activities and internal intervention within judicial organs due to the administrative management style. Although the guiding case system is not designed to address these administrative issues, it is intended to address problems of differential judicial rulings arising from the lack of more detailed regulations.

The guiding case system has in fact become the third source of regulation besides laws and judicial interpretations in China. Of course, the rules mapped out in the guiding case system are specific implementing rules derived from the sentencing principles of guiding cases and are therefore more applicable to judicial practice.

The SPC and the SPP issue guiding cases sporadically when they see a need for them. These cases are first selected on the basis of certain criteria and then are examined following prescribed procedures. Finally, they are issued through authoritative media. As set forth in relevant regulations of the SPC and the SPP, China's guiding case system presents the following characteristics.[2]

The Authority Bodies of Guiding Cases

Under the Regulations, only the SPC and the SPP have the authority to issue guiding cases; courts and procuratorates at lower levels are not authorized to do so. It is a rather rare feature that the SPP shares the authority to issue guiding cases in China because the power of issuing guiding cases rests almost exclusively in the hands of the supreme court in many other countries. In China, however, both the SPC and the SPP are supreme judicial organs and enjoy judicial interpretation rights. Nevertheless, the guiding cases issued by them carry different effects. While the guiding cases issued by the SPC are binding for courts' sentencing activities, the cases issued by the SPP are binding on the prosecution's work.

The Selection Criteria for Guiding Cases

The purpose of the guiding case system is to create rules for judicial activities. The Regulations issued by the SPC and the SPP specify the selection procedure for the guiding cases. I have noted five categories of cases that serve as the main criteria for selecting the guiding cases: (1) influential cases (cases that draw wide public attention and reaction); (2) application cases (cases that serve as a guideline on how to apply abstract laws to the specific case context); (3) typical cases (cases that have common applications); (4) difficult and complicated cases; and (5) emergent cases (cases that are new but typical). These five types of cases sometimes overlap, but their primary function is to create rules on how to apply and interpret the law in specific cases.

The Scope of Authority

On the scope of the guiding case authority, Article 7 of the SPC's Regulations stipulates that they are to be applied to "similar" cases, while Article 15 of the SPP's Regulations stipulates that they shall be applied to cases of "same or similar" types. Thus, in essence, the guiding cases are applicable only to cases of the same or similar types.

The Regulating Effect of Guiding Cases

The SPC's Regulations use the words "[The lower courts] shall make reference to" on the effect of guiding cases. Here, "shall" means "must," while "make reference to" means "refer to or to comply with." In other words, when judges are adjudicating cases that are similar to the guiding cases, they are expected to comply with the sentencing yardsticks and criteria of the guiding cases. Although guiding cases are not legally binding, this stipulation implies that they are binding in actuality.

The Referral Procedure of Guiding Cases

In China, guiding cases are not necessarily cases adjudicated or handled by the supreme judicial organs. Rather, most of them come from local judicial organs. Both the SPC and the SPP have set up guiding case work units, which are responsible for the selection of guiding cases. Therefore, according to the Regulations of the SPC and the SPP, courts at various levels and representatives of the National People's Congress are both entitled to refer cases to the SPC and the SPP for the purpose of selecting guiding cases.

The Review Procedure of Guiding Cases

The review procedure for the guiding cases is the procedure by which cases referred to be guiding cases are further examined and selected. The SPC has adopted a two-step review procedure. The first is the preliminary examination by the Work Office of Guiding Cases. This office primarily determines whether the selected cases merit submission to the Adjudication Committee of the SPC for further discussion. The second phase involves the final review of the referred cases by the adjudication committee. The adjudication committee is the SPC's full-time adjudication organization and has the final authority regarding the guiding cases.

The Issuance Procedure of Guiding Cases

The issuance procedure of guiding cases is the procedure by which selected guiding cases are issued in a specific way. Guiding cases are issued publicly in principle and occasionally internally (as exceptions). Only after publication can guiding cases be made known and serve as guidance in adjudication and prosecution.

The stipulations on death penalty imposition in the Chinese Criminal Law are rather abstract. For example, Clause 1, Article 48, of the Criminal Law stipulates: "The death penalty is only applicable to those extremely heinous criminals. Unless it is imperative to have them executed immediately, criminals who shall be sentenced to death may be sentenced to the death penalty with a two-year suspension." This stipulation covers the two most important components of China's death penalty system: (1) the requirements for imposition of the death penalty and (2) the requirements for imposition of the death penalty with a two-year suspension (DPWTYS). On the requirements for imposition of the death penalty, the Criminal Law stipulates that the crime must be "extremely heinous"; meanwhile, the specific provisions of the Criminal Law generally use terms such as "circumstances of the crime are extremely severe," "the amount of criminal gain is extremely huge," and "the consequences are extremely grave" as requirements for the imposition of the death penalty for specific crimes. These stipulations are quite abstract, and their interpretation can be controversial. For instance, Chinese legal scholars often have mixed opinions on whether the "extremely heinous" requirement stipulated by Article 48 means extremely severe social harm in the objective sense or also includes the subjective culpability of the criminal (see Ren 2012:148).

The DPWTYS is a unique part of China's death penalty system and is intended to reduce the number of cases of the death penalty with immediate execution (DPWIE). Criminals sentenced to the DPWTYS will generally have their sentence commuted to life imprisonment or fixed-term imprisonment at the end of the two-year suspension. Article 48 stipulates that the imposition criterion of the DPWTYS is "[when it is] not imperative to execute." This general statement leaves broad discretion to judicial organs when they essentially make a life-and-death decision. Therefore, how judicial organs handle the demarcation between the two becomes critically important.[3]

The stipulations of China's Criminal Law on the death penalty and imposition of the DPWTYS are very abstract and general, but China's death penalty practice is also heavily influenced by criminal justice policies. Under the influence of the strike-hard policy, for example, death penalty laws were interpreted very broadly, and the DPWTYS was meted out with much scrutiny.[4] Within this context, the guiding cases could potentially provide much clearer instructions on how death sentences are supposed to be meted out under specific conditions. In addition, evidentiary requirements for death penalty cases, as stipulated in China's Criminal Procedure Law, are also quite abstract and general. Therefore, the guiding cases may provide guidance in this regard too.

As of May 2015, three of the published guiding cases were death penalty cases. These cases dealt with issues of imposition of the death penalty and admissibility of evidence. However, in the author's opinion, none of these three cases created new rules for future cases to follow because the sentencing principles extracted from these three cases remain largely reiterations of existing judicial interpretations. Rather, they merely set examples of how to handle death penalty cases properly. Nevertheless, the issuance of these three cases was groundbreaking and paved the way for a more uniform sentencing system in China.

WANG ZHICAI'S HOMICIDE CASE: THE DIFFERENTIATION BETWEEN THE DPWIE AND THE DPWTYS

Because of the traditional notion "Killers shall be killed," intentional homicide is one of the crime types that receive the most death sentences in China. As a result, it is a challenge for China's judicial organs to restrict imposition of the death penalty in such cases. If a victim died in a homicide case, sentencing is mainly a matter of choice between the DPWIE and the DPWTYS. This is what happened in Wang Zhicai's case.

As mentioned before, the use of the DPWTYS is of critical importance to the reduction of the use of the DPWIE, but the key premise is the correct differentiation between these two. According to Article 48 of China's Criminal Law, the differentiating criterion is "[when it is] not imperative to execute," and the question is how to interpret this criterion in capital cases. The ruling in Wang's homicide case issued by the SPC (SPC guiding case no. 4, issued on December 20, 2011) shed light on this question.

The defendant, Wang, and the victim, Zhao (female, aged 26), were in a romantic relationship, but later Zhao wanted to break up. In a rage, Wang stabbed Zhao in her dorm on her neck, chest, abdomen, and back with a knife, leading to hemorrhagic shock and death. At about 8:30 A.M. the next morning, Wang attempted suicide by drinking pesticide but failed and was arrested by the police. Wang had previously behaved well (with no criminal record), confessed to his crime after his arrest, and together with his family offered compensation to the victim's family but failed to reach a compensation agreement.

The Intermediate Court of Weifang City in Shandong Province sentenced Wang to the DPWIE, and Wang appealed. The High People's Court of Shandong Province rejected his appeal, upheld the original verdict, and requested approval from the SPC. The SPC did not approve the DPWIE sentence and sent the case back to the Shandong High Court for retrial. After the retrial, the Shandong High Court resentenced Wang to the DPWTYS, along with deprivation of his political rights for life and restricted commutation (see Li Fei's case, examined later, for discussion of restricted commutation). In the retrial, the Shandong High Court held that Wang's actions constituted intentional homicide. The crime was extremely heinous, and he deserved to be sentenced to death. However, because this case was triggered by relationship and marriage disputes (i.e., Wang's courtship failed, and he became enraged and decided to kill), and because Wang confessed after his arrest, actively compensated the victim's family, and had behaved well before the crime, the death penalty could not be executed immediately. At the same time, considering that Wang's method of killing was extremely cruel, and that the victim's family did not forgive him and demanded harsher punishment, in order to solve social problems, the High Court sentenced Wang to the DPWTYS with restricted commutation.

The SPC extracted the following sentencing principle from this case: "For intentional homicide triggered by relationship and marriage disputes, where the defendant's method of killing is cruel and he or she deserves to be sentenced to death in terms of the crime itself, if the defendant, however, has mitigating circumstances such as confession, remorse, active compensation, but at the same time the victim's family demands harsher sentences, the people's court, based on the nature of the case, crime circumstances, damage severity, and the defendant's subjective culpability and propensity to dangerousness, may sentence the defendant to the DPWTYS with restricted commutation in order to solve social problems and promote social harmony."

In this case, without making arguments that this crime was extremely heinous, the trial court drew the conclusion that the defendant should be sentenced to death immediately. This has to do with the stipulated punishments for homicide crimes in Article 232 of the Criminal Law, which are listed in order from the most to the least severe, including "the death penalty, life imprisonment, or over-ten-year fixed-term imprisonment." Such stipulated punishments in the specific provisions of China's Criminal Law are unique (in comparison with other provisions of the Criminal Law) and signify that the legislature deems intentional homicide the most severe crime in China's Criminal Law; thus, the most severe punishments shall apply. That is, in intentional homicide crimes, as long as someone is killed, the death penalty is generally applicable. This legislative spirit coincides with Chinese public opinion on intentional homicide crimes. Under China's current death penalty restrictions, it is advisable to reduce greatly the number of death penalties applied to nonviolent crimes, but restrictions on the death penalty in intentional homicide cases should still be approached with extreme caution. In the death penalty abolition experiences of various other countries, intentional homicide is the last fortress of abolition. In China, because there is still a large number of nonviolent crime cases for which the death penalty is imposed, if capital punishment for intentional homicide crimes is recklessly reduced, that is going to cause a public opinion uproar, which should be guarded against. Of course, this does not mean that the death penalty, especially the DPWIE, should be meted out for every intentional homicide crime. Because the number of death penalties incurred by intentional homicide constitutes a large proportion of the overall number of death penalties, if nothing is done with regard to the imposition of the death penalty on intentional homicide cases, reduction of overall imposition of the death penalty will be ineffective. Therefore, a cautious but reliable approach should be adopted in meting out the death penalty for intentional homicide crimes.

Therefore, it is imperative to reduce the imposition of the DPWIE and increase the imposition of the DPWTYS in intentional homicide cases, and the demarcation between the DPWIE and the DPWTYS becomes more important in homicide cases. In China's judicial practice, the major legal policy grounds for the imposition of the death penalty for intentional homicide is the SPC's Meeting Minutes of the National Courts' Criminal Adjudication Work for Maintaining Rural Stability (Quanguo fayuan weihu noncun wending xingshi shenpan gongzuo zuotanhui jiyao), issued on October 27, 1999 (hereafter the Minutes). In addressing the imposition of the death penalty for intentional homicide, the Minutes pointed out: "Whether the death penalty should be meted out depends not only on whether a death is incurred, but also on the overall circumstances of the case. With regard to intentional homicide crimes aggravated by marriage, family, and neighborly disputes, extreme caution should be exercised. These cases should be treated differently from other intentional homicide cases that seriously endanger social security. Cases where the victim is clearly at fault or is directly responsible for aggravating the dispute, or the defendant has mitigating circumstances, shall not be sentenced to the DPWIE." According to the Minutes, in deliberating whether the death penalty should be meted out for intentional homicide cases, the following three factors should be considered:

The Nature of the Crime, Determined by the Cause of Killing

The cause of killing refers to the objective reasons for killing. To a certain extent, the cause of killing determines the nature of the crime. The Minutes differentiates two types of homicide: (1) intentional homicide aggravated by marriage, family, and neighborly disputes, and (2) intentional homicide that seriously endangers social security. The Minutes believes that there is a fundamental difference in the nature of these two types. This difference has to be considered in meting out the death penalty.

The major differences between the two types of homicide lie in the cause of killing. The former is triggered by marriage, family, and neighborly disputes, while the latter is caused by other reasons. Among homicides caused by civil disputes, the Minutes lists two special circumstances, marriage or family and neighborly disputes. Homicides triggered by marriage and family disputes refer to disputes due to improper handling of marriage and family matters, which further escalate into homicide. In such cases, the defendant(s) and victim(s) have close personal relationships or are even relatives. For example, in homicide cases that happen between married couples, the parents and children of the couple are the defendant's relatives and the victim's relatives.

Homicides triggered by neighborly disputes refer to cases where there are neighborly relationships between the defendant(s) and the victim(s). These two types of homicide are both criminal cases that escalate from civil disputes, and both occur among acquaintances. In other words, these types of homicide are a simple kind of homicide that infringes on the right to life of other individuals.

In contrast to homicides triggered by civil grudges that escalated from marriage, family, and neighborly disputes, other intentional homicides that seriously endanger public security exhibit two characteristics: first, the location of the crimes is public; second, they seriously endanger public security. Of course, of the two characteristics, the former is superficial, but the latter is of real substance. These two characteristics determine that these two types of intentional homicide are different in the cause of killing. For instance, intentional homicide resulting from provocation, brawling, or retaliation not only infringes on the victim's right to life but also seriously endangers public security. Because the victims of this type of homicide are uncertain, this type of homicide causes terror and instills fear in the general public. Therefore, the two types of homicide are different in nature and thus should be treated differently in sentencing.

The Victim's Fault

In intentional homicide cases, a victim's fault means that the victim is partially responsible for the killing. In deliberating whether the death penalty will be imposed, judges should take into account whether the victim is at fault and to what extent the fault affects the imposition of the death penalty.

It should be pointed out that on imposition of the death penalty, what makes a difference in judiciary discretion is not the victim's fault in an ordinary sense but the victim's severe and obvious fault. Severe fault means that the victim's fault is fundamentally provocative for the defendant to commit homicide. For instance, the victim blackmailed the defendant repeatedly, prompting the defendant to kill the victim. This is one kind of severe fault, since blackmailing is against the law and is thus a crime. In cases of regular insult and language provocation that resulted in killing, although the victim is at fault to a certain extent, the fault is minor and not severe. Obvious fault denotes the degree of the victim's fault and the obviousness of the fault; that is, a reasonable person would deem the victim at fault, not just the defendant himself or herself. Therefore, in judging whether the victim is at fault, it is logical to adopt the reasonable person's criterion rather than the defendant's criterion.

The victim's fault can affect imposition of the death penalty in intentional homicide cases because it reflects the defendant's subjective culpability. The subjective culpability is the defendant's mentality for his or her behavior and the corresponding social harmfulness. To some extent, it reflects the possibility of the defendant's reformation. Homicide triggered by the victim's fault reveals that the defendant is of lesser culpability. Therefore, in meting out the death penalty for intentional homicide, the victim's fault and its extent should be an important factor, especially when differentiating between the DPWIE and the DPWTYS.

Statutory Mitigating Circumstances

Whether there exist statutory mitigating circumstances is also significant for death penalty decisions. The statutory mitigating circumstances (*fading congqing qingjie*), in contrast to discretionary mitigating circumstances (*zhuoding congqing qingjie*), usually refer to voluntary surrender, meritorious services, and confession, all of which are clearly defined in the Criminal Law. How to use such statutory mitigating circumstances correctly in death penalty cases is a question that merits further research. In judicial practice, defendants who committed a murder but voluntarily surrendered, unless the circumstances are especially severe and the consequences especially grave, generally will not receive the DPWIE. In cases where relatives turned the defendant in or helped arrest the defendant, the defendant shall be deemed to have "surrender[ed] oneself to the police" as well and shall be sentenced more leniently in general. Defendants in homicide cases who rendered meritorious services generally shall be treated less harshly and may be spared from the DPWIE. However, if the circumstances are especially severe and the consequences are especially grave, defendants shall not be treated leniently even if they rendered meritorious services.

Wang's homicide case went through a change from the DPWIE to the DPWTYS, indicating the necessity to properly differentiate these two sentencing options. Wang's case incorporates both mitigating circumstances and aggravating circumstances. Mitigating circumstances included the following: (1) the crime was triggered by relationship and marriage disputes; (2) the defendant confessed and showed repentance after the arrest; (3) the defendant actively compensated the victim's family; and (4) the defendant behaved well before the crime. Aggravating circumstances included that the victim's family did not forgive and demanded harsher punishment.

Among these circumstances, the fact that this case was triggered by relationship and marriage disputes reflects its fundamental nature; that is, Wang's homicide resulted from escalated civil disputes rather than being a homicide that seriously endangered public security. Confession and remorse showed the defendant's good attitude after the crime (indicating that the defendant was not very dangerous to society) and therefore constituted mitigating circumstances. Active compensation for the victim's economic loss is also part of the defendant's good behavior after the crime. Typically, compensating the victim's economic loss wins the forgiveness of the victim's family and thus becomes a mitigating circumstance. In this case, however, the victim's family refused to forgive the defendant, which is also the main reason for the imposition of the DPWIE by courts of both the first and second instances. In China's judicial practice, imposition of the death penalty is, to a large extent, affected by factors on the victim's side. In homicide cases in particular, whether the victim's side (mainly the relatives of the deceased) forgives the defendant is one of the important factors that the court considers in its sentencing. Some victims' families do not forgive the defendant and demand that the court mete out the DPWIE. In extreme cases, they gather in front of the court and create a disturbance or petition courts or governments at higher levels (even as far as the capital, Beijing) to exert pressure on the court. In Wang's case, the DPWIE was meted out by courts of both the first and second instances, but the SPC did not approve the death penalty, and the sentence was revised to the DPWTYS. Were it not for the SPC's final power of review and approval, Wang would have been executed.

In this case, the SPC established the following significant guidelines for the imposition of the DPWTYS in homicide cases: in meting out the death penalty in homicide cases, if there are mitigating circumstances, such as confession, remorse, and active compensation, but at the same time, the victim's family demands harsher punishment, the court may sentence the defendant to the DPWTYS with restricted commutation on the basis of the nature and circumstances of the crime, harmfulness, and the defendant's culpability. This guideline is important for the reduction of the use of the DPWIE.

LI FEI'S HOMICIDE CASE: THE COMMUTATION RESTRICTION SYSTEM

Limiting the use of the death penalty is part of China's current policy of Balancing Severity with Leniency, and the SPC has played a significant role in this process. However, attempts to restrict the application of the death penalty face tremendous pressure from society and especially from victims. Cases punishable by the DPWIE but where the defendant has received the victim's party's forgiveness are generally given the DPWTYS. It is difficult, though, to mete out the DPWTYS in homicide cases where the victim's party refuses to forgive. In such cases, the first-instance court (the intermediate court in the Chinese system) and the second-instance court (the provincial high court) often give in to pressure from the victim's party and mete out the DPWIE. Wang's case and Li's case are such examples. Given the circumstances, the national SPC becomes the ultimate gatekeeper for the policy of Balancing Severity with Leniency.

One year after the issuance of Wang's case, the SPC issued Li's intentional homicide case (SPC guiding case no. 12, issued on September 18, 2012). In fact, Li's case resembles Wang's case in many ways, such as nature, circumstances, and prosecution procedure. The SPC's intention in issuing this case was to provide another example of how to exercise judicial discretion in death penalty cases. This time the guiding case focuses on the commutation restriction (*xianzhi jianxing*) system.

The defendant, Li, and the victim, Xu (female, aged 26), were in a romantic relationship that later turned sour. Li entered Xu's bedroom by force, hit Xu on the head multiple times, and hit Xu's cousin, Wang, on her head and hands multiple times with a hammer. Later, Li hit Xu and Wang on their heads again, causing Xu to die on the spot and leaving Wang with minor injuries. The Intermediate Court of Harbin City in Heilongjiang Province sentenced Li to the DPWIE along with deprivation of political rights for life. Li appealed. The High Court of Heilongjiang Province rejected Li's appeal, upheld the original sentence, and sent the case to the SPC for final review and approval. The SPC disapproved Li's death sentence and sent the case back to the Heilongjiang High Court for retrial. After the retrial, the Heilongjiang High Court resentenced Li to the DPWTYS along with deprivation of political rights for life and also put a restriction on Li's potential commutation in the future.

In the retrial, the high court held that Li's actions constituted intentional homicide. His crime was extremely heinous, and he deserved to be sentenced to the death penalty. This case, however, was triggered by civil disputes. After the crime, Li's mother, Liang, voluntarily and promptly reported the case to the police after finding out Li's whereabouts, and she worked with the police to have Li captured. When Li was captured, he was submissive and did not fight against the police, and he also confessed to his crimes consistently and showed good attitude. During the trial, Li's mother compensated the victim's economic loss. Although Li was a recidivist, the circumstances of his prior larceny were not very grave. In view of these circumstances, a relatively lenient punishment might be meted out, and Li might be spared from the DPWIE. On the other hand, because his method of killing was cruel, he was a recidivist, and the victim's family refused to forgive, the High Court resentenced him to the DPWTYS with restricted commutation.

The SPC extracted the following sentencing principle from this case: "In intentional homicide cases triggered by civil disputes where the defendant's method of killing is cruel and the defendant is a recidivist, he or she deserves to be sentenced to death. However, if the defendant's family actively assisted the police in arresting the defendant and actively compensated the victim, the court, on the basis of the specific circumstances of the crime, for the purpose of resolving social problems, may sentence the defendant to the DPWTYS with restricted commutation."

Li's case includes the following mitigating circumstances: (1) this case was triggered by civil disputes; (2) after the crime, Li's mother, Liang, reported the case to the police actively and promptly after learning about Li's whereabouts and worked closely with the police to have Li captured; when Li was captured, he was submissive and did not fight against the police; he also confessed to his crimes consistently and showed good attitude; and (3) during the trial, Li's mother compensated the victim's economic loss on behalf of Li.

The aggravating circumstances are that (1) the defendant was a recidivist and (2) the victim's family refused to forgive the defendant. Li's case shares some similarities with Wang's case in discretionary circumstances; for example, both cases were triggered by civil disputes, and both victims' families refused to forgive the defendant. But the two cases also differ; for example, Li was a recidivist. In light of the circumstances of Li's case, the sentencing principle of this guiding case maintains that the DPWTYS shall be imposed, and at the same time, commutation restrictions shall be meted out.

The commutation restriction was introduced in the Eighth Amendment to the Criminal Law (2011). According to Clause 2, Article 50, of the new Criminal Law, "With regard to a recidivist sentenced to the death penalty with suspension and a criminal so sentenced for committing intentional homicide, rape, robbery, kidnapping, arson, explosion, spreading hazardous materials, or organizing violent crimes, a people's court may impose commutation restriction depending upon the circumstances of the crimes." According to Section 3, Clause 2, Article 78, of the Criminal Law, the actual term of punishment for criminals with commutation restriction shall observe the following rules: "After commutation, the term of punishment to be actually executed may not be less than 25 years, applicable where the criminal is sentenced to the death penalty with suspension and is restricted for commutation by the people's court in accordance with Clause 2 of Article 50 herein, and he or she is commuted to life imprisonment upon the expiration of the suspension period; or 20 years if he or she is commuted to fixed-term imprisonment of 25 years upon the expiration of the suspension period."

The commutation restriction was introduced to resolve a dilemma in the death penalty system. Before the commutation clause was introduced, there was no buffering mechanism to bridge the harshness of the death penalty and the leniency of non–death penalty sentences because the prison sentence that a defendant served for a suspended death sentence could be under 20 years with good behavior. This, in the public and policy makers' view, did not reflect the true principle of just deserts. The commutation restriction is likely to restrict the use of the death penalty by increasing the length of the minimum prison sentence for serious offenders, thus addressing the public safety concern, as well as the concern for justice. Increasing punishment for severe crimes should include both violent crimes and nonviolent crimes. After transitioning from the previous DPWIE sentence to the DPWTYS, the degree of punishment should be increased. In the author's view, most of those sentenced to the DPWTYS should be incarcerated for life, and those few who are granted commuted sentences or parole should be incarcerated for no less than 30 years. Most of those who are sentenced to life should be incarcerated for life, while the rest may be commuted to serve no less than 20 years of incarceration. The upper limit of fixed-term imprisonment should be increased to 25 years, and a combined punishment for multiple offenses should not exceed 30 years (see X. Chen 2007:20).

Note that the author's proposal to increase punishment for nondeath sentences is fundamentally intended to reduce the application of the death penalty and to restructure China's punishment framework (to make it more feasible). During the legislative discussion of the Eighth Amendment to the Criminal Law, there was a transition from "no commutation" to "commutation restriction" on how to increase punishment for nondeath sentences. In this regard, Professor Gao Minxuan made the following remarks: "In the initial draft [of the amendment], the preference was to allow 'no commutation' to reflect the criminal policy of balancing severity with leniency. But some believe this is too harsh, as it emphasizes only the retributive side of criminal punishment and is thus not in line with China's goal of reforming people. The legislative organs eventually changed the original 'no commutation' to 'commutation restriction,' after combining opinions of various sources. The amendment was passed in the end. Though only a legislation measure aimed at moderately increasing nondeath punishment, it is nevertheless effective for the reduction of death penalty imposition" (Huang 2007:230).

The commutation restriction added another layer of discretion to the difference between the DPWIE and the DPWTYS. That is, the DPWTYS is now divided into two categories because of the commutation restriction: the DPWTYS without commutation restriction and the DPWTYS with commutation restriction. The question becomes how to decide whether commutation restriction should be imposed.

It is not necessary to impose commutation restrictions on all criminals sentenced to the suspended death penalty. Rather, commutation restrictions should be reserved for criminals who should have been given the DPWIE were it not for mitigating circumstances, and where the suspended death penalty would not reflect the principle that punishment fits the crime. However, commutation restriction remains a challenge for the judiciary in practice.

Both Wang's and Li's cases were triggered by marriage, family, and neighborly disputes. In addition, in Li's case, Li's mother reported to the police voluntarily and in timely fashion and worked closely to have Li arrested; Li surrendered himself to the police, confessed his crime honestly and consistently, and had a good attitude. Although his behavior was not deemed "voluntary surrender," the effect was the same. However, in both cases, there were aggravating circumstances. For example, Li was a recidivist, and the victim's family refused to forgive him. Under such circumstances, it is reasonable to impose the DPWTYS with commutation restriction—it not only avoided the imposition of the DPWIE but also was a relatively harsher punishment that answered the victim's family's concerns. In contrast, if Li had not been a recidivist and had obtained forgiveness from the victim's family, commutation restriction might not have been needed. Li's case thus provides a reference for judges when they consider whether and under what conditions commutation restriction should be applied.

XIN YUANLONG'S KIDNAPPING CASE: THE ADMISSIBILITY OF EVIDENCE

Besides assessing whether to impose the DPWIE or the DPWTYS, judges must determine the admissibility of evidence in death penalty cases. While the former is a matter of the Criminal Law, the latter is governed by the Criminal Procedure Law. The Xin Yuanlong case issued by the SPP (SPP guiding case no. 2, issued on December 31, 2010) mainly concerns the admissibility of evidence in death penalty cases.

Defendant Xin came up with the idea of kidnapping children and blackmailing their parents for money because of financial hardship. He familiarized himself with the possible sites in Cixi City in Zhejiang Province and looked for potential victims on multiple occasions. On the morning of August 18, 2005, Xin kidnapped a girl named Yang (female, born June 1, 1996) in his van. Later that night, he killed the girl by stifling her on her nose and mouth and buried her. Afterward, he blackmailed Yang's family over a cell phone and was captured.

On January 17, 2006, the Intermediate Court of Ningbo City in Zhejiang Province sentenced Xin to the DPWIE, along with deprivation of political rights for life and confiscation of all personal property. Xin appealed to the Zhejiang Province High People's Court. The high court ruled that Xin's act of kidnapping and killing people for blackmailing purposes constituted the crime of kidnapping. The circumstances of the crime were extremely serious, and the social harm was especially grave. Accordingly, he deserved to be severely punished. However, given the specific circumstances of the case, it was not necessary to have him executed immediately. The high court sentenced Xin to the DPWTYS along with deprivation of political rights for life.

After reviewing the high court's decision, the Zhejiang Province High People's Procuratorate held that it was wrong for the high court to revise the trial court's sentences and requested that the national SPP lodge a protest (*kangsu*) in accordance with the procedure for trial supervision. The SPP sent special delegates to Zhejiang Province to verify the circumstances of this case. The procuratorial committee of the SPP discussed the case twice and deemed the facts of the crime clear and the evidence authentic and sufficient. Thus Xin should be sentenced to the DPWIE, and it was wrong for the Zhejiang High Court to revise Xin's sentence to the DPWTYS on the grounds of "considering the specific circumstances of the case." On October 22, 2008, in accordance with Clause 3, Article 205, of China's Criminal Procedure Law, the SPP lodged a protest with the SPC. On March 18, 2009, the SPC directed the Zhejiang High Court to form a new collegial panel to conduct a retrial for this case.

On May 14, 2009, the Zhejiang High Court formed a new collegial panel and opened a court session to retry the case. After the retrial, the high court held that Xin's act of kidnapping and killing people for blackmailing purposes constituted the crime of kidnapping. In addition, the method of committing the crime was cruel, the circumstances were flagrant, the social harm was grave, and the defendant lacked repentance; therefore, he should be harshly punished. The prosecutorial organ's opinion to correct the second-instance judgment was justified. Xin and his attorney's request to uphold the second-instance verdict lacked proper grounds and should not be granted. On June 26, 2009, the Zhejiang High Court sentenced Xin to the DPWIE, along with deprivation of political rights for life and confiscation of all personal property. The SPC approved the Zhejiang High Court's retrial judgment, and Xin was executed accordingly on December 11, 2009.

The SPP extracted the following principle from this case: "As to the protest of death penalty cases, it is imperative to grasp the terms of death penalty sentences, follow stringent evidence standards, and perform the legal supervision functions of criminal adjudication in accordance with law."

The Xin kidnapping case is one where the SPP protested, and the major reason for the protest concerned the admissibility of evidence. The admissibility of evidence concerns the life and death of the defendant and thus should be treated with great caution. The evidence criterion of China's Criminal Procedure Law is that the facts be "clear" and the evidence "authentic and sufficient." However, this criterion is relatively abstract. In death penalty cases, in particular, how to ascertain whether evidence is "authentic and sufficient" is a matter worth attention. Hence, legal scholars propose to discriminate between the evidence standard of death penalty cases and that of regular criminal cases and to raise the evidence bar for the former (see, e.g., Z. Yang 2008).

On July 1, 2010, the SPC, the SPP, the Ministry of Public Security, the Ministry of National Security, and the Ministry of Justice jointly promulgated the Rules on Certain Issues Concerning Examination and Judgment of Evidence in Death Penalty Cases (Guanyu banli sixing anjian shencha panduan zhengju rugan wenti de guiding, hereafter Death Penalty Evidentiary Rule). This is one of the efforts by Chinese judicial authorities to specify and standardize evidence standards for death penalty cases. Although it is not a law made by legislative organs, in China's current power framework, the Death Penalty Evidentiary Rule, as a regulatory document jointly promulgated by the five departments, has factual regulatory effect.[5] The Death Penalty Evidentiary Rule consists of three sections with a total of 41 articles: general rules, evidence review and admissibility by category, and overall review and use of evidence. Given that China has yet to draft a comprehensive evidentiary rule, the Death Penalty Evidentiary Rule is no less than a mini–evidence law that will have a profound guiding effect on the examination and judgment of death penalty evidence in China. Even after the adoption of the Second Amendment to the Criminal Procedure Law on March 14, 2012, the Death Penalty Evidentiary Rule still plays a tremendous role.

Clause 2, Article 5, of the Death Penalty Evidentiary Rule specifies the standard of death penalty evidence: "Evidence being 'authentic and sufficient' refers to: (1) There is evidence to prove the facts utilized to convict and sentence the defendant; (2) All evidence used to convict has been proven authentic in accordance with legal procedures; (3) There is no contradiction among evidence and facts, or contradiction is reasonably excluded; (4) In joint crimes, the defendant's position and role have been ascertained; (5) The process in which evidence is used to establish facts is logical and conforms to empirical rules; conclusions derived from evidence are the only conclusion." As an explanation of the abstract rule of evidence in the Criminal Procedure Law, this specification is applicable to the examination and judgment of evidence not only for death penalty cases but also for other criminal cases.

In addition, the Second Amendment to the Criminal Procedure Law in 2012 incorporated the preceding rule and established for the first time the evidence examination and judgment standard to exclude reasonable doubt. In particular, Clause 2, Article 53, of the new Criminal Procedure Law prescribes: "In order for evidence to be reliable and sufficient, it shall satisfy the following requirements: (1) There is evidence to prove the facts used to convict and sentence [the defendant]; (2) Evidence used to establish facts has all been verified in accordance with legally prescribed process; (3) On the basis of overall evidence, reasonable doubt has been excluded from established facts." Some Chinese scholars maintain that "the 2012 Criminal Procedure Law specified the evidence standard that 'the facts are clear and evidence is reliable and sufficient.' In particular, the introduction of the rule of 'excluding reasonable doubt' into this highest evidence standard marked a step forward to the maturity of China's evidence standard system" (R. Chen 2012:254). Thus, starting from the evidence standard in death penalty cases, the Chinese criminal evidence standard is becoming more concrete, which is significant for the perfection of China's criminal justice system.

With regard to the scope of evidence admissibility in death penalty cases, Clause 3, Article 5, of the Death Penalty Evidentiary Rule clearly prescribes: "Evidence for the following facts shall be reliable and sufficient: (1) the occurrence of the crime being charged; (2) the crime committed by the defendant, and the time, place, method, consequences, and other circumstances of the crime; (3) the identity of the defendant that might impact conviction; (4) the defendant has the capability of taking criminal responsibility; (5) the defendant's fault; (6) if it is joint crime, and if so, the defendant's position and role in joint crime; (7) aggravating circumstances." In other words, all this evidence, which concerns whether death penalty eligible charges can be applied and whether the death penalty shall be imposed, shall be reliable and sufficient.

The Xin kidnapping cases took place before the promulgation of the Death Penalty Evidentiary Rule and the Second Amendment to the Criminal Procedure Law, but this case was issued as a guiding case by the SPP after the promulgation of the Death Penalty Evidentiary Rule but before the Second Amendment to the Criminal Procedure Law. This time frame is of reference value for our understanding of the death penalty evidence standard involved in the Xin case.

Xin was sentenced to the DPWIE by the court of first instance, but the second-instance court revised the sentence to the DPWTYS on grounds of "the specific circumstances of the crime." However, the "specific circumstances" were not specified in the second-instance verdict. The SPP pointed out clearly in its protest that the so-called specific circumstances of the crime referred to the following two evidentiary problems of the case: first, witness Fu Shihong, who sold Xin the cell phone, stated in her testimony that the serial number of that cell phone was different from that of the phone seized by the police, and thus whether it was the same phone remained a question; second, two other witnesses testified that on the day of the crime, they saw a middle-aged woman taking away a little girl with the same characteristics as those of the victim; therefore, the likelihood of others committing this crime could not be excluded.

The first question concerns the reliability of material evidence. The cell phone used to extort money was important material evidence for the case. Evidence on file also included the secondhand commodity trading voucher when the cell phone was sold to Fu. The error in the serial number was merely due to the fact that when the police were questioning Fu, they erroneously took the ID number of the cell phone's old owner as the cell phone's serial number. If this circumstance was true, this error indeed would not affect the conviction. However, why did the police not spot this error then? How to correct flawed evidence once it enters the judicial process? These key questions remain unresolved in this case.

The second question concerns whether the offender could be another person. If this doubt could not be excluded, it would overthrow the conviction. With regard to the testimony that a middle-aged woman was seen taking away a little girl with the same characteristics as those of the victim on the day of the crime, the prosecutors argued it was irrelevant and should be excluded. In addition to discrepancies between the time and place of the crime and the time and place from the testimony above, the conviction evidence also included two pieces of objective evidence: the defendant identified the place where the body was buried, a body was indeed uncovered there, and two traces of hair were extracted from defendant's van; forensic DNA testing proved that the body and hair belonged to the victim, Yang. Hence the likelihood of others committing the crime could be eliminated. This analysis supported the opinion in the protest. Eventually, the SPC upheld the protest. Xin was resentenced to the DPWIE, the SPC approved the death penalty, and the execution was carried out.

In the trial of second instance, since the court believed that there was reasonable doubt that could not be excluded, it should have pronounced the defendant innocent. However, why did the second-instance court not pronounce the defendant innocent but instead revise the judgment to the DPWTYS? This is a customary practice of the Chinese judiciary that is called the death penalty with suspension leaving some leeway for uncertainty.

There are two different types of the death penalty with suspension leaving some leeway in Chinese judicial practice. The first type occurs when conviction evidence is reliable and sufficient, but evidence influencing sentencing remains reasonably dubious. Under such circumstances, the DPWTYS instead of the DPWIE is the way out. This type of the death penalty with suspension leaving some leeway is accepted by judicial interpretations. For example, Article 35 of the Opinion on Further Strictly Enforcing the Law to Ensure the Quality of Death Penalty Cases (2007) promulgated jointly by the SPC, the SPP, the Ministry of Public Security, and the Ministry of Justice prescribes: "The people's court shall make judgment on the basis of already ascertained facts, evidence and related laws and provisions in accordance with the law. If the facts of a case are clear, the evidence is reliable and sufficient, and the defendant is found guilty in accordance with the law, he shall be pronounced guilty accordingly; if the defendant is found innocent in accordance with law, he shall be pronounced innocent accordingly; if the evidence is insufficient and thus the defendant cannot be found guilty, he shall be pronounced innocent accordingly on account of the facts that the evidence is insufficient and the accusation is unfounded; if the conviction evidence is clear, but evidence influencing sentencing remains dubious, *leeway* shall be given when sentencing."

In contrast, the second type occurs when reasonable doubt has not been eliminated from conviction evidence, but a defendant is still pronounced guilty. In order to avoid wrongful executions and to leave some leeway, the defendant is sentenced to suspended death. Such a practice obviously lacks legal basis but is common in China's judicial practice. Further, it is customarily referred to as "in light of the specific circumstances of the case" in judgments. Chinese scholars usually name the first circumstance "the death penalty with suspension leaving some leeway" and the second circumstance "doubtful criminal cases." Further, they deem the second circumstance a wrongful application of the death penalty with suspension leaving some leeway (see, e.g., Ma 2006:244).

The author believes that even if the second circumstance does erroneously use the death penalty with suspension leaving some leeway, it is nevertheless still the death penalty with suspension leaving some leeway. The issue of "being right and wrong" is a judgment of values. To judge from the results, the first type of the death penalty with suspension leaving some leeway is obviously fine because it is of benefit to the defendant. Problems, however, arise from the second type of the death penalty with suspension leaving some leeway. If a court metes out the death sentence with suspension, leaving some leeway when reasonable doubt has not been eliminated from conviction evidence, there may be two circumstances. First, the defendant may gain an unfair advantage; that is, in a death penalty case with reliable and sufficient conviction evidence, because of mistaken opinions of the court, which deems that reasonable doubt has not been eliminated, only the DPWTYS is meted out when the DPWIE should have been given. The second circumstance is a wrongful conviction; that is, in a case where reasonable doubt in conviction evidences has not been eliminated and the defendant thus should not be convicted, the defendant is convicted and sentenced to the death penalty with suspension leaving some leeway.

Xin's kidnapping case belongs to the first situation, and after the procuratorial organs protested the verdict, it was corrected. In judicial practice, however, there are a large number of cases of the second situation, which are not remedied effectively. Only in a few cases where the real criminals were discovered later has the wrongful conviction been exposed and corrected.

It is thought-provoking that two wrongful convictions in Zhejiang Province in 2013 that shocked the nation belonged to the aforementioned second type of the death penalty with suspension leaving some leeway; that is, reasonable doubts in conviction evidence had not been eliminated, but the defendants were convicted and sentenced to the death penalty with suspension. The cases were overturned after the real criminals surfaced later.

The first is the robbery and homicide case of Chen Jianyang and codefendants in Xiaoshan, Zhejiang Province. In 1995, there were two separate counts of robbery and homicide against taxi drivers in Xiaoshan, and the procuratorate accused Chen and codefendants of both counts. In July 1997, the Hangzhou Intermediate Court sentenced Chen and two other defendants to the DPWIE, one defendant to the DPWTYS, and another defendant to life imprisonment. In December 1997, in the second-instance trial, the Zhejiang High Court revised the sentences of the first three persons to the DPWTYS on grounds of "the specific circumstances of the case" and upheld the sentences of the other two persons. In the spring of

2012, via fingerprint comparison, the Zhejiang police found that another criminal suspect, Xiang, had committed one of the robbery and homicide crimes. On May 30, 2013, the Jiaxing Intermediate Court of Zhejiang Province sentenced Xiang to the DPWTYS. Chen was convicted solely on the basis of his confession without any objective evidence. The one fingerprint left on the dead person's vehicle matched none of the fingerprints of the five defendants on file. The police did not admit this important exculpatory evidence in favor of the defendants, nor did they give any reasonable explanation afterward. Further, there were obvious coerced confessions during police investigation. Actually, during the second-instance trial, the court found it difficult to convict with the available evidence but nevertheless revised the sentence to the death penalty with suspension leaving some leeway and ended the case.

The second wrongful conviction is that in the Zhangs' rape case in Zhejiang Province. In May 2003, truck drivers Zhang Hui (nephew) and Zhang Gaoping (uncle) from Anhui were suspected of raping and killing a female college student who rode in their truck. In April 2004, the Hangzhou Intermediate Court sentenced Zhang Hui to the DPWIE and Zhang Gaoping to life imprisonment. In October 2004, the Zhejiang High Court revised Zhang Hui's sentence to the DPWTYS and Zhang Gaoping's sentence to imprisonment for 15 years. In November 2011, it was found that the DNA of residual in the victim's fingernails matched that of Gou, another criminal executed a few years earlier on rape charges. Although the DNA results did not match the DNA of both Zhangs, they were still convicted by the court on the grounds that "it is unable to rule out the possibility of [the victim] touching others in real life." In the trial of second instance, the judges noticed this suspicion but nevertheless convicted the defendants on the ground of "the specific circumstance of the case" and revised the sentences of both Zhangs.

These two wrongful convictions are both death penalty cases where, because reasonable doubt had not been ruled out, sentences were revised to the death penalty with suspension leaving some leeway on the grounds of "the specific circumstances of the case." The Zhejiang High Procuratorate did not lodge protests against either of these two cases but instead upheld the rulings of the second-instance court. After these two wrongful convictions were exposed in 2013, the vice president of the SPC was grateful that the defendants had not been erroneously executed thanks to revising sentences to the death penalty with suspension leaving some leeway.[6]

Xin's kidnapping case is a guiding case issued by the SPP. It is intended to advocate the role of the procuratorate's protest, which secured a revised sentence from the court. Therefore, the principle of this case is: "For the protest of death penalty cases, it is imperative to grasp the requirements of death penalty sentences, follow stringent evidence standards, and perform the legal supervision functions of criminal adjudication." Discussing how to avoid wrongful convictions, the vice chief procurator of the procuratorate talked about "how to avoid dwelling on confounding minor details and as a result indulging criminals."[7] In Xin's case, the court did dwell on minor details. However, in view of the fact that the two wrongful conviction cases exposed later both took place in Zhejiang, it should be clear that the procuratorate should carry out the death penalty evidence standard, and it is more important to follow the evidence standard strictly than to avoid dwelling on minor details. On the issue of evidence admissibility, the court was obviously under pressure from the procuratorate and thus was unable to safeguard the evidence standard. Instead, as a compromise, it revised the sentence to the DPWTYS and made a huge mistake. The lesson is very grave. We should not look at Xin's kidnapping case separately from the others. Combining it with the two wrongful conviction cases, we get a bigger picture of the situation.

* * *

It has been only a few years since China systematized the imposition of the death penalty via guiding cases. Two of the six criminal guiding cases issued by the SPC are death penalty cases, signifying the emphasis on the death penalty. Because of the different standpoints between the SPC and the SPP, the SPC's effort in restraining the death penalty is obvious in the aforementioned death penalty guiding cases. The SPP's guiding case, however, is about a revised judgment from the DPWTYS to the DPWIE and mainly concerns the problem of evidence admissibility. In a way, the messages that the SPC and the SPP intended to send are somewhat contradictory.

Both the SPC and the SPP are attempting to standardize the imposition of the death penalty through guiding cases. Theoretically speaking, it is straightforward to demonstrate the specific rules of the imposition of the death penalty through guiding cases, and it is easy to compare them to other similar cases. Therefore, the guiding cases are expected to have a positive impact on China's death penalty practice. However, China's death penalty imposition is affected by various complicated factors, such as the public security situation at a given time, the political need to maintain social stability, public opinion uproar, and pressure from victims. Therefore, the restraining effect of guiding cases on imposition of the death penalty could remain rather limited.

The establishment of the guiding case system is one of the highlights of China's legal reform, although the system itself is largely administrative. For example, guiding cases are issued by the SPC and the SPP irregularly, and they are limited in number and thus necessarily have limited roles. Only a sufficiently large number of cases can provide enough references for judicial organs at lower levels based on the specific circumstances of the cases. Further, it is worth mentioning that the principles of current guiding cases are mostly repetitions of the prescriptions of existing laws and judicial interpretations, without creating new rules. Under these conditions, the role of the guiding cases will be limited. Of course, China's guiding case system is still at a nascent phase, and it will improve over time.

NOTES

1. As of May 2015, when this chapter was finished, the SPC had issued a total of 52 guiding cases in 10 batches, among which 9 are criminal guiding cases. The SPP had issued a total of 19 guiding cases in 5 batches, all of which are criminal cases.
2. For a detailed discussion of the guiding case system, see X. Chen (2013).
3. For a regional positivist study of the DPWTYS, see Huang (2007).
4. On the impact of the strike-hard campaigns on the imposition of the death penalty, see W. Yang (2011).
5. On the effect of guiding opinions on the imposition of the death penalty jointly formulated and signed by judicial organs, see J. Chen (2005:50).
6. For instance, Shen Deyong, vice president of the SPC, even stated that "the adjudicating court rendered meritorious services at the time, or at least, its contributions outweighed its mistakes; otherwise, the defendant would have been executed long ago." See "How to Avoid Wrongful Convictions," *People's Court Daily*, May 6, 2013, p. 2.
7. See Zhu Xiaoqing, "Several Comments on Safeguarding the Bottom Line to Prevent Wrongful Convictions," *Procuratorate's Daily*, July 8, 2013, p. 3.

REFERENCES

Chen, J. (2005). *Lun sixing shiyong de biaozhun* [On the Standard of the Death Penalty Imposition]. Beijing: People's Court Press.

Chen, R. (2012). *Xingshi zhengju faxue* [Criminal Evidence Law]. Beijing: Peking University Press.

Chen, X. (Ed.). (2007). *Kuanyan xiangji xingshi zhengce yanjiu* [A Study on the Criminal Policy of "Balancing Severity with Leniency"]. Beijing: People's University of China Press.

Chen, X., Zhang, J., & Hu, Y. (Eds.). (2013). *Renmin fayuan xingshi zhidao anli caipan guize tongzuan* [China's Guiding Case System: A study on the Rules of Adjudication of People's Courts]. Beijing: Peking University Press.

Huang, W. (2007). *Sihuan zhidu de dangdai jiazhi* [The Contemporary Value of the Sihuan System]. Beijing: Kexue chubanshe.

Ma, S. (2006). *Sixing sifa kongzhi yanjiu* [Research on the Judicial Control of the Death Penalty]. Beijing: The Law Press.

Peng, Y. (2011). Sixing anjian susong chengsxu yanjiu [A Study on the Criminal Procedure in Death Penalty Cases]. Beijing: China University of Political Science and Law Press.

Ren, Z. (2012). *Sixing shiyong wenti yanjiu* [Research on the Imposition of Death Penalty]. Beijing: Intellectual Property Press.

Yang, W. (2011). *Sixing yanbian yaolue* [A Brief Introduction to the Evolvement of the Death Penalty]. Beijing: People's Public Security University of China Press.

Yang, Z. (2008). *Sixing de chengxu xianzhi* [The Procedural Limit of the Death Penalty]. Beijing: People's Public Security University of China Press.

8

The Death Penalty After the Restoration of Centralized Review

AN EMPIRICAL STUDY OF CAPITAL SENTENCING

▸ MOULIN XIONG

ALTHOUGH GLOBAL EXPERTS have been trying to decipher the number of executions in China over the past few decades, secrecy surrounding this issue prevents the public from knowing how many offenders were actually executed every year. Because of the inaccessibility of official data, criminologists have been unable to specify what crimes tend to result in the death penalty in practice. Organizations such as Amnesty International also struggle to obtain reliable statistics to tell the real story (Bakken 2004; Hood 2001, 2009; Hood & Hoyle 2008; Johnson & Zimring 2009; Macbean & Li 2003; Nathan & Gilley 2003). Still, scholars have tried their best to estimate that China has accounted for 93% of executions in Asia and has ranked at the top of the world in that category since the start of the new millennium (Johnson & Zimring 2009).

Earlier capital punishment policies in China were deemed to be inadequate in meeting the requirements of international standards, such as that of the International Covenant on Civil and Political Rights, because of the opaque procedures caused by state secrecy (Lu & Miethe 2007; Trevaskes 2012). Under mounting pressure from the international society and from domestic stories of wrongful convictions, the years since 2007 have witnessed strong reforms in capital policy in China (Wang 2008). After the approval of procedural reforms of the death penalty on October 31, 2006, there was at least a 25% reduction in death penalty cases approved by the Supreme People's Court of China (SPC), and this helped China maintain an atmosphere of "killing fewer and killing cautiously" (*shao sha shen sha*) (Hood 2009; W. Li 2008; Smith 2009; Trevaskes 2012). In February 2011, the National People's Congress passed the Eighth Amendment to the Criminal Law (hereafter the Eighth Amendment), which eliminated the death penalty for 13 nonviolent and economic crimes (Xie 2009).

On March 14, 2012, the National People's Congress passed the Second Amendment to the Criminal Procedure Law, which further improved the transparency of and placed greater weight on the review system for the death penalty. It stipulated that the SPC must inquire about the defendant and hear the defense lawyer's opinion if the lawyer so requests. On July 17, 2013, SPC judges held an open appellate hearing for Yang Fangzheng's death sentence review. Yang, though innocent, had been tortured and sentenced to the death penalty with a two-year suspension by the Huanghua Intermediate Court in Hebei Province. In their review, the SPC judges applied the criminal procedure of the second instance (appeals), and such an open trial, rarely used before, is viewed as a major reform move in China's death penalty practice (China Court Online 2013).

With these policy changes, the recent numbers of China's death penalty cases, as estimated by the Dui Hua Foundation, indicate a clear trend of reduction from 6,500 executions in 2007 to 3,000 in 2012, because China promised to be more cautious about using capital punishment (Amnesty International 2013; Dui Hua Foundation 2014; Johnson & Zimring 2009; World Coalition 2014). The reduced number of executions in China possibly reflected the improvement of human rights status and China's response to international pressure and to abolition advocacy by international scholarship and organizations (Hood & Hoyle 2008; Johnson & Zimring 2009; Placais 2014).

In fact, the idea of abolition was debated by some Chinese scholars who argued that China should keep its death penalty because of considerations based on traditional values, such as deterrence and the strong notion of retribution held by Chinese citizens (Lu & Miethe 2007). Nowadays the accepted theory of Chinese academics is that outright abolition in current China is impractical. Nevertheless, scholars in China are pursuing measures to improve the current system, such as increased transparency and gradual abolition of the death penalty for nonviolent crimes (Bakken 2011; R. Liu 2005; Y. Liu 2007; Yu 2009; Zhao & Yin 2013).

A key empirical question, yet to be addressed, is whether national policies and academic theories are making an actual impact on the application of capital punishment in practice, since official reports often disclose little reliable information and very few empirical studies have been published (Johnson & Zimring 2009; Lu & Miethe 2007; Trevaskes 2008, 2012). In this study, I attempt to test how Chinese judges in lower criminal courts have carried out the national policy of "killing fewer and killing cautiously" on the basis of empirical data, because such data may provide insights for possible reform in the future. As a result, I address the following questions specifically:

1. What crimes frequently result in the death penalty in China? Although many crimes are eligible for the death penalty under the Criminal Law, not all of them play a significant role in practice. A clear understanding of the actual distribution of capital crimes may shed light on future reforms.

2. What is the percentage of immediate executions in all death penalty cases? Unlike other countries where a death sentence means that the offender will be executed if all appeals are exhausted, China's practice of the death penalty with suspension (*sihuan*), though technically a death sentence option in law, results only in life imprisonment in reality in the absence of new offenses (see more discussion later). The use of the death penalty with suspension therefore plays a key role in assessing the reality of the death penalty in China.

3. Has the number of death penalty cases in China been reduced in recent years? Do we witness empirical support for the government's claim of killing fewer?

In the rest of this chapter, I will briefly review policy changes with regard to the death penalty since 1979, when the first Criminal Law was passed. Then I will compare the two death penalty options: the death penalty with suspension and the death penalty with immediate execution (*sixing liji zhixing*), because the former is a unique practice in China's context. Next, I will turn to the empirical data and present major findings based on the research questions. In conclusion, I discuss potential policy implications based on my findings.

POLICY CHANGES AND DEATH SENTENCE OPTIONS
Death Penalty Policy Changes, 1979-2013

In China, the death penalty is applied only to extremely serious crimes, although the crimes subject to such legislative and judicial interpretation have varied from time to time, given the emphasis of criminal justice policies. For instance, Article 43 in the 1979 Criminal Law provided that the death penalty be applied to those offenders who committed serious crimes with severe heinousness (*zuida e'ji*). Article 48 in the 1997 Criminal Law also declared that the death penalty applies to offenders who commit extremely serious offenses (*zuixing jiqi yanzhong*).

The first Criminal Law in 1979 implied that the death penalty applied only to serious offenses with such terrible consequence as loss of human life or to crimes of a "counterrevolutionary nature" (Liang et al. 2006; Lu & Zhang 2005; Trevaskes 2012). However, this restrictive requirement was lifted in 1982, when the Standing Committee of the National People's Congress (SCNPC) decided to extend the use of the death penalty to crimes that would not normally result in the death penalty under 1979 Criminal Law. For example, the death penalty would not be applicable to theft according to the 1979 Criminal Law, but the SCNPC stipulated in 1983 that theft with serious circumstances (*qingjie yanzhong*) would qualify for the death penalty (SCNPC 1983). Similarly, there was no legally stipulated capital punishment for drug crimes, corruption, and bribery in the 1979 Criminal Law, but these crimes were made death eligible in 1982, and the death penalty was indeed used frequently for them from then on, after some provincial high courts were authorized to approve death sentences (SCNPC 1982).

China's criminal justice policy since 1979 has experienced a zigzag with almost 30 years of strike-hard campaigns (*yanda*). The strike-hard campaigns, which first began in 1983, were nationwide campaigns during which criminal laws were applied to the utmost stringent degree to inflict the most severe punishment on offenders in order to crack down on crimes. During the height of these campaigns, offenders were sentenced and executed for such common offenses as theft, hooliganism, and drug offenses (Hood 1996, 2009; Liang et al. 2006; Trevaskes 2012). At the national level, the 1979 Criminal Law stipulated 28 death-eligible crimes, which accounted for one-fifth of of the number of acts designated as crimes under the law (Chen & Zhou 2011; Y. Wang 2008). Moreover, several provincial high courts, such as those in Sichuan, Guizhou, Yunnan, and Guangxi, were granted the right to review and approve death sentences for violent crimes in 1981 in order to implement the strike-hard policy (Hood 2009; Trevaskes 2012). As a result, both legislative interpretations and provincial practices made capital punishment so prevalent that 71 crimes were qualified for the death penalty before the 1996 criminal procedure reform and the passage of the 1997 Criminal Law (R. Liu 2004; Zhao 2005a). The death penalty was also used to combat drug-related crimes, and the final review and approval authority for the death penalty was delegated to provincial high courts in 1991 and 1993 in the heat of the nationwide war on drugs.

In retrospect, the adoption of the Criminal Procedure Law in 1996 could have presented an opportunity to reclaim the review and approval authority from provincial high courts. Unfortunately, they still exercised the approval authority to grant the death penalty when the strike-hard campaigns continued with another round in 1996 (and another one from 2001 to 2003). The 1997 Criminal Law expanded the use of the death penalty to 68 crimes (accounting for about one-sixth of all 452 crimes). The wide and unrestrained use of the death penalty continued with large volumes of executions and little due procedure protection (Chen 2013; Hood 1996; Shao 2005).

Major breakthroughs occurred from 2006 on. In 2006, in a significant event in the history of China's criminal justice system, the SCNPC decided to end the decentralized death penalty review and give the review and approval power back to the SPC to tighten the use of the death penalty. In 2007, the SPC issued a new judicial decision to end provincial high courts' review and approval power for the death penalty with immediate execution. The latest revision of the People's Republic of China's Criminal Law, the Eighth Amendment in 2011, abolished 13 nonviolent and economic crimes previously qualified for the death penalty, leaving 55 crimes eligible for the death penalty in the current code.

Death Penalty with Immediate Execution or with Suspension

Unlike other nations, China's Criminal Law presents two possible options for criminals who are sentenced to the death penalty, the death penalty with immediate execution and the death penalty with a two-year suspension. The former results in immediate execution once the offender exhausts all possible appeals and review options. In contrast, the death penalty with suspension means that the criminal will not be executed unless he or she intentionally commits new crimes during the two-year suspension. Unlike countries such as Malaysia, Thailand, and Singapore, where the king or the president has the power to grant clemency to criminals on death row, the death penalty with suspension in China is automatically commuted to life imprisonment by an intermediate court at the end of the two-year suspension. Despite the obvious difference between life and death, both the death penalty with suspension and the death penalty with immediate execution are regarded as capital punishment in China (Chen & Zhou 2011; Trevaskes 2012).

In addition, the review and approval processes for these two forms of the death sentence are different. The death penalty with immediate execution requires a stricter review process than that of the death penalty with suspension. Before submission to the SPC for its final review and approval, cases of immediate execution must first be reviewed by the provincial high court, whether or not the offender appeals to the high court (Criminal Procedure Law, Article 236). Only when the provincial high court approves the capital punishment will the case be eligible for the SPC's final review and approval. In any event, all executions require final endorsement by the SPC. In contrast, cases where the offenders are sentenced to the death penalty with suspension will be reviewed by the provincial high court but not necessarily by the SPC, because the execution is suspended in these cases. It is therefore important to distinguish these two different practices, and it is of vital importance to contrast the total number of death penalty sentences (including both practices) with the number of actual executions (including only the death penalty with immediate execution).

DATA AND METHODOLOGY

Compared with theoretical essays, empirical studies of China's death penalty are rather limited (Johnson & Zimring 2009; Nie 2008; Trevaskes 2012). In the English-language literature, a few studies have focused on public opinion on the death penalty on the basis of survey results. For instance, Liang and his colleagues published their research about the difference of attitudes toward the death penalty between Chinese and overseas students (Liang et al. 2006). Jiang and his colleagues published a few articles comparing college students' and ordinary citizens' attitudes toward the death penalty in China (e.g., Jiang, Lambert, & Nathan 2009; Jiang et al. 2010).

In the Chinese-language literature, Mo and her research group conducted their investigation in Beijing and Hebei Province to analyze judicial participants' attitudes toward the death penalty, using survey data from lawyers, judges, police officers, and procurators (Mo & Zeng 2009). In addition to these survey studies, Amnesty International computed the annual number of executions in China on the basis of published sources, such as news reports (Roney 2014). A few publications in China have found that executions in China resulted mainly from such violent crimes as homicide, robbery, kidnapping, rape, and drug-related crimes (S. Li 2011; Qi 2007; Zhang 2011; Zhao & Yin 2011).

I take a different approach in this study and have conducted empirical research by collecting judicial judgments (*panjue shu*), which are published on court websites from eight courts in five provinces, including Guangzhou and Zhanjiang in Guangdong Province in southern China, Shanghai, Hangzhou in Zhejiang Province in eastern China, Kaifeng and Jiaozhuo in Henan Province in northern China, and Lanzhou in Gansu Province in western China. Given the fact that other access to meaningful data is lacking, research relying on published judicial documents has proved fruitful in recent years (e.g., He & Su 2013; Xiong 2013; Xiong, Jiang, & Chen 2013).

Publication of Capital Judgments by Courts

Criminal justice policies in China have made great strides toward more formalization and transparency in recent years. Compared with decades ago, China's supreme justice organs (the SPC and the Supreme People's Procuratorate) today publish more reports and annual statistics in order to better inform citizens and scholars of ongoing legal changes. However, the *Statistical Yearbooks* or other annual reports at the national level publish very little useful information about the death penalty. Fortunately, court websites at the city, county, and provincial levels turn out to be very helpful. With the advance of new technology, almost all intermediate courts (excluding Tibet) have constructed their own websites in order to publish judicial works and display their human resources, judgments, and other documents. In 2013, for instance, the SPC encouraged lower courts to publish all judgments online in order to revitalize "judicial openness" (*si fa gong kai*) (Supreme People's Court 2013). Some courts in China had already

TABLE 8.1   Intermediate Courts Explored in This Study
(Number of Intermediate Courts = 365)

PROVINCE	NUMBER	PROVINCE	NUMBER	PROVINCE	NUMBER
Sichuan	22	Hubei	14	Fujian	9
Guangdong	22	Hunan	14	Qinghai	8
Henan	19	Inner Mongolia	13	Tibet[a]	7
Shandong	18	Jiangsu	13	Ningxia	5
Yunnan	17	Jiangxi	13	Chongqing	5
Gansu	17	Shanxi	12	Hainan	5
Heilongjiang	16	Jilin	11	Beijing	4
Liaoning	16	Hebei	11	Shanghai	3
Anhui	16	Shaanxi	11	Tianjin	2
Guangxi	15	Zhejiang	11		
Xinjiang	14	Guizhou	9		

[a] No website was found in 6 intermediate courts of Tibet; only two criminal judgment documents were published on the website of the Ngari Intermediate Court.

Note: The Railway Intermediate Court is included, but the Maritime Court and the Military Court are excluded.

published online, either in whole or selectively, judicial documents and judgments before 2013.

According to Article 20 of the Criminal Procedure Law, cases regarding crimes punishable by death must be tried by courts of intermediate level or higher. I therefore searched intermediate courts nationwide for judgments with death sentences (table 8.1). As expected, the publishing of such judgments varied greatly from one jurisdiction to another. Most courts located in less developed provinces in western or central China did not publish such judgments at all. Some courts, such as courts in coastal areas and more developed provinces, such as Beijing, Fujian, and Shenzhen, selectively published a few civil and criminal judgments, but death penalty judgments were specifically excluded. Some courts published a very small number of death penalty judgments, but I cannot tell whether the publication is complete (most likely not). For example, Jiaozhuo Intermediate Court of Henan Province published a few death penalty judgments from 2006 to 2010, but nothing was published in 2011 and 2012. In contrast, some other courts, such as those in Guangzhou and Shanghai, published many more judgments, and the Guangzhou Intermediate Court even claimed to have published all of its judgments.

Another layer of complication is added when several courts did not publish capital judgments directly. Rather, these courts published some capital judgments indirectly, that is, via publication of cases with incidental civil procedure to criminal cases (*xingshi fudai minshi panjue shu*). In China, civil compensation of criminal judgments arises from the need to compensate victims of criminal offenses, and these cases are tried by criminal judges. We are able to search online cases with civil compensation of criminal judgments because these judgments may reveal some basic information about capital cases, such as how and why the victim was killed, injured, or raped, and what punishment was applied to the offender(s). Courts publishing capital judgments rarely use real names, with the exception of the Guangzhou Intermediate Court. The two intermediate courts in Shanghai published some of their capital judgments anonymously (e.g., using "XXX" for names) and revealed only family names in other cases. In the case of sex crimes or crimes involving state secrets (particularly death penalty cases), protective measures are taken before the judgments are posted, such as deleting key information if secrets are involved, and replacing real names if privacy issues are involved.

One would assume that judgments published on court websites, if available, are necessarily selective because of the state secrecy surrounding the death penalty. To my surprise, however, it appears that some courts actually try to publish all criminal judgments. For instance, during a personal interview in 2013, a judge who works at the Guangzhou Intermediate Court informed me that the court indeed publishes all judgments, because the court asks all judges to upload all their judgments to the official website of the court in order to help parties track the status of the case.[1] I also double-checked the serial numbers of cases I downloaded (and the content of publications): it appears that the serial numbers are sequential, which seems to confirm that the court has indeed been publishing all cases. In addition, news reported online also suggested that the Guangzhou Intermediate Court has tried its best to publish all judgments since 2004 (J. Lin 2004).

In contrast, criminal judgments from Shanghai are quite complicated because capital judgments are not published directly but through cases with incidental civil procedure to criminal cases. Five other courts in Gansu, Henan, and Zhejiang Provinces are similar to Shanghai. It is quite obvious that these courts published their judgments rather selectively. For example, because published cases are so scanty in Hangzhou in Zhejiang Province, it is inconceivable that a big metropolitan city such as Hangzhou had only a few capital sentences in 2009 and 2010 and no death sentences in 2011 and 2012. As a result, although I include data from all courts (a total of eight) in my analyses, I single out three courts in Guangzhou and Shanghai for comparison purposes.

Because this is an exploratory study, I am fully aware that it is difficult, if not impossible, to validate my research conducted on local courts at its current stage. As a result, I caution readers that my research very likely runs the risk of underestimating the scale and scope of the death penalty in China.

Data Sample

I successfully retrieved capital judgments from eight intermediate courts in five provinces (see table 8.2). I downloaded every available capital judgment with at least one defendant sentenced to a death sentence or suspended death sentence and coded relevant information from these eight intermediate courts. As table 8.2 indicates, I obtained information on 552 offenders (samples) from 521 capital judgments (in 31 of which two or more offenders were sentenced to death). Among them, 93.1% of the offenders (514) were generated from Shanghai and Guangzhou, 50.5% (279) were collected from criminal judgments, and 49.5% (273) were gathered from cases with civil compensation of criminal judgments. Note that in three of the five provinces (Henan, Gansu, and Zhejiang), data are very limited: only 4 cases in Hangzhou Province, 16 cases in Henan Province, and 10 cases in Gansu Province. The scarcity of available data shows that judicial openness is still largely out of reach with regard to the death penalty in China. Nevertheless, I display results from all eight courts for data distribution purpose and single out data from Guangzhou and Shanghai for comparison purposes in my analyses.[2]

Because these cases had yet to be reviewed by provincial high courts or the SPC at the time when the data were collected, the judgments did not indicate whether the executions were actually carried out or suspended. However, I decided to focus on capital cases tried by the first-instance courts in this study in order to assess the general patterns of initial death sentence decisions. Ideally, it would be more precise and revealing to collect data on death penalty judgments reviewed by provincial high courts and the SPC to estimate more accurately the number of people executed in China.

TABLE 8.2 Death Penalty Sample by Jurisdiction
(Number of Defendants = 552; Number of Cases = 521)

PROVINCE	CITY (INTERMEDIATE COURT [IC])	JUDGMENT SOURCE		YEAR								TOTAL
		CJ[a]	CICJ[b]	2005	2006	2007	2008	2009	2010	2011	2012	
Guangdong	Guangzhou	162	167	2	—	1	9	100	74	97	46	329
	Zhanjiang	3	5	—	—	—	1	4	—	—	3	8
Shanghai	Shanghai First IC	41	46	—	1	5	12	20	32	10	7	87
	Shanghai Second IC	58	40	—	—	2	17	30	26	18	5	98
Zhejiang	Hangzhou	3	1	—	1	—	—	1	2	—	—	4
Henan	Kaifeng	0	4	—	—	1	—	1	3	—	—	4
	Jiaozhuo	8	4	—	1	1	2	5	3	—	—	12
Gansu	Lanzhou	4	6	—	—	—	—	—	2	—	8	10
TOTAL		279	273	2	3	9	41	161	142	125	69	552

[a] CJ is short for criminal judgments.
[b] CICJ is short for criminal incidental civil judgments.

MAJOR FINDINGS

The Criminal Law of the PRC contained 68 capital offenses before the 2011 revision and now contains 55 capital offenses. Little information exists on how death penalty sentences are distributed among these offenses. To answer this question, I coded crimes for which judges rendered the death penalty (both suspension and immediate execution) in my sample. If the offenders committed multiple offenses, I coded only the offense(s) for which the death penalty was rendered, omitting offenses that were not sentenced to the death penalty (there were 125 offenders with capital sentences who also committed other crimes that resulted in sentences of incarceration for various numbers of years or life imprisonment).

Frequency of Capital Crimes in Eight Courts

Table 8.3 provides the distribution of death penalty crimes. It clearly shows that 99.5% of capital crimes in practice come from violent crimes (65.6%) and drug crimes (33.9%). Among violent crimes, murder, robbery, and assault are the top three in numbers, accounting for 40.9%, 10.9%, and 10% of all crimes, respectively. Drug-related crimes mainly consisted of crimes covered in Article 347 of the Criminal Law, that is, selling, smuggling, trafficking, and manufacturing of drugs. Among drug crimes with death sentences, drug selling and smuggling are the top two, accounting for 16.8% and 11.4%, respectively, of all capital crimes in my sample.

It is impossible, however, from table 8.2 and table 8.3 to accurately describe the capital crime distribution because of the sampling problems identified earlier. Such problems are obvious in several crime categories. For example, I found rape cases only in the Second Intermediate Court of Shanghai but not in the other seven courts, and illegal fund-raising cases only in the Hangzhou Intermediate Court. One potential reason for the rarity of rape cases, as scholars have pointed out, is that rape does not automatically result in a death sentence unless the victim dies (Nie 2008; Zhao & Yin 2011). On June 12, 2014, the SPC disproved death sentences for two principal offenders who committed rape against a 10-year-old girl after the case was reviewed and approved by the Hunan High Court (Yuan 2014). In this case, the two offenders, Zhou Junhui and Qin Xing, ran a criminal gang of organized prostitution and forced the victim to be a prostitute, who was gang-raped by several

TABLE 8.3   Crimes in Which Offenders Were Sentenced to the Death Penalty
(2005–2012: Eight Immediate Courts)
(Samples = 552; Cases = 521)

CRIME[a]	FREQUENCY	PERCENT	CUMULATIVE PERCENT	RANK
Murder	226	40.9	40.9	1
Assault	55	10.0	50.9	5
Robbery	60	10.9	61.8	4
Kidnapping	20	3.6	65.4	6
Rape[b]	1	0.2	65.6	9
Illegal fund-raising[c]	1	0.2	65.8	9
Counterfeiting money[d]	1	0.2	65.9	9
Trading and trafficking of illegal Explosives[e]	1	0.2	66.1	9
Drug selling[f]	93	16.8	83.0	2
Drug smuggling[f]	63	11.4	94.4	3
Drug trafficking[f]	19	3.4	97.8	7
Drug manufacturing[f]	12	2.2	100.0	8
TOTAL	552	100	100	—

[a]   Main offenses for which the offender received the death penalty, excluding noncapital offences that the offender committed.

[b]   The offender was convicted of rape in 2011 by the Shanghai Second Intermediate Court, and the victim was assaulted and killed during the course of the crime.

[c]   The offender was convicted of illegal fund-raising in 2006 by the Hangzhou Intermediate Court.

[d]   The offender was convicted of counterfeiting money in 2011 by the Guangzhou Intermediate Court.

[e]   The offender was convicted of trading and trafficking illegal explosives in 2008 by the Jiaozhuo Intermediate Court.

[f]   Forty-eight offenders committed multiple drug offenses. Article 347 of the Criminal Law of the People's Republic of China deals with drug selling, smuggling, trafficking, and manufacturing. Official charges are determined by specific offenses committed but converged into one crime if the offender has more offenses (see table 8.5 for the distribution of multiple drug offenses).

men in the course of work. The SPC rejected the two principals' death sentences and reasserted the criminal policy of no application of the death penalty in rape cases without the death of the victim. This case has been very influential and widely discussed and reported in China. To many, this is a sign that China has already been tightening its use of the death penalty. To gain a better assessment of the capital crime distribution, I next turn to capital crime distributions in Guangzhou and Shanghai.

Three Courts in Shanghai and Guangzhou

Table 8.4 displays the capital crime distribution of cases collected from the First and Second Intermediate Courts of Shanghai and the Guangzhou Intermediate Court (the Zhanjiang Intermediate Court in Guangdong Province is excluded because of the extremely small and unreliable sample). A total of 514 offenders in 485 cases were sentenced to death, and these cases constituted the bulk of my data. I broke down the data by jurisdictions (the three courts), and the overall pattern of the table across jurisdictions leads to the same conclusion as that from the preceding analysis, that is, criminals receiving the death penalty are mainly charged with murder, assault, drug selling, and drug trafficking. A close examination of the table shows that 31.3% of death penalty cases in the Guangzhou Intermediate Court, 54.1% in the First Intermediate Court of Shanghai, and 54% in the Second Intermediate Court of Shanghai were murder cases (39.5% of the combined capital cases in the three courts). The data show a similar pattern for assault: 10% in Guangzhou, 10.2% in the First Intermediate Court of Shanghai, and 9.2% in the Second Intermediate Court of Shanghai (9.9% of the combined capital cases in the three courts). Again, the trend for drug-related crimes is consistent with the data for the eight courts discussed earlier: drug selling, smuggling, trafficking, and manufacturing accounted for significant portions of all death penalty cases in these three courts, with percentages of 17.7%, 12.3%, 3.5% and 2.3%, respectively (table 8.4, last column). This is not surprising, given that the data from the three courts in Shanghai and Guangzhou represent approximately 93% of the total cases in this study.

The fact that Article 347 of the Criminal Law covers several drug offenses creates some complications in the calculation of capital drug crimes. In practice, official charges are determined by specific offenses committed, but if an offender has committed multiple offenses under Article 347, they are combined into one crime. For instance, if an offender has committed drug selling, trafficking, and manufacturing, he or she will be charged with the mixed crime of drug selling, trafficking, and manufacturing under Article 347 (therefore, officially there is one crime). I display in table 8.5 the specific content of the offenses under Article 347 if the offenders committed two

TABLE 8.4 Distribution of Crime Type Among Death Penalty Cases (2005–2012) (Shanghai and Guangzhou Intermediate Courts) (Samples = 514; Cases = 485)

CRIME	GUANGZHOU IC		SHANGHAI FIRST IC		SHANGHAI SECOND IC		THREE COURTS	
	FREQUENCY	PERCENT	FREQUENCY	PERCENT	FREQUENCY	PERCENT	FREQUENCY	PERCENT
Murder	103	31.3	53	54.1	47	54.0	203	39.5
Assault	33	10.0	10	10.2	8	9.2	51	9.9
Robbery	51	15.5	2	2.0	4	4.6	57	11.1
Kidnapping	13	4.0	1	1.0	3	3.4	17	3.3
Rape	—	—	1	1.0	—	—	1	0.2
Counterfeiting money	1	0.3	—	—	—	—	1	0.2
Drug selling	51	15.5	26	26.5	14	16.1	91	17.7
Drug smuggling	59	17.9	—	—	4	4.6	63	12.3
Drug trafficking	7	2.1	4	4.1	7	8.0	18	3.5
Drug manufacturing	11	3.3	1	1.0	—	—	12	2.3
TOTAL	329	100	98	100	87	100	514	100

TABLE 8.5 Coexistence of Drug Offenses Among Death Penalty Cases (2005–2012)
(Shanghai and Guangzhou Intermediate Courts)
(Samples = 47; Cases = 36)

DRUG OFFENSE	DRUG SMUGGLING	DRUG TRAFFICKING	DRUG MANUFACTURING	SUM
Drug selling	5	27	10	42
Drug smuggling	0	2	0	2
Drug trafficking	2	0	1	3
Sum	7	29	11	47

offenses. Note that it is possible that the offenders committed more than two drug offenses (36 cases in my sample), but the situations would be handled exactly the same. Table 8.5 confirms that many drug offenders receiving the death penalty in China indeed committed a combination of various offenses prescribed in Article 347, including drug selling with smuggling (5), drug selling and manufacturing (10), and particularly the juncture of drug selling and trafficking (27).

I also found significantly more capital cases for drug smuggling in Guangzhou than in Shanghai (see table 8.4). A possible explanation is that drug transactions in Guangzhou are much more rampant than they are in Shanghai, given the location of Guangzhou, where it is easier to smuggle drugs from countries in Southeast Asia into southern China.

Drug crimes are the second-largest category of death sentences in my data. In line with the international movement toward abolishing capital punishment for drug-related offenses (Donovan 2012; Edwards et al. 2010; Gallahue & Lines 2013), it is quite obvious that the use of the death penalty would decrease significantly if China abolished capital punishment for drug-related crimes.

Death Penalty with Suspension or Immediate Execution

The death penalty with suspension is a unique practice in China. Table 8.6 presents information from the three courts in Shanghai and Guangzhou with regard to this practice in contrast to the death penalty with immediate execution.

TABLE 8.6 Distribution of Death Penalty Options by Crime (2005–2012) (Shanghai and Guangzhou Intermediate Courts) (Samples = 513)

CRIME	DEATH PENALTY WITH IMMEDIATE EXECUTION		DEATH PENALTY WITH SUSPENSION		TOTAL
	FREQUENCY	PERCENT	FREQUENCY	PERCENT	
Murder	58	28.6	145	71.4	203
Assault	6	11.8	45	88.2	51
Robbery	23	41.1	33	58.9	56
Kidnapping	11	64.7	6	35.3	17
Rape	1	100.0	0	0.0	1
Counterfeiting money	1	100.0	0	0.0	1
Drug selling	27	29.7	64	70.3	91
Drug smuggling	7	11.1	56	88.9	63
Drug trafficking	2	11.1	16	88.9	18
Drug manufacturing	1	8.3	11	91.7	12
TOTAL	137	26.7	376	73.3	513

Note: One case in Guangzhou was excluded here because the data set does not indicate whether the offender was sentenced to the death penalty with immediate execution or with suspension.

First, the number of cases of the death penalty with suspension in my sample (376) is almost threefold that of cases of the death penalty with immediate execution (137). In other words, 26.7% of all capital offenders in my sample would potentially be executed in Guangzhou and Shanghai if their death sentences were approved in appellate reviews, while the rest, 73.3%, were sentenced to the death penalty with suspension. This disproportionate use of the death penalty with suspension seems to indicate that both the stricter review and approval system by the SPC (after it took back the final review and approval power in 2007) and the current guiding policy of "killing fewer and killing cautiously" are playing a part in helping judges exercise more caution when they impose capital punishment. The gap of 46.6% between suspension cases and immediate execution cases confirms that China is making an effort to control and limit the use of the death penalty, especially the death penalty with immediate execution. One criminal judge working in the SPC pointed out that the percentage of immediate execution cases was greater than suspension cases nationwide before 2007, but the trend was reversed immediately in the first quarter of 2007 (W. Li 2008).

Second, table 8.6 shows that offenders who committed the most violent crimes are more likely to receive immediate execution than offenders who committed other crimes (e.g., drug-related crimes). To my surprise, kidnapping and robbery are seemingly the top two capital crimes in terms of the likelihood of execution[3] if the offender killed the victim or the victim died afterward, or when other conditions prescribed in the law were satisfied. In my data, 64.7% of kidnapping offenders and 41.1% of robbery offenders were sentenced to immediate execution, compared with 28.6% of all murder offenders. It is important to point out that the differential rates of the death penalty with immediate execution for violent crimes and drug crimes may well reflect the doctrine of using the death penalty only for extremely heinous crimes (Zhao & Yin 2011). Combining the national policy of gradual abolition and the actual figures of the death penalty with suspension in practice, I recognize a possibility for China to abolish the death penalty, or at least the death penalty with immediate execution, for drug crimes (particularly nonviolent drug offenses) in the future (Donovan 2012; Edwards et al. 2010; R. Liu 2004, 2005; Zhao & Yin 2013).

Third, in frequency (i.e., measured by numbers), murder and drug selling accounted for the bulk of executions if the offender was sentenced to the death penalty with immediate execution. Fifty-eight murder offenders and 27 offenders of drug selling made up 62% (85 out of 137) of all potential executions if they were approved by the SPC. For murder, the traditional concept of retribution plays a vital role in guiding judges to apply the death penalty (Lu & Miethe 2007; Lu & Zhang 2005; Trevaskes 2012). Although there is no evidence to prove the deterrence effect of capital punishment in violent crimes, the death penalty in China is designed to deter potential murderers and maintain social order (Donohue & Wolfers 2006; Kirby 2013; Lu & Zhang 2005; Trevaskes 2012). Compared with the high percentage of nonsuspension judgments for murder, the rest of the data in table 8.6 indicate that offenders in cases of crimes other than murder would hardly be sentenced to immediate execution if the offense was not extremely heinous (Qi 2007). This finding lends support to arguments that offenders with extenuating circumstances, for example, when the victims are at fault, cases arise from family and neighborhood disputes, or the offender turned himself or herself in, should not be sentenced to immediate execution under the influence of "killing fewer and killing cautiously" (Chen & Zhou 2011).

Fourth, among offenders who were sentenced to the death penalty with suspension, drug smuggling (88.9%), trafficking (88.9%), and manufacturing (91.7%) ranked as the top three crimes in which the offenders were most likely to be sentenced to the death penalty with suspension in both Guangzhou and Shanghai. This finding, again, could imply a possible change of criminal justice policy for drug crimes. In terms of frequency, violent crimes and drug-related crimes constituted the majority of death penalty judgments with suspension, which suggests that capital punishment in China has been applied to a narrower scope of offenses in recent years in operation, compared with its random and broader sweep during the era of strike-hard campaigns.

I also paid particular attention to both financial crimes and other white-collar crimes in my research. Only one capital case of money counterfeiting (financial crime) was found in Guangzhou, while none was found in Shanghai, Gansu, Henan, and Zhejiang. Similarly, I found only one capital case of illegal fund-raising in Hangzhou, Zhejiang Province. This scarcity of white-collar crimes may have two explanations. First, crimes of this nature are handled through a different system or are treated as top secret, therefore evading observation. Second, the death penalty is rarely used in these types of crimes in China, and more effort has been made to exclude more and more financial and white-collar crimes from the scope of the death penalty in the past 10 years (R. Liu 2004; Mo & Zeng 2009; "36 representatives" 2014; Zhao & Li 2010). Although it is most likely that the scarcity of such cases in my sample is due to both reasons, there is some evidence that lends support to the second explanation.

Take the famous Wu Ying case, for example. Wu, a 26-year-old woman when she was arrested, raised more than 389 million yuan by borrowing money from hundreds of rich people in several provinces. In the trial of first instance, the Jinhua Intermediate Court of Zhejiang Province convicted her of fraud and illegal fund-raising and sentenced her to immediate execution. On appeal, the (provincial) High Court of Zhejiang Province upheld Wu's sentence. However, the SPC rejected her death sentence with immediate execution in 2012, and the Zhejiang High Court then changed her sentence to the death penalty with suspension on May 21, 2012. Whatever the real reasons might be behind the Wu case's decision (because there are different political implications of Wu's conviction and sentencing), the SPC's rejection of her immediate execution may indicate another national policy change in limiting the use of the death penalty for economic crimes. The abolition of the use of the death penalty for nonviolent economic crimes by the Eighth Amendment in 2011 also indicates a sign that the Chinese government might be taking steps toward abolishing the death penalty for crimes of an economic nature.

Death Penalty Reduction

Figure 8.1 displays the decreasing trend of death penalty use from 2009 to 2012 based on yearly distribution of my data, especially in Guangzhou and Shanghai. The numbers fluctuated during this period, making the decrease less obvious. However, the reduction can be seen by comparing the number of death penalty cases in 2009 and 2012: there were 100 offenders who received capital punishment in Guangzhou and 50 more offenders in Shanghai (20 from the First Intermediate Court and 30 from the Second Intermediate Court) in 2009 (a total of 150); subsequently, the numbers sharply decreased to 46 offenders in Guangzhou and 12 offenders in Shanghai in 2012 (a total of 58). Similarly, data from all eight courts showed that the total number of offenders who were sentenced to the death penalty decreased from 161 in 2009 to 69 in 2012. Corroborating the estimates by the Dui Hua Foundation and Amnesty International (Amnesty International 2013; Death Penalty Worldwide 2014; Dui Hua Foundation 2014), my exploratory research reinforces the conclusion that the use of capital punishment is on the decline in China. Moreover, the reduction appears to occur for both types of death sentences, because the numbers of both immediate execution and suspension cases in Guangzhou and Shanghai exhibited a similar trend of reduction from 2009 to 2012.

In particular, the death penalty with suspension has been considered an effective tool to implement the policy of leniency (Trevaskes 2012). As table 8.6 indicates, 73.3% of capital cases in my sample are death penalty with suspension cases. Figures 8.1 and 8.2 reveal that the percentage of suspension cases was increasing and the number of immediate executions decreasing yearly. In 2009, the percentage of death penalty with suspension cases was 60.9% in eight courts and 61.3% in the Guangzhou and Shanghai intermediate courts, while the percentages of death penalty with immediate execution cases were 39.1% and 38.7%, respectively. By 2012, the percentage of death penalty with suspension cases increased to 82.6% in eight

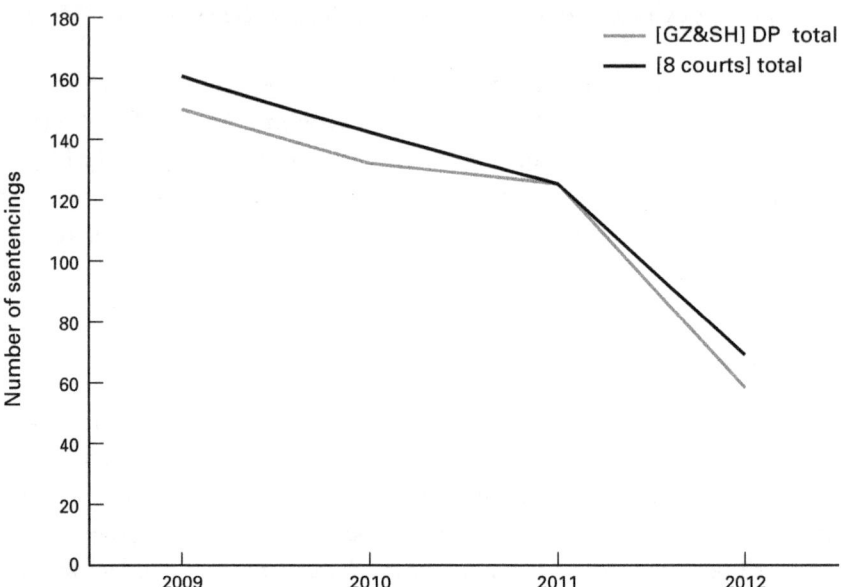

FIGURE 8.1A **Decline of Death Penalty Use in China, 2009–2012.** This chart shows the decline in death penalty sentences between 2009 and 2012 for only the eight surveyed courts and Guangzhou and Shanghai courts.

Note: GZ&SH: Guangzhou and Shanghai; DP: death penalty.

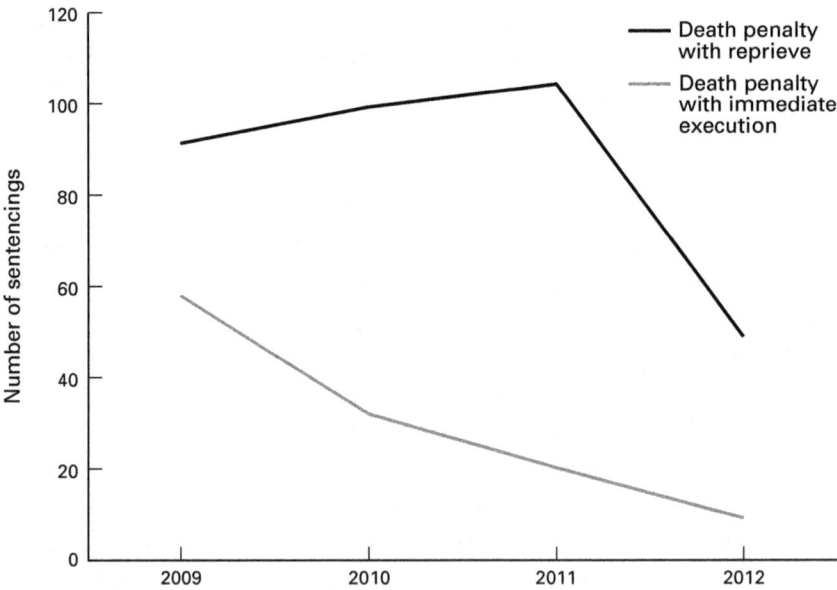

FIGURE 8.1B **Death Penalty with Immediate Execution Versus Suspension in Guangzhou and Shanghai, 2009–2012.** This figure illustrates the change in death penalty sentencing in Guangzhou and Shanghai: the rise of sentencing with suspension and the fall of immediate executions from 2009 to 2012.

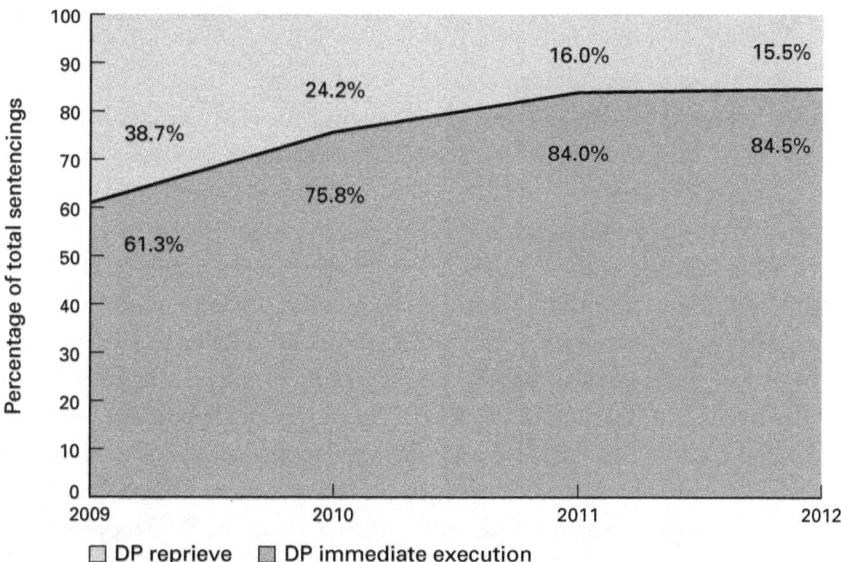

FIGURE 8.2A **Percentages of Death Penalty with Suspension and Immediate Execution in Guangzhou and Shanghai, 2009–2012**

Note: Samples for Guangzhou and Shanghai courts: 465.

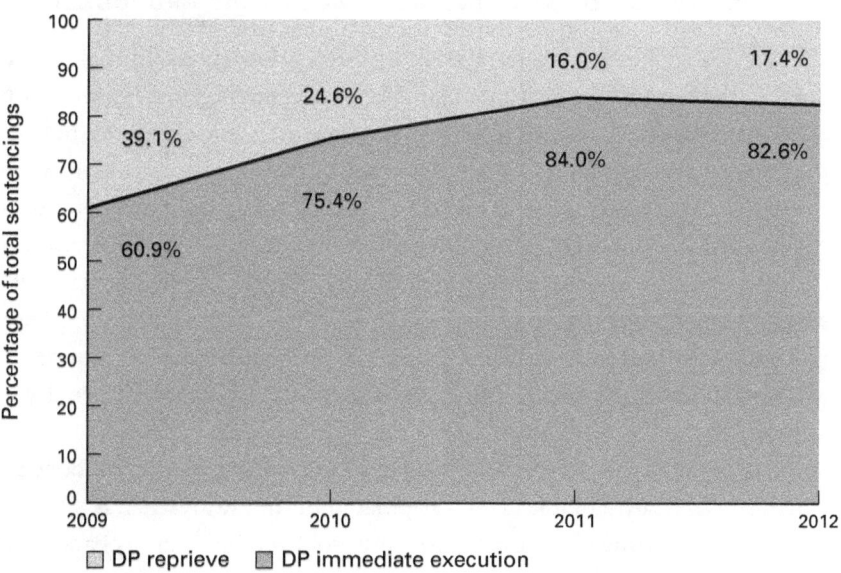

FIGURE 8.2B **Percentages of Death Penalty with Suspension and Immediate Execution in Eight Courts, 2009–2012**

Note: Samples for the eight courts: 497.

courts, and the percentage of death penalty with immediate execution cases decreased to 15.5% in courts from Guangzhou and Shanghai. To those who advocate mercy to offenders, the increasing percentages and total numbers of death penalty with suspension cases lend support again to the impact of the national policy of "killing fewer and killing cautiously."

In sum, the use of the death penalty in China shows a completely different trend from that in Iran, where the application of capital punishment rebounded again in 2013 (Iran Human Rights 2014). However, I am anxious that use of death penalty may have increased in 2014 in China because the war on terror seems to be on the rise. Terrorists have committed a number of high-profile violent crimes, such as the Kunming Railway Station massacre on March 1, 2013, the Tiananmen Square attack on October 28, 2013, and the Kashgar terrorist attack on August 20, 2013. The SPC reported that eight offenders involved in these violent events were executed on August 24, 2014. How these incidents will affect the use of the death penalty in China requires further analysis.

DISCUSSION OF KEY FINDINGS AND FUTURE PROPOSALS

There is no other country that raises more international concern than China does on the issue of the death penalty. Among 58 retentionist nations, only 21 countries carried out executions in 2012 and 2013. As a response to both proponents and opponents of the death penalty, how Chinese judges apply the death penalty to convict and sentence offenders is an important question. My empirical inquiry therefore focused on the actual judicial operation of the death penalty system in China, especially after the implementation of a series of reforms beginning in 2006. Though my data are nonrepresentative and very limited in many respects, the analysis presents a number of reassuring findings with regard to the reduced use of the death penalty in China.

First, my data show that the death penalty was rarely used in practice for a majority of death-eligible crimes stipulated in the law. Rather, it was limited to violent crimes (e.g., murder, assault, robbery, kidnapping) and drug crimes (e.g., drug selling, smuggling, trafficking, and manufacturing). The rationale for the frequent application of the death penalty to violent crimes is the likelihood of such crimes causing the victim's death. Retribution is deemed achieved by the application of the death penalty in these cases. The traditional concept of justice demands that the killer pay with his or her life for what he or she did (Bakken 2011; Liang et al. 2006; Lu & Miethe 2007; Mo & Zeng 2009; Trevaskes 2012). China's political ideology also suggests that only harsh punishment can suppress heinous crimes and promote societal stability, and this policy has led Chinese judges to inflict extreme punishment, especially in the era of strike-hard campaigns (Bakken 2008; Miao 2013). Although the strike-hard campaigns were largely discontinued after 2003, their impact still lingers on. For instance, according to an officially issued report, Wang Shengjun, then chief justice and president of the SPC, asked all judges to increase the use of the death penalty for serious violent crimes in 2008 ("China's chief justice" 2008).

Drug offenses are the second most common capital crimes after violent crimes in my sample. Although scholars advocate gradual restriction and ultimate abolition of capital punishment for drug-related crimes (R. He 2013; He & Mo 2012; Zhao & Yin 2013), drug crimes are still heavily targeted in China (S. Li 2011; Zhang 2011). With the increasing trend of drug use and the apparent ineffectiveness of drug control, the Chinese government regarded combating drug crimes as a very important part of its anticrime campaigns (Mei & Xu 2006). Liu Yuejin, director of Narcotics Control Bureau, pointed out in 2012 that China was experiencing a serious situation where crimes related to drug abuse steadily increased ("Growing" 2012). This is also evident in the growing volume of drug cases. For example, a judge in the Zhongshan Intermediate Court in Guangdong Province pointed out that cases of drug selling increased from 286 in 2007 to 376 in 2011 (D. Hu 2012).

It is interesting that my empirical data showed very little use of the death penalty for economic crimes. Many have already argued that it is very important that China abrogate the death penalty for crimes such as theft, fraud, and smuggling, in line with a general trend to abolish the death penalty for economic crimes (R. Liu 2004, 2005; Zhao 2005a). Although the Eighth Amendment abolished 13 capital crimes (12 of which were nonviolent economic crimes) in the 2011 Criminal Law, the remaining 55 crimes eligible for the death penalty still leave much room for further discussion, considering the call for total abolition by the international community.

Second, when I compare the use of the death penalty with suspension to the use of the death penalty with immediate execution, my data show that the former far outnumbered the latter in these jurisdictions since 2009, perhaps because of the influence of the new "kill fewer" policy. In frequency rank, murder and drug selling accounted for the bulk of cases of the death penalty with immediate execution. In other words, offenders in these two types of crimes would likely face a high risk of execution if they were convicted. Unfortunately, as discussed earlier, these two types of crimes will most likely present the toughest challenges if China continues its abolition effort down the road.

Third, given the overall reduction trend (measured by reduced numbers) from 2009 to 2012 in both immediate execution and suspension cases and the increased percentage of death penalty with suspension cases (in contrast to cases of immediate execution), my data seem to lend support to the governmental statement that the "killing fewer and killing cautiously" policy has successfully reduced the use of capital punishment in China since the review and approval authority was reclaimed by the SPC in 2007. I truly welcome this trend and hope for more similar moves in the near future.

In discussing any proposal to abolish the death penalty in China, it is important to put things into perspective, given China's economic, political, legal, social, and cultural conditions. Before the passage of the Eighth Amendment to the Criminal Law, some Chinese scholars had already called for reform to abolish the death penalty, but opponents argued that it was too early for outright and complete abolition (R. Liu 2004; Zhao 2005a, 2005b). Within the academic community, it is now widely accepted that China should abolish its death penalty eventually, but that this requires gradual steps. As the chairmen of the Criminal Law Association (an official organization in China) and drafters of the Eighth Amendment, Gao Mingxuan and Zhao Bingzhi put forward a plan to abolish gradually the death penalty for nonviolent crimes and limit the use of the death penalty only to violent crimes (Gao, Su, & Yu 2010; Zhao 2005b). As for future plans, Gao insisted that crimes of corruption should still qualify for the death penalty (L. Wang 2011). In contrast, Zhao rejected the universal application of capital punishment for corruption cases and argued that capital punishment should be reserved for the most serious corruption cases, based on a case-by-case review (Zhao & Li 2010). In 2013, Zhao further argued that China should abolish the death penalty for drug crimes as well (Zhao & Yin 2013), which could be the future direction of death penalty reform in China.

Given the likely decline in executions in recent years, it seems that proposals by scholars such as Gao and Zhao have already broken ground, because Chinese judges are shown to have cut back the actual use of the death penalty, at least for some crimes. If this is true, more realistic proposals are needed, and, more important, these proposals need to be evaluated by the government and put into practice with the goal of gradually moving toward abolition of the death penalty in the long run, from fewer executions to no executions.

Any good proposal must be empirically based and tested, as I have tried to achieve in this chapter. What is needed is transparency and availability of reliable data. My statistical analysis of judgments in eight intermediate courts provides a glimpse into what is still regarded as a state secret in China. The global human rights movement has already prompted China to readjust its way of dealing with the death penalty. I am looking forward to the day when more reliable national statistics on the death penalty become available.

As my empirical data reveal, the death penalty in China is mainly applied to violent crimes and drug-related crimes. In my judgment, there is no doubt that China is capable of stopping the use of the death penalty for nonviolent crimes, such as economic crimes and corruption crimes, in practice (Y. Liu 2007; Yang 2013). To achieve gradual abolition, it is time to consider abolishing the death penalty for all crimes that are stipulated in law but never or rarely result in death sentences in practice. Special attention should also be given to drug crimes, since they represent a significant portion of the current death penalty regime in China. Therefore, as Zhao and Yin proposed, I hope that China will be able to abolish the death penalty for drug-related crimes no later than 2020 (Zhao & Yin 2013).

Although criminologists and legislators have expressed strong concern over the use of the death penalty for nonviolent crimes in China, their silence on violent crimes in past decades has not been helpful to China's restriction of the death penalty. I believe that it is time to turn our attention also to violent crimes because of the high ratio of executions that they account for. As Professor Mo's investigation indicated, 90.1% of practitioners in the criminal justice system (lawyers, judges, and procurators) agreed that the death penalty is legally appropriate for murder (Mo & Zeng 2009). There is still a long way to go before China abolishes capital punishment for violent crimes, which is not likely to happen unless the notion of retribution is changed or dampened (Y. Hu 1995; R. Liu 2005; Xia 2004). I am concerned that the current war on terror may lead to another round of strike-hard campaigns and increased use of the death penalty, negating what has been achieved in recent years, if the government chooses capital punishment to suppress the collective violence without showing mercy to guide the masses toward nonviolence.

Last but not least, wrongful convictions in capital cases in China (a topic not addressed in this chapter) have also pushed the SPC to review these cases with greater caution. Although many judgments of immediate execution were changed to the death penalty with suspension in wrongful conviction cases, convictions based on evidentiary and factual defects revealed the miscarriage of justice in China. How judges in intermediate and high courts acquit the innocent (many of whom have been jailed for a long time) is also significantly affecting criminal justice in China. Facing the war on terror and frequent terrorist attacks, how China will avoid resorting to a new wave of strike-hard campaigns and upholds the "killing fewer" policy toward the death penalty remains to be seen.

NOTES

1   It is asserted on the website of the Guangzhou Intermediate Court (http://www.gzcourt .org.cn/cpws/cpws/) that the judgments published in this column are designed for the inquiry of lawsuit parties or other citizens only, and that other uses are prohibited.
2   I reran my analyses with data from the Guangzhou Intermediate Court only (because the Guangzhou sample is the most representative one) and found similar patterns. As a result, I did not further distinguish Guangzhou data from Shanghai data.
3   Note that offenders who committed rape and money counterfeiting were all sentenced to the death penalty with immediate execution. However, the statistics are unreliable because there was only one offender for each of these two crimes.

REFERENCES

Amnesty International. (2013). *Amnesty International Report 2013: The State of the World's Human Rights*. Retrieved from http://files.amnesty.org/air13/Amnesty InternationalAnnualReport2013_complete_en.pdf.

Bakken, B. (2004). Moral panics, crime rates and harsh punishment in China. *Australian and New Zealand Journal of Criminology, 37*, 67–89.

Bakken, B. (2008). The culture of revenge and the power of politics: A comparative attempt to explain the punitive. *Journal of Power, 1*, 169–189.

Bakken, B. (2011). China, a punitive society? *Asian Journal of Criminology, 6*, 33–50.

Chen, X. (2013). Sixing zhengce zhi fali jiedu [Death penalty policies: A jurisprudential perception]. *Journal of Renmin University of China, 6*, 2–9.

Chen, X., & Zhou, G. (2011). *Xingfa shiyong zonglun jingshi* [Explaining General Part of Criminal Law]. Beijing: People's Court Press.

China Court Online. (2013, June 19). Zuigao fayuan kaiting fuhe sixingan, xi shouhui sixing hezhunquan hou shouci [Supreme Court reviews death penalty by trial, the first time after taking approval back]. Retrieved from http://www.chinacourt.org/article/detail/2013/06/id/1014830.shtml.

China's chief justice has harsh words for killers. (2008, April 12). *Eyewitness News*. Retrieved from http://abclocal.go.com/kabc/story?section=news/worldnews&id=6077085.

Death Penalty Worldwide. (2014, April 10). *China*. Retrieved from http://www.deathpenalty-worldwide.org/country-search-post.cfm?country=China.

Donohue, J., & Wolfers, J. (2006). Uses and abuses of empirical evidence in the death penalty debate. *Stanford Law Review, 58*, 791–846.

Donovan, S. (2012, December 11). Singapore to abolish death penalty for some drug couriers. *ABC News*. Retrieved from http://www.abc.net.au/news/2012-12-11/singapore-to-abolish-death-penalty-for-some-drug/4422304.

Dui Hua Foundation. (2014, August 2). *Criminal Justice: Death Penalty Reform*. Retrieved from http://duihua.org/wp/?page_id=136.

Edwards, G., Babor, T., Darke, S., Hall, S., Marsden, J., Miller, P., & West, R. (2010). Drug trafficking: Time to abolish the death penalty. *International Journal of Mental Health and Addiction, 8*, 616–619.

Gallahue, P., & Lines, R. (2013, October 24). The death penalty for drug offences: Global view 2010. International Harm Reduction Association. Retrieved from http://www.hrdp.org/files/2013/10/24/IHRA_DeathPenaltyReport_2010.pdf.

Gao, M., Su, H., & Yu, Z. (2010). Congci tashang feichu sixing de zhengtu sixing wenti sanren tan [On the way of abolishing the death penalty: Discussion of Criminal Law Eighth Amendment]. *Journal of Legal Science, 9*, 3–15.

The growing synthetic drug crimes and abusers in China [Zhongguo hecheng dupin fanzui anjianshu chixu shangsheng, xiaofei renqunduo]. (2012, July 3). *China*

News. Retrieved from http://www.chinanews.com/fz/2012/07-03/4003772 .shtml.

He, R. (2013). Dangqian woguo dupin fanzui sixing xianzhi yu feichu de zhuyao zhangai yu duice [The block and countermeasure toward abolishing and restricting the death penalty for drug crime]. *Journal of Fazhi, 6,* 25–32.

He, R., & Mo, H. (2012). Dupin fanzui sixing de guoji kaocha jiqi dui woguo de jiejian [A review of the death penalty for drug crimes and what China should learn from international society]. *Journal of Huazhong University of Science and Technology (Social Science), 2,* 66–71.

He, X., & Su, Y. (2013). Do the haves come out ahead in Shanghai Court? *Journal of Empirical Legal Studies, 10,* 121–146.

Hood, R. (1996). Death penalty: The USA in world perspective. *Journal of Transnational Law and Policy, 6,* 517–542.

Hood, R. (2001). Capital punishment: A global perspective. *Punishment and Society, 3,* 331–354.

Hood, R. (2009). Abolition of the death penalty: China in world perspective. *City University of Hong Kong Law Review, 1,* 1–21.

Hood, R., & Hoyle, C. (2008). *The Death Penalty: A Worldwide Perspective* (4th ed.). New York: Oxford University Press.

Hu, D. (2012, June 13). Fayuan: dupin fanzuian zhunian shangsheng [Court: Growing cases of drug crimes]. *China Daily.* Retrieved from http://www.chinadaily .com.cn/hqgj/jryw/2012-06-13/content_6166782.html.

Hu, Y. (1995). *Sixing tonglun* [A General Discussion of the Death Penalty]. Beijing: China University of Political Science and Law Press.

Iran Human Rights. (May 28, 2014). *Annual Report on the Death Penalty in Iran 2013.* Retrieved from http://iranhr.net/wp-content/uploads/2014/03/Rapport -iran-2014-GB-030314-bd-e.pdf.

Jiang, S., Lambert, E., & Nathan, V. (2009). Reasons for death penalty attitudes among Chinese citizens: Retributive or instrumental? *Journal of Criminal Justice, 37,* 225–233.

Jiang, S., Lambert, E., Wang, J., Saito, T., & Pilot, R. (2010). Death penalty views in China, Japan and the U.S.: An empirical comparison. *Journal of Criminal Justice, 38,* 862–869.

Johnson, D., & Zimring, E. (2009). *The Next Frontier: National Development, Political Change, and the Death Penalty in Asia.* New York: Oxford University Press.

Kirby, J. (2013, October 30). Death penalty support vs. violent crime: Two graphs with very similar arcs. *New Republic*. Retrieved from http://www.newrepublic.com/article/115—405/death-penalty-support-and-violent-crime-there-correlation.

Li, S. (2011). *Dupin fanzui xingfa wenti yanjiu* [Research on Issues Relating to Drug Crime in the Criminal Law]. Beijing: China Procuratorial Press.

Li, W. (2008). Cong sixing zhuangkuang kan zhongguo renquan [Studying the human rights of China by the death penalty]. *Modern China Tribune, 8*, 77–79.

Liang, B., Lu, H., Miethe, T., & Zhang, L. (2006). Sources of variation in pro-death penalty attitudes in China: An exploratory study of Chinese students at home and abroad. *British Journal of Criminology, 46*, 119–130.

Lin, J. (2004, April 12). Guangzhou zhongyuan panjueshu 'wuyi' qi shangwang shimin ke chaxun [Citizens can access online judgments in Guangzhou Intermediate Court after May 1st]. *Neteasy*. Retrieved from http://tech.163.com/04/0412/10/0JOT3FQB00-0915CN.html.

Liu, R. (2004). Sixing zhengce: quanqiu shiye ji zhongguo shijiao [A global view of death penalty policy and China's perspective]. *Journal of Comparative Law, 4*, 77–89.

Liu, R. (2005). Sixing yanjiu fangfalun [Research methodology of the death penalty]. *Peking University Law Journal, 5*, 631–639.

Liu, Y. (2007). Jingji fanzui sixing lifa de duowei fenxi [Multidimensional analysis for the death penalty legislation of economic crimes]. *Modern Law Science, 6*, 176–182.

Lu, H., & Miethe, T. (2007). *China's Death Penalty: History, Law, and Contemporary Practices*. New York: Routledge.

Lu, H., & Zhang, L. (2005). Death penalty in China: The law and the practice. *Journal of Criminal Justice, 33*, 367–376.

Macbean, N., & Li, Q. (2003, December). The death penalty in China: A baseline document—Strengthening the defence in death penalty cases in the People's Republic of China. European Initiative for Democracy and Human Rights. Retrieved from http://www.ecba.org/extdocserv/DP_Baseline.pdf.

Mei, C., & Xu, Y. (2006). Dupin fanzui de xingfa shiyong wenti sikao: jianlun dupin fanzui shiyong sixing [On applying penalty to drug crimes: The death penalty for drug crimes]. *Journal of Gansu Institute of Political Science and Law, 3*, 93–98.

Miao, M. (2013). Capital punishment in China: A populist instrument of social governance. *Theoretical Criminology, 17*, 233–250.

Mo, H., & Zeng, Y. (2009). Zhongguo sixing wenti shizheng yanjiu: dui jing e falv shiwujie de diaocha fangtan [Empirical studies on the issues of applying the death penalty in China: A survey of professionals in Beijing and Hubei Province]. *Journal of Henan Administrative Institute of Politics and Law, 3*, 14–19.

Nathan, A., & Gilley, B. (2003). *China's New Rulers: The Secret Files*. New York: New York Review of Books.

Nie, L. (2008). Woguo qiangjie zui sixing shiyong kongzhi yanjiu [Investigation into judicial controls on the application of the death penalty for robbery crimes in China]. *Political Science and Law, 11*, 21–25.

Placais, A. (2014, March 24). China rejects all UN recommendations on death penalty use. *World Coalition*. Retrieved from http://www.worldcoalition.org/china-un-death-penalty-upr-recommendations-capital-crimes.html.

Qi, J. (2007). Sixing wenti diaocha baogao [Investigative report on death penalty issues]. In W. Gao et al. (Eds.), *Zhongguo sixing wenti de shehuixue yanjiu* [Social Science Research on Issues of the Death Penalty in China] (pp. 198–222). Beijing: Peoples' Public Security University Press.

Roney, T. (2014, March 28). China dismisses Amnesty's death penalty report: China rejects an Amnesty International report naming China the world's top executioner in 2013. *Diplomat*. Retrieved April 25, 2014, from http://thediplomat.com/2014/03/china-dis—misses-amnestys-death-penalty-report/.

Shao, X. (2005). Sixing Fuhequan xiafang yu huishou de sanwei sikao [A three-dimensional thinking of death penalty: Authorizing lower court and taking back]. *Peking University Law Journal, 5*, 585–597.

Smith, C. (2009, October 24). China must show mercy. *Guardian*. Retrieved May 21, 2014, from http://www.guardian.co.uk/commentisfree/libertycentral/2009/oct/24/china-death-penalty.

Standing Committee of the National People's Congress. (1982, March 8). *Guanyu yancheng pohuai jingji de zuifan de jueding* [Decree on severely punishing criminals who disturb national economic order]. Retrieved from http://www.npc.gov.cn/wxzl/gongbao/2000-12/06/content_5004412.htm.

Standing Committee of the National People's Congress. (1983, September 2). *Guanyu yancheng yanzhong weihai shehui zhian de fanzui fenzi de jueding* [Decree on severely punishing criminals who threaten public security]. Retrieved March 22, 2014, from http://www.npc.gov.cn/wxzl/gongbao/2000-12/06/content_5004438.htm.

Supreme People's Court of the People's Republic of China. (2013, November 13). *Guanyu renmin fayuan zai hulianwang gongbu caipan wenshu de guiding* [Rules about court publishing judgments online]. No. 26 Law-Interpretation 2013. Retrieved April 26, 2014, from http://www.chinacourt.org/article/detail/2013/11/id/1152212.shtml.

36 representatives of NPC submitting proposal to call for abolishing death penalty for illegal fund-raising [36 ming quanguo renda daibiao lianhe tiyi feichu jizi zhapianzui sixing]. *Dahe*. Retrieved March 10, 2014, from http://law.dahe.cn/108/20140310/455466.html.

Trevaskes, S. (2008). The death penalty in China today: Kill fewer, kill cautiously. Asian Survey, 48, 393–413.

Trevaskes, S. (2012). *The Death Penalty in Contemporary China*. New York: Palgrave Macmillan.

Wang, L. (2011, March 11). Zhongguo xingfaxue kaituozhe Gao Mingxuan: tanfu zuixing buyi quxiao sixing [The pioneer of Chinese Criminal Law Gao Mingxuan suggests not abolishing the death penalty for corruption crimes]. Retrieved May 8, 2014, from http://news.eastday.com/c/2011lh/u1a5776032.html.

Wang, Y. (2008). The death penalty and society in contemporary China. *Punishment and Society, 10*, 137–151.

World Coalition. (2014, April 10). *China, Asia (Eastern Asia)*. Retrieved from http://www.worldcoalition.org/China.

Xia, Y. (2004). Zhongguo feichu sixing yingyou de guannian zhunbei [Proper conceptive preparation for abolishing the death penalty in China]. In X. Chen (Ed.), *Sixing wenti yanjiu* [Research on Death Penalty Issues] (pp. 257–267). Beijing: Chinese People's Security University Press.

Xie, C. (2009, July 29). Fewer executions expected, top judge says. *China Daily*. Retrieved from http://www.chinadaily.com.cn/china/2009-07/29/content_8484062.htm.

Xiong, M. (2013). Woguo fajinxing zai renshi: jiyu kuaguo bijiao de zhuizong yanjiu (1945–2011) [Rethinking of fine in China: A cross-national perspectives tracking (1945–2011)]. *Tsinghua Law Review, 5*, 86–111.

Xiong, M., Jiang, L., & Chen, S. (2013). Shengming zhouqi yanjiu: xingbie, nianling yu fanzui [Research on the life span: Gender, sex and crime in China]. *Juvenile Delinquency Issues, 1*, 75–82.

Yang, M. (2013, September 3). Zhongguo sanshinian nei buhui quxiao tanwu huilu zui sixing [China would not abolish the death penalty of embezzlement and bribery-taking within thirty years]. *Legal Daily*, p. A004.

Yu, Z. (2009). Abolition or retention: Rethinking the death penalty in China. *China Social Science, 2*, 178–190.

Yuan, D. (2014, June 2). Zuigaofa xiangjie weihezhun Tang Hui nüer bei qiangpo maiyinan liang zhufan sixing yuanyou [Supreme People's Court explains the reason: Why it disapproved the death penalty to two principals who forced Tang Hui's daughter to prostitution]. Retrieved from http://www.legaldaily.com.cn/index_article/content/2014/06/12/content_5592604.htm.

Zhang, H. (2011). *Dupin fanzui zhengyi wenti yanjiu* [A Study on the Contesting Issues Relating to Drug Cases]. Beijing: China Law Press.

Zhao, B. (2005a). Zhongguo zhubu feizhi sixing lungang [Abolition of the death penalty in China]. *Law Science, 1,* 55–62.

Zhao, B. (2005b). Lun zhongguo feibaoli fangzui sixing de zhubu feizhi [On abolition of the death penalty of nonviolent crimes in China]. *Tribune of Political Science and Law, 1,* 92–99.

Zhao, B., & Li, H. (2010). Tanwu huilu fanzui sixing de sifa kongzhi: yi xingshi shitifa kongzhi wei shijiao [Judicial control of the death penalty for corruption and bribery crimes: A perspective on the criminal law]. *Journal of People's Procuratorial Semimonthly, 15,* 12–19.

Zhao, B., & Yin, J. (2011). Guyi sharen zui sixing sifa kongzhi lungang [Outline of judicial controls relating to intentional homicide in death penalty cases]. In B. Zhao (Ed.), *Sixing shiyong biaozhun yanjiu* [Research on Standards for Application of the Death Penalty] (pp. 161–172). Beijing: China Legal.

Zhao, B., & Yin, J. (2013). Lun zhongguo dupinfanzui sixing de zhubu feizhi [Abolishing death penalty for drug crimes in China step by step]. *Law Science Magazine, 5,* 1–12.

9

Public Opinion and the Death Penalty

▸ SHANHE JIANG

PUBLIC OPINION IS AN IMPORTANT FACTOR that affects the death penalty, although it is not a determining factor. In a democratic society, government officials, legislators, and jurists often use public opinion as a factor to determine whether capital punishment should be retained or abolished (Schabas 2004). In a socialist society such as China, government officials, lawmakers, and courts also frequently use public opinion to guide death penalty law and policy (Lu & Miethe 2007). In addition, both retentionists and abolitionists use public opinion to defend their arguments on capital punishment (Schabas 2004).

Although there are many polls on the death penalty in the United States, no similar national polls have been conducted in China. Using the traditional case study approach, the Chinese government may have investigated its citizens' attitudes toward capital punishment, but no statistical data are available for the general public (Jiang & Wang 2008; Lu & Miethe 2007). Besides polls, there are many empirical studies of capital punishment in the United States. However, survey-based studies of the death penalty are rare in China.

China is one of the oldest civilized countries and a Confucian society. Confucianism strongly believes that social order should be maintained through education and family rather than punishment (Jiang, Lambert, & Wang 2007). China is also a socialist country. "Socialist countries were generally committed to the abolition of the death penalty" (Lu & Zhang 2005:368). However, China has used capital punishment for thousands of years (Jiang et al. 2007; Liang, Lu, Miethe, & Zhang 2006; Lu & Miethe 2007), although it may have experienced some short periods of death penalty abolition in its history (Johnson & Zimring 2009; Wang 2004).[1] According to Hewitt, Regoli, Regoli, and Iadicola (2004), China's death penalty can be traced back to the Xia dynasty (2207–1766 B.C.). In the Shang dynasty (sixteenth to eleventh centuries B.C.), the legal code included capital punishment as one of its Old Five Punishments (face tattooing, nose amputation, feet amputation, castration, and the death penalty) (Liang et al. 2006; Lu & Miethe 2007). Although China's legal code changed from time to time, the death penalty was retained as one punishment before the People's Republic of China (1949–present). Major reasons for supporting the death penalty throughout Chinese history have been its functions, including deterrence, retribution, and incapacitation (Jiang et al. 2007).

Like traditional China, the People's Republic of China continues to use the death penalty. The current government and many legal scholars strongly believe that the death penalty has general deterrence and educational values (Hu 2002). They also believe that executing a person will prevent him or her from killing again (Jiang & Wang 2008). The deputy director of China's Supreme People's Court, Wan E'xiang, argued in 2005 that abolishing the death penalty is almost beyond discussion in China because of the millennium-old notion of retribution in people's minds (Jiang et al. 2007). Today, China executes more people than any other country (Bakken 2012).[2] Do China's current death penalty law and practice reflect its people's views or attitudes toward capital punishment? If so, is their support level higher than that of their counterparts in other nations? Why do Chinese people support the death penalty? This chapter will address these questions by reviewing previous empirical research, published in extant studies of death penalty views.

Before presenting empirical findings from extant studies, it is helpful to clarify what is meant by *public opinion*. Literally, *public opinion* means opinions of the public. Public opinion is a form of collective views, expressed by those who are debating or talking about a given social issue at any one time. Given this definition, there are many publics. This chapter focuses on the quantitative analyses of citizens' attitudes toward the death penalty from extant studies. The public will include college students and the general public, as well as criminal justice professionals in China. Relative to the general public, opinions of criminal justice professionals and governmental officials would potentially have greater impact on lawmaking and implementation and sway opinions of laypeople. Also, existing research on death penalty views has limited coverage of criminal justice professionals and governmental officials, and opinions from some influential legal professionals and officials will be elaborated in the discussion section.

SURVEYS OF THE DEATH PENALTY: DESCRIPTIVE SUMMARY OF DIFFERENT STUDIES

Support Level for the Death Penalty in China

Table 9.1 shows 13 studies of death penalty views based on 10 surveys of Chinese people. These 10 surveys were intermittently conducted from 1988 to 2008. Most surveys used the nonrandom sampling method due to limited funding or the sensitivity of the topic in China. Among the 10 surveys, 6 surveyed college students, 3 surveyed ordinary Chinese citizens, and 1 surveyed criminal justice professionals. General support for the death penalty varied from 58 to 97%. Comparatively, college students had lower levels of support than ordinary citizens and criminal justice professionals.

Question Wording and Support for the Death Penalty

A respondent's support for the death penalty may be affected by question wording (Cullen, Fisher, & Applegate 2000; Ellsworth & Ross 1983; Hewitt et al. 2004; Oberwittler & Qi 2009). Table 9.2 lists questions regarding death penalty views from studies in table 9.1. Findings from Liang et al. (2006), Qi and Oberwittler (2009), and Oberwittler and Qi (2009) indicate that question wording does make a difference. All three studies show that when life imprisonment, especially life imprisonment without parole, was used as an alternative sanction, support for the death penalty decreased (see Oberwittler & Qi 2009 for references). Moreover, descriptive statistics and qualitative information shown in tables 9.1 and 9.2 indicate that even though the same question or very similar questions are used, support for the death penalty varies by time, space, and type of respondents. For example, college students generally had lower levels of support for the death penalty than ordinary citizens. Overseas Chinese students were more likely to support the death penalty than their counterparts in China.

TABLE 9.1 Surveys of Death Penalty Views Among Chinese People in China and Overseas

STUDY	RESPONDENTS	SAMPLE AND SURVEY YEAR	SAMPLE SIZE	SUPPORT FOR DEATH PENALTY (%)
Hu (2000)	Citizens	Not clear	5,006	97
Cao & Cullen (2001)	College students	Nonrandom, 1988	203	78.2
Jia (2005)	College students	Nonrandom	1,873	75.8
Liang, Lu, Miethe, & Zhang (2006)	Two samples of Chinese students: 60 from China and 57 from the United States	Nonrandom, 2004	117	83 for the sample in the United States; 62.7 for the sample in China
Jiang, Lambert, & Wang (2007)	College students	Nonrandom, 2005	524[a]	70
Jiang & Wang (2008)	College students	Nonrandom, 2005	524[a]	70
Qi & Oberwittler (2009)	Chinese students in Germany	Nonrandom, 2007	896	69
Oberwittler & Qi (2009)	Citizens	Random sample from Hubei, Guangdong, and Beijing, 2007–8	4,472	57.8
Jiang, Lambert, & Nathan (2009)	College students and ordinary citizens	Nonrandom, 2006	109	83.5
Kuang, Zeng, Li, Liu, Chen, Dai, & Zhang (2010)	Criminal justice professionals	Nonrandom, 2007–8	455	91.2
Jiang, Lambert, Wang, Saito, & Pilot (2010)	College students	Nonrandom, 2005	524[a]	70
Wu, Sun, & Wu (2011)	College students	Nonrandom, 2008	422	71–77
Lambert, Jiang, Elechi, Khondaker, Baker, & Wang (2014)	College students	Nonrandom, 2005	524[a]	70

[a] These four studies in this table used the same data set.

TABLE 9.2 Question Wording and Support for Capital Punishment

STUDY	QUESTION	SUPPORT FOR DEATH PENALTY (%)
Hu (2000)	What is your attitude toward the death penalty?	97
	a. Too many death penalties.	3.1
	b. Not too many death penalties.	42.2
	c. The number of death penalties is appropriate.	31.4
	d. Too few death penalties.	22.5
	e. Death penalty may be imposed on any kind of crime.	.8
Cao & Cullen (2001)	I believe that capital punishment should be used because people who take a life deserve to be punished by having their own life taken.	
	a. agree	78.2
	b. undecided	7.4
	c. disagree	14.4
Jia (2005)	Do you support the death penalty? (yes/no)	75.8
Liang, Lu, Miethe, & Zhang (2006)	1. Are you in favor of the death penalty as punishment for a criminal offense? (yes/no)	83/62.7[a]
	2. What do you think should be the penalty for the most serious offense (e.g. murder)?	
	a. death penalty	68.4/52.6[a]
	b. life imprisonment/other	31.6/47.4[a]
Jiang, Lambert, & Wang (2007)	I support the death penalty (Likert scale).	70
Jiang et al. (2008)	I support the death penalty (Likert scale).	70
Qi & Oberwittler (2009)	1. In general, do you favor or oppose the death penalty?	
	a. yes	69.0
	b. not sure	11.8
	c. no	19.3
	2. Do you oppose the abolition of the death penalty if an alternative to the death penalty is	
	a. life imprisonment without parole	about 52[b]
	b. life imprisonment with parole	about 65
	c. (a) plus prisoners' earning are given to the victims	about 50
Oberwittler & Qi (2009)	1. In general, do you favor or oppose the use of the death penalty?	
	a. yes	57.8
	b. not sure	28.2
	c. no	14.0

Continued

TABLE 9.2 *(Continued)*

STUDY	QUESTION	SUPPORT FOR DEATH PENALTY (%)
	2. Do you oppose the abolition of the death penalty If an alternative to the death penalty is	
	a. life imprisonment without parole	About 30[b]
	b. life imprisonment with parole	About 37
	c. (a) plus prisoners' earning are given to the victims	About 24
Jiang, Lambert, & Nathan (2009)	I support the death penalty (Likert scale).	83.5
Kuang, Zeng, Li, Liu, Chen, Dai, & Zhang (2010)	In general, do you favor or oppose the death penalty? (yes/no)	91.2
Jiang, Lambert, Wang, Saito, & Pilot (2010)	I support the death penalty (Likert scale).	70
Wu, Sun, & Wu (2011)	(1) The death penalty is necessary to maintain law and order.	
	a. strongly disagree	7.8
	b. disagree	20.9
	c. agree	28.0
	d. strongly agree	43.4
	(2) The death penalty should be used because people who take a life or bring severe harm to others and the society deserve to be punished by having their own life taken.	
	a. strongly disagree	5.9
	b. disagree	16.8
	c. agree	34.4
	d. strongly agree	42.9
	(3) No one including the State has the right to take away life.	
	a. strongly disagree	30.8
	b. disagree	46.9
	c. agree	15.9
	d. strongly agree	6.4
Lambert, Jiang, Elechi, Khondaker, Baker, & Wang (2014)	I support the death penalty (Likert scale).	70

[a] The first number is for the U.S. sample, while the second number is for the Chinese sample.

[b] The percentages were not provided in the studies, so they were estimated from an eyeball observation of the graph. In addition, in the data from China, about 26% of the respondents were undecided about the question.

Types of Offenses and Support for the Death Penalty

Four of these studies surveyed death penalty views on different crimes. Results in table 9.3 clearly indicate that the types of offenses matter with regard to death penalty views. It is no surprise that support for the death penalty for murder is higher than for any other offenses among the four studies in the table. Support for the death penalty for rape or sexual abuse of a girl under the age of 14 is the second highest among the list of offenses in the table and is consistent among the four studies. Among criminal justice professionals surveyed by Kuang et al. (2010), support for the death penalty for robbery was higher than that for economic crimes, such as corruption and embezzlement. However, it is surprising that support for capital punishment for economic crimes was higher than that for robbery among college students and ordinary citizens. With regard to capital punishment for intentional assault resulting in death, there was also a significant difference between criminal justice professionals and citizens who were not criminal justice professionals. That is, the support level among ordinary citizens and students was higher than that among criminal justice professionals. The majority of criminal justice professionals (Kuang et al. 2010) and college students (Qi & Oberwittler 2009) supported capital punishment for terrorism (82% and 81%, respectively), whereas fewer than 50% of ordinary citizens (Oberwittler & Qi 2009) did so.

GENERAL PERSPECTIVES AND CORRELATES OF DEATH PENALTY VIEWS

In Western societies in general and in the United States in particular, four major conceptual perspectives are found to be related to attitudes toward the death penalty: deterrence, retribution, incapacitation, and rehabilitation (Bohm 1987; Jiang et al. 2007; Lambert, Clarke, & Lambert, 2004; Miethe & Lu 2005).

The fundamental idea of the deterrence perspective is based on utilitarian philosophy, in which "individuals freely choose between alternative courses of action to maximize pleasure and minimize pain" (Miethe & Lu 2005:20). The core idea of the deterrence perspective is that a society "must punish offenders to discourage others from committing similar offenses; we punish past offenders to send a message to potential offenders"

TABLE 9.3 Support for the Death Penalty for Specific Offenses

	QI & OBERWITTLER (2009)		OBERWITTLER & QI (2009)		JIA (2005): SHOULD THE LAW HAVE THE DEATH PENALTY FOR THE FOLLOWING OFFENSES? (%)			KUANG, ZENG, LI, LIU, CHEN, DAI, & ZHANG (2010) (% OF SUPPORT BELOW)	
OFFENSES	SUPPORT LEVEL <50%	SUPPORT LEVEL =50% OR HIGHER	SUPPORT LEVEL <50%	SUPPORT LEVEL =50% OR HIGHER	SHOULD	NO OPPOSITION	SHOULD NOT	DEATH PENALTY	OTHER PENALTY
Murder	—	x	—	x	58.3	35.8	6	89.9	10.1
Intentional assault resulting death	n/a[a]	—	—	x	—	—	—	37.1	62.9
Drug dealing	—	x	—	x	41.1[b]	35.7	22.7	75.7	24.3
Sexual abuse of a girl under age 14	—	x	—	x	52.9	32.4	14.4	62.7	37.3
Terrorism	—	x	x	—	—	—	—	82.0	18.0

Producing fake medicines	x	—	n/a	—	—	—	47.9	52.1
Counterfeiting	x	—	x	—	—	—	15.2	84.8
Theft	x	—	x	—	—	—	29.6	70.4
Corruption	x	—	x	41.1[b]	35.7	22.7	36.1	63.9
Raping an adult woman	x	—	x	52.9	32.4	14.4	32.7	67.3
Embezzlement	x	—	n/a	41.1[b]	35.7	22.7	31.7	68.3
Organizing prostitution	x	—	x	—	—	—	23.0	77.0
Espionage	x	—	x	48.4	30.6	20.3	40.9	59.1
Robbery	x	—	x	27.3	49.8	22.9	68.6	31.4
Intentional assault	x	—	n/a	—	—	—	—	—
Military crimes	x	—	n/a	36.5	41.4	21.6	—	—

[a] N/a = not applicable.
[b] For Jia's study (2005), the reason for three rows with the same numbers in this table is that different offenses in those rows were surveyed by a single question.

(Radelet & Borg 2000:44). In regard to the death penalty, this general deterrence is based on whether executing convicted murderers (with great certainty and swiftness) will prevent other people from committing murder (Bohm 1987; Radelet & Borg 2000).

Retribution is a perspective that influences what people regard as just and moral punishments for a crime (Jiang & Wang 2008; Radelet & Borg 2000). Its punishment philosophy lies in equity, proportionality, and blameworthiness. It is related to people's attitudes toward punishment in general and capital punishment in particular. This perspective is based on the principle of the *lex talionis*, or "an eye for an eye." It refers to the idea that "if a person takes a life, then he or she must sacrifice his or her own life" (Lambert et al. 2004:7).

The third general perspective on capital punishment is incapacitation. Like deterrence, the fundamental idea of incapacitation is based on utilitarian philosophy. According to this perspective, the ultimate goal of punishment is to eliminate an individual's opportunity to commit a crime through a variety of physical restraints on his or her actions (Meithe & Lu 2005). People in China who hold this perspective believe that executing a person is the most effective way to prevent him or her from killing again because "the murderers sentenced to life may be released again to prey upon innocent citizens" (Jiang & Wang 2008:26).

The fourth perspective associated with people's attitudes toward capital punishment is rehabilitation. According to this perspective, "We [society] punish for the treatment and reform of offenders.... The ultimate goal of rehabilitation is to restore a convicted offender to a constructive place in society through some combination of treatment, education, and training" (Miethe & Lu 2005:22). Proponents of the rehabilitation perspective tend to view offenders as sick people and in need of help. The goal of rehabilitation is to help offenders reenter society, not to permanently remove them (Jiang et al. 2007). Given these underlying principles of rehabilitation, scholars argue that people who support rehabilitation are more likely to oppose the death penalty than those who do not support rehabilitation (Jiang et al. 2007; Jiang & Wang 2008; Lambert et al. 2004).

Scholars of China suggest that the views of deterrence, retribution, and incapacitation have long existed in China. For example, a general deterrence perspective is reflected in the Chinese popular sayings "Executing one deters one hundred" and "killing a chicken to scare the monkey" (Jiang &

Wang 2008; Jin 1997; Liang et al. 2006; Lu & Zhang 2005; Ma 1997). Similarly, the sayings "A tooth for a tooth" and "The killer should be killed" reflect a retribution perspective (Jiang & Wang 2008; Jin 1997; Liang et al. 2006). Retribution is an obvious reason for Chinese officials' support for the death penalty in today's China (Jiang & Wang 2008). Jiang and Wang (2008) suggest that incapacitation is also an important reason that the Chinese support the death penalty. Since money and personal connections in China can manipulate the early release of inmates sentenced to imprisonment for life, many Chinese people believe that only the death penalty can take evildoers away from society permanently (Jin 1997).

A few empirical studies have examined the prevalence of the four general perspectives of punishment and their impact on death penalty views in China. Table 9.4 lists the findings of prevalence of the four perspectives. Cao and Cullen (2001) reported that the majority of the respondents considered retribution (78.2%), deterrence (53%) and incapacitation (82.1%) the reasons that they supported the death penalty. Liang et al. (2006) found that on average, more than 50% of the respondents cited deterrence as the reason for their support of capital punishment. Furthermore, Chinese college students in the United States were more likely to cite deterrence as the reason for their support of the death penalty than their counterparts in China. Jiang et al. (2007) used multiple questions to measure deterrence and retribution. According to table 9.4, answers to three of the four questions indicate that the majority of respondents considered deterrence the reason for their support for capital punishment. In addition, answers to deterrence-related questions indicate that question wording affects the result, even though all four questions measure deterrence based on a factor analysis. In the same study, three questions were used to measure retribution, and only one question received a 50% or higher level of "agree" or "strongly agree," indicating that question wording matters. Table 9.4 also shows that more than 60% of the respondents chose incapacitation as a reason for supporting capital punishment.

Jiang, Lambert, and Nathan (2009) used the same questions as Jiang et al. (2007) to measure deterrence, retribution, and incapacitation. Although the latter surveyed only college students, the former surveyed both college students and urban and rural residents in China. For all four questions measuring deterrence, more than 50% of respondents believed that capital punishment has a deterrent effect. Compared with Jiang et al. (2007), Jiang et al.

TABLE 9.4 Prevalence of Deterrence, Retribution, Incapacitation, and Rehabilitation (%)

STUDIES AND ITEMS	STRONGLY DISAGREE	DISAGREE	UNDECIDED	AGREE	STRONGLY AGREE
CAO & CULLEN (2001)					
Retribution: Capital punishment should be used because people take a life deserve to be punished by having their own life taken.	—	14.4	7.4	78.2	—
Deterrence: Punishing criminals more harshly would reduce crime by setting an example and showing others in society that crime does not pay.	—	33.7	13.4	53.0	—
Incapacitation: Even if prisons cannot deter or rehabilitate criminals, long prison sentences are needed so that we can keep habitual and dangerous offenders off our streets.	—	12.4	5.5	82.1	—
LIANG, LU, MIETHE, & ZHANG (2006)					
General deterrence (China sample)	—	25.0	31.7	43.3	—
General deterrence (overseas students in the United States)	—	17.5	19.3	63.2	—
Specific deterrence (China sample)	—	15.0	30.0	55.0	—
Specific deterrence (overseas students in the United States)	—	8.8	24.6	66.7	—
JIANG, LAMBERT, & WANG (2007)					
Deterrence items					
The death penalty is a more effective deterrent than life imprisonment.	4	25	20	30	21
I feel that the death penalty deters others from commiting crimes.	4	21	21	43	10

The death penalty punishment is a powerful deterrent to crime.	2	11	14	54	20
The death penalty will deter people from committing murder.	3	23	28	39	7
Retribution items					
I believe in the idea of an eye for an eye, a life for a life.	10	39	21	24	5
Society has a right to seek revenge on violent criminals.	5	25	19	39	11
Murderers deserve the death penalty since they took a life.	4	28	30	29	9
Incapacitation item					
Death is the ultimate incapacitation of a violent criminal.	3	22	13	44	18
Rehabilitation item					
The main goals for dealing with criminals should be to treat and rehabilitate them.	3	12	16	49	20
JIANG, LAMBERT, & NATHAN (2009)					
Deterrence items					
The death penalty is a more effective deterrent than life imprisonment.	3.7	17.4	12.8	36.7	29.4
I feel that the death penalty deters others from committing crimes.	2.8	10.1	11.9	48.6	26.6
The death penalty punishment is a powerful deterrent to crime.	2.8	19.3	27.5	37.6	12.8
The death penalty will deter people from committing murder.	1.8	8.3	9.2	70.6	10.1
Retribution items					
I believe in the idea of an eye for an eye, a life for a life.	13.8	30.3	16.5	24.8	14.7
Society has a right to seek revenge on violent criminals.	9.2	30.3	9.2	39.4	11.9
Murderers deserve the death penalty since they took a life.	1.8	1.0	20.2	44.0	22.9

Continued

TABLE 9.4 (Continued)

STUDIES AND ITEMS	STRONGLY DISAGREE	DISAGREE	UNDECIDED	AGREE	STRONGLY AGREE
Incapacitation item					
Death is the ultimate incapacitation of a violent criminal.	1.8	13.8	8.3	56.9	19.3
Oberwittler & Qi (2009)					
Deterrence items					
The abolition of the death penalty would immediately cause an increase of crime in China.	—	17.4	19.0	63.6	—
Among all the variable punishments, the death penalty deters crimes most.	—	22.4	19.0	58.6	—
Retribution items					
People who take a life deserve to be punished by having their own life taken.	—	12.4	9.4	78.1	—
The death penalty restores feelings of right and wrong in our society.	—	23.2	28.4	48.4	—
Incapacitation item					
Only execution can guarantee that a serious offender will not commit further crime.	—	35.6	17.9	46.5	—
Rehabilitation item					
Criminals can all be rehabilitated, so execution is unnecessary.	—	37.2	20.3	42.5	—

(2009) found a higher level of overall agreement on the deterrence questions, indicating that ordinary citizens may be more supportive of the death penalty than college students. Jiang et al. (2009) also found a higher level of overall agreement on the three retribution questions and a higher level of agreement on the incapacitation question.

The last study shown in table 9.4 is that of Oberwittler and Qi (2009). For the two questions measuring deterrence, approximately 60% of respondents believed in the deterrent effect of the death penalty. For the two retribution items, 78% of respondents agreed that "people who take a life deserve to be punished by having their own life taken," while only 48% of respondents agreed that "the death penalty restores feelings of right and wrong in our society." Oberwittler and Qi (2009) also found that about 47% of respondents believed in the incapacitation effect of capital punishment, a percentage lower than those reported by Cao and Cullen (2001), Jiang et al. (2007), and Jiang et al. (2009).

Table 9.5 presents the predictors of death penalty views in China. Results shown in the table are taken from five studies. All five of these studies used multiple regressions. Liang et al. (2006) found that perceived crime prevalence led to more support for the death penalty, and male respondents were more likely to support the death penalty than their female counterparts. Jiang and Wang (2008) found that college students who believed in the deterrent effect of capital punishment were more likely to support the death penalty than those who did not believe in it. Also, college students who believed in retribution had higher levels of support for the death penalty than those who did not. Compared with other studies shown in table 9.5, Qi and Oberwittler (2009) included fewer predictors in their regression model and found that a punitive orientation in sentencing led to higher levels of support for the death penalty among Chinese students studying in Germany. Finally, Wu, Sun, and Wu (2011) found that several variables, including victimization and three attitude variables, were related to death penalty views among college students in China. However, none of them measured the four general perspectives of punishment: deterrence, retribution, incapacitation, and rehabilitation.

TABLE 9.5 Correlates of Death Penalty Views in China

VARIABLES / STUDIES	LIANG, LU, MIETHE, & ZHANG (2006)	JIANG & WANG (2008)	JIANG, LAMBERT, & NATHAN (2009)	QI & OBERWITTLER (2009)	WU, SUN, & WU (2011)
Deterrence	.74[a]	.231***	.174*	—	—
Retribution	—	.228***	.156*	—	—
Incapacitation	—	.108	-.138	—	—
Rehabilitation	—	-.268	—	-.05	—
Wrongful execution	—	-.082	.084	—	—
Crime severity	1.28*	.032	.093	—	—
Confidence in government	—	.158	—	—	—
Fear of crime	.72	—	—	-.04	.01
Victimization	1.43	—	—	—	.08**
Crime-control orientation	—	—	—	—	.09**
Punitiveness in sentencing	—	—	—	.40***	.19***
Punitiveness in incarceration	—	—	—	—	.26***
Age	—	.050	.016	—	-.04
Gender (male = 1)	1.53*	-.268	.486	—	.11***
Class	—	—	—	—	.01
Education	—	—	.026	—	—
Religion	—	.035	—	—	—

[a] Refers to general deterrence and absolute support for the death penalty.
*p < 0.05; **p < 0.01; ***p < 0.001.

Note: Jiang and his associates published more than one article on death penalty views based on the same data set. Articles based on cross-national studies are shown in Table 9.6.

COMPARATIVE DEATH PENALTY VIEWS

Generally speaking, comparative studies "help to reveal not only intriguing differences between countries and cultures, but also aspects of one's own country and culture that would be difficult or impossible to detect from domestic data alone" (Jowell 1998:168). In addition, cross-national studies are helpful in narrowing the gap between nations and building bridges so that information flows more freely (Cao & Cullen 2001). These general significances of cross-national research are also applicable to death penalty views. Accordingly, this section reviews empirical studies on attitudes toward capital punishment and the reasons behind those attitudes.

There are several empirical studies comparing support levels of capital punishment between China and other nations. The first is Cao and Cullen (2001). On the basis of data collected from 203 college students in China and 101 college students in the United States, Cao and Cullen found that 78.2% of the Chinese respondents agreed that capital punishment should be used for murderers, while 59.4% of their American counterparts expressed the same opinion. When these students were asked whether the death penalty should be abolished entirely, 63.3% of the respondents in the United States disagreed, while 87.6% of the respondents in China disagreed. These findings suggest that Chinese college students were more likely to support the death penalty than their American counterparts were.

Qi and Oberwittler (2009) collected data from 896 Chinese college students who were studying in Germany and 509 German college students in Germany. The authors asked the students a simple question: "In general, do you favor or oppose the death penalty?" Among the Chinese respondents, 69% favored the death penalty, while only 10.5% of the German respondents did so, indicating that support for the death penalty among Chinese students was much higher than that among German students.

Jiang, Lambert, Wang, Saito, and Pilot (2010) compared death penalty views in three nations: China, Japan, and the United States. They used the same questionnaire to collect data in the three nations. In China, 524 college students completed the questionnaire; in Japan, 267 college students participated in the survey; and in the United States, there were 484 usable questionnaires from college students. Two statements were used to measure attitudes toward the death penalty: (1) "I support the death penalty"; and (2) "I am in favor of the death penalty." Slightly more than 69% of the

Chinese respondents agreed or strongly agreed with the first statement, and 65% of the respondents agreed or strongly agreed with the second statement. In Japan, these numbers were approximately 59% and 63%, respectively. In the United States, the corresponding numbers were 57% and 64%, respectively. On average, the support level for all the three nations was slightly more than 60%, with the highest support level from Chinese college students.

Wu et al. (2011) compared the support level for capital punishment of Chinese and American college students. A total of 422 Chinese students and 425 U.S. students completed the survey. This study asked the respondents whether they agreed with three statements: (1) "The death penalty is necessary to maintain law and order"; (2) "The death penalty should be used because people who take a life or bring severe harm to others and the society deserve to be punished by having their own life taken"; and (3) "The death penalty should be abolished entirely because no one has the right to take away another's life." For the first statement, 71% of the respondents in China agreed or strongly agreed, while 43% of the respondents in the United States did so. The results for the second statement were that 77% of the respondents in China agreed or strongly agreed, while 65% of their American counterparts did so. Findings for the third statement were that 78% of the Chinese respondents opposed the abolition of capital punishment, while 74% of their American counterparts opposed the abolition.

In summary, all these studies revealed that Chinese respondents had higher levels of support for the death penalty than their counterparts in Germany, Japan, and the United States. In the following section, I examine the reasons behind the attitudes toward the death penalty in China and other nations.

Table 9.6 presents findings of regression analyses from three studies of the predictors of death penalty views with a cross-national approach. Qi and Oberwittler (2009) compared China and Germany. Their study found that a punitive orientation in sentencing led to higher levels of support for the death penalty in both nations. In addition, German college students who believed in rehabilitation were less likely to favor the death penalty among German students, but this relation did not exist for their Chinese counterparts. This study included a few predictors in the regression model but missed some important ones.

Jiang et al. (2010) examined the predictors of death penalty views among college students from three countries: China, Japan, and the United States.

TABLE 9.6 Predictors of Death Penalty Views Between China and Other Nations

	QI & OBERWITTLER (2009)		JIANG, LAMBERT, WANG, SAITO, & PILOT (2010)			WU, SUN, & WU (2011)	
CORRELATES\STUDIES	CHINA	GERMANY	CHINA	JAPAN	USA	CHINA	USA
Deterrence	—	—	.26***	.23***	.14***	—	—
Retribution	—	—	.22***	.27***	.41***	—	—
Incapacitation	—	—	—	—	—	—	—
Rehabilitation	-.05	-.15**	-.22**	-.27*	-.28***	—	—
Wrongful execution	—	—	-.21*	-.38**	-.13	—	—
Crime severity	—	—	.05	.09	-.17	—	—
Confidence in government	—	—	—	—	—	—	—
Fear of crime	-.04	-.01	—	—	—	.12*	-.08
Victimization	—	—	—	—	—	.49*	.43
Barbarity	—	—	-.39***	-.62***	-.62***	—	—
Punitiveness in sentencing	.40***	.29***	—	—	—	.70***	.69***
Punitiveness in incarceration	—	—	—	—	—	.35***	.55***
Age	—	—	.03	-.01	-.02	-.02	-.05
Gender (male = 1)	—	—	-.18	.32	-.02	.46*	.73**
Class	—	—	—	—	—	.18	-.16
Education	—	—	—	—	—	—	—
Religion	—	—	.46	-.36	.19	—	—

*p<0.05; **p<0.01; ***p<0.001.

Their study found that predictors of death penalty views were very similar for the three nations. For example, in all three nations, beliefs in deterrence and retribution led to higher levels of support for the death penalty. Belief in rehabilitation and the view that the death penalty was barbaric (e.g., executions set a violent example that leads to further violence) led to lower levels of support for the death penalty. The three nations differed on the relationship of wrongful execution to death penalty views. That is, beliefs that wrongful executions occur led to lower levels of support for capital punishment in China and Japan but not in the United States.

Wu et al. (2011) investigated the reasons for death penalty views among Chinese and American college students. They did not include general perspectives of punishment in their study but did include several other frequently used variables. Their study found that a punitive orientation in sentencing and a punitive orientation in corrections were positively related to support for capital punishment in both China and the United States. Male respondents were more likely to support capital punishment in both nations as well. In addition, fear of crime and victimization led to higher levels of support for the death penalty in China, but these relationships did not exist among American college students.

It is worth noting that these comparative studies were based on surveys of college students. It is not clear whether these findings are applicable to ordinary citizens. Although the comparative investigation of death penalty views among Asian countries in Johnson and Zimring's book (2009) did not come directly from an empirical study, their book does provide helpful information. In Asia, public support for the death penalty is high. In this regard, China does not differ significantly from other Asian countries, but government is a "major shaper of death penalty policy" (Johnson & Zimring 2009:295). Thus, "public opinion supports capital punishment for serious crime all over the region, but executions occur frequently only in the PRC, Singapore, and (probably) Vietnam and North Korea" (Johnson & Zimring 2009:296). Overall, the comparative study of death penalty views in Asia is sparse. Further comparative research on death penalty views, especially ordinary citizens' views, is needed in the future.

DISCUSSION

Caution must be exercised in assessing the findings from the studies reviewed in this chapter. Among 10 surveys reviewed in this chapter, only 1 used a random sample of three provinces; 6 were conducted among college students only; 3 included ordinary citizens; and 1 was conducted among criminal justice professionals. Like information from case studies, findings from nonrandom samples may be informative but cannot be statistically generalized to a larger population. In addition, findings from the random sample of three provinces allow us to infer citizens' attitudes toward the death penalty only in those three provinces. More surveys of death penalty opinion based on random sampling are needed in the future.

Several issues merit further discussion. The first is the function of the general public's attitudes toward capital punishment in retaining or abolishing the death penalty. All the studies reviewed in this chapter indicate that the majority of Chinese citizens support the death penalty. This is one of the reasons that the Chinese government retains the death penalty (Hood 2009; Qi & Oberwittler 2009). Should death penalty policy be determined by polls or citizens' attitudes toward the death penalty? There is no doubt that in either a democratic society or a socialist society, citizens' death penalty views will affect governmental policy of capital punishment to some degree. However, legislatures, courts, and the government often have the final say in retaining or abolishing capital punishment or in halting an execution (Schabas 2004). A well-known example is that in 1981, even though 63% of the general public supported capital punishment, President François Mitterrand of France opposed the death penalty during his reelection campaign (Hood 2009). Some nations, including France, Germany, the United Kingdom, and Canada, abolished capital punishment when a majority of the general public supported the death penalty (Johnson & Zimring 2009; Liang et al. 2006). Thus, Hood argues that "it has needed political leadership and judicial support to bring about abolition" (2009:7).

It is commonly agreed that China is an authoritarian society, and that the government plays a key role in policy development, including death penalty policy. What is the government's attitude toward the death penalty? The founder of the People's Republic of China, Mao Zedong, supported retaining the death penalty along with the idea of "killing fewer, killing carefully, and preventing wrongful killing" (Zhang & Zhao 2014). His views heavily affected China's official attitudes toward the death penalty in his era and even today's death penalty policy. After his death, Deng Xiaoping, senior leader after Mao, held a similar view of the death penalty to Mao's (Gao 2005). Deng's successors pretty much have held the same views as their predecessors. Lu and Miethe (2007) summarize the death penalty views of several leaders, including the past president of the Chinese Communist Party, Hu Jintao; the past premier, Wen Jiabao; and the past president of the Supreme Court, Xiao Yang. The current president of the Supreme Court, Zhou Qiang, believes that the death penalty should be retained for the most serious offenders ("Death Penalty" 2014). Chinese officials believe that the death penalty helps control crimes, especially serious crimes. They also stress Mao's approach of killing fewer, killing carefully, and preventing wrongful killing in death penalty policy.

Second, findings from regression analysis (Jiang et al. 2010) indicated that deterrence was the strongest predictor of attitudes toward capital punishment in China, while retribution was the strongest predictor in the United States. Why does deterrence strongly affect public attitudes toward the death penalty in China? One possible explanation is that deterrence may be more socially acceptable in China than retribution (Jiang et al. 2010). Another possible explanation may be related to knowledge about the functions of capital punishment. In the United States, there are many scientific studies on the deterrence effect (or lack thereof) of capital punishment. Therefore, citizens, including college students, are likely at least to be aware of different findings on the deterrent effect of capital punishment and to make their own judgment. In contrast, China lacks published scientific research on the deterrence effect of capital punishment. Thus, students in the United States may be better informed on this topic than students in China, who may simply accept a deterrence effect, whether it is real or not, because that is the official position (Hood & Hoyle 2008). Alternatively, Chinese students may feel intuitively that members of the general public are deterred from committing crime because of the threat of capital punishment (Schabas 2004). If knowledge of the lack of the deterrence effect of capital punishment reduces support for the death penalty, more scientific research on the deterrence of capital punishment is needed in China.

Then the question is whether information on the death penalty affects people's attitudes toward it. In 1972, U.S. Supreme Court justice Thurgood Marshall postulated that information about the death penalty might reduce people's levels of support for it. Several studies (Bohm 1989; Lambert, Camp, Clarke, & Jiang 2011; Sandys 1995; Zeisel & Gallup 1989) found that information on deterrence, innocence, and other issues related to capital punishment reduced people's support for the death penalty. Is this relationship applicable to China? Findings from a random sample of 4,472 people in 2007 in three provinces of China (Oberwittler & Qi 2009) suggested that knowledge about wrongful convictions and inequality in death sentences could decrease support for the death penalty (Hood 2009). However, as shown in table 9.2, a survey of 455 Chinese judges, policemen, procurators, and lawyers indicates that criminal justice practitioners had a higher level of support for the death penalty (Kuang et al. 2010: 91.2%) than the general public had (Oberwittler & Qi 2009: 57.5%). There is no doubt that these practitioners had more knowledge about capital punishment than the general public had in China. This finding suggests that more information on capital punishment does not necessarily lead to a reduction in death penalty support. Thus, a direct test is needed for the impact of information on people's support for the death penalty among people with different backgrounds in China.

Literature shows that in the West, when a life sentence or a life sentence without parole is presented as an alternative sanction, people are less likely to support the death penalty (Hewitt et al. 2004; see Oberwittler & Qi 2009 for references). Scholars of China also have found that when a life sentence is listed as an alternative punishment for serious crimes, support for the death penalty decreases (Liang et al. 2006; Oberwittler & Qi 2009; Qi & Oberwittler 2009). However, even when a life sentence is listed as an alternative sanction, support for the death penalty is still above 50% in these studies. One reason for this situation may be people's low confidence in the fairness of the Chinese criminal justice system (Oberwittler & Qi 2009). In China, offenders and/or their families who have money, a personal network, or power may receive lighter punishment. So it is reasonable to assume that enhanced public confidence in courts and corrections would potentially help reduce support for the death penalty when a life sentence is an alternative.

• • •

There is a global trend toward the abolition of capital punishment (Hood 2009; Johnson & Zimring 2009). Attitudes of the general public, government officials, legislators, judges, and lawyers toward capital punishment may all affect the development of death penalty law and practice. Traditional values such as revenge, scientific research on the deterrence effect of the death penalty, beliefs such as rehabilitation and incapacitation, wrongful convictions, and crime prevalence and the related fear of crime could also affect the future direction of the death penalty. In current China, both the general public and government authorities strongly support retaining the death penalty. Although China has recently been moving toward a more cautious approach in the imposition of a death sentence and the majority of Chinese legal scholars believe that capital punishment will be abolished in the future, abolition is likely to be in the far-distant future (Hood 2009).

Nevertheless, several factors may help accelerate China's progress toward abolishing the death penalty. The first factor is change in the public's views of punishment. When people consider a life sentence an adequate replacement for the death penalty, they are less likely to support the death penalty. When Chinese people begin to value freedom and life more, they may see that a life sentence is more painful and costly. The second factor is to establish the connection between human rights and capital punishment. To many Chinese, capital punishment is only an issue of penal policy, not an issue of human rights. Advocacy of abolition of the death penalty is needed in China. As Schabas argues, when people adopt two views, "1. Everyone has the right to life. 2. No one shall be condemned to the death penalty, or executed," they will be less likely to support retaining capital punishment (Schabas 2004:321). Scientific research on the functions of the death penalty in general and the deterrence effect of the death penalty in particular is another factor that may reduce death penalty support in China. As noted earlier, Chinese people intuitively believe in the deterrence effect of the death penalty. If scientific research finds no or little deterrence effect of capital punishment, Chinese people may be less likely to support it.

NOTES

Many thanks go to Starr Jiang for his proofreading of a previous edition of this chapter.

1   Johnson and Zimring (2009) argue that political factors are the only reasons that China retains capital punishment. Government officials use public opinion as an excuse for executions.
2   Bakken (2012) argues that even though China has long used the death penalty, Chinese people's death penalty views are not necessarily rooted in Chinese traditional culture.

REFERENCES

Bakken, B. (2012). Zhongguoren de sixingguan [Chinese people's death penalty views]. *Qingshaonian fanzui wenti* [Juvenile Delinquency and Crime], *6*, 28–36.

Bohm, R. M. (1987). American death penalty attitudes: A critical examination of recent evidence. *Criminal Justice and Behavior, 14*, 380–396.

Bohm, R. M. (1989). The effects of classroom instruction and discussion on death penalty opinions: A teaching note. *Journal of Criminal Justice, 17*, 123–131.

Cao, L., & Cullen, F. T. (2001). Thinking about crime and control: A comparative study of Chinese and American ideology. *International Criminal Justice Review, 11*, 58–81.

Cullen, F. T., Fisher, B. S., & Applegate, B. K. (2000). Public opinion about punishment and corrections. *Crime and Justice, 27*, 1–79.

The death penalty is retained for the most serious offenders. (2014). Xinhua Network. Retrieved September 18, 2014, from http://www.022net.com/2014/3-10/483866202439164.html.

Ellsworth, P. C., & Ross, L. (1983). Public opinion and capital punishment: A close examination of the views of abolitionists and retentionists. *Crime and Delinquency, 29*, 116–169.

Gao, Y. (2005). Deng Xiaoping de sixingguan [Deng Xiaoping's death penalty views]. Retrieved September 18, 2014, from http://www.aisixiang.com/data/8495.html.

Hewitt, J. D., Regoli, A., Regoli, R. M., & Iadicola, P. (2004). A comparison of death penalty opinion among university students in the U.S. and Taiwan. *Crime and Criminal Justice International, 3*, 73–102.

Hood, R. (2009). Abolition of the death penalty: China in world perspective. *City University of Hong Kong Law Review, 1*, 1–21.

Hood, R., & Hoyle, C. (2008). *The Death Penalty: A Worldwide Perspective* (4th ed.). New York: Oxford University Press.

Hu, Y. (2002). Application of the death penalty in Chinese judicial practice. In J. Chen, Y. Li, & J. M. Otto (Eds.), *Implementation of law in the People's Republic of China* (pp. 247–275). Boston: Kluwer Law International.

Jia, Y. (2005). Sixing shizheng yanjiu zhi sixingguan de diaocha baogao [Death penalty views among college students in China: An empirical study]. *Faxue pinglun* [Legal Science Review], *3*, 20–33.

Jiang, S., Lambert, E., & Nathan, V. (2009). Reasons for death penalty attitudes among Chinese citizens: Retributive or instrumental? *Journal of Criminal Justice, 37*, 225–233.

Jiang, S., Lambert, E., & Wang, J. (2007). Capital punishment views in China and the United States: A preliminary study among college students. *International Journal of Offender Therapy and Comparative Criminology, 51,* 84–97.

Jiang, S., Lambert, E., Wang, J., Saito, T., & Pilot, R. (2010). Death penalty views in China, Japan and the U.S.: An empirical comparison. *Journal of Criminal Justice, 38,* 862–869.

Jiang, S., & Wang, J. (2008). Correlates of support for capital punishment in China. *International Criminal Justice Review, 18,* 24–38.

Jin, J. (1997). *Jianyuxue zonglun* [On Prisons]. Beijing: Law Press.

Johnson, D. T., & Zimring, F. E. (2009). *The Next Frontier: National Development, Political Change, and the Death Penalty in Asia.* New York: Oxford University Press.

Jowell, R. (1998). How comparative is comparative research? *American Behavioral Scientist, 42,* 168–177.

Kuang, L., Zeng, Y., Li, K., Liu, S., Chen, M., Dai, C., & Zhang, X. (2010). Zhuanye renshi sixing taidu diaocha baogao [A survey on criminal justice professionals' attitudes toward the death penalty]. In H. Mo (Ed.), *Zhongguo Sixing Taidu Diaocha Baogao* [A Survey Report on the Death Penalty in China] (pp. 63–224). Taipei: Yuanzhao.

Lambert, E. G., Camp, S. D., Clarke, A., & Jiang, S. (2011). The impact of information on death penalty support, revisited. *Crime and Delinquency, 57,* 572–599.

Lambert, E. G., Clarke, A., & Lambert, J. (2004). Reasons for supporting and opposing capital punishment: A preliminary study. *Internet Journal of Criminology,* 1–34. Retrieved from http://www.internetjournalofcriminology.com/.

Lambert, E. G., Jiang, S., Elechi, O. O., Khondaker, M., Baker, D., & Wang, J. (2014). A preliminary study of gender differences on death penalty views of college students from Bangladesh, China, Nigeria, and the United States. *Journal of Ethnicity in Criminal Justice, 12,* 44–68.

Liang, B., Lu, H., Miethe, T. D., & Zhang, L. (2006). Sources of variation in pro-death penalty attitudes in China. *British Journal of Criminology, 46,* 119–130.

Lu, H., & Miethe, T. D. (2007). *China's Death Penalty: History, Law, and Contemporary Practices.* New York: Routledge.

Lu, H., & Zhang, L. (2005). Death penalty in China: The law and the practice. *Journal of Criminal Justice, 33,* 367–376.

Ma, X. (1997). *Zhongguo Gudai Shehui de Faluguan* [China's Traditional Legal Views]. Zhengzhou, Henan, China: Daxiang.

Miethe, T. D., & Lu, H. (2005). *Punishment: A Comparative Historical Perspective.* New York: Cambridge University Press.

Oberwittler, D., & Qi, S. (2009). *Public Opinion on the Death Penalty in China: Results from a General Population Survey Conducted in Three Provinces in 2007/08.* (Forschung Aktuell/research in brief 41). Freiburg, Germany: Max Planck Institute for Foreign and International Criminal Law. Retrieved from https://www.mpicc.de/files/pdf2/forschung_aktuell_41.pdf.

Qi, S., & Oberwittler, D. (2009). On the road to the rule of law: Crime, crime control, and public opinion in China. *European Journal of Criminal Police Research, 15,* 137–157.

Radelet, M., & Borg, M. (2000). The changing nature of death penalty debates. *Annual Review of Sociology, 26,* 43–61.

Sandys, M. (1995). Attitudinal change among students in a capital punishment class: It may be possible. *American Journal of Criminal Justice, 20,* 37–55.

Schabas, W. A. (2004). Public opinion and the death penalty. In P. Hodgkinson & W. A. Schabas (Eds.), *Capital Punishment: Strategies for Abortion* (pp. 309–331). Cambridge: Cambridge University Press.

Wang, D. D. (2004). *The Monster That Is History: History, Violence, and Fictional Writing in Twentieth-Century China.* Berkeley: University of California Press.

Wu, Y., Sun, I. Y., & Wu, Z. (2011). Support for the death penalty: Chinese and American college students compared. *Punishment and Society, 13,* 354–376.

Zeisel, H., & Gallup, A. (1989). Death penalty sentiment in the United States. *Journal of Quantitative Criminology, 5,* 285–296.

Zhang, H., & Zhao, Y. (2014). Mao Zedong de sixingguan [Mao Zhedong's death penalty views]. Retrieved September 18, 2014, from http://www.flzx.com/lawyer/lgrui20020924/blog/234107.html.

10

Between Deference and Defiance

COURTS AND PENAL POPULISM IN CHINESE CAPITAL CASES

▸ HUALING FU

WHEN 21-YEAR-OLD Yao Jiaxin stepped out of his car on the evening of October 20, 2010, to stab Zhang Miao to death after his car accidentally struck her,[1] he could not have foreseen that his act would cause nationwide outrage. The case offers a textbook example of the decisive influence that public opinion may have on court decisions. Yao's explanation was as offensive as his crime was brutal: he stabbed the already injured Zhang eight times because she, who looked like a migrant worker, might make unreasonable demands for compensation because of the traffic accident. The Chinese Internet went viral on Yao's case, and angry Internet users demanded the death penalty for Yao with immediate execution. Calls for caution and reason were quickly silenced, and courts seemed to have no other choice except to comply with the demand of a bloodthirsty public. At one stage, Yao's family had intended to compensate the victim's family in exchange for forgiveness. Forgiveness is a necessary and frequently sufficient condition to reduce the sentence from death with immediate execution. There were signs that the victim's family would have been receptive to such a settlement if it had been done properly and promptly, as is done frequently in many of China's capital cases. No deal was reached in this case, however, because public opinion was so overwhelming that the court and the victim's family were not willing or able to risk offending public sentiment. Yao's case appears to be a perfect storm: public opinion rose spontaneously and affected the court's decisions decisively. Either representing China's democratic awakening or an altered form of a more traditional mob culture, public opinion is a powerful force in China, with which decision makers in the party-state have to reckon.

Yao's case illustrates the tension that faces China's politically weak judiciary struggling to reinvent itself (McConville & Pils 2013; Peerenboom 2009). It is well known that Chinese courts lack independence and are vulnerable to outside interference. It is equally well known that the Chinese judicial system has been undergoing reform and is asserting autonomy through developing professionalism. Judges may be vulnerable to outside interference, including that from public opinion, but they also endeavor to resist interference when it appears. In death penalty cases in particular, the courts are torn by two contradictory imperatives.

On the one hand, the professional imperative, either imposed by the Supreme People's Court (SPC) and the legislature or derived from the professional calling, demands the application of legal principles and rules in the imposition of the death penalty. In particular, the professional imperative requires a steady decrease in imposition of the death penalty and the application of a penal policy of combining severity and leniency across all criminal cases.

On the other hand, the populist imperative, coupled with political conservatism, demands the application of a political standard in death penalty cases and a decision that will satisfy public wrath (Trevaskes 2012). When Xiao Yang became the president of the SPC in 1998, the SPC demanded that lower courts tighten up death penalty procedures to reduce the number of judicial executions in China. With the support of the party, China has been able to make a significant reduction in death penalty cases. Interestingly, the reduction has been occurring at a time when the general public is at its most vocal and victim advocacy is at its most aggressive in influencing judicial decisions. How have Chinese courts reconciled the two conflicting imperatives and achieved the impressive reduction in the number of death penalty cases while facing unprecedented public pressure to impose harsh penalties?

This chapter studies the organization of public opinion surrounding the application of the death penalty in China and the judicial strategies to cope with the pressure of public opinion. The chapter makes two principal arguments. First, public opinion has become influential and has had a significant impact on judicial decisions (Liebman 2005, 2011). Although public opinion is multilayered, multifaceted, varied in scale, and fraught with complexity, close examination reveals that it is often the product of diligent organization and is often well structured. Public opinion is not limited to the views of victims and their families, but in most of the capital cases in which public opinion has a role to play, the opinion of the victims and families is instrumental in shaping public opinion and is at the pivotal center of the death penalty debate. In this chapter, this victim-generated stream of public opinion, which is proactive, aggressive, and effective in its mobilization, is referred to as *penal populism*.

Second, the courts, situated at the final stage in the criminal process, have to deal directly with the wrath of public opinion. Within China's pro–death penalty context, it is difficult for a court to defy popular demand for the death penalty in any potential capital case. Yet over the past decade, the Chinese courts have developed agency in managing and capturing public opinion. Although the courts are not able to defy popular opinion in its entirety, they are able to use different strategies to deflect, incorporate, or otherwise cope with public opinion so as to reduce the number of death penalty cases and at the same time manage not to offend public sensitivity. The scheme of cash for clemency, in which a defendant compensates the victim's family, mostly in homicide cases, in exchange for a sentence that is less than the death penalty, is one of the successful strategies.

CHINESE PENAL POPULISM IN COMPARISON

The criminal justice system in Western democracies has experienced an unprecedented level of popular resentment and distrust. Galvanized by personal tragedies often caused by violent crimes, victim advocacy groups and activist citizens have mobilized significant social and political support in challenging the established criminal justice system. The criminal justice policies made by professionals are seen as detached from ordinary people and clearly favoring criminals at the cost of law-abiding citizens (Pratt 2007). Penal populism, defined as "expressions of anger, disenchantment and disillusionment with the criminal justice establishment," has swept major Western democracies (ibid.:12) and is particularly influential and occasionally decisive in shaping penal policies (Garland 2001; Pratt 2007; Roberts, Stalans, Indermaur, & Hough 2003).

It is a new phenomenon that public opinion plays a proactive role in shaping governmental decisions in China. The expansion of civil society and the availability of information technology since the late 1990s have been instrumental in that development. Chinese penal populism, like its counterpart in Western democracies, originates from and is rooted in the groundswell of the people and evolves largely independent of state control. Therefore, Chinese penal populism differs fundamentally from what is referred to as *authoritarian populism*, in which the state first stirs up public anger, creates a moral panic among the masses, and then taps into the popular will to legitimize state penal policies (Hall 1979; Roberts & Hough 2002). Indeed, the Chinese propaganda state can no longer manipulate and rein in popular opinion as it used to do, but has to respond to popular issues in the vibrant social media (Reilly 2011; Stockmann 2013).

Compared with the more entrenched penal populism in major democracies, the United States in particular, the Chinese counterpart demonstrates some unique characteristics. In the United States, penal populism often reflects a deep fear of social disintegration and a feeling of all-around insecurity, along with anger and desperation that the institutions have failed the people (Garland 2001; Pratt 2007; Roberts et al. 2003). Penal populism in general is largely fear driven and anger motivated and represents the eventual outburst of the otherwise silent majority against the seeming expansion of the rights of criminal offenders. Tough anticrime legislation represents those deep hostilities toward those who have taken undue advantage of the system at the expense of their victims and society at large, and it demonstrates the clear determination of the dissatisfied public to address their concerns through direct democracy (Garland 2001; Logan 2011; Pratt 2007; Roberts et al. 2003).

Chinese populism has fundamentally different manifestations. Instead of a silent majority who reclaims its right to security against criminals, Chinese populism, typified by Yao's case, is geared in a different direction and represents the anger and frustration of the underdogs toward the more privileged class in Chinese society. The criminal justice system and the political system are seen as captives of political elites, bureaucratic powers, business interests, or otherwise privileged classes. People mobilize around individual cases under the banner of equality and egalitarianism to correct a perceived structural defect in the criminal process. Populism is a grassroots force seeking to rebalance power relations.[2]

In the Chinese debate on capital cases, penal populism pitches the poor against the rich, the powerless against the powerful, or individuals against the state. Even in the case of Wu Ying, a multibillionaire who was initially sentenced to death for financial fraud, Wu was portrayed as a weak party who was persecuted by predatory government officials (see further discussion in chapter 12). As Belkin (2014:28) points out: "In China, the broader social narrative includes a general resentment against wealth and power and a sense that the system is rigged against the ordinary citizen. Thus, defendants . . . can receive public support if their cases are put into this narrative of ordinary citizens being taken advantage of by more powerful forces." Who deserves sympathy in the criminal process is never a straightforward issue, but Chinese penal populism is firmly embedded in the strongly held suspicion that the criminal justice system serves the interests of the powerful and the rich. The demand of Chinese penal populism is case specific; it may be lenience in one case but harshness in another, all depending on how the power balance between the parties is played out in a particular case.

A populist demand influences either the individual case or legislative and policy changes beyond an immediate case. A defining characteristic of Western penal populism is its objectives and its ability to change penal legislation, leading to certain structural and sustained changes in penal practices. Victim advocacy is embedded in a particular political system in which the advocacy occurs. In democracies with an open political process and meaningful political participation, victim advocacy groups naturally channel their demands directly through the political process, leading to harsh anticrime legislation, such as the three-strikes law (Zimring, Hawkins, & Kamin 2001; for the anticrime referendum in New Zealand, see Pratt 2007) and legislation against sexual predators (Filler 2001). The sharp increase in the prison population in the past few decades in major Western democracies can be attributed to the powerful movement of penal populism and its ability to create tough anticrime laws and policies (Enns 2014). Around the globe, victims' families have advocated legal changes, and, in response, politicians are under pressure to demonstrate their toughness on crime and their willingness to work with victim advocacy groups (Blacker & Griffin 2010; Pratt 2007; Roberts et al. 2003; for a critique of the punitive culture in the West and an alternative conceptual framework, see Lacey 2008).

Chinese penal populism targets individual cases and is consequently limited to judicial disposal of those cases. Indeed, penal populism in China rarely offers a structural solution. Since the political channel is firmly closed to victims' families, they naturally focus their attention on the more vulnerable courts, which have to make decisions on the case at hand. This special focus on the courts and the disposal of individual cases is not surprising because of the strong state control over society and the lack of nongovernmental organizations in China. There is virtually no organization that pays sustained attention to issues relating to victims' rights and moves beyond dealing with individual cases on an ad hoc basis. Victims and their supporters barely have the will or the capacity to develop a long-term interest in promoting legal changes. Compared with Western populism, the Chinese counterpart is more spontaneous than structural and more case oriented than policy focused.[3]

ORGANIZATION OF PENAL POPULISM

Political scientists used to debate whether public opinion is the opinion of the public, or what passes for it, is actually the view of the elite in society, broadly defined to include politicians, community leaders, or newspaper editors (Blumer 1948; Converse 1987). Notwithstanding the improvement in the quality of public opinion surveys, there is still a lingering concern that what matters in shaping legislation and policies is not public opinion per se but effective opinion, which is the opinion of advocates who can put their thoughts into action and can organize themselves and mobilize public support (Reilly 2011). Generally, public opinion is better known in democracies with an open political process, a free press, and a strong civil society where public opinion can be freely expressed, accurately measured, and more effectively responded to. Friedman, for example, is confident that in the American democracy, the Supreme Court is able to locate, capture, and reflect mainstream public opinion through the open-ended judicial processes (Friedman 2009). In contrast, in nondemocracies, expression of public opinion is opaque. There, public opinion is ordinarily hidden and even invisible until it suddenly surfaces in response to certain scandals or tragic events.

Penal populism is a structured process with a particular origin, actors for its promotion, and sustained public interest. It is important to identify the source of penal populism, the actors involved in its development, and the factors that shape its direction. Generally, penal populism has three stages of development: a tragic event, effective victim advocacy, and sustained public response. Each of these stages will be discussed in turn.

First, penal populism in general has its origin in tragic crimes that shock the conscience of a community. Indeed, penal populism feeds on tragic or drastic events. U.S. legislation against sexual predators and the three-strikes law would not have come into existence without the tragic death of those young victims whose names were commemorated through legislation. Victims, their supporters, the media, and interested politicians united around some tragic events to make some moral claims for greater public good.

Again, there is an interesting difference. Western penal populism honors the victims whose names loomed so large that the identities of the perpetrators vanished quickly from public view. In contrast, the Chinese counterpart tends to focus on the identity of the offenders for hatred or sympathy: Yang Xia's killing of six police officers in Shanghai in 2007, Xia Junfeng's murdering of two urban enforcement officers in Shenyang in 2009, and Deng Yujiao's stabbing a thuggish cadre to death in Hubei in 2009 (for a succinct summary of some of the high-profile legal cases, see Belkin 2014). Rarely do the victims come to the attention of public discussion. This difference may reflect the priority and the ultimate goal that penal populism aims to achieve. Western penal populism finds its way into the political process, leading ultimately to legislative change, whereas Chinese penal populism narrowly focuses on the fate of individual offenders.

Second, tragedy does not trigger public outcry automatically. Penal populism is the result of victim activism, through which actors and agents frame tragic events and then mobilize and shape public opinion. Victims' voices and actions matter most in the development of penal populism. As the American victims' movement demonstrates, success depends on the extraordinary dedication of individuals, and many core leaders in these movements were themselves victims of brutal crimes.[4] Through creating victim advocacy groups, reaching out for societal support, organizing campaigns, and lobbying representatives, victims and their supporters in democracies struggle to advance their causes (for a case study of the three-strikes law in California, see Zimring 1996).

How do victims' families mobilize public opinion support in China without an open political process and effective entry points into the system? Grassroots mobilization and petitions seem to be the answer. In the infamous case of She Xianglin,[5] the victim's family and relatives gathered 220 signatures in the village in support of She's death penalty and then presented them to the trial and appellate courts to demand She's immediate execution. In Ge Bin's case, the victim's family gathered the signatures of 235 villagers to demand the death penalty. Family members of the deceased went door-to-door to gather signatures, and many agreed to put their names on the petition out of sympathy.[6] The petition, often supported by local government officials, became part of public opinion. As the judges admitted, both the trial and appellate courts were placed under great pressure to impose the death penalty. In the case of Feng Fu, in demanding the death penalty, the victim's family gathered 10 petitions signed or fingerprinted by family members and fellow villagers. The trial judge recalled that during the trial, the mother of the deceased stood in front of the courthouse wearing funeral clothing and demanding the imposition of the death penalty.[7] Defendants and their representatives also use similar strategies in petitioning the court. In the case of Teng Xingshan in Hunan, for example, the defendant was convicted of murdering Shi Xiaorong in 1989 and was sentenced to death with immediate execution. During the appeal, Teng's defense lawyer gathered more than 100 signatures from Teng's fellow villagers to testify to Teng's innocence. The appellate judges dismissed the appeal before they were able to read the petition. The victim was found alive in Guizhou in 2005 (see Yu 2006:479).

A defining characteristic of effective lawyering in sensitive cases in China is to try a case in the court of public opinion and then bring the pressure of public opinion to bear on courts (see Fu & Cullen 2008). When help from journalists is not forthcoming, victims' families, with the support of lawyers where available, resort to social media and upload their grievances to the Internet to attract attention. The family in the Li Changkui case publicized the gruesome murder online and eventually attracted attention that was too powerful to be controlled.[8] In the Yao Jiaxin case, a family friend of the deceased single-handedly mobilized the immense public outcry against Yao and his family, leading to Yao's execution. Going one step further, families of victims and defendants are known to seek assistance from professional "online pushers" to promote their causes, just as professional protesters would do in settling other disputes (Liebman 2013).

The determination and strong will of the victims and their supporters are crucial for a tragedy to receive wide public attention and support for victims. Activism is thus the root of penal populism and provides life to public opinion. Tragedies abound, but it is difficult to frame them in a way that grabs popular attention. Sympathy comes and goes, but whether a case can attract sustained attention and resilient support depends on how the issue in that case is framed. Most tragic events do not develop an effective entry point to the domain of public opinion. In an open political process in democracies, victims must be able to articulate clear demands for reform and offer sound justification for the necessity and reasonableness of the proposed reform. In China's case, since strong public opinion is able to swing courts' decisions, victims and defendants will do as much as possible to attract public attention and stir up public anger, even misinforming the public, if necessary, as the agent for the victim's family in the Yao Jiaxin case did in exaggerating the wealth and influence of the offender's family (Belkin 2014).

Chinese penal populism can, to a significant degree, be reduced to the demands of the victims' families and the views of local communities that the families are able to solicit. There are exceptional cases in which scholars and rights lawyers may step in to play a surrogate function in mobilizing public support on behalf of defendants who may have suffered from gross injustice. Most people are bystanders and strangers in the virtual world who express their literally virtual sympathy and support from a distance. The media hype on sensational crime news may have roots in the actual events of real people (Garland 2001), but it is the victims themselves and a few dedicated supporters who painstakingly and carefully advocate for certain decisions and policy changes. Organization matters a lot in presenting effective public opinion (Reilly 2011). It is normally not public opinion in a general sense that concerns Chinese judges. The single most important issue for Chinese judges is to pacify the victim's family and the immediate support it solicits in order to impose a lesser sentence than immediate execution.

The final stage in penal populism is full-fledged public participation in deliberating tragic events, allocating responsibilities, and proposing possible legislative and policy reforms. Generally, social media go viral on tragic cases; Internet users passionately engage in debates; advocacy groups are formed with professional and expert input; the press demonstrates sustained interest in the issues and keeps them alive; government departments start to respond to the bottom-up demand for action; and influential political leaders seize the opportunity and bring the matter forward in the political process. In the Chinese case, party leaders finally get to know what the people want and then give instruction to the courts. As Belkin points out, "Since the Party, the government and the court leadership can directly influence, or more accurately, simply direct the court to decide a case a certain way, public opinion has an official and a practical role in court decisions in high-profile criminal cases" (2014:29).

It is impossible to determine which cases will attract sustained media attention to influence a decision. Victims' families may have done their best, but it is up to the media, the public, and the government to respond. But once the matter is in the public domain, the public will claim ownership of the matter, leaving victims' families largely in the shadow of the public debate. For victims' families, going public needs to be handled with caution if the demand for the death penalty is actually a bargaining chip for more payment. The original appeal for sympathy and support may have been, in part, to maximize a cash payment, but once the case has attracted public attention, the case develops a life of its own. The original family may lose control over the process. The court and the political authority behind the court may make a decision in direct response to public opinion rather than a hidden wish of the family.

THE LAW AND PENAL POPULISM IN CHINA

Victims in Chinese Law

Public opinion is important to China's authoritarian state. The Communist Party's legitimacy relies to a significant degree on the regime's performance, including maintaining social order, public perception of the state's governance capacity, and effectiveness in maintaining order (Gilley 2009; Stockmann 2013). Authoritarian regimes regularly create comprehensive social control mechanisms to preempt and control crime and react quickly to assuage public anger after serious crimes take place. The level of institutionalization in the legal system is low, and legal institutions can respond to populist demands quickly and flexibly (Liebman 2005). It is in this political context that legal rules in support of victims' rights are understood.

Chinese criminal law, largely in line with the civil law tradition, allows a larger role for victims and their families than the common law in formal criminal proceedings. Under Chinese criminal procedures, the victim of a crime is a formal party to the criminal proceeding and enjoys the right to participate throughout the process. For example, victims can retain legal representatives to participate in the legal process and have the right to be informed of prosecution decisions (Criminal Procedure Law, Article 44); in reviewing cases, prosecutors are required to hear and keep a record of the views of the victims or their legal representatives (Article 170); victims have the right to petition the prosecution at the next higher level to reconsider a nonprosecution decision and the right to apply for judicial review if they are dissatisfied with the decision after reconsideration (Article 176); victims have the right to examine and cross-examine witnesses during trial (Article 59); and victims have the right to comment on the bill of prosecution and question the defendant during trial (Article 186).

In sentencing, the court is legally required to consider two factors relating to victims: (1) whether the victim is meaningfully compensated by the defendant considering the defendant's ability to pay, and (2) whether the victim or his or her family has forgiven the defendant considering the nature of the offense that has been committed (Supreme People's Court [SPC] 2010). In the Chinese sentencing process, victims and their families can speak directly to the court in influencing sentencing. Common law courts grapple with the weight to be given to a family statement of the impact of the offense in murder cases (Kirchengast 2011); Chinese law, being less structured, takes for granted such impact statements, including the harm to the individuals, harm to the community, societal outrage, and public condemnation.

In capital cases, there has been a standing requirement that courts are to take views of victims' families into consideration. This is not surprising, given the formal position of victims in the criminal process. Victims take parts in the trial, and their voices must be heard and considered when judges make decisions. In practice, a court, in cases where the death penalty is applicable, will find it difficult not to impose the death penalty if a victim's family demands it. The offender's life in such cases may be spared only if the victim's family has expressed its consent not to execute.[9] This practice is from time to time reinforced by the political requirement that judges must consider the feeling of the public in deciding death penalty cases (Belkin 2014). Interestingly, the pro-victim law also gives victims a choice to opt out of harsh punishment, and the otherwise harsh law against offenders can be softened through a cash payment.

Penal Populism, Social Impact, and Vulnerable Courts

Penal populism in China works though courts instead of the legislative process because China's democratic deficit necessarily narrows the channel of political participation. Short of political advocacy on policy and lawmaking, frustration can be channeled only to the judiciary, with a special focus on individual cases. Courts in China, more than in many democracies, are at the receiving end of public wrath. It is difficult for a court that is directly facing a populist demand to stand firm by legal rules and act contrary to the pressure. As weak institutions in the political system, courts are vulnerable to outside interference, principally from the ruling party but also from the influence of public opinion. Chinese law gives victims full legal status in the criminal process, but the open-ended nature of the Chinese legal system invites political and public intrusion into the legal process.

The court is politically, as well as legally, vulnerable to penal populism. Where a case has attracted public attention, there is likely to be intense public discussion in both the virtual and real worlds, and online discussion may lead to offline mobilization. The concerns for the ruling party are that, sooner or later, victims and their families and supporters will act to show their solidarity. In the eyes of the party-state, social mobilization of any kind may erode its remaining legitimacy and has the potential to destabilize social order and put the party's legitimacy at risk (Fu 2014). To defuse a potential social and political crisis, the party demands that legal institutions, courts in particular, cave in to public demand by rendering decisions that satisfy the popular demand. As the party reminds the courts, the legal consequence of a court decision must coincide with its political impact, and judges should keep the larger picture in mind in rendering legal decisions. At the end of the day, politics still takes command in China, and legal rules are secondary considerations in special cases involving broad public interest.

The fact that courts are politically weak and have a low institutionalization level does not necessarily mean that they have no agency and therefore defer to political order and public opinions blindly. Since Xiao Yang's presidency of the SPC in 1998, the judiciary under the leadership of the SPC has been embarking on a professional enterprise in particular to enhance judges' professional standing. The agenda is that a professionalized body will develop its own identity, code of conduct, institutional interest, and professional autonomy. A key legacy of that emerging professionalism is the SPC's ability to tighten procedures to standardize the application of the death penalty with the ultimate goal of reducing its use. The SPC has, in general, called for caution and restraint in death penalty cases, both procedurally and substantively. Procedurally, there has been a significant reform that allows the SPC to centralize death penalty review. Substantively, the SPC, through judicial interpretation of the criminal law, has successfully reduced the application of the death penalty in certain cases, in particular, homicide cases taking place within families and between neighbors, despite political suspicion and public outcry (for a detailed review of the legal development and the corresponding academic debate, see Trevaskes 2012).

RESPONDING TO PENAL POPULISM

Facing the demands of victims' families, courts have three options: to defer to public opinion, to act against public opinion, or to strategically engage and to capture public opinion through institutional design.

Deferring to Public Opinion

The first choice is the default position where public opinion counts the most and is able to swing a court's decision. Without further legislative change on the use of the death penalty, a court will impose the death penalty on a wide range of homicide cases if victims' families strongly insist. Historically, Chinese courts were required to take public wrath into consideration in death penalty decisions, and cash for clemency was not politically possible. Populist demand in the form of authoritarian populism contributed significantly to the high execution rate in China's criminal justice system. Within the authoritarian tradition to kill more and kill expediently, the choice of deferring to public opinion represents the correct political line. Indeed, many have argued that the imposition of the death penalty after mass demand for retribution may have enhanced the legitimacy and resilience of the Communist Party (Miao 2013). The offender and his or her family may defend legally but do not stand on high moral ground to challenge a decision to execute. The death penalty is also an easier choice for judges to make. After all, who is likely to criticize a judge for being harsh on murderers and for following the routine? Barring exceptional cases, a death sentence with immediate execution easily satisfies political leaders and, most important, pacifies victims' families and the masses (ibid.).

A key concern in China's political system is the demand of the victims' families in homicide cases. Victims' families who lost loved ones immediately shift to the court to vent their anger if a death penalty is not forthcoming (Zhang 2012). Because of the political accountability and the vulnerable position of Chinese courts, as mentioned earlier, judges are sensitive to the feelings and demands of victims' families and are willing to compromise. In the Li Huailiang case, where the father of a murder victim aggressively demanded Li's death sentence,[10] there was allegedly even a written promise by a court to the father of the deceased that the court would try to impose a severe sentence, likely the death penalty, if the father would cease to petition further (Ng & He 2013). As one high court judge stated explicitly:

> Judges ... often receive pressure from victims who actively demand heavy punishment for defendants, on the one hand, and demand compensation from them for their economic losses, on the other. If their demand is not met, they would disrupt the court, make repeated petitions, and severely disturb social stability. (quoted in Zhang 2012:1029)

There is a larger political implication than mere disturbance of court order by victims' families. Although judges are bound to follow the law, they have to take social impact and political stability into account. In the eyes of the government, organized petitions by victims' families and their supporters present an instability factor, and the court handling the case must address the concerns. There is thus a high likelihood that the persistent demands of victims' families may attract serious political attention and have an overriding impact on the death penalty decision. Facing intense public attention and strong demands for execution, judges react conservatively and may intentionally overlook some statutory mitigating factors, such as voluntary surrender or confession, and impose the death penalty merely to pacify the victims' families. Judges often concede that although there are legal rules to follow in sentencing, there is also a political demand, which has a higher priority, to deliver a good social impact. Indeed, in many cases, the demand to execute by the victim's family is the only hurdle for a decision not to execute, and the hurdle often cannot be conquered (ibid.).

What, then, explains the policy change in the judiciary and the shift from killing more to killing fewer and killing cautiously? Current literature focuses on the institutional self-interest of the court in brokering a deal between offenders and their victims so that the case ends once the money changes hands. The victims receive much-needed compensation, the defendant has his or her life spared, and the court can avoid further appeals from the defense or petitions from the victim's family. In sum, the court generally benefits from the informality that the deal brings about, hence the incentives (Ng & He 2013).

What has been underestimated is the professional aspiration within the judiciary to reduce and restrict the use of death penalty. Efforts to control the use of the death penalty began under Xiao Yang's leadership and have continued under his successors. The court has been able to persuade the Communist Party of the virtue of more cautious use of the death penalty in creating social harmony and has created institutions such as cash for clemency to conquer resistance (Trevaskes 2012). Brokering a deal between victims and their offenders in murder cases is a delicate, time-consuming, and risky business. In a significant way, behind mere self-interest, the court has made an extraordinary effort to control China's use of the death penalty.

Defiance of Public Opinion

There is occasionally a moment when legal rules matter and judges decide on death penalty cases according to their understanding of law in defiance of popular outcry. Li Changkuai's case well demonstrates a moment of judicial defiance of public opinion calling for the death penalty. In that case, the Yunnan Provincial High Court initially defied public outcry and the demand for immediate execution and reduced the sentence to death with a two-year suspension. The deputy president of the court, Tian Chengyou, held the strong view that a court should decide a case on the basis of law rather than public opinion, and that victims cannot dictate a court's decision. Tian spoke provocatively that there should not be execution "under a lynch mentality":

> We can no longer be indifferent as used to be the case. The old idea of a life for a life and sentencing someone to death without careful deliberation should be changed.... Our country needs to calm down, and our nation needs to calm down.... We will not execute a person simply because everyone demands killing.[11]

Tian went on to use the case to engage in a dialogue with the public on the death penalty and to guide public opinion. He believed that history was on the side of the court:

> Ten years later, many people would have changed their hearts. Now we are facing tremendous pressure, but the case will be a landmark and a model to follow in ten years' time.[12]

The Yunnan court, as it turned out, was not able to resist the social and political forces to execute Li. Tian's open defiance provoked fierce criticism from the public and allegedly censure from the party authority. Just over one month after Tian made his spirited statement, the high court reopened the case on its own for retrial and humbly admitted and corrected the error by reimposing the death penalty with immediate execution. The SPC soon duly approved the death penalty.

No court has been able to resist immense public pressure and subsequent political demands. Judicial compliance, that is, the imposition of the death penalty (or not) due to public opinion, and consequently political pressure, can happen at the highest level, as in the 2002 case of Liu Yong, a Mafia chief from Shengyang. The public was outraged by the appellate court's decision in that case to reduce the sentence from immediate execution to the death penalty with a two-year suspension because of apparent evidence of torture during interrogation. Facing mounting pressure from the public and apparently under the instruction of the party's political-legal authority, the SPC initiated an extraordinary proceeding of a new trial, found Liu guilty, and sentenced him to death on the same day.[13]

Judges will continue to defy public opinion and may even succeed in certain cases. A firm defiant position taken by a court institutionally may be possible only after significant legislative changes reducing and restricting the use of the death penalty, the development of a more independent and powerful court system, and sufficient institutional designs, such as insurance or state compensation for victims' families.

Engaging Public Opinion

Chinese courts are trying to find the right balance between deference and defiance in dealing with victims' claims for justice and potential populist backlash by actively engaging and absorbing public opinion. To enhance their credibility and legitimacy, courts have been instituting public participation programs, for example, by inviting influential individuals to serve as lay judges, law professors to serve as advisers, and other public figures to serve as special supervisors. In Henan province, the courts set up a special jury system in which selected individuals were invited to observe criminal trials and to give advisory opinions after a trial (for an overview of judicial measures to improve public relations and better reflect public opinion in judicial work, see SPC 2009). Although the opinions were not binding on the court, judges had to give explanations if the opinions were not followed.[14]

In order to bring the general public, victims' families in particular, on board in reducing the use of the death penalty, the SPC has formally endorsed a cash-for-clemency scheme for a limited number of death penalty cases.

Despite strong doubts about the legitimacy and legality of cash for clemency (for the academic and public debate on this matter, see Trevaskes 2015), there are three broad political-intellectual sources in support of this scheme in China. First, there is the political demand for a harmonious society since 2003. In regard to penal policies, and death penalty policies in particular, the SPC has demanded a more careful balancing between severe punishment for some offenders and lenient treatment for others. In capital cases, the SPC, through a series of judicial interpretations and guiding cases, has called for caution in using the death penalty in cases where there was some ongoing relationship between victims and offenders, where the offenders repented and agreed to compensate the victims' families, and where the victims' families were willing to accept a lesser punishment (SPC 1999; Chen 2013). Although the SPC has always allowed cash for leniency and clemency in limited circumstances, the harmonious society policy provided much-needed political legitimacy for the SPC to be clear and firm in supporting the cash-for-clemency scheme.

Second, there is an intellectual source that supports reconciliation throughout the criminal process. Victim-offender reconciliation (VOR) in China started as local initiatives under the influence of restorative justice and later received legislative endorsement in handling a wide range of minor offenses. VOR operates to create a system of diversion of criminal cases from prosecution and trial. Although VOR is designed to rehabilitate offenders who have committed minor offenses, its modus operandi provides some intellectual support for its use in cases of more serious offenses, including capital offenses (Wong & Mok 2010).

Third, there is an institutional source to support cash for clemency. Cash for clemency provides the right incentives to solve a particularly serious legal difficulty facing Chinese courts in enforcing civil damages that they award. In criminal cases, civil damage caused by a crime does not have an independent cause of action and is instead included within the criminal trial as a supplementary civil action. In the vast majority of cases, damages that are awarded to the victims or their families cannot be enforced for a variety of reasons, a situation that leads to repeated complaints and petitions by victims of crime to the trial courts. Insurance is generally not available or reliable in criminal cases; although a local scheme of state compensation exists, it offers a limited amount of assistance and pales in comparison with the huge demand. In the Chinese socialist tradition, the state habitually shifts the burden of a wide range of social security matters to families and local communities. When push comes to shove, local governments can be forced to step in to offer some payment to victims in high-profile cases. To ameliorate the difficulties of victim compensation, courts offer a reduction in sentencing to lure offenders, or their families in most of the cases, to offer financial payment to their victims. That proves to be a huge success when destitute victims and their families receive a cash payment and then leave the court alone to render a reduced sentence.

Compensation of victims' families in homicide cases becomes the other side of the death penalty debate. Indeed, penal reformers in Western democracies are well aware of the resistance on the part of victims' families to abolishing the death penalty and have tried to address issues on both sides of the debate: the state's interest in abolishing state killing and the emotional and financial interest of victims' families. It is not a coincidence that leading penal reformers, such as Margery Fry, campaigned not only for the abolition of the death penalty but also for the creation of state compensation for victims of crime.[15]

When the SPC demanded a reduction in use of the death penalty, compensation to victims' families naturally became an integral part of the process. Given the importance of a cash payment in exchange for forgiveness, defendants and their defense lawyers are eager to explore the possibility of a settlement, that is, to accept the possibility of a sentence other than death with immediate execution. VOR, which was commonly used for minor offenses, soon was extended to capital cases. To reduce the number of death penalty cases, the SPC has proactively designed and used a cash-for-clemency scheme in which victims' families cease their demand for immediate execution in exchange for a cash payment and an accompanying apology. To guide the courts in the country, the SPC has issued a number of guiding cases to promote and guide settlement between victims' families and offenders, along with subsequent cash for clemency (Trevaskes 2012).

Given the strong political, intellectual, and institutional support for cash for clemency, the practice has been widely used for certain capital offenses. Ng and He (2013) have forcefully argued that cash for clemency is a traditional practice and has been frequently used and well debated in China. It is a familiar practice for all the parties involved in the criminal process (Ng & He 2013). The practice was officially endorsed in 2003 as a response to the harmonious society policy and started to be used more frequently. In one of the centrally controlled cities, the number of cases involving cash for clemency in the high court (appellate court) was 2 in 2003, 3 in 2004, 4 in 2005, and 11 in 2006. Between 2007 and 2011, the same high court regularly conducted cash-for-clemency mediation, and as a result, the sentence was reduced from immediate execution to death with two-year suspension or from death with two-year suspension to a lower sentence in 83 cases after proper compensation was made. Interestingly, victims' families have also started to initiate cash for clemency on their own, although in the vast majority of cases, mediation has been initiated and facilitated by the court (Zhang 2012:1040). In Chongqing, another centrally controlled city, in the majority of cases, reduction from death with immediate execution to the death penalty with a two-year suspension was triggered by compensation made by the defendants to victims' families. There is sufficient evidence to indicate that cash for clemency happens regularly in Chinese courts, and voluntary payment to victims' families offers the highest likelihood of a sentence less than the death penalty with immediate execution (Zhao & Peng 2010).

The negotiation process involves two interrelated questions: does the victim's family need the money, and is the offender able to pay? It is often said that murder cases involve strong emotions, and it is hard to persuade the victim's family to accept cash for clemency. It is a delicate psychological process that needs careful planning and caution in handling. But the matter is often more straightforward than expected. For destitute families who lose an able-bodied member, as is often the case, there may not be another option. There are multiple variations in reconciling the need for money and the ability to pay, and the particular dynamics naturally vary from one case to another. Some defendants and their families offer more than they are willing or able to pay at the outset but then try to bargain the price down in subsequent negotiation. Others take an incremental approach and increase the offer as the negotiation evolves. Victims' reactions vary. For some, it is extremely difficult to start a conversation on cash for clemency; others proactively pursue a settlement. Even in cases where victims' families adamantly demand immediate execution, there have been attempts to reach a settlement.[16]

An example may illustrate the process. After some minor disputes, Ma Tao stabbed three of his fellow workers and killed one of them.[17] He was convicted of murder and sentenced to death with immediate execution at trial, and his appeal was dismissed. On review by the SPC, an SPC judge was reluctant to approve the death penalty on the ground that Mao had no criminal record; he regretted and repented; the killing was caused by trivial disputes among workers; and, more important, Ma's father and sister were willing to compensate the victim's family. Ma's father expressed his willingness to sell his house to cover the civil damage awarded to the victim's family. The judge then traveled to Henan to persuade Ma's sister, who was a schoolteacher, to pay another 150,000 yuan to the victim's family to save her brother's life.

After consulting the trial judges and appeal judges in the case, the SPC judges traveled to Sichuan, where the deceased's father resided. There the judges were able to secure written consent from the destitute father not to request the death penalty on condition that the offender's family would make payment as promised. After some difficult negotiations, money changed hands, and the SPC then decided not to approve the death penalty.

Money is not the only concern in the bargaining process. Ng and He (2013) noted that other factors beyond the amount of money also matter, such as the cultural and moral value, including the effort made by offenders and their families in raising the money and their attitude in dealing with victims' families. Yao Jiaxin's family failed to settle with the victim's family in part because of the perception that Yao's parents had behaved arrogantly at an earlier stage of the case. Like the son who killed the victim, the parents looked down on migrants. The strong view of the victim's family in the Li Changkui case was that Li's family did not care.

• • •

Public opinion matters in different regime types, and an authoritarian state like China is as deeply concerned with opinions of its citizens as democracies are. Popular opinion as reflected in victims' petitions and sympathy in social media is an influential force for Chinese courts to reckon with in making decisions. In the end, death penalty decisions require the broad support of society and cannot be left merely to judges to decide. This chapter has argued that Chinese penal populism occurs in a different cultural context. Chinese penal populism challenges principally the perceived abuse of power and addresses the issue of social inequality, with Chinese egalitarianism as the backdrop; in contrast, its Western counterpart pitches the silent majority against the interest of criminals and what are perceived to be soft-on-crime penal policies.

This chapter also argues that what passes for public opinion in China is really the opinions of victims, defendants, and their respective supporters who advocate for certain specific positions—either for lenience or for harshness in sentencing and either for or against the death penalty. Piercing the veils of public opinion in the Yao case and many other sensational cases, one can quickly realize that public opinion may not be as spontaneous as it initially appears to be. Behind public agitation and outcry, victims' families and their supporters actively mobilize and exploit the sympathy of the general public, tactically frame their tragedies, and aggressively push a particular line with the explicit aim of bringing public pressure to bear on decision makers. There are professional middlemen for hire who can fan public emotion and bring the case to a higher profile. The perfect storm would not have formed without painstaking, persistent, and aggressive organization of public opinion. The storm can then shape the political agenda and override the judicial decision-making process.

Having identified the core of penal populism, Chinese courts have to face the challenges in a particularly Chinese style. The courts may defer to the populist demand and render a compliant decision, or they may ignore it and stand firm on what is regarded as professional principles and rules. Neither choice satisfies the competing imperatives of killing more and killing less. That dilemma between populist demand and professional requirements eventually compels the court to identify the origin of public opinion, address it tactically, and successfully capture it to the court's advantage. As is often the case, victims' families are at the heart of public opinion in support of the death penalty. The lack of meaningful state compensation and societal support for victims' families place them in a precarious position. The vulnerability of victims' families easily attracts the sympathy and support of the general public, which rallies behind the call for the imposition of the death penalty with immediate execution. The court seizes that opportunity and exploits the vulnerability by aggressively implementing the cash-for-clemency scheme. The monetary compensation, accompanied by the cultural value, often assuages the emotions of the victims' families, softens their demands, and preempts populist protests. In the end, this judiciary-facilitated compromise of cash for clemency works to reduce the use of the death penalty in a country where a weak court has to face powerful public opinion.

NOTES

1. See M. Wines, "Execution in a Killing That Fanned Class Rancor," retrieved September 1, 2014, from http://www.nytimes.com/2011/06/08/world/asia/08china.html?_r=0.
2. The call for equity vanishes quickly, however, in cases relating to ethnic minorities. Chinese Internet users, for example, are nationalistic and chauvinistic in debating the death penalty that was imposed on Uyghurs (a local ethnic group) for the alleged terrorist offenses in Xinjiang.
3. Li (2015) is of the view that there is penal populism in China only in a weak sense because of the lack of political space for advocacy.
4. See M. Young, "History of Victims Movement—U.S.A.," retrieved September 1, 2014, from http://www.iovahelp.org/About/MarleneAYoung/USHistory.pdf.
5. She was charged with the offense of murdering his wife in 1994 and was finally convicted of the same offense in 1998, but the victim was actually alive and returned home in 2005.
6. This case involved a suicide pact of two persons in love who were not able to marry because of the objection of the woman's parents. Ge killed his lover and then tried to commit suicide. See Trevaskes (2014).
7. During a dispute over an agreement between two families to build residential houses on farmland, Feng stabbed three members of the other family, leading to the death of one of them. See ibid.
8. The case happened in a remote village in Yunnan, where the Li and Wang families had been engaged in family feuds. On May 14, 2009, fresh fighting erupted that led to Li Changkui's return from the city in which he worked. On May 16, 2009, Li Changkui accosted the Wangs' 19-year-old daughter, Wang Jiafei, and her 3-year-old brother. A fight ensued, and Li raped Wang Jiafei and then killed both her and her brother. For a brief introduction to the lengthy procedure of this case, see "Li Changkui," retrieved October 15, 2014, from http://baike.baidu.com/subview/634081/6124609.htm.
9. As stated in the judgment sentencing Yao Jiaxin to death with immediate execution, "Although Yao Jiaxin and their parents are willing to pay the economic loss of the plaintiff in the supplementary civil litigation, the plaintiff however declined to accept the compensation that may serve to reduce the sentencing. The offer to compensate therefore cannot be used to reduce Yao Jiaxin's punishment." Cited in Zhang (2012).
10. Li was eventually found not guilty because of lack of evidence after a 12-year detention. See "Sixing baozhengshu an dangshiren Li Huailiang shoudao 980,000 guojia peichang" [Li Huailiang, the defendant in the 'death penalty undertaking' case, receiving 980,000 in state compensation], retrieved September 1, 2014, from http://news.163.com/14/0303/03/9MCQ09RV00014Q4P.html.
11. See "Yunnan gaoyuan fuyuanzhang tan Li Changkui an: buhui yinwei dou hansha er pan sixing" [Deputy president of Yunan High Court on the Li Changkui case: Cannot execute a person simply because everyone so demands], retrieved September 1, 2014, from http://news.ifeng.com/society/1/detail_2011_07/14/7694927_0.shtml.

12 Ibid.
13 For an analysis of the legal process of the case, see "Liaoning heishehui laoda Liu Yong sixing gaipan sihuan shijian zhenxiang" [The truth behind the change from death penalty with immediate execution to one with a two-year suspension for Shengyang's Mafia chief Liu Yong], retrieved September 1, 2014, from http://www.china.com.cn/chinese/2003/Aug/392917.htm. For a critical view of the Liu Yong case by a death penalty judge at the SPC, see Lu (2009).
14 See J. A. Cohen, "A 'People's Jury' Trial for China's Criminal Defendants," retrieved September 1, 2014, from http://usali.org/media-entities/a-peoples-jury-trial-for-chinas-criminal-defendants/.
15 Fry was a leading prison reformer in the United Kingdom in the early twentieth century who effectively advocated for a more humanitarian penal system. See Jones (1966).
16 In the Yao Jiaxin case, the victim's family made it clear that Yao's parents should have made their apology and offered compensation much earlier instead of waiting until the trial was about to start. Yao's family claimed to be acting on their lawyer's advice to wait for a better moment to negotiate. They eventually asked the police to serve as the middlemen for the negotiation, but the police declined. In the Li Changkui case, the trial judge imposed the death penalty with immediate execution only after the court tried to mediate a settlement on compensation but failed. According to the victims' family, Li's family neither had the ability to pay nor demonstrated any willingness to pay.
17 See "Faguan kua sansheng diaojie Ma Tao an qisihuisheng: yifa buhezhun sixing dianxing anli 1" [Judges travelling across three provinces to mediate a case and to bring Ma Tao back to life from dead: Standard case of non-approval of death sentence: Case 1], retrieved September 1, 2014, from http://www.legaldaily.com.cn/misc/2009-10/30/content_1174648.htm.

REFERENCES

Belkin, I. (2014, July 10–11). The seeds of democracy or mob justice? The influence of Chinese public opinion on criminal cases. Paper presented at the workshop *Justice: The China Experience* at Griffith University, Australia.

Blacker, K., & Griffin, L. (2010). Megan's law and Sarah's law: A comparative study of sex offender community notification schemes in the United States and the United Kingdom. *Criminal Law Bulletin, 46*, 987–1008.

Blumer, H. (1948). Public opinion and public opinion polling. *American Sociological Review, 13*, 542–549.

Chen, X. (2013). Sixing de sifa kongzhi [Judicial control of death penalty]. *Faxue* [China Legal Science], *2*, 43–57.

Converse, P. (1987). Changing conceptions of public opinion in the political process. *Public Opinion Quarterly, 51*, 12–24.

Enns, P. K. (2014). The public's increasing punitiveness and its influence on mass incarceration in the United States. *American Journal of Political Science, 58*, 857–872.

Filler, D. M. (2001). Making the case for Megan's law: A study in legislative rhetoric. *Indiana Law Journal, 76*, 315–366.

Friedman, B. (2009). *The Will of the People: How Public Opinion Has Influenced the Supreme Court and Shaped the Meaning of the Constitution.* New York: Farrar, Straus & Giroux.

Fu, H. (2014). Politicized challenges, de-politicized responses: Political monitoring in China's transitions. In F. Davis, N. McGarrity, and G. Williams (Eds.), *Surveillance, Counter-Terrorism, and Comparative Constitutionalism* (pp. 296–312). New York: Routledge.

Fu, H., & Cullen, R. (2008). *Weiquan* (rights protection) lawyering in an authoritarian state: Building a culture of public interest lawyering. *China Journal, 59*, 111–127.

Garland, D. (2001). *The Culture of Control.* New York: Oxford University Press.

Gilley, B. (2009). *The Right to Rule: How States Win and Lose Legitimacy.* New York: Columbia University Press.

Hall, S. (1979). *Drifting into a Law and Order Society.* London: Cobden Trust.

Jones, E. H. (1966). *Margery Fry: The Essential Amateur.* Oxford: Oxford University Press.

Kirchengast, T. (2011). The landscape of victim rights in Australian homicide cases—Lessons from the international experience. *Oxford Journal of Legal Studies, 31*, 133–163.

Lacey, N. (2008). *The Prisoners' Dilemma: Political Economy and Punishment in Contemporary Democracies.* Cambridge: Cambridge University Press.

Li, E. (2015). The cultural idiosyncrasy of penal populism: The case of contemporary China. *British Journal of Criminology, 55*(1), 146–163.

Liebman, B. (2005). Watchdog or demagogue? The media in the Chinese legal system. *Columbia Law Review, 105*, 1–157.

Liebman, B. (2011). A populist threat to China's courts? In Mary Gallagher & Margaret Woo (Eds.), *Chinese Justice: Civil Dispute Resolution in Post-Reform China* (pp. 259–313). Cambridge: Cambridge University Press.

Liebman, B. (2013). Medical mobs: Malpractice dispute resolution in China. *Columbia Law Review, 113*, 181–264.

Logan, W. A. (2011). Megan's law as a case study in political stasis. *Syracuse Law Review, 61*, 371–411.

Lu, J. (2009). On the application of the death penalty and public opinion. *Chinese Sociology and Anthropology, 41*(4), 66–79.

McConville, M., & Pils, E. (Eds.). (2013). *Comparative Perspectives on Criminal Justice in China*. Cheltenham: Edward Elgar Publishing.

Miao, M. (2013). Capital punishment in China: A populist instrument of social governance. *Theoretical Criminology, 17*, 233–250.

Ng, K., & He, X. (2013). The limits of legal commensuration: Blood money and negotiated justice in China. Paper on file with the author.

Peerenboom, R. (2009). *Judicial Independence in China: Lessons for Global Rule of Law Promotion*. New York: Cambridge University Press.

Pratt, J. (2007). *Penal Populism*. London: Routledge.

Reilly, J. (2011). *Strong Society, Smart State: The Rise of Public Opinion in China's Japan Policy*. New York: Columbia University Press.

Roberts, J., & Hough, M. (Eds.). (2002). *Changing Attitudes to Punishment: Public Opinion, Crime and Justice*. Cullompton: Willan.

Roberts, J. V., Stalans, C., Indermaur, D., & Hough, M. (2003). *Penal Populism and Public Opinion: Lessons from Five Countries*. Oxford: Oxford University Press.

Stockmann, D. (2013). Media Commercialization and Authoritarian Rule in China. New York: Cambridge University Press.

Supreme People's Court. (1999, October 27). *Quanguo fayuan weihu nongcun wending xingshi shenpan gongzuo zuotanhui jiyao* [Notice to circulate the minutes of the conference on the role of criminal trial in maintaining rural stability]. Retrieved October 7, 2014, from http://wenku.baidu.com/view/08995b166edb6 f1aff001faa.html.

Supreme People's Court. (2009, April 13). *Zuigao renmin fayuan guanyu jinyibu jiaqiang minyi goutong gongzuo de yijian* [Notice of the Supreme People's Court on issuing the opinions on further strengthening the communication with public opinion]. Available at http://china.findlaw.cn/fagui/p_1/12640.html.

Supreme People's Court. (2010, October 1). *Renmin fayuan liangxing zhidao yijian (shixing)* [Guidance opinions for People's Courts on sentencing (provisional)]. Available at http://www.360doc.com/content/10/0806/17/2587284_44136882 .shtml.

Trevaskes, S. (2012). *The Death Penalty in Contemporary China*. New York: Palgrave Macmillan.

Trevaskes, S. (2014). Death sentencing for stability and harmony. In S. Trevaskes, E. Nesossi, S. Biddulph, & F. Sapio (Eds.), *The Politics of law and Stability in China*. Cheltenham: Edward Elgar Publishing.

Trevaskes, S. (2015). Lenient death sentence and the "cash for clemency" debate. *The China Journal, 73*, 38–58.
Wong, D. S., & Mok, L. W. (2010). Restorative justice and practices in China. *British Journal of Community Justice, 8*, 23–35.
Yu, J. (Ed.). (2006). *Sixing yanjiu* [A Study of Death Penalty]. Beijing: Falv chuban she [Law Press].
Zhang, X. (2012). Sixing anjian caipanzhong fei xingfa guifan yinsu kaoliang [Extra–criminal law consideration in death penalty decisions]. *Zhongwai faxue* [Peking University Law Journal], *5*, 1021–1045.
Zhao, B., & Peng, X. (2010). Lun minshi peichang yu sixing de xianzhi zuoyong [On civil compensation and limiting the application of the death penalty]. *Zhongguo faxue* [China Legal Science], *5*, 52–62.
Zimring, F. E. (1996). Populism, democratic government, and the decline of expert authority: Some reflections on "three strikes" in California. *Pacific Law Journal, 28*, 242–256.
Zimring, F. E., Hawkins, G., & Kamin, S. (2001). *Punishment and Democracy: Three Strikes and You're Out in California*. Oxford: Oxford University Press.

11

Chinese Capital Punishment in Comparative Perspective

▸ DAVID T. JOHNSON *and* MICHELLE MIAO

WHAT IS SEEN and stressed in Chinese capital punishment depends on how one looks. As David Garland (2007:439) observes:

> There is no one "right way" to think historically and comparatively about capital punishment (or about any other subject for that matter). There are multiple vantage points, multiple perspectives, and multiple interpretations, each of which is more or less useful, more or less appropriate, more or less persuasive. The choice of perspective depends on the stakes and the purposes involved. How we think about capital punishment depends on how we contextualize it. Significance depends on context; comparison depends on the choice of comparison group. We conventionally compare the United States to other developed Western nations, or to liberal democracies, but it might also make sense to compare it to other federated nations, or to states with very large populations, or to high-crime societies, or to postcolonial societies, or to nations characterized by fundamentalist religious belief. Each of these comparisons would alter our sense of where America stands on the capital punishment continuum.

In China, too, there is no one right way to think about capital punishment. There are, rather, multiple vantage points, perspectives, and interpretations. This chapter adopts three of them in order to suggest where the People's Republic of China (PRC) stands in comparative perspective. Comparative analysis is about "discovering both surprising differences and unexpected similarities" (Nelken 2010:32). Two other aims of this chapter are to discern what is peculiar in Chinese capital punishment and also what is ordinary.

The first section of this chapter compares capital punishment in contemporary China with capital punishment in the Chinese past, a perspective that reveals both striking continuities and remarkable changes. The second section compares the PRC with the "other Chinas," namely, Hong Kong, Taiwan, and Singapore, a comparison that highlights the importance of international norms and national reputation as influences on death penalty policy and practice. The third section compares China with the Communist countries of Vietnam and North Korea, an approach that suggests that the future of capital punishment in Asia depends on the fate of the last remaining authoritarian regimes in the region.

PERSPECTIVES FROM CHINA'S PAST

At the time of this writing in June 2014, two contrasting facts about capital punishment in China deserve emphasis. First, China remains by a large margin the most frequent user of the death penalty in the modern world. State secrecy and the manipulation of information continue to frustrate efforts to describe the empirical contours of capital punishment in the PRC, but best estimates suggest that in 2012 the country probably executed about 3,000 persons—around four times more judicial executions than were carried out by the rest of the world combined (Areddy 2013; "Death penalty" 2013; Hands off Cain 2013). In absolute numbers, China remains the world's execution leader—and second place is not close.

Second, executions in China have also declined rapidly since the turn of the millennium, from a total of 15,000 or so in 2000 to perhaps 20% of that total in 2012. The magnitude of this plunge in executions rivals "the great American crime decline" that have occurred in the United States (Zimring 2007) and New York City (Zimring 2012) in recent decades, and China's decline has been driven in part by the perception of leaders in the Chinese Communist Party (CCP) that the country's outlier status with respect to capital punishment undermines the quest to receive the respect and recognition they feel the PRC deserves. Worldwide, moral revolutions against dueling, slavery, foot binding, and other practices now deemed barbaric were often rooted in a "deep and persistent concern with status and respect" and the powerful human need for recognition and honor (Appiah 2010:xiii), and the same seems to be true of China's execution decline. As Bakken (2007:182) observes, "The fact that China today executes many more people than the rest of the world combined is one that today shames the country internationally more than any other single question." At the same time, China's execution drop suggests that capital punishment in the PRC is rapidly changing even while the country remains a death penalty giant.

How did China become the world's most aggressive death penalty state? One prominent account of modern Chinese history argues that "in trying to understand China today we need to know about China in the past; but how far back we carry that search remains, in a sense, the central question" (Spence 1990:xix). Arguments to the contrary notwithstanding (Lu & Miethe 2007:27–48), understanding the origins of China's death penalty exceptionalism does not require a return to ancient emperors or mandarins. China's modest death penalty totals in the early twentieth century contrast starkly with the death penalty rate for common crimes in the early years of the twenty-first century (Johnson & Zimring 2009:253). Among other puzzles, how did the country go from only 122 death sentences in 1933 to 100 times or more that many in 2000?[1]

The origins of China's present death penalty policy can be found in the political carnage of postrevolutionary China and in the transitions in criminal justice and governance during the reform years of the 1980s that turned judicial execution into a frequent form of criminal punishment. More specifically, the founding fathers of execution policy in the PRC are Joseph Stalin, Mao Zedong, and Deng Xiaoping. In asserting the obvious importance of this triumvirate, we are not advancing a great-man theory of history; we are merely recognizing that some individuals can be powerful agents of change (Tucker 1995). These three leaders represented and created social forces that helped determine the shape of capital punishment in present-day China.

Stalin (1879–1953) was the originator and first great practitioner of mass killing as an instrument of Communist governance. Although he never made Chinese policy, his design and administration of mass extermination in the Soviet Union from the time he took control of the party and government in 1929 until his death in 1953 were in many ways the model Mao adopted. The highest levels of violence under Stalin were far removed from the years of the Russian Revolution and were attached to a wide variety of agendas, from agrarian reorganization to the removal of political threats. Although most killings were governmental, they frequently failed to observe the principles or pretenses of legal authorization of criminal sanctions (Bullock 1998).

The truest heirs of Stalin were not the Soviet leaders who followed him, for they had no grand political scheme other than keeping the Soviet Union afloat. For huge Stalinist projects aimed at remaking society, one must turn to the Asian cases of Mao Zedong (1893–1976) in China and Pol Pot (1925–1998) in Cambodia. Cambodia abolished the death penalty after a holocaust that killed 1.5 million people out of a total population of only 7 million. The main point of that abolition was to "mark with a powerful symbol" the end of Pol Pot's vicious regime (Hood and Hoyle 2008:85). Cambodia's abolition was confirmed in 1993 when its new constitution mandated that "there shall be no capital punishment" (Cambodian League for the Promotion and Defence of Human Rights 2007).

The death penalty in China, by contrast, outlived Mao with a vengeance not seen in the Soviet Union after Stalin. Mao has been called "the most destructive tyrant in recorded history," and intentional killing was one hallmark of his rule (Mirsky 1994). This view has been contested by those who believe that Mao belongs in a different category from other twentieth-century tyrants because, unlike Stalin and Hitler, he had a utopian dream to transform his country, and because he never lost his belief in the efficacy of thought reform and the possibility of redemption. In the end, however, both Mao and Stalin had many people killed in an effort to expand their personal power, so it is difficult to see a big difference between them. Of course, there were numerous actors and factors besides Mao that made the twentieth century such a terrible one for so many Chinese, including the savagery of Japan's assault on China, the depth of peasant deprivation in Republican China, the collapse of local order and the spread of banditry in the early Republican period, the strength of criminal gangs in many parts of the country, the large-scale extrajudicial killing by Chiang Kai-shek and his Nationalist Party, and the means-justify-the-ends mentality of Mao's comrades in the Communist Party. This was the milieu in which Mao emerged, and accounts of his acts and influences must attend to these formative forces (Johnson & Zimring 2009:257). In the end, however, Mao had more control over more people than any other leader in human history, and how he exercised that control was strongly shaped by his direct and indirect relationships with Joseph Stalin and by his decisions to adopt many of the Soviet dictator's methods (Chang & Halliday 2005:337). In particular, Mao employed Stalin's model of death as an instrument of political action, both during the long civil war of Communist ascendancy and throughout his nearly three decades of rule thereafter. In much of this Maoist period, legal forms and judicial authority were not regarded as important or even necessary elements of political killing because the authority of the Communist power structure was considered sufficient to provide whatever legitimacy the act required. As with Stalin, when terror was a weapon of state, legitimacy was not a pressing issue. And as with Stalin, the death toll generated by Mao's policies is difficult to determine with precision but certainly numbered in the many millions (Zhang 2008).

Two years after Mao's death in 1976, Deng Xiaoping (1904–1997) assumed leadership of China. When he died in 1997, an obituary in the *New York Times* stated that "if you look at the 150 years of modern China's history since the Opium Wars, then you can't avoid the conclusion that the last 15 years [under Deng] are the best 15 years in China's modern history" (Tyler 1997). In the nearly two decades during which Deng was the PRC's premier leader, his economic pragmatism helped nourish a boom that greatly improved the lives of hundreds of millions of Chinese (Vogel 2011). But if Deng's economic pragmatism diverged from Mao's ideological extremism, there were significant continuities between the two leaders in politics and criminal justice (Pan 2008). Most fundamentally, both strongly resisted democratic stirrings, and both insisted on the preeminence of the Communist Party. The capital punishment policies of Mao and Deng did differ in some respects. Most notably, the blurry line between judicial and extrajudicial killing that existed under Mao became clearer under Deng as he pushed for the development of some legal institutions, and the volume of extrajudicial executions decreased dramatically after Mao died and the Cultural Revolution ended. Nonetheless, the death penalty similarities between Mao and Deng are striking and substantial. In our view, the following are 10 of the most salient death penalty resemblances (Johnson & Zimring 2009:263–264):

1 A strong reliance on harshness in punishment, including the frequent use of execution as a criminal sanction

2. The use of execution targets and quotas, with different regions of the country sometimes competing against one another
3. The decentralization of most death penalty decision-making power
4. The orchestration of mass campaigns to crack down on people and activities deemed threatening, the enlistment of mass involvement in these campaigns, the routinization of the campaigns, and faith in the general deterrent effects of public degradation rituals
5. The leading role of the Communist Party in capital punishment policy making and the frequent intervention of party officials in individual cases
6. A view of law as an elastic instrument for achieving party and regime purposes
7. Speedy decision making in individual cases, with little allowance for aggressive defense lawyering or meaningful appeal
8. Heavy dependence on confessions for evidence and the routine use of torture to obtain them
9. Frequent recourse in official rhetoric to "popular will" and "public support" as reasons for harsh punishment policies
10. Extreme secrecy about death penalty statistics

In short, Deng had a golden opportunity to change Chinese death penalty policy after he came to power in 1978, but he chose not to (Bakken 2004:79). The year 1978 marked a turning point for China in many ways, economically and socially, of course, but also in the crime field, because the belief that the nation was experiencing a large increase in crime rapidly became orthodox. The belief may not have been well grounded, but things that are defined as real can have real consequences, and that is what happened here. By the early 1980s, concerns about deteriorating public security prompted Deng and his comrades in the CCP to declare that they would "reverse the present abnormal situation" by showing "absolutely no mercy in striking determined blows against criminal elements" (quoted in Tanner 1999:83). Thus was born the first of China's strike-hard (*yanda*) campaigns. They would become a perpetual feature of China's crime-control policy for the next two decades.

To say that Deng continued many of Mao's execution policies is not to say that the two leaders were death penalty twins. Crime was not a central concern of the first two founding fathers (Stalin and Mao), nor was execution as a specific judicial sanction its central form. Moreover, it was Deng and his cadre who engineered the transformation of judicially ordered execution into a frequently used instrument of crime control. Little is known about the level of executions in China immediately before this change or about the peak rates that were reached after strike-hard campaigns took effect. What we do know, however, is that rising crime became an important public and governmental concern in the early 1980s, and the central government responded by mandating severe punishments and implementing changes in the legal process that would reduce the costs and increase the rates of execution. The most important of these Deng-era changes was the 1983 decision to decentralize the administration of capital punishment by relocating authority for reviewing death sentences from the Supreme People's Court (SPC), the nation's top judicial organ, to local courts at the provincial level. This decentralization stimulated a large increase in the use of capital punishment (Trevaskes 2012:28).

The big difference between the scale of political killing in the era of terror under Mao and the much smaller number of state executions during the strike-hard campaigns under Deng suggests that political killing can provide a precedent for broad campaigns of judicial execution. The same contrast helps explain how Deng and his successors could regard their crackdowns as moderate. Compared with 300,000 or 500,000 political killings per year, 15,000 executions of convicted criminals do not seem extreme. In comparison with the scale of state killings under Mao and their often dubious legality, even five-digit execution totals seem like small beer, especially if they are accompanied by some signs of legality.

But if state killing today is less common and more governed by law than it was under Mao, and if most Chinese citizens support capital punishment, then what explains the state secrecy that continues to surround the number of executions in China? The core answer is the sensitivity of China's government to critical foreign opinion (Miao 2013b), but the connection between political killing and judicial execution may provide additional insight into this secrecy policy. If political authorities like Deng regarded these two genres of state killing as linked, the practice of treating political killing as an appropriate secret of government may have carried over to the practice of judicial execution. In this way, a central fact about state power—how often is it used to kill?—may be kept secret as much out of inertia as out of fear of foreign criticism framed in terms of human rights.[2]

Tradition is also used to explain and justify the frequent use of capital punishment in contemporary China, but the high current rate of execution has its proximate roots in the government that came to power in the mid-twentieth century rather than in ancient practices or enduring propunishment values. Long-standing patterns of Chinese culture may have contributed to the political appeal and public tolerance of Mao's practices and tactics. If so, then China's "legalist" tradition of reliance on harsh punishment for order could have played an indirect role in the exceptional policies of the present (Lu & Miethe 2007:31). Even if this is true, the most important causes of China's present system of capital punishment are less than 70 years old and are political at their core (Bakken 2013). The CCP continues to encourage and enforce forgetfulness about the most painful parts of this recent history, but most of China's present leaders were in their teens or twenties when the brutalizing class warfare of the Cultural Revolution occurred, and they would not be human if the scars did not run deep. The culture of violence of Mao's Communist Party not only shaped the death penalty sensibilities of China's current leaders but also dominated the thinking and feeling of the old men—Mao's comrades—who ordered the killings at Tiananmen in 1989 and the crackdown on Falun Gong ten years later (Johnson & Zimring 2009:229). For these reasons, one might expect strike-hard campaigns to "continue to be used as the key political response to social change in China well into the first decades of the new century" (Trevaskes 2002:692). Another reason to expect more of the same is that crime is considered a primary threat to China's economic development and social stability, and therefore, crime control is widely regarded as the nation's top priority (Osnos 2014). What Jiang Zemin stressed when he was in power (1993–2003) remains a watchword today: "Stability overrides everything" (Gilley 1998:170).

No matter how reasonable these expectations for more Maoist capital punishment may seem, they are being complicated and confounded in several ways. Since the early years of the twenty-first century, a remaking of China's death penalty regime has unfolded in top-down fashion. The reforms, which were launched by China's political and legal authorities at the national level, were backed by elites in academic and judicial circles. Concerns about China's international reputation as the global champion of execution were shared by members of this reform-minded elite community (Miao 2013a), and China launched these reforms only a few years after the global campaign against the death penalty started gathering momentum in this country around the turn of the century (Hood 2009). Another important motivating factor for the reforms was domestic criticism after several miscarriages of justice in capital cases were revealed in the early years of the twenty-first century (Scott 2010:72–74).

The elite-led reconfiguration of Chinese capital punishment is composed of five main reforms: restricting the scope of capital offenses in Chinese criminal law, replacing shooting with lethal injection as the main execution method, increasing the use of suspended death sentences, encouraging "cash for clemency," and, most important, the recentralization of judicial review in capital cases.

The term *death-eligible offenses* in China's Criminal Law (1997) covers a wide range of crimes, including theft and smuggling wildlife across national borders. Although the Criminal Law stipulates that only those who "commit extremely serious crimes" are subject to the ultimate punishment, the ambit of this category in practice is extremely broad. The Criminal Law of 1997 was promulgated at the height of the second wave of nationwide strike-hard campaigns. Incorporating no fewer than 68 capital offenses into this law reflected a widening of the net of penal control in that era.

For more than a decade after 1997, the number of capital offenses in Chinese criminal statutes remained unchanged. Then in 2011, 13 nonviolent economic crimes were removed from the list of capital offenses (Hogg 2011; Stack 2010). Interviews conducted by the second author of this chapter found that in some Chinese provinces, most of these 13 offenses were seldom subject to capital punishment before their abolition (Miao 2013c:504). The approach taken by Chinese reformers is to progressively restrict the scope of capital offenses, starting with those that are least controversial and of marginal importance to the actual operation of the criminal justice system. But even since the 2011 change, capital punishment remains on the books for 55 crimes, of which 31 are nonviolent offenses. If the draft Ninth Amendment to the Criminal Law is approved by the national legislature later this year, the number of capital offenses will be further reduced to 46. At present, the most frequently prosecuted capital crimes in China are murder, robbery, intentional infliction of physical harm, and drug offenses. Death sentences are seldom sought or imposed for other offenses (Miao 2013b), but there remains a large gap between China's notion of "most serious crimes" and the interpretation of this notion by the United Nations Economic and Social

Council Safeguards, which guarantees the rights of persons facing capital punishment.

The main method of execution in China has slowly shifted from shooting to lethal injection. In contrast to the United States, where lethal injection has been challenged for inflicting extreme pain on prisoners, in China it is considered a more humane method than death by a bullet to the back of the head. But the legitimacy of lethal injection in China has been challenged as a privilege reserved for a small number of death row inmates, especially corrupt officials and condemned offenders whose cases attracted nationwide publicity. It appears that most condemned inmates are not offered a choice between lethal injection and a firing squad in provincial areas where the judicial budget is tight, but wealth and connections apparently can be used to obtain the more medicalized method (MacLeod 2006; Xiong 2009). The use of lethal injection is motivated by domestic and international concerns (Bezlova 2008; Johnson & Zimring 2009:275). In particular, the two main forces driving this reform are heightened concern about the negative impact on China's reputation of execution by firing squad and the shift of cultural sensibilities toward compassion and sympathy for persons sentenced to death.

The most important reform in Chinese capital punishment was the 2007 recall of review power in capital cases to the SPC. If the delegation of this review power to provincial courts in 1983 was the "clearest case of explicit encouragement for an aggressive execution policy" (Johnson & Zimring 2009:270), the retrieval of it by China's top court is a major milestone in China's death penalty reform. This particular reform is also a product of domestic and international forces. Public discourse about capital punishment in the middle of the first decade of the twenty-first century was brimming with anger and discontent over miscarriages of justice that had occurred in capital cases (Lu & Miethe 2007:130; Yardley 2005). Restoring review power to the SPC was a response to these concerns about accuracy in fact finding. At the same time, international pressure on China to restrict its use of capital punishment also shaped political and legal decision making on this issue. Indeed, according to the then president of the SPC, the restoration of review power was an essential step toward improving the fairness of capital trials and curtailing the use of capital punishment in the PRC (Xiao 2006).

In China's criminal justice system, the top judiciary has broad authority to influence and even determine the general policies and specific decisions of lower courts. Most notably, the SPC has directed lower courts to implement a policy of "kill fewer, kill cautiously" (*shao sha shen sha*) and thereby to move toward moderation in the use of capital punishment. If the SPC finds that fact finding or the application of law by a lower court is flawed, or if it finds that a defendant sentenced to death should have received a lesser punishment, it is likely to overturn the decision or send it back to the lower court for retrial (Xinhua News Agency 2007). As a result, lower-court judges in the postreform era exercise greater care in deciding capital cases (Scott 2010). A complementary way of interpreting this change is to say that the recentralization of review power in capital cases has to some extent freed judicial decision making in capital trials and appeals from the control of local networks of corruption and patronage, which have long been influential in China's judiciary (Miao 2013b).

Elite interviews carried out by the second author found that since the recall of review power to the SPC, the number of cases sent back to lower courts for retrial or overturned by the SPC on the grounds of wrongful application of the law or erroneous admission of evidence has gradually declined over time. Hence, further restriction on the use of capital punishment no longer depends on appellant reviews, which focus mainly on correcting wrongful convictions. Instead, increasing the use of noncapital sanctions through guidelines issued in the reform era, such as "The defendant should not be subject to the death penalty if he or she can be sentenced to lesser punishment according to law," became the most effective approach to reducing the number of defendants subject to capital punishment. This in turn led to judicial reinterpretation of the Criminal Law and a rise in the number of offenders given a suspended sentence of death (*sihuan*), a form of penal punishment one level below the death penalty in China's hierarchy of criminal statutes.

A suspended death sentence can be used as an alternative to the death penalty even for serious criminal offenses, such as murder, rape, and kidnapping. In practice, there has been a huge gap in the severity of punishment between a death sentence and a suspended death sentence, for the average time served by inmates sentenced to the latter is about 16 years (Huang 2011). It is therefore surprising that there are few official sentencing guidelines for judicial decision making in capital cases. The discretionary power of lower-court judges is guided mainly by instructions from the SPC, which are often expressed in ambiguous language. As a result, defendants committing comparable offenses can be sentenced to very different sanctions, and sometimes offenders who committed less serious crimes are sentenced to capital punishment while those who deserve more serious punishment are treated with greater leniency. This threat to the principle of proportionality in capital sentencing has been widely debated in China (Trevaskes 2012:115–142). One solution recently proposed by academics was to increase the severity of the suspended sentence of death so as to reduce the gap between a suspended death sentence and a death sentence eligible for immediate execution. In 2011, the SPC, through the Eighth Amendment to the Criminal Law and a related legal ordinance, stipulated that for serious crimes, such as murder, rape, robbery, and kidnapping, lower courts may place limitations on the conditions under which a suspended death sentence can be commuted to a lesser punishment. Under the new rule, defendants subject to a suspended death sentence will have to spend at least 25 years in prison in addition to the initial 2-year probationary period. It remains to be seen what the practical effects of this enhancement will be, and the same can be said about the collateral consequences of reduced reliance on capital punishment for the rest of China's criminal justice system.

"Cash for clemency" is another mechanism through which Chinese reformers have promoted more restricted use of capital punishment (Johnson & Zimring 2009:277). For political and legal authorities, coping with the demands of victims' families for justice and revenge has been a major concern, not least because these aggrieved families can cause serious disruptions to social stability (Miao 2013c:509). One practical strategy for reducing the volume of capital sentences, therefore, is to offer monetary compensation to the families of victims so that they will agree to judicial decisions to impose a suspended sentence of death. Although financial restitution of this kind is an effective tactic for fostering forgiveness and settlement in some cases, concerns about fairness and just deserts mean that cash for clemency has in practice been highly controversial, especially when the punishment meted out corresponds more to the wealth of the defendant's family than to the harmfulness or culpability of his or her conduct. Some Chinese courts restrict the compensation that can be demanded or offered (Johnson & Zimring 2009:277), and the interviews conducted by the second author confirm that there are large regional disparities in cash-for-clemency practices and outcomes.

China's capital punishment reforms are important for symbolic and practical reasons. As described earlier in this section and elsewhere in this book, there has been a large decline in the use of capital punishment in China since these reforms started. But in addition to this primary practical impact, China's top-down death penalty reforms signify the willingness of the party-state to adapt its policies, laws, and practices to changing contexts and conditions—and, in particular, to the need for a better-functioning and less error-prone death penalty system. Even on the politically charged issue of capital punishment, China's penal policies and practices have proved to be responsive to international opinion and to the push for more effective domestic governance.

PERSPECTIVES FROM OTHER CHINAS

Perspectives from China's past reveal significant continuities in the PRC's death penalty policy and practice, but also significant changes. Views from the "other Chinas," that is, Hong Kong, Taiwan, and Singapore, provide additional insight by suggesting some of the trajectories that capital punishment in the PRC may travel in the years to come, for all three of these countries are well ahead of the PRC in economic and political development.

Singapore, of course, is not another China except in the critical sense of the authoritarianism of its one-party political system. In this respect, Singapore may be "a post-Maoist model of the Chinese future" (Buruma 2001:125). With respect to capital punishment, one sees even larger declines of death penalty usage in the city-state that Lee Kuan Yew built than in the PRC. Singapore was long considered the world capital of capital punishment. Indeed, in the mid-1990s it executed at a per capita rate that was almost double the execution rate during China's strike-hard campaigns of the same decade. Today, Singapore's government claims that little has changed with respect to capital punishment, but this obscures major change in its death penalty system. A new normal for capital punishment is emerging in Singapore, the first signs of which started to appear after Amnesty International released a critical report in 2004, thereby catapulting the country to "global attention as the jurisdiction with 'possibly the highest' per capita execution rate in the world" (Hor 2013:141). In "an age of abolition" (Garland 2010), this was intensely unwelcome attention.

There are several signs of change in Singapore's death penalty. Defense attorneys are more aggressively challenging the state's case in capital trials and the institution of capital punishment itself. Courts are starting to recognize that because "death is different" (Bedau 1987), special procedures and protections are required for defendants in capital cases. Domestic discussions about the death penalty have become more frequent, intense, and sophisticated. Singapore's state had a difficult time finding a new hangman when the veteran executioner retired (Darshan Singh hanged about 1,000 persons during his 48 years of service). Singapore's system of mandatory capital punishment is softening, especially for drug crimes, as law and practice move toward a system in which judges have discretion to decide between capital and lesser sentences. And in a striking break with previous practice, Singapore's government released execution figures on at least two occasions: in 2006, to the *Straits Times* newspaper; and in 2011, in response to a question in Parliament.

But the most important sign of Singapore's new normal is a sharp decline in executions that has occurred since Amnesty International issued its critical report in 2004. The evidence is imperfect, especially for the period before that report (when Singapore's government released no numbers at all), but executions apparently peaked during a war on drugs in the mid-1990s, with an average of 66 per year from 1994 to 1996. The annual number of executions dropped nearly two-thirds in the first years of the new millennium (2000–2003) and then fell into the single digits, averaging 5.4 per year since 2004. In 2010, while the Court of Appeals was considering a constitutional challenge to mandatory capital punishment in the drug case of a Malaysian defendant, Singapore's government carried out no executions at all—the country's first zero year since 1987 (D. T. Johnson 2013). The main cause of this remarkable decline in Singapore's execution rate is prosecutorial discretion. Prosecutors in Singapore have been avoiding capital trials by instituting so-called 14.99 charges, which posit that a defendant possessed just under the amount of drugs required to render his or her crime capital. In this way, mandatory capital punishment, which was for decades a pillar of Singapore's system of capital punishment, is not really mandatory at all (Hor 2013:163). The lesson for China is that informal practices, especially when they are directed from the center of government (as was the Singapore shift in prosecution), can transform the administration of capital punishment. In a context where the imperative to appear tough on crime is strong and hence legal change is difficult, the Singapore story suggests further possibilities for change in Chinese capital punishment.

The recent history of capital punishment in Hong Kong reveals two additional possibilities that may also pertain to the PRC. The first concerns deterrence, which is one major justification for China's retention and frequent use of the ultimate punishment. For the crime of homicide, Singapore's death penalty system, even during its years of highest use in the mid-1990s, did not deter any better than the penal regime in Hong Kong, a similar city that performed its last execution in 1966 and abolished capital punishment in 1993. Although Hong Kong and Singapore have radically different death penalty policies, their homicide curves have traveled remarkably similar trajectories for the past 40 years (Zimring, Fagan, & Johnson 2010). If Singapore benefits from capital punishment, the effect is invisible for the crime of homicide. If the deterrent effect of an aggressive execution policy is invisible in the capital of capital punishment, why should one suppose that it is large and important in cities such as Beijing, Shanghai, and Chengdu?

The second lesson from Hong Kong's history of capital punishment concerns public opinion and the political possibility of death penalty change. There is no clear difference between public attitudes toward the death penalty in the PRC and public sentiments on the same topic elsewhere in Asia (Oberwittler & Qi 2009). If anything, general support for the death penalty seems a little lower in China than in some other places (such as Hong Kong and South Korea) and a lot lower than in places such as Taiwan, Thailand, Japan, and the Philippines (Johnson & Zimring 2009:302). Moreover, compared with other policy questions, capital punishment receives little attention from most Chinese citizens—it is not a salient issue. Public opinion is not a major influence on rates of executions in Asia. For the most part, executions are common when authoritarian governments wish to have a lot of them (as in China, Vietnam, North Korea, and Singapore), and they decline when political regimes became more democratic or (for international or domestic reasons) more reluctant to kill. Crucially, changes in death penalty policy are seldom inspired by public sentiment. Leadership from the front is the norm, and the efforts of governments to alter death penalty policy are usually tolerated by the citizenry. In this regard, Hong Kong may be an important precedent for the impact of death penalty abolition in the PRC. As measured by publications in two Hong Kong newspapers (*South*

China Morning Post and *Singtao Daily*), the political backlash to Hong Kong's abolition in 1993 was so mild that it could almost be called nonexistent (Johnson & Zimring 2009:372–377). More broadly, the impact of Hong Kong's moratorium on executions (which began in 1966) on crime rates and perceptions of public safety was negligible. In these criminological and social senses, abolition in Hong Kong can be called a quiescent success. This should be good news for people seeking to abolish the death penalty in the PRC, and it is highly relevant news for those who claim that the roots of the PRC's prodigious rates of execution are Chinese cultural values.

To mainland China, the most important "other China" is Taiwan, where, despite a rebound in executions that started in 2010, the changes that have occurred in death penalty policy and practice are as remarkable as those in any other nation. In the White Terror campaign[3] of the 1950s, there was as much per capita state killing in Taiwan—judicial and extra-judicial—as there was in the PRC under Mao and Deng. But as Taiwan democratized, the death penalty declined, reaching a nadir of zero executions during the four years from 2006 through 2009. This decline had several causes, including revisions to Taiwan's capital statutes (e.g., the abolition of mandatory death sentences) that significantly narrowed the scope and scale of capital punishment, and amendments to the Code of Criminal Procedure that altered the balance of power in the criminal process among prosecutors, judges, and defense lawyers. Ultimately, though, the critical force driving the downsizing of Taiwan's death penalty has been leadership from the front by political elites. At present, public opinion in Taiwan supports capital punishment, much as it has throughout the recent decades of democratization, but at several key points in recent history, Taiwan's political leaders have tried to reduce the country's reliance on state killing. In leading this way, those leaders were motivated by two main desires: to pull away from the excesses and associations of the country's authoritarian past and to push toward a different identity in the world as a state committed to human rights—and as a Chinese state more respectful of human rights than is its huge sibling to the west. From a Taiwanese perspective, thinking about the possibilities for capital punishment in mainland China's future requires recognition of the critical importance of democratization and human rights, for these are two main drivers of deep death penalty change in many countries and contexts (Hood & Hoyle 2009; Johnson & Zimring 2009:290–304).

PERSPECTIVES FROM OTHER COMMUNIST COUNTRIES

The rise of Marxist ideology was a "historical tsunami" that is breathtaking in both its "total human impact" and its lethality (Pinker 2011:343). The three deadliest post–World War II conflicts were "fueled by Chinese, Korean, and Vietnamese communist regimes" that acknowledged that the lives of their citizens meant little (Pinker 2011:308). As Mao put it, "We have so many people. We can afford to lose a few. What difference does it make?" (quoted in Glover 1999:297). But communism—"the single most important cause of mass killing in the twentieth century"—appears to be fading into history (Valentino 2004:150). With it, the high execution rates in China, Vietnam, and North Korea may also fade into the past.

Of the 13 nations in Asia that retain capital punishment and continue to carry out executions on a regular basis, only 4 conduct executions with any frequency—as a regular criminal sanction rather than a one-in-a-thousand penalty of chiefly symbolic importance. The high-rate execution states are China, Vietnam, North Korea, and Singapore: three authoritarian states on the left and one on the right, where, as we have seen, executions have declined markedly in recent years. In Asia, as in most of the rest of the world, capital punishment remains strongest where democracy is weakest. China, Vietnam, and North Korea are all characterized by low respect for human rights, few restraints on government power, and single-party dominance. They also remain Communist states in two important senses: the ruling party and the state are so closely connected that it makes sense to speak of a party-state, and the ruling party regards itself as the vanguard of the people.

In Vietnam, Ho Chi Minh (1890–1969) was not as enthusiastic a proponent of Stalinist methods of state killing as his counterparts were in China and Cambodia, but he was strongly influenced by the Russian dictator's approach to governing and executing—and by Maoist methods as well. The result is a system of capital punishment that in many respects looks a lot like China's, with a wide range of capital offenses, many death sentences and executions, heavy reliance on confessions, few due process protections, strict control of information about capital punishment, little tolerance for criticism of the nation's death penalty, and a leading role for the Communist Party in death penalty decision making, both at the policy level and in individual cases (Johnson & Zimring 2009:381–396). In Vietnam, as in China, recognizing the relevance of the recent past is a necessary step toward understanding the prominence of capital punishment in the present. As commitments to communism collapse, so will some of these hallmarks of Communist capital punishment.

As for North Korea, it is impossible to say much about capital punishment in a country that is called "the hermit kingdom" and "a kingdom of lies," but there is enough evidence to support a few generalizations about the death penalty in Asia's most authoritarian state. For starters, executions in North Korea occur at high rates that are rivaled in Asia only by those in China and Vietnam. The Kim dynasty's regime maintains a wide range of capital crimes, including the expansive offense of "conspiracy against state power," which was used to justify the executions in December 2013 of Kim Jong-un's once powerful uncle (Jang Song-thaek) and several of his relatives (Choe 2013; Choe & Sanger 2013). Capital punishment in North Korea is deeply political, and the party-state's purge of disloyal subjects may be even more brutal than what occurred in China's Cultural Revolution. As for criminal investigations and evidence, North Korean authorities frequently use torture to extract confessions, and some persons are executed without even receiving a fair trial, much less due process. A principle of collective responsibility makes every member of a household accountable for the conduct of his or her kin, so the deviance of one may become the calamity of all. Conversely, criminals with "good" family backgrounds are often able to escape punishment. Executions in North Korea are sometimes staged in public, as occasionally still occurs in the PRC ("Kokai shokei" 2013). Some public executions are aimed at instilling fear in the public in order to dampen discontent about a regime that fails to provide many of the essentials of a decent life. Finally, in addition to the execution of political prisoners and ordinary offenders, an estimated 100,000 to 300,000 persons are incarcerated in North Korea's gulag. For persons imprisoned in these "hard labor zones," one purpose of work is to drive them to an early grave (Kang & Rigoulot 2001:xi, 144). Incarceration of this kind can be called capital punishment on the installment plan (Harden 2012).

Looking back at the recent history of death penalty practices in North Korea, Vietnam, and China, one sees striking similarities. In all these Communist countries, one finds death penalty targets and quotas, the orchestration of campaigns and crackdowns and the enlistment of mass participation in them, a central distinction between "friends" and "enemies," the treatment of law as an elastic instrument for achieving party purposes, extreme secrecy about state killing, and routine recourse in official rhetoric to "public support" for the party-state's harsh punishment practices. There are also differences between these countries. Most notably, capital punishment in North Korea is less governed by law and more likely to target political enemies than is the case in Vietnam and China. In the end, however, the similarities are most significant. East Asia is almost the only place on earth where Communists continue to rule, and it is no coincidence that some of the world's most aggressive capital punishment practices are concentrated in these countries.

The affinity of Communist governments for capital punishment is more a matter of practice than principle. Communist theory (which hopes for a "withering away" of the state) typically advocates the ultimate abolition of executions, and the rhetoric of eventual abolition is already manifest in China and Vietnam, as it was in the Soviet Union under Stalin and Lenin. In practice, however, hard-line Communist governments tend to use the death penalty aggressively (Courtois et al. 1999). But if hard-line regimes tend to endorse capital punishment and resist limits on its application, the prospects for further decline in Asian capital punishment are closely linked to the behavior of Communists in power because hard-line regimes of the Right in the region have already been replaced or softened, as in South Korea, Taiwan, Indonesia, Malaysia, Thailand, and the Philippines. In these countries, when regimes of the Right were displaced by more democratic governments, the death penalty declined or disappeared. Time will tell what happens to capital punishment when Asian regimes of the Left liberalize, but there are some hopeful signs. The changes in China described earlier in this chapter mainly push in the direction of reduction, restraint, and refinement of the death penalty, and some of the Chinese reforms have parallels in Vietnam (Johnson & Zimring 2009:387–395). In 2010, for example, Vietnam significantly reduced the number of offenses that carry capital punishment, and a year later it changed its execution method from firing squad to lethal injection, a switch that led to an 18-month pause in executions after the European Union banned the export of chemicals used for lethal injections (Cumming-Bruce 2013). Even the rogue regime of North Korea, which defies international norms in many areas, from nuclear weapons and narcotics to trade and terrorism, frequently declares that it is a decent state when it comes to capital punishment (Johnson & Zimring 2009:359). This posturing is a window into the symbolic importance of capital punishment, even in the most closed state in the world (Zimring 2003:40). It is also a testament to the power of international human rights norms and the logic of appropriateness to shape the death penalty sensibilities of leaders in repressive regimes (Bae 2007).

In China and Vietnam, change is a pervasive feature of national existence in every sphere of society, from agriculture to industry and from sex to sects. Capital punishment in these societies is also changing, and the key causes of change are political and international, not cultural. The fact that China executes more people than the rest of the world combined brings dishonor on the nation (Appiah 2010). And in Vietnam, the Communist Party's cautious approach to capital punishment for foreign offenders seems to reflect the party-state's need—economically and politically—to avoid censure by abolitionist nations to which its future development is linked. Fear of censure also helps explain why Vietnam was the only retentionist nation in Asia that did not oppose a United Nations resolution in 2007 calling for a worldwide moratorium on executions with an eye toward abolition (it abstained).

The Communist countries of China, Vietnam, and North Korea remain exceptional in their frequent use of capital punishment, but they will become more normal death penalty nations when their leaders acquire the political will to move toward the terrain that the rest of Asia inhabits. "Culture" will not be irrelevant—and the cultural forces that matter most will affect political elites (Garland 2010:143)—but it will play a secondary role. China is no more "Chinese" than Taiwan (where executions dropped during democratization) or Hong Kong (which has not executed since 1966). Similarly, no two countries on earth share more history and culture than North Korea and its sibling to the south, which has not executed since 1997. One does not need to invoke "culture" to explain why Asia's Communist states lead the region in the use of capital punishment. One only needs to recognize the primary role that political leadership plays in shaping death penalty policy and practice in states of all kinds.

○   ○   ○

Like Tolstoy's families in *Anna Karenina*, "Abolitionist nations all seem alike, but every death penalty nation is retentionist in its own way" (Garland 2010:22). The People's Republic of China is indeed retentionist in its own way. There, history matters immensely, because the effects of the Communist revolution and its Maoist aftermath carry large parts of the past into the present. In this chapter, we have compared the PRC of the present with China of the recent past and with other "Chinas" in the Asia region and other Communist countries. What we stressed depended on how and where we looked. We could have focused on how Chinese capital punishment compares with death penalty regimes in other large nations, such as the United States and Japan. Had we adopted those vantage points, more emphasis would have been placed on the capacity of powerful countries to resist the influence of the human rights dynamic that is driving the death penalty downward in many parts of the world (Hood & Hoyle 2009). In China, as in other powerful countries, the use of international human rights pressure to try to influence death penalty practice can be "a double-edged sword" (Miao 2013a:67). This approach can transform capital punishment, but it can also deepen the distrust and disapproval of political elites and thereby induce more aggressive and secretive death penalty policies.

In contrast to the human rights approach, a different agent of change for Chinese capital punishment could be—as China's party-state prefers—the gradual evolution of public opinion about penalty toward more lenity and less severity. Public views of capital punishment in China are changing rapidly (Bakken 2013:196), but experience in the rest of the world—including the United States and Japan—suggests that attempts to convert a public majority into opposing the death penalty are probably "doomed to fail" (Hammel 2010:1). In this respect, public education seems to be a "hollow hope" (Hammel 2010:40). In our view, the most viable route to death penalty reform in China runs through the continued influence of human rights frames and claims—notwithstanding the risks of backlash acknowledged earlier.

We conclude with an irony that proceeds from the premise that "the straightest road to abolition involves bypassing public opinion" (Hammel 2010:236). This finding, derived from studies of abolition in Germany, France, and the United Kingdom, generates the counterintuitive possibility that China may be a better candidate for abolition than the United States and Japan precisely because it is less democratic. Chinese leaders cannot ignore public opinion altogether (I. Johnson 2004:25), but in charting their country's future, they are less constrained by it than are their counterparts in more democratic nations. China also possesses another precondition of abolition that was important in the European context (and is absent in the United States): a unified national penal code (Hammel 2010:234). The story of Hong Kong's abolition suggests that if China's party-state decided to eliminate the death penalty, there would be little public backlash. Considering the sensitivity of China's state to foreign criticism of its human rights policies, abolishing the death penalty could be a low-cost way "to project a more sympathetic image on the world stage" (Hammel 2010:235) and to obtain more of the status and respect its people strongly desire (Schell & Delury 2013). A concern for honor drives many moral revolutions. At the turn of the twentieth century, Chinese women were freed from the horrors of foot binding when reformers emphasized that nothing made China more an object of international ridicule than this barbaric practice (Appiah 2010:53–100). At the turn of the twenty-first century, few things make China more an object of international rebuke than its death penalty exceptionalism. This fact is not lost on its leaders. The open question is, what will they do about it?

NOTES

1 Of course, factors such as population growth, crime increases, and the decline of extrajudicial killing also help explain the huge increase in death sentences, but a change in penal policy is the primary proximate cause (Johnson & Zimring 2009:253).
2 Because China is a large and developing country, it is difficult for its central government to produce reliable national crime statistics, but we know that the Supreme People's Court keeps reliable statistics about the number of death sentences and executions (authors' interviews, 2007–2012).
3 The White Terror campaign was launched in the 1950s by the Kuomintang against intellectuals, activists, and political dissidents. Thousands were imprisoned or executed for their opposition (or perceived opposition) to the government of Chiang Kai-shek (Roy 2003:90).

REFERENCES

Appiah, K. A. (2010). *The Honor Code: How Moral Revolutions Happen*. New York: Norton.

Areddy, J. T. (2013, September 25). Chinese vendor's execution unleashes outrage. *Wall Street Journal*. Retrieved May 12, 2015, from http://www.wsj.com/articles/SB10001424052702304795804579097032715327984.

Bae, S. (2007). *When the State No Longer Kills: International Human Rights Norms and Abolition of Capital Punishment*. Albany: State University of New York Press.

Bakken, B. (2004). Moral panics, crime rates and harsh punishment in China. *Australian and New Zealand Journal of Criminology, 37*, 67–89.

Bakken, B. (2007). Review of *Die Todesstrafe in der VR China* [The Death Penalty in the People's Republic of China]. *China Journal, 57*, 180–182.

Bakken, B. (2013). Capital punishment reform, public opinion, and penal elitism in the People's Republic of China. In R. Hood & S. Deva (Eds.), *Confronting Capital Punishment in Asia: Human Rights, Politics, and Public Opinion* (pp. 187–204). New York: Oxford University Press.

Bedau, H, (1987). *Death Is Different: Studies in the Morality, Law, and Politics of Capital Punishment*. Boston: Northeastern University Press.

Bezlova, A. (2008, June 14). China: Will the people choose the death penalty? Inter Press Service. Retrieved May 12, 2015, from http://www.ipsnews.net/2008/06/china-will-the-people-choose-the-death-penalty/.

Bullock, A. (1998). *Hitler and Stalin: Parallel Lives*. London: Fontana.

Buruma, I. (2001). *Bad Elements: Chinese Rebels from Los Angeles to Beijing*. New York: Vintage Books.

Cambodian League for the Promotion and Defence of Human Rights. (2007, January). "Abolition of death penalty: Ratification of second optional protocol to the ICCPR and Cambodia." Phnom Penh.

Chang, J., & Halliday, J. (2005). *The Unknown Story of Mao*. New York: Knopf.

Choe, S. (2013, December 13). Leader's uncle executed as a traitor, North Korea says. *New York Times*, p. A14.

Choe, S., & Sanger, D. E. (2013, December 24). Korea execution is tied to clash over businesses. *New York Times*, p. A1.

Courtois, S., Werth, N., Panne, J., Paczkowski, A., Bartosek, K., & Margolin, J. (1999). *The Black Book of Communism: Crimes, Terror, Repression*. Cambridge, MA: Harvard University Press.

Cumming-Bruce, N. (2013, August 10). Human rights office criticizes Vietnam as executions resume. *New York Times*, p. A8.

The death penalty: Strike less hard; Most of the world's sharp decline in executions can be credited to China. (2013, August 3). *Economist*. Retrieved May 12, 2015, from http://www.economist.com/news/china/21582557-most-worlds-sharp-decline-executions-can-be-credited-china-strike-less-hard.

Garland, D. (2007). The peculiar forms of American capital punishment. *Social Research, 74*, 435–464.

Garland, D. (2010). *Peculiar Institution: America's Death Penalty in an Age of Abolition*. Cambridge, MA: Belknap Press of Harvard University Press.

Gilley, B, (1998). *Tiger on the Brink: Jiang Zemin and China's New Elite*. Berkeley: University of California Press, 1998.

Glover, J. (1999). *Humanity: A Moral History of the Twentieth Century*. New Haven, CT: Yale University Press.

Hammel, A. (2010). *Ending the Death Penalty: The European Experience in Global Perspective*. New York: Palgrave Macmillan.

Hands off Cain. (2013, July 27). Hands off Cain presents 2013 report on the death penalty worldwide. *Hands off Cain News*, no. 31. Retrieved May 12, 2015, http://deathpenaltynews.blogspot.hk/2013/07/hands-off-cain-presents-2013-report-on.html.

Harden, B. (2012). *Escape from Camp 14: One Man's Remarkable Odyssey from North Korea to Freedom in the West*. New York: Penguin Books.

Hogg, C. (2011, February 25). China ends death penalty for 13 economic crimes. *BBC News*. Retrieved May 12, 2015, http://www.bbc.com/news/world-asia-pacific-12580504.

Hood, R. (2008). *The Death Penalty: A Worldwide Perspective* (4th ed.) (p. 85). New York: Oxford University Press.

Hood, R. (2009). Abolition of the death penalty: China in world perspective. *City University of Hong Kong Law Review, 1*, 1–21.

Hood, R., & Hoyle, C. (2009). Abolishing the death penalty worldwide: The impact of a "new dynamic." *Crime and Justice: A Review of Research, 38*(1), 1–63.

Hor, M. (2013). Singapore's death penalty: The beginning of the end? In R. Hood & S. Deva (Eds.), *Confronting Capital Punishment in Asia: Human Rights, Politics, and Public Opinion* (pp. 141–167). New York: Oxford University Press.

Huang, T. (2011). Xingfa xiuzhengan ba jiedu [Interpreting the Eighth Amendment to the Criminal Law in China]. *Renmin jiancha* [People's Procuratorial], *6*, 5–20.

Johnson, D. T. (2013, March). The jolly hangman, the jailed journalist, and the decline of Singapore's death penalty. *Asian Journal of Criminology, 8*(1), 41–59.

Johnson, D. T., & Zimring, F. E. (2009). *The Next Frontier: National Development, Political Change, and the Death Penalty in Asia*. New York: Oxford University Press.

Johnson, I. (2004). *Wild Grass: Three Portraits of Change in Modern China*. New York: Vintage Books.

Kang, C., & Rigoulot, P. (2001). *The Aquariums of Pyongyang: Ten Years in the North Korean Gulag*. New York: Basic Books.

Kokai shokei: Chugoku nao [Public punishment in China again]. (2013, September 22). *Asahi shimbun.*

Lu, H., & Miethe, T. D. (2007). *China's Death Penalty: History, Law, and Contemporary Practices.* New York: Routledge.

MacLeod, C. (2006, June 14). China makes ultimate punishment mobile. *USA Today.* Retrieved May 12, 2015, http://usatoday30.usatoday.com/news/world/2006-06-14-death-van_x.htm.

Miao, M. (2013a). Examining China's responses to the global campaign against the death penalty. In R. Hood & S. Deva (Eds.), *Confronting Capital Punishment in Asia: Human Rights, Politics, and Public Opinion* (pp. 46–67). New York: Oxford University Press.

Miao, M. (2013b). *The Politics of Change: Explaining Capital Punishment Reform in China.* Unpublished doctoral thesis, St. Anne's College, Oxford University.

Miao, M. (2013c). The politics of China's death penalty reform in the context of global abolitionism. *British Journal of Criminology, 53*(3), 500–519.

Mirsky, J. (1994, November 17). Unmasking the monster. *New York Review of Books.* Retrieved May 12, 2015, http://www.nybooks.com/articles/archives/1994/nov/17/unmasking-the-monster/.

Nelken, D. (2010). *Comparative Criminal Justice.* Thousand Oaks, CA: Sage.

Oberwittler, D., & Qi, S. (2009). Public opinion on the death penalty: Results from a general population survey conducted in three provinces in 2007/08. Freiburg, Germany: Max Planck Institute for Foreign and International Criminal Law. Retrieved June 14, 2014, from http://www.mpicc.de/shared/data/pdf/forschung_aktuell_41.pdf.

Osnos, E. (2014). *Age of Ambition: Chasing Fortune, Truth, and Faith in the New China.* New York: Farrar, Straus & Giroux.

Pan, P. P. (2008). *Out of Mao's Shadow: The Struggle for the Soul of a New China.* New York: Simon & Schuster.

Pinker, S. (2011). *The Better Angels of Our Nature: Why Violence Has Declined.* New York: Viking.

Roy, D. (2003). *Taiwan: A Political History.* Ithaca, NY: Cornell University Press.

Schell, O., & Delury, J. (2013). *Wealth and Power: China's Long March to the Twenty-First Century.* New York: Little, Brown.

Scott, K. (2010). Why did China reform its death penalty? *Pacific Rim Law and Policy Journal, 19,* 63–80.

Spence, J. (1990). *The Search for Modern China.* New York: Norton.

Stack, M. K. (2010, August 25). China reviews death penalty. *Los Angeles Times.* Retrieved May 12, 2015, http://articles.latimes.com/2010/aug/25/world/la-fg-china-death-penalty-20100825.

Tanner, H. M. (1999). *Strike Hard! Anti-Crime Campaigns and Chinese Criminal Justice, 1979–1985.* Ithaca, NY: Cornell University East Asia Program.

Trevaskes, S. (2002). Courts on the campaign path in China: Criminal court work in the "yanda" 2001 anti-crime campaign. *Asian Survey. 42*(5), 673–693.

Trevaskes, S. (2012). *The Death Penalty in Contemporary China.* New York: Palgrave Macmillan.

Tucker, R. C. (1995). *Politics as Leadership* (rev. ed.). Columbia: University of Missouri Press.

Tyler, P. E. (1997, February 20). Deng Xiaoping: A political wizard who put China on the capitalist road. *New York Times.* Retrieved May 12, 2015, http://www.nytimes.com/1997/02/20/world/deng-xiaoping-a-political-wizard-who-put-china-on-the-capitalist-road.html.

Valentino, B. A. (2004). *Final Solutions: Mass Killing and Genocide in the 20th Century.* Ithaca, NY: Cornell University Press.

Vogel, E. (2011). *Deng Xiaoping and the Transformation of China.* Cambridge, MA: Belknap Press of Harvard University Press.

Xiao, Y. (2006). Zuigao renmin fayuan yuanzhang Xiao Yang zai zuigao renmin fayuan xingshi faguan dahuishang de jianghua (jielu) [Speech at the Supreme People's Court Conference for Criminal Judges (excerpt)]. Beijing: Supreme People's Court. Retrieved June 18, 2014, from http://law.legaldaily.com.cn/law_content.php?law_id=f1a688df668aefd59b89a01135ce71de24347&key_word=.

Xinhua News Agency. (2007). New regulation guarantees death penalty review. Retrieved June 18, 2014, from http://www.china.org.cn/english/government/200973.htm.

Xiong, H. (2009). Liangzhong sixing zhixing fangshi bingxing shi'ernian: zhuanjia cheng zhushe sixing shangque biaozhun [Two methods of execution coexisted for 12 years: Experts pointed out the lack of relevant standards]. Xinhua News Agency. Retrieved June 18, 2014, from http://news.xinhuanet.com/legal/2009-06/16/content_11549071.htm.

Yardley, J. (2005, November 12). Desperate search for justice: One man vs. China. *New York Times.* Retrieved May 12, 2015, http://www.nytimes.com/2005/11/12/international/asia/12china.html?pagewanted=all.

Zhang, N. (2008). The political origins of death penalty exceptionalism: Mao Zedong and the practice of capital punishment in contemporary China. *Punishment and Society, 10*, 117–136.

Zimring, F. E. (2003). *The Contradictions of American Capital Punishment*. New York: Oxford University Press.

Zimring, F. E. (2007). *The Great American Crime Decline*. New York: Oxford University Press.

Zimring, F. E. (2012). *The City That Became Safe: New York's Lessons for Urban Crime and Its Control*. New York: Oxford University Press.

Zimring, F. E., Fagan, J., & Johnson, D. T. (2010). Executions, deterrence, and homicide: A tale of two cities. *Journal of Empirical Legal Studies, 7*(1), 1–29.

12

China's Death Penalty in the Twenty-First Century

▸ BIN LIANG and HONG LU

THE MAIN GOAL of this collection is to examine China's death penalty practice within the dramatically changing social, political, and legal context of China and under the influence of the global abolition movement. In this concluding chapter, we first review two prominent cases in the 2000s to highlight major problems and challenges of the existing death penalty system in China. We then examine gaps between China's current practices and international standards. We conclude by speculating on the future prospects for death penalty reforms in China.

TWO MORE CASES

In this section, we discuss two high-profile cases, the Tang Hui case and the Wu Ying case, to put China's death penalty reforms into larger context.

Tang Hui Case

The Tang Hui case involved both Tang Hui and her daughter (nicknamed Lele in news reports for protection purposes), who lived in Yongzhou City, Hunan Province. On October 1, 2006, one defendant, 19-year-old Zhou Junhui, met then 10-year-old Lele at an ice-skating rink and took her to his apartment and had sex with her. Two days later, in the name of finding her a job, Zhou took Lele to a local hair salon that was actually an underground brothel run by two codefendants, Qin Xing (female) and Chen Gang. After that, Lele (now 11 years old) was coerced to work there as a prostitute and was even gang-raped once by four other defendants (Liu Run, Jiang Junjun, Lan Xiaoqiang, and Qin Bin) in December. On December 30, Lele was finally rescued by the police after Tang Hui learned about Lele's whereabouts and tipped them off. Court records indicated that Lele was forced to see over 100 customers in about three months, was infected with sexually transmitted diseases, and suffered mental damage as well.

On December 31, Tang went to the local police station to demand official action against the suspects, but her request was dismissed by the police officer in charge, Yang Junxiang, who claimed that the case was "too trivial with insufficient evidence to press charges" (Yang was disciplined internally later for his misbehavior). Tang then turned to other authorities to demand action, and finally a case was officially filed on January 5, 2007.

In April 2008, the Yongzhou People's Procuratorate indicted six defendants (Zhou, Qin Xing, Chen, Liu, Jiang, and Lan) for various offenses, including organizing prostitution, forcing a minor into prostitution, rape, and assault. Tang demanded the death penalty against all defendants and 1.8 million yuan for civil compensation. On June 6, 2008, the Yongzhou Intermediate Court sentenced Zhou and Qin Xing to death with immediate execution, Liu and Chen to life imprisonment, and Jiang and Lan to 16 and 15 years of imprisonment, respectively, and ordered a combined compensation of 90,000 yuan. Afterward, the Yongzhou Intermediate Procuratorate protested the trial court's decision on the grounds that Jiang and Lan's sentences were too light. All six defendants appealed as well.

On August 8, 2008, the Hunan Provincial High Court sent the case back to the intermediate court for retrial because of the technical error that Zhou was not provided with an appointed defense lawyer at the trial (therefore, his due process rights were violated). After the retrial, the intermediate court upheld the original convictions and sentences on February 21, 2009. Nevertheless, the high court once again sent the case back for another retrial on the grounds that the facts were unclear and the evidence was not sufficient on October 25, 2009. When the intermediate court started its third trial (i.e., the second retrial) on December 23, 2010, all defendants except Zhou retracted their testimony. The courtroom was at one time out of control. On March 28, 2011, the intermediate court resentenced Zhou and Qin Xing to death with immediate execution, Chen, Liu, Jiang, and Lan to life imprisonment, and the seventh defendant, Qin Bin (who had been arrested and was in custody now) to 15 years of imprisonment. Both sides appealed again, and this time the high court sustained both the convictions and the sentences on June 5, 2012.

On June 12, 2014, the national Supreme People's Court (SPC) conducted its review of Zhou and Qin's death sentences, annulled both death sentences, and sent the case back to the Hunan High Court for retrial on the grounds that Zhou and Qin Xing's crimes were not serious enough to warrant the death sentence with immediate execution. Apparently, there was some ambiguity whether Lele was completely coerced during her "abduction" and whether Qin Xing had performed meritorious service while she was in detention (thus warranting a sentence reduction). On September 5, 2014, the Hunan High Court resentenced Zhou and Qin to life imprisonment after its retrial.

Besides Lele's criminal case, what happened to Tang Hui equally grabbed the media's attention. As soon as Lele's case started, Tang had a very rough relationship with the local police. Feeling that she did not get support and full attention from the police (not to mention the alleged favorable treatment received by the defendants because of their supposed connection with local police, as Tang suspected), Tang as a good mother tried all means to press for official charges and demand the death penalty against all defendants, including turning to the media and continuously petitioning higher-level governmental branches both in Hunan and in Beijing. On August 3, 2012, Tang was sentenced to 18 months of reeducation through labor (*laodong jiaoyang* in Chinese)[1] by the Lingling Police Department in Yongzhou City. The official justification was that her protests "seriously disturbed the social order and exerted a negative impact on society," including an egregious 15-day stay at the Youngzhou Intermediate Court in order to exert pressure on the trial court in March 2011.

Nevertheless, Tang's case and Lele's case had drawn enormous attention from the media and the public, and many voiced their sympathy toward Tang and Lele. As lawyers representing Tang exposed her story on microblogs (*weibo*) to spark a public outcry, hundreds of thousands of weibo users reportedly called for Tang's release and demanded that authorities stop their unfair treatment of her. Ten days later, on August 13, the reeducation decision was rescinded by the Hunan Reeducation Management Committee (hereafter the Reeducation Committee). In January 2013, Tang petitioned the Reeducation Committee for state compensation, but her petition was rejected. Tang immediately filed an administrative lawsuit against the

Reeducation Committee with the Yougzhou Intermediate Court but lost her case in April 2013. In her appeal, Tang turned down mediation offers by the Hunan High Court and eventually won her appeal in July 2013. The high court awarded Tang 1,941 yuan for infringement of her freedom and another 1,000 yuan for her mental suffering. Her request for a written apology from the Reeducation Committee, however, was rejected. As Tang said, "It is normal for a victim's mother to wish for the severest punishment on the criminals. It would be abnormal to do otherwise. The law cannot control my heart, while my heart cannot change the law."[2]

As dramatic as it is, the Tang Hui case is not the most heinous violent case in which the defendants were eligible for the death penalty in China's recent decades. However, it has grabbed national attention because of Tang's relentless effort to petition to the government and to mobilize public support. This case sheds light on several aspects of China's current death penalty practice. First, the lengthy judicial proceeding in this case reveals potential legal loopholes in the Criminal Law. On the one hand, nonmurder offenses, such as forcing a minor into prostitution and rape, could potentially subject offenders to the death penalty in China. Given the ambiguity of the law and broad discretion possessed by the police, the procuratorate, and the judiciary, judicial sentences are often subject to circumstantial interpretations. On the other hand, such leeway allows the high court and the SPC to correct errors by the trial court and to limit the use of the death penalty (see relevant discussions in chapter 5). For example, the Hunan High Court cited the lack of legal representation in its first appellate review and unclear facts and insufficient evidence in its second review to reject the trial court's decisions. Such judiciary efforts to some extent reflect progress made in the past 10 years in safeguarding both procedural and substantive justice.

Second, this case clearly shows the vulnerability of the Chinese judiciary system, often subject to external influences. Distrusting the system, Tang had to rely on the media and personal petitions to draw the attention of the central government to put more pressure on the police and the court. The outcome of such a strategy, however, is often unpredictable (see chapter 10). Tang's effort seemingly worked in her favor against local protectionism (e.g., harsh penalties were meted out against almost all defendants) and won the support of the public. Nevertheless, her allegedly troublemaking behavior also led to action against her (the sentence to reeducation through labor), although her punishment was finally overturned by the court. The clash between local protectionism and upper-level review and supervision, coupled with the uncertainty of death penalty reforms, perhaps all contributed to the judiciary's indecisiveness in this case.

Third, the SPC appeared to have exercised its review authority independently in this case and closely adhered to the current policy of "killing fewer and killing cautiously." In an interview with the media, one of the SPC judges elaborated on the court's interpretation of Article 358 of the Criminal Law regarding the crime of forcing others into prostitution. As stated by the judge, only when circumstances are extremely severe (e.g., the leader of an organized criminal group forces a large number of people or several minors into prostitution, abducts several individuals in public and forces them into prostitution, or uses methods that are extremely cruel or cause serious illness or death) shall the death sentence be warranted.[3] The SPC's opinion sent a strong signal of resolute execution of the current "killing fewer" policy.

Last but not least, the vindictiveness displayed by Tang and her supporters to some extent reflected public support for the use of harsh punishment against criminals, including the death penalty. As Tang said, "I know it is impossible to sentence all of them to death. But my daughter's life is ruined, and I want the criminals to die. I'm afraid they might harm more people if they are out there."[4]

Wu Ying Case

Wu Ying was born in May 1981 to a farmer's family in the city of Dongyang in Zhejiang Province. After graduating from a middle school in 1997, Wu dropped out of high school and started working at a beauty salon. Later she opened her own beauty parlor and made huge profits by selling beauty products before she turned to other businesses (e.g., running car rental agencies and hotels). In 2005, Wu founded the Bense Group in Dongyang and in the following year registered 15 separate companies under the group with a total registered capital of 300 million yuan. In 2006, at the age of 25, she was ranked the 6th-richest woman and the 68th-richest person in China, with a net worth of 3.6 billion yuan. Her sudden wealth and fame caused a sensation in the Chinese media, and there were wild speculations about the source of her wealth.

In December 2006, Wu went missing for a week in Wenzhou (a famous entrepreneurial city near Wu's hometown) and later claimed that she had been abducted by a few of her creditors, who forced her to sign blank documents and took from her both the business license and the seal of the Bense Group. Wu reported her abduction to the police, but they took no action. This incident, however, may have triggered the financial crisis of the Bense Group.

Wu was suddenly arrested in February 2007 for illegal collection of public funds (*feifa xishou gonggong cunkuan zui*) and fraudulent fund-raising (*jizi zhapian zui*) and was tried in April 2009 in the Jinhua Intermediate People's Court, whose jurisdiction governs Dongyang. She was initially charged with illegal collection of public funds (which is subject to a maximum sentence of 10 years' imprisonment under Article 176 of the Criminal Law) along with seven other codefendants, but her charges were later singled out and changed to the more serious crime of fraudulent fund-raising, which is subject to the death penalty (Articles 192 and 199). The other seven codefendants were all convicted of illegal collection of public funds in January 2009 and were sentenced to terms ranging from 22 months to 6 years, along with criminal fines ranging from 20,000 yuan to 300,000 yuan.

The official indictment against Wu alleged that between May 2005 and February 2007, Wu had illegally raised 770 million yuan from the public by promising high investment returns (e.g., annual rates of 50% to 100%) and running a Ponzi scheme. When she was arrested, only 380 million yuan was recovered. Wu's defense claimed that the money was merely borrowed from 11 of her friends and invested in legitimate, profitable businesses. Nevertheless, Wu was found guilty at trial and was sentenced to death with immediate execution in December 2009. The Zhejiang Provincial High Court upheld Wu's conviction and death sentence in January 2012.

Like the Tang Hui case, Wu Ying's conviction and death sentence generated an outpouring of sympathy from the public, as well as Chinese media. Wu's supporters argued that her sentence was much harsher than that of corrupt officials, and many called for leniency and abolition of capital punishment for economic crimes (Gao 2012; Luo 2013). In March 2012, then Chinese prime minister Wen Jiabao commented on the Wu Ying case at a news conference and mentioned that "the case should be carefully handled by the SPC." On April 20, 2012, the SPC upheld Wu's conviction but overturned the immediate death sentence and sent her case back to the

Zhejiang High Court for resentencing. On May 21, 2012, Wu's sentence was reduced to death with a two-year suspension, and it was further commuted to a life sentence on July 11, 2014, at the expiration of the two-year suspension.[5]

The Wu Ying case is one of the most controversial death penalty cases and probably the best-known economic death penalty case in recent years. First, what triggered the massive interest was the controversial nature of Wu's financial loans and business transactions and the extremely severe punishment associated with them. Court records showed that all financial assets of Wu Ying's Bense Group came from private financing except a short-term loan of 15.5 million yuan from the Dongyang branch of the Industrial Commercial Bank of China. Reportedly, private financing through high-interest loans is very popular in China, and in Zhejiang Province (particularly in a manufacturing city such as Wenzhou), underground lending markets catering to ambitious entrepreneurs have always been widely present. One major reason that such private financing continues to exist in China is that private entrepreneurs often have a tough time getting financing from state banks, which often prefer to lend to state-owned enterprises. It was reported that "at least one trillion yuan in funds has been utilized for private financing in China. If people like Wu Ying would be subject to criminal punishment, how many bank employees, guarantors, and even public servants would be forced to go to prison?"[6] Prime Minister Wen Jiabao well acknowledged this concern during the previously mentioned news conference in March 2012 and pointed out that "private financing should be further studied, regulated and protected by law." As a matter of fact, the SPC issued the Notice on Proper Handling of Cases of Private Financing (in Order to Maintain Social Stability) in December 2011, before it disapproved Wu's death sentence in 2012.[7] Although Wu's life was spared, she was unfortunately caught in the crossfire between a dramatically changing economy and slowly reactive law.

Second, the Wu Ying case once again opened up the discussion on the scope of China's death penalty application. Although the trajectory of death penalty reform seems to indicate more restrictive use for economic offenses (e.g., the removal of 13 nonviolent and economic offenses in 2011), 9 of the 55 existing death-eligible offenses remain economic in nature,[8] including fraudulent fund-raising, with which Wu Ying was charged. Moreover, the impact of the Wu Ying case on other nonviolent capital offenses is not clear.

Notice that the general sentiment in Wu's case (as in economic cases in general) seemed very different from that in corruption cases, because there is seemingly a high level of consensus to retain the death penalty for public official crimes, such as corruption (Liu 2013).

Third, like the Tang Hui case, the Wu Ying case also showed signs of local protectionism and external influence on judicial decision making. It was speculated that some local governmental officials connected with the case pressed the court to sentence Wu to death. These officials wanted Wu dead so that no incriminating information could leak out. In fact, upon Wu's arrest, she cooperated with law enforcement authorities, and as a result, several officials were arrested and subsequently punished.

In sum, both the Tang Hui and the Wu Ying cases showed a cautious approach to the use of the death penalty by the Chinese judiciary, particularly the SPC. More important, these cases revealed some fundamental issues and challenges (e.g., judicial independence and the public's lack of confidence in the judicial system) faced by China's death penalty reforms. Despite the unique Chinese characteristics of these problems, an examination of these problems within the global context will be fruitful, given the influence of the global abolition movement.

CHINA'S PRACTICES AND INTERNATIONAL STANDARDS

Although China's practice of the death penalty has made significant progress over the decades, it is useful to identify existing, substantive gaps between China's practice and international standards in order to draw up potential plans for future reforms.

As has been pointed out (Hood 2009; Su 2011), three key documents are particularly relevant to setting international standards with regard to the practice of the death penalty: the International Covenant on Civil and Political Rights (ICCPR) adopted by the United Nations General Assembly in 1966 (of which China is a signatory),[9] the Safeguards Guaranteeing Protection of the Rights of Those Facing the Death Penalty (the Safeguards) adopted by the United Nations Economic and Social Council in 1984,[10] and the Second Optional Protocol to the ICCPR (the Second Optional Protocol), adopted by the United Nations General Assembly in 1989.[11]

In the new century, Chinese scholars have already produced seminal works to examine gaps between China's existing legal system and requirements based on the ICCPR (Chen, Cheng, & Yang 2002; Chen & Yang 2005). Both the revised Criminal Law (2011) and the revised Criminal Procedure Law (2012) also address some concerns raised in these studies and seek to further improve China's criminal justice system. Our discussions focus on the death penalty and contrast key standards based on the three international documents with China's current practice based on the existing Criminal Law and Criminal Procedure Law.

First, in regard to the stance on capital punishment, the ICCPR states clearly that "every human being has the inherent right to life" and "no one shall be arbitrarily deprived of his life" (Article 6, paragraph 1). Further, the Second Optional Protocol explicitly expresses its desire for abolition, believing it to be a contribution to "enhancement of human dignity" and "development of human rights" (preamble). In contrast, as the largest executioner in the world, the Chinese government has never seriously considered abolition. Even among the progressive academic circle, a retention consensus has seemingly been reached based on considerations of China's current situation (see chapter 6). The retention argument often draws on China's history, culture, and politics and on practical reasons as justifications.

Second, on the scope of capital punishment, both the ICCPR (Article 6, paragraph 2) and the Safeguards (paragraph 1) demand that capital punishment, if retained, shall be imposed only for the "most serious crimes." The Safeguards further provides that the scope of serious crimes "should not go beyond intentional crimes with lethal or other extremely grave consequences" (paragraph 1). By law, China limits the use of the death penalty only to criminals who commit the "most heinous crimes" (Criminal Law, Article 48). Nevertheless, China's definition of the most heinous crimes is still very broad and elastic: despite the most recent reduction of 13 previous capital offenses, the existing Criminal Law still carries 55 potential capital crimes (31 of which are nonviolent). As a result, economic and nonviolent offenders such as Wu Ying and some of those in the Tang Hui case can still be punished with the extreme measure.

Third, the ICCPR (Article 6, paragraph 5) demands that juvenile offenders (below 18 years of age) and pregnant women be exempt from capital punishment, and the Safeguards further expands that exemption to cover new mothers or persons who have become insane (paragraph 3) and recommends establishment of a maximum age beyond which no death sentence and execution shall be imposed and carried out (Safeguards, 1989 revision).

In contrast, China's Criminal Law exempts juvenile offenders, pregnant women, and seniors above 75 (unless the crime is committed in an extremely cruel manner) (Article 49). However, no official protection is provided for new mothers and insane persons, even though Article 18 of the Criminal Law leaves open the possibility that mentally insane individuals may have their criminal liabilities exempted or reduced.

Fourth, both the ICCPR and the Safeguards set up a number of important due process protections, including, but not limited to, the following: (1) all persons shall be treated equally (ICCPR, Article 14, paragraph 1); (2) capital judgment be rendered by a competent, independent, and impartial tribunal on the basis of clear and convincing evidence leaving no room for alternative explanation of the facts (ICCPR, Article 6, paragraph 2, and Article 14, paragraph 1; Safeguards, paragraphs 4 and 5); (3) everyone shall have the right to be presumed innocent until proved guilty and not be compelled to testify against oneself (ICCPR, Article 14, paragraphs 2 and 3(g)); (4) everyone shall be informed promptly about the nature and cause of charges against him or her and shall be tried without undue delay (ICCPR, Article 14, paragraph 3(a)); (5) everyone shall have the assistance of legal counsel (ICCPR, Article 14, paragraphs 3(b) and (d); Safeguards, paragraph 5); (6) everyone shall have the right to confront and cross-examine adversary witnesses and utilize witnesses in one's favor (ICCPR, Article 14, paragraph 3(e)); (7) everyone shall have the assistance of an interpreter if language presents a problem (ICCPR, Article 14, paragraph 3(f)); (8) everyone shall have the right to appeal the trial court's decision to a higher tribunal (ICCPR, Article 14, paragraph 5; Safeguards, paragraph 6); (9) everyone shall have access to state compensation in case of a miscarriage of justice (ICCPR, Article 14, paragraph 6); (10) everyone shall have the right to avoid facing double jeopardy (ICCPR, Article 14, paragraph 7); and (11) everyone shall have the right to avoid negative retroactive penal punishment (Safeguards, paragraph 2).

An examination of China's existing Criminal Law and Criminal Procedure Law shows *legal compliance* with all these standards except the presumption of innocence and double-jeopardy protections (items 3 and 10).[12] Article 4 of the Criminal Law stipulates that "all persons shall be equal before the courts and tribunals," and Article 12 of the Criminal Procedure Law stipulates that "no one shall be found guilty without a legal verdict by the people's court." Nevertheless, lack of fundamental judicial independence has always been a major concern for China's criminal justice system, and extralegal influences may play a determining role in cases with death sentences and executions (as witnessed in both the Wu Ying and the Tang Hui cases, for example).

On the issue of burden of proof, Article 195 of the Criminal Procedure Law requires that "the facts of the case are clear and the evidence reliable and sufficient (for a conviction)." Article 53 further clarifies "reliable and sufficient evidence" as follows: (1) all conviction facts are corroborated by evidence, (2) all evidence is verified through legal procedures, and (3) taken as a whole, reasonable suspicion has been ruled out. In addition, newly added safeguards aim to tackle long-existing problems, such as police torture and coerced confessions, by mandating full audio or video recording of police interrogation of criminals facing a potential death sentence (Article 121) and exclusion of illegal evidence extracted through torture (Article 54). The effect of these new measures, however, remains to be seen, and the court is still experiencing difficulty in upholding the strictest evidence standards in practice (as seen in the Nian Bin case discussed in chapter 2).

A number of articles of the Criminal Procedure Law (e.g., Articles 83 and 182) stipulate specific time limits within which the authoritative body (e.g., the police, the procuratorate, the court) shall provide timely notice to the suspect or defendant's family members and defense attorneys. Whether such notice would allow sufficient time for the preparation of the defense is still subject to debate. For instance, Article 182 requires delivery of a copy of the bill of procuratorial prosecution to the defendant no later than 10 days before the opening of the court session, but how such a 10-day advance notice affects defense preparation of the trial is not clear.

The current Criminal Procedure Law specifically mandates legal representation for defendants facing a potential death sentence or life imprisonment (Article 34) and guarantees the defense's right to cross-examine adversary witnesses and evidence (Article 59). As seen in the Tang Hui case, lack of legal representation can be used as a legal ground to reject death sentences, and this marks a significant improvement with regard to procedural justice in China's practice. Nevertheless, defense lawyers continue to face obstacles in their criminal defense work (Fu 2007; Liu & Halliday 2011; Lu & Drass 2002; Lu & Gunnison 2003; Lu & Miethe 2002; Michelson 2007; Ran 2008; Yu 2002). The most notorious are the so-called three difficulties (*sannan*), referring to the difficulties in meeting with detained clients without police supervision, obtaining a copy of the prosecutor's case files, and gathering evidence and cross-examining witnesses at trial, and they consistently raise deep concerns for defense work in reality (Halliday & Liu 2007; Liu & Halliday 2009; Lynch 2011). The existing Criminal Procedure Law adopted new measures in 2012 to tackle some of these difficulties. For instance, the new law grants lawyers early intervention in the investigation stage (e.g., Articles 33 and 36), simplifies the procedure for lawyers to meet with detained clients without police supervision (e.g., Article 37), and adopts exclusionary rules against evidence illegally obtained through torture (e.g., Articles 50, 53, 54). The effect of these new measures again remains to be seen.

To China's credit, the Criminal Procedure Law stipulates that members of (ethnic) minority groups enjoy the right to use their own native language in lawsuits (Article 9). Chapter 4 of the law specifically deals with the appellate review process for death penalty cases and mandates appellate review by the court of second instance (i.e., provincial high courts in death penalty cases). In addition, all cases in which defendants are sentenced to death with immediate execution are subject to final review and approval by the SPC. In case of a miscarriage of justice (e.g., wrongful convictions), state compensation is available under the State Compensation Law (in particular, Chapter 3 on criminal compensation). On the issue of potential retroactive penal punishment, Article 12 of the Criminal Law stipulates that criminal punishment may be imposed only for a crime for which the punishment is prescribed by law at the time of its commission, and if, subsequent to the commission of the crime, a newer legal provision is adopted with no or a lighter penalty, the new provision shall apply (and therefore benefit the defendant).

In contrast, China is still struggling with the principle of presumed innocence and the principle against self-incrimination (Chen et al. 2002:27, 264–270; Chen & Yang 2005:31–34 and chapter 12). The Criminal Procedure Law carries no specific language with regard to presumed innocence. Instead, Article 12 ("No one shall be found guilty without a legal verdict by the people's court") is often argued to provide this protection. Further, Article 195 provides that in case of insufficient evidence, the court shall find a not-guilty verdict. Whether the combined effect of both articles is equivalent to the presumed-innocence standard is subject to scholarly debate (Liang 2008:140), but lessons from wrongful conviction cases in recent years have raised serious questions about the practical effect of the Chinese style of presumed innocence. Similarly, there is no legal stipulation that one has the right to remain silent. Indeed, one's "voluntary cooperation" is traditionally encouraged in exchange for lighter punishment (Criminal Procedure Law, Article 118). The lack of presumed innocence and protection against self-incrimination presents arguably the biggest gap between China's current practice and international standards.

On the principle of double jeopardy, neither the Criminal Law nor the Criminal Procedure Law contains a relevant stipulation. The main reason for this gap lies in the fundamental structure of the Chinese system, modeled on the European civil (i.e., continental) system instead of the common law system. In a common law system, more safeguards are set up to protect the defendant's rights, and as a result, the double-jeopardy principle aims to limit the power of the prosecution procedurally. In contrast, in a civil legal tradition under the impact of an inquisitorial model, the goal is to seek factual truth, correct any (factual and legal) errors, and protect judiciary authority and maintain the stability of the system. As a result, both the prosecution and the defense are granted rights to appeal incorrect decisions.[13] Although the 2012 Criminal Procedure Law adopts some measures limiting retrials (Chapter 5, "Procedure for Trial Supervision"), no protection against double jeopardy is adopted.

Fifth, both the ICCPR (Article 6, paragraph 4) and the Safeguards (paragraphs 7 and 8) demand that one have the right to seek pardon, amnesty, or commutation of a death sentence. Unfortunately, no Chinese laws provide that criminals sentenced to death have this right (see discussions in Chen et al. 2002:26, 99; and Chen & Yang 2005:59–60, 66). Although offenders sentenced to death with a two-year suspension may have their sentence commuted on expiration of the suspension period, the commutation can be initiated only by the government, and the right to make this request is not granted to citizens (Su 2011:445).

Last, the Safeguards (paragraph 9) demands that capital punishment, if it occurs, be carried out so as to inflict the minimum possible suffering. As discussed in chapter 1, lethal injection is authorized by Chinese law (Criminal Procedure Law, Article 252) and is praised as a means of humane and scientific execution in China. This claim has not met any theoretical or empirical challenge in China so far.

THE FUTURE OF CHINA'S DEATH PENALTY REFORM

There is little doubt that China has made considerable strides in improving its death penalty system in the past 20 years. Although many newly instituted reform measures remain to be fine-tuned (e.g., how the SPC interrogates the defendant and hears the defense counsel's opinion during its death sentence review and approval), additional reform initiatives need to be proposed and adopted to allow China to continue on the path toward restricting its use of the death penalty and providing more procedural safeguards for death penalty cases.

Many Chinese scholars have already proposed various blueprints for China's death penalty reform, and the majority of reform proposals have focused on either legislative or judicial measures. For instance, Zhao (2005) suggests that the legislative abolition of China's death penalty be carried out in three phases to target nonviolent capital offenses, violent offenses that do not result in loss of human life, and all capital offenses, respectively. X. Chen (2006) recommends that the gap between life punishment and the death penalty be reduced legislatively, so that harsh life punishment (e.g., life imprisonment without parole) can eventually replace the death penalty. In contrast, M. Wang (2009) focuses on judicial practices and suggests that the judiciary should tighten the burden of proof required for death penalty cases. In this section, we focus on major challenges faced by both the legislature and the judiciary in pursuing future reforms. Moreover, we specifically examine what needs to be accomplished in order to reduce the gap between international standards and China's practices.

Legislative Measures

Legislative efforts to further overhaul Chinese laws are critical for China's death penalty reform. As we have learned from domestic experiences (e.g., the SPC's reform measures in recent years) and foreign experiences (e.g., the U.S. Supreme Court's struggles with capital punishment), the effect of judicial efforts to limit and regulate capital punishment can be short-lived and subject to personnel and political changes and influences. For instance, Wang Shengjun, the successor of Xiao Yang as the president of the SPC (2008–2013), was noticeably less progressive in pursuing the "killing fewer" policy.

In addition to other obstacles, one major legislative challenge is the traditional notion that capital punishment is not a human rights issue but merely a tool to serve party-state policies (so-called instrumentalism). This is the reason that abolition is never an urgent agenda for the Chinese government and lawmakers. Rather, the expansion or limitation of the scope of capital punishment is at the mercy of the government on the basis of its assessment of a given situation (see chapter 4).

Nevertheless, adoption of further reform measures to comply with international standards is technically feasible, and there is hope that it can be carried out (Chen et al. 2002; Chen & Yang 2005). To do so, the Chinese legislature needs first to gradually abolish the death penalty for nonviolent, economic, and drug crimes and limit its use to the most heinous crimes that result in loss of human life. Although recent decisions rendered by the SPC (e.g., in the Wu Ying case and the Tang Hui case) showed clear signs of moving in this direction, legislative changes are necessary to bring about full compliance with international standards and minimize the possibility of potential backlash or reversion (especially given the weak status of the Chinese judiciary). What accompanies the abolition of the death penalty in these crimes could be expanded use of the suspended death sentence, which is already in place as a viable alternative. Empirical data (see, e.g., chapter 8) have shown that these crimes represent only a small percentage of actual executions in practice, and it should therefore be possible to eliminate immediate death sentences legislatively in those crimes.

Second, the Chinese legislature needs to expand protection of special vulnerable groups and exempt new mothers and the mentally insane in particular. Although no empirical data are available, it is very unlikely that either group represents a significant proportion of China's death row inmates. As witnessed in the exemption for seniors over 75 in 2011, it should not be controversial to extend such protection to cover new mothers and the mentally insane.

Third, with regard to the presumption of innocence and the double-jeopardy principle, it is also possible for the Chinese legislature to adopt further reform measures to comply with both standards. For instance, revisions of both the Criminal Law and the Criminal Procedure Law have already included elements that aim to protect criminal suspects or defendants from being coerced to confess and to prohibit use of illegally extracted evidence. Some progressive Chinese scholars have already called for adoption of one's right to remain silent in order to comply with the principle against self-incrimination (Chen et al. 2002:516; Chen & Yang 2005:Chapter 12). Similarly, it is also likely that the Chinese legislature will adopt further procedural protections to limit the abuse of prosecutorial power in amending official charges against defendants (especially after a final verdict has been announced). Although the Chinese criminal justice system is still largely built on an inquisitorial model, adversarial elements from the common law system have already been integrated into the newly revised Criminal Law and Criminal Procedure Law.

Last, to comply with ICCPR requirements, Chinese scholars have also proposed that the legislature grant convicted capital defendants the right to seek official pardon, amnesty, or commutation (Chen et al. 2002:26, 99; Chen & Yang 2005:59–60, 66). If this right is to be established, a related issue is the extremely short time between death sentence approval by the SPC and execution (only seven days; Criminal Procedure Law, Article 251). A meaningful review of any petition for pardon, amnesty, or commutation would require a significant extension of this period.

In sum, all these legislative changes are necessary to bring China's practice into full compliance with international standards. At this moment, however, it is unclear whether the Chinese government is willing and ready to accept all or part of these changes. It is worth noting that China has not yet ratified the ICCPR, although it became a signatory in 1998. The true challenge is not technical but political: whether the Chinese legislature will be willing to exercise its political power to pursue such reform measures (see chapter 11).

Judicial Measures

As the final gatekeeper of the criminal justice system, the judiciary eventually bears the full burden of rendering death sentences. Nevertheless, lack of fundamental judicial independence presents the greatest challenge to judicial practice and often leaves ample room for external influence. Despite strenuous efforts led by the SPC in recent years, the Chinese judiciary has essentially no power to break down the framework of the death penalty system. Rather, in a time of crisis (e.g., the increased terrorist threats in 2014), the judiciary often follows the directive of the government to beef up its use of capital punishment.

As legal scholars have discussed (Chen & Yang 2005:Chapter 10), given the lack of judicial independence, the Chinese judiciary faces potential influences from several sources in its daily practice. First, the internal administrative structure within the judiciary often presents opportunities for intervention from court superiors, such as the president of the court and the adjudication committee.[14] In complicated cases, particularly death penalty cases, it is common that presiding judges who run the trial do not make the final sentencing decision; instead, other superiors who do not try the case make the final decision (a problem called *shenzhe bupan, panzhe buzhen*). Further, in these complicated cases, it is also common for lower courts to seek advice or guidance from higher-level courts as a way to avoid potential reversals. In 1998, the SPC issued the Approach on the Accountability of Judges' Illegal Judicial Behavior (Trial) and the Approach on the Disciplinary Punishment in People's Court. These two regulations officially institutionalized a system of investigation of misjudged cases (*cuo'an zhuijiu zhidu*). Although it meant more protection for defendants (via curbing misjudged cases), this system (linked with judges' evaluation, promotion, and wages) further weakened judges' independence because cases reversed by appellate courts are considered misjudged cases. As a result, judges are turning more to their superiors for instruction and guidance to avoid potential mistakes in complicated and controversial cases (B. Wang 2010).

Second, the notion of checks and balances is fundamentally lacking in the Chinese political and legal system, and as a result, the courts also face potential external influences from other local governmental agencies (e.g., political-legal committees) because the Chinese judiciary often relies on the (financial and administrative) support of the local government, and it is the court's responsibility to work collectively with other governmental branches. The notion of "checks and balances" is fundamentally lacking in the Chinese political and legal system. As a result, courts are subject to influences by other governmental agencies. In such cases, presiding judges are deprived not only of their capability to adjudicate cases independently but also of their professional development opportunities because of a narrow path of upward mobility through administrative ranks only. Because of this situation, coupled with heavy caseloads and disjunction between their authority and their responsibility, judges' morale has been low, and turnover has been high among judges in recent years (Ren 2014).

Third, in death penalty cases in particular, Chinese judges also face pressure from the central government when they have to answer the call to help "build a harmonious society." Judges routinely agonize over the need to adhere to the law and the need to meet the political mission. Within the current political context of maintaining social stability, judges must ensure that a decision based on law simultaneously satisfies demands from the victim's family or public opinion at large (see chapter 10). In the Tang Hui case, for example, her open and public demand for the death penalty for all defendants and her persistent petitioning exerted tremendous pressure on the courts' decisions. In such cases, courts are likely to be hijacked by the demands of the victim's family or public opinion. As a result, the high court sometimes sends a tough case back to the trial court for reconsideration numerous times (as occurred in the Tang Hui case and the Nian Bin case), an indication of the challenge faced by the Chinese judiciary as it tries to reach a compromise among upholding the law, meeting the demands of the parties, and taking responsibility for its decision.

Realizing the problems, the Chinese government and the judiciary are trying to make improvements. The fourth Five-Year Reform Plan (2014–2018), issued by the SPC in July 2014, adopted several measures to address this issue.[15] The proposed judicial reform was also echoed at the Fourth Plenary Session of the 18th Chinese Communist Party Central Committee, featuring the theme of the rule of law, held in October 2014. In particular, proposals aimed at establishing professional judgeship target two barriers that have traditionally interfered with judicial independence: local and administrative interferences ("Judicial reform" 2014). First, the delocalization (*qu difanghua*) proposal suggests that provincial governments, not local governments, shall exercise authority over budgetary and personnel decisions concerning the courts. It is hoped that if administrative ties between the court and the local government are severed, less interference from the local government will ensue. Second, the deadministrationalization (*qu xingzhenghua*) proposal deals with both external and internal interference. The proposal aims to separate judges from the ordinary state functionary system and set them on a professional path. For example, Shanghai has started a pilot program that ties judges' authority, responsibility, and incentives together. The presiding judge under the new system will make legal rulings independently and will be held responsible for the decisions. To enhance job performance, the presiding judge is provided with legal assistants and other support staff. A promotion system is also set up to allow judges to have upward mobility in professional development (Q. Chen 2014).

Granted, the changing roles and reallocated personnel and resources in these proposals may not be the panacea for the complex problems and challenges faced by the Chinese judiciary and the larger legal system. Making a fundamental difference will require more structural and cultural changes (e.g., a more transparent and independent system, a strong culture of legal professionalism, and further promotion of respect for law and adjudication). Nevertheless, these are critical steps toward a more independent court system and may have an effect that could potentially trickle down to other branches of the legal system. For example, an independent judicial system may become more effective in correcting errors or abuse by the police. It may also help the court withstand better the political pressure that demands it be tough on crime during anticrime campaigns.

It should also be noted that China's political system remains socialist. Any call to remove the instrumental function of adjudication and law (Jiao 2014) will go against the fundamental design of a socialist system (Minas 2009). In other words, an independent judiciary can be effective only to the extent that it serves the functions of the socialist agenda (and also the party's agenda). When there is a conflict between politics and law, politics will likely prevail. This has been evident in several high-profile death penalty cases in the past two decades. This systematic limitation poses a serious challenge to building an independent judiciary, especially in extraordinary cases when the court faces tremendous pressure from different government branches, the victim's family, and the public in general.

To comply with international standards, the Chinese judiciary first should strictly adhere to safeguards already in place to maximize protections for capital offenders. For instance, the judiciary should use Article 195 of the Criminal Procedure Law to find the defendant not guilty when there is insufficient evidence (see the Nian Bin case in chapter 2). Moreover, the judiciary should turn to Article 54 to exclude illegal evidence extracted through torture. These measures have great potential to stop wrongful convictions, but the real challenge is whether the judiciary will be willing and able to use them effectively, given its close relationship with the police and the procuratorate and interference from other powerful players and agencies.

In the absence of legislative amendments, the judiciary has been very creative in implementing the "killing fewer" policy in recent years (see chapter 5).

New guidelines from the SPC (e.g., via guiding cases; see chapter 7) and new practices to limit immediate executions (e.g., cash for clemency; see chapter 10) all have helped bring down the numbers of death sentences and executions. The judiciary should continue its laudable efforts in case the legislature is hesitant to take on reform moves.

Granted, reforms of China's death penalty system must be part of the reform of China's criminal justice system in general. Without reforms of the criminal justice system in the last three and a half decades, China's death penalty would have never reached its present stage. To make China's death penalty reform effective, a holistic approach is desirable to involve players beyond the legislature and the judiciary. For example, the central government should restrain itself from intervening in adjudication, reduce or stop anticrime campaigns, and increase governmental transparency (e.g., make death sentence information available to the public). More measures are also needed to adjust the traditional *gongjianfa* relationship among the judiciary, the police, and the procuratorate and to maximize the judicial review function to avoid the effect of the assembly line among these three players.

Future death penalty reform in China will face many challenges. The outlook is intriguing but hopeful. The recently elevated status of the rule of law under the Xi Jinping administration shows promising signs for a more functional and independent judiciary. This new development will likely reaffirm the death penalty policy of "killing fewer and killing cautiously." Right around the time when we were finishing this closing chapter, news broke out that the draft of the Ninth Amendment of the Criminal Law (currently under consideration by the Chinese National People's Congress) proposed a further reduction of nine more capital offenses (including organizing prostitution and forcing others into prostitution, as seen in the Tang Hui case, and fraudulent fund-raising, as seen in the Wu Ying case). Given China's continuing role as an economic powerhouse in the twenty-first century and the Chinese government's keen awareness of international criticisms of its human rights record and death penalty policies, China's death penalty reform is expected to continue on the path of closing the gap between China's practice and international standards without complete abolition.

NOTES

1. Introduced in 1957, reeducation through labor was an administrative measure directly handled by the police in China without intervention by the judiciary. Its practice was seriously questioned both domestically and internationally. In December 2013, the Standing Committee of the National People's Congress passed a decision to end this practice.
2. For a detailed description of the case, see the following reports: Bianca Ortega, China's Supreme Court overturns death sentence in high-profile rape case, retrieved October 8, 2014, from http://www.chinatopix.com/articles/3099/20140613/china-s-supreme-court-overtur-death-sentence.htm; chankaiyee2, China: "Petition mother" Tang Hui's determined fight for justice over daughter's rape, retrieved October 4, 2014, from https://tiananmenstremendousachievements.wordpress.com/2013/04/27/china-petition-mother-tang-huis-determined-fight-for-justice-over-daughters-rape/; and the Tang Hui case, retrieved October 8, 2014, from http://zh.wikipedia.org/wiki/%E5%94%90%E6%85%A7%E6%A1%88.
3. See Attorney Liu, The Supreme People's Court answered related questions on the final review and approval of two defendants in the Tang Hui case, retrieved October 8, 2014, from http://club.kdnet.net/dispbbs.asp?id=10129523&boardid=25&read=1.
4. See chankaiyee2, China.
5. Information on the Wu Ying case is gathered from the following reports, the Wu Ying case, retrieved on October 4, 2014, from http://www.baike.com/wiki/%E5%90%B4%E8%8B%B1%E6%A1%88; Xinian Tao, The full record of the Wu Ying case: Crime and punishment of the billionaire, retrieved October 4, 2014, from http://news.qq.com/a/20091228/001582.htm; The Wu Ying case: Death sentence should not be rendered, retrieved October 4, 2014, from http://news.ifeng.com/opinion/special/wuyingan/; Xiangyang Tang and Ruoji Tang, Considered opinion: The Wu Ying case (by), retrieved October 4, 2014, from http://www.eeo.com.cn/ens/Politics/2011/04/19/199377.shtml; Edward Wong, Chinese court overturns a young tycoon's death sentence, retrieved October 4, 2014, from http://www.nytimes.com/2012/04/21/world/asia/china-court-overturns-death-penalty-for-tycoon-in-fraud-case.html?_r=1; and Who goes to the gallows? Concern over a high-profile death penalty, available at http://www.economist.com/node/21543593.
6. Tang and Tang, Considered opinion.
7. The full text of the SPC notice is available at http://china.findlaw.cn/lawyers/article/d164947.html (retrieved October 8, 2014).
8. These nine capital offenses include six crimes of undermining the socialist market economic order, robbery, graft, and bribe taking (see chapter 2, table 2.3). This categorization follows an expansive definition of economic crimes used by Chinese scholars (Liu 2013:41; Su 2011; Zhao & Wan 2009).
9. The full text of the ICCPR is available at http://www.ohchr.org/EN/Professional Interest/Pages/CCPR.aspx (retrieved September 29, 2014).

10 The full text of the Safeguards is available at http://www.ohchr.org/EN/Professional Interest/Pages/DeathPenalty.aspx (retrieved September 29, 2014). Note that the 1984 Safeguards was further expanded and supplemented twice, in 1989 and 1996.
11 The full text of the Second Optional Protocol is available at http://www.ohchr.org/EN/ProfessionalInterest/Pages/2ndOPCCPR.aspx (retrieved September 29, 2014).
12 We emphasize *legal compliance* (i.e., compliance stipulated in the law) because what is practiced in reality can be very different from what is stipulated in the law. Indeed, although the Chinese law largely complies with the requirements of the ICCPR, there still exist significant gaps between the standards and actual practice in China (see relevant discussions in Chen et al. 2002 and Chen & Yang 2005).
13 Please see R. Chen (2003) for a detailed discussion of issues with regard to repeat petitioning in criminal cases and his suggestions to reform Chinese criminal procedure on the basis of lessons from both the common law and the civil legal traditions. See also discussions in Chen et al. (2002: 329–340) and Chen and Yang (2005: Chapter 14).
14 The adjudication committee is the highest decision-making body in Chinese courts, and it reviews and rules on the most complicated and controversial cases behind closed doors. For an empirical study of the adjudication committee, see He (2012).
15 For a detailed discussion of the reform plan, see The SPC's fourth Five-Year Reform Plan (2014–2018) is adopted, retrieved October 8, 2014, from http://www.dffyw.com/fazhixinwen/sifa/201407/36477.html; and Lubman (2014).

REFERENCES

Chen, G., Cheng, W., & Yang, V. C. (Eds.). (2002). *Gongmin quanli he zhengzhi quanli guoji gongyue pizhun yu shishi wenti yanjiu* (A Study on the Issues of Ratifying and Implementing of International Covenant on Civil and Political Rights). Beijing: China Legal Publishing House.

Chen, G., & Yang, Y. (Eds.). (2005). *Gongmin quanli he zhengzhi quanli guoji gongyue yu woguo xingshi susong* (The International Covenant on Civil and Political Rights and China's Criminal Procedure). Beijing: Commercial Press.

Chen, Q. (2014, August 1). Court reform in Shanghai. *Jiefang ribao*. Retrieved October 2014, from http://www.jfdaily.com/shanghai/bw/201408/t20140801_617954.html.

Chen, R. (2003). Issues with regard to repeat petitioning in criminal procedure. Retrieved December 2013, from http://www.acla.org.cn/article/2003-12-16/10819.html and http://www.acla.org.cn/article/2003-12-18/10856.html.

Chen, X. (2006). Destiny of the death penalty in China in the contemporary era. *Frontier Law China, 1*, 53–71.

Fu, H. (2007). When lawyers are prosecuted... The struggle of a profession in transition. *Journal of Comparative Law, 2,* 95–132.

Gao, Y. (2012). Beyond the regulation on financial fraud and illegal fundraising: Crime and punishment in the Wu Ying case. *Peking University Law Journal, 24*(2), 411–439.

Halliday, T. C., & Liu, S. (2007). Birth of a liberal moment? Looking through a one-way mirror at lawyers' defense of criminal defendants in China. In T. C. Halliday, L. Karpik, & M. M. Feeley (Eds.), *Fighting for Political Freedom: Comparative Studies of the Legal Complex and Political Liberalism* (pp. 65–107). Oxford: Hart.

He, X. (2012). Black hole of responsibility: The adjudication committee's role in a Chinese court. *Law and Society Review, 46*(4), 681–712.

Hood, R. (2009). Abolition of the death penalty: China in world perspective. *City University of Hong Kong Law Review, 1,* 1–21.

Jiao, H. (2014). Success of judicial reform relies on court reform. Retrieved October 2014, from http://www.cntaoxue.com/zx/rdzz/2014-10-18/25518.html.

Judicial reform—Let judges be judges. (2014, October 17). *Xinhua News.* Retrieved October 2014, from http://news.163.com/14/1017/07/A8O88VC200014AED.html.

Liang, B. (2008). *The Changing Chinese Legal System, 1978–Present: Centralization of Power and Rationalization of the Legal System.* New York: Routledge.

Liu, R. (2013). *Sixing de quanqiu shiye: Zhongguo yuejing* [A Global Vision of the Death Penalty and the Chinese Context]. Beijing: China Social Science.

Liu, S., & Halliday, T. C. (2009). Recursivity in legal change: Lawyers and reforms of China's criminal procedure law. *Law and Social Inquiry, 34*(4), 911–950.

Liu, S., & Halliday, T. C. (2011). Political liberalism and political embeddedness: Understanding politics in the work of Chinese criminal defense lawyers. *Law and Society Review, 45,* 831–864.

Lu, H., & Drass, K. A. (2002). Transience and the disposition of theft cases in China. *Justice Quarterly, 19,* 69–96.

Lu, H., & Gunnison, E. (2003). Power, corruption, and the legal process in China. *International Criminal Justice Review, 13,* 28–49.

Lu, H., & Miethe, T. D. (2002). Legal representation and criminal processing in China. *British Journal of Criminology, 42,* 267–280.

Lubman, S. (2014, July 10). Power shift: Hopeful signs in China's legal reform plan. *China Real Time.* Retrieved from http://blogs.wsj.com/chinarealtime/2014/07/10/power-shift-hopeful-signs-in-chinas-legal-reform-plan/.

Luo, J. (2013). Qianzha changing de luoji beilun yu daode kunjing: cong Zeng Chengjie Wu Ying deng an tan jizi zapianzui sixing de feichu [Debt repaid with life, the logical paradox and moral dilemma: On abolition of the death penalty in financial fraud cases such as Zeng Chengjie and Wu Ying]. *Journal of Southwest University for Nationalities (Humanities and Social Science Edition), 12*, 90–94

Lynch, E. M. (2011). China's rule of law mirage: The regression of the legal profession since the adoption of the 2007 Lawyers Law. *George Washington International Law Review, 42*, 535–585.

Michelson, E. (2007). Lawyers, political embeddedness, and institutional continuity in China's transition from socialism. *American Journal of Sociology, 113*(2), 352–414.

Minas, S. (2009). "Kill fewer, kill carefully": An analysis of the 2006 to 2007 death penalty reforms in China. *UCLA Pacific Basin Law Journal, 27*, 36–70.

Ran, Y. (2008). When Chinese criminal defense lawyers become the criminals. *Fordham International Law Journal, 32*, 988–1042.

Ren, Z. (2014). Chen Ruihua discusses death penalty review reforms—Defense opinion is the best help for the judge. *Southern Weekend*. Retrieved October 2014, from http://blog.sina.com.cn/s/blog_63aeaff70102v3rz.html.

Su, C. (2011). The present and future: The death penalty in China's penal code. *Oklahoma City University Law Review, 36*(2), 427–450.

Wang, B. (2010, April 6). Faguan xiaoyong hanshu yu faguan xingwei [Judges' utility function and judges' behavior]. *Chinese Social Science Today*, p. 10.

Wang, M. (2009). On the "criterion" of proof in capital cases and the revision of the Criminal Procedure Law. *Social Science in China, 30*(2), 138–151.

Yu, P. (2002). Glittery promise vs. dismal reality: The role of a criminal lawyer in the People's Republic of China after the 1996 revision of the Criminal Procedure Law. *Vanderbilt Journal of Transnational Law, 35*, 827–864.

Zhao, B. (2005). Lun zhongguo feibaoli fangzui sixing de zhubu feizhi [On abolition of the death penalty of nonviolent crimes in China]. *Tribune of Political Science and Law, 23*(1), 92–99.

Zhao, B., & Wan, Y. (2009). On limiting and abolishing the death penalty for economic crimes in China. *Chinese Sociology and Anthropology, 41*(4), 14–40.

CONTRIBUTORS

XINGLIANG CHEN is professor of law at Beijing University School of Law. He is also a selected Chang Jiang Scholar in China and a leading scholar on China's study of the death penalty. His research interests cover a broad range of issues in criminal law. He has published numerous books and research articles.

HUALING FU is professor of law at the University of Hong Kong. His research interests include constitutional law and human rights, with a special focus on the criminal justice system and media law in China.

CHARLOTTE HU is an MA student in the Department of Criminal Justice at the University of Nevada, Las Vegas. She has copresented two papers at professional conferences and is currently working on a master's thesis examining corruption and criminal sentencing in China.

SHANHE JIANG is professor of criminal justice at Wayne State University and a visiting chair professor at Central China Normal University. He has organized a survey of seven nations on public opinion on crime, crime control, and punishment (including the death penalty). He has published several articles on the death penalty in China, the United States, Japan, India, and other countries. He is conducting ongoing collaborative research on community corrections with scholars in China.

DAVID T. JOHNSON is professor of sociology at the University of Hawaii at Manoa and former coeditor of *Law and Society Review*. He is the author of three books: *The Japanese Way of Justice: Prosecuting Crime in Japan* (Oxford University Press, 2002), *The Next Frontier: National Development, Political Change, and the Death Penalty in Asia* (Oxford University Press, 2009, with Franklin E. Zimring), and *Koritsu Suru Nihon no Shikei* [Japan's isolated death penalty] (Gendai Jinbunsha, 2012, with Maiko Tagusari).

YUDU LI is a doctoral student in the Department of Criminal Justice at Sam Houston State University. He was the recipient of a fellowship from the International

Institute of Education of the Ford Foundation. He has published two peer-reviewed journal articles and one book review and has presented papers at professional conferences. He is working on a project examining eyewitness lineups using data collected by the Houston Police Department Robbery Division and another project on public attitudes toward the police.

BIN LIANG is associate professor of Sociology at Oklahoma State University. His current research interests include globalization and its impact on the Chinese legal system, crime and deviance in China, and comparative studies in criminology and criminal justice. He is the author of three books: *The Changing Chinese Legal System, 1978–Present: Centralization of Power and Rationalization of the Legal System* (Routledge, 2008), *China's Drug Practices and Policies: Regulating Controlled Substances in a Global Context* (Ashgate, 2009, coauthored), and *Jurisprudence* (Renmin University of China Press, 2012, coedited, in Chinese).

HONG LU is professor of criminal justice at the University of Nevada, Las Vegas. She has published scholarly works in the areas of comparative criminology and sociology of law and has authored or coauthored three books: *Punishment: A Comparative and Historical Perspective* (Cambridge University Press, 2005), *China's Death Penalty: History, Law, and Contemporary Practices* (Routledge, 2007), and *China's Drug Practices and Policies: Regulating Controlled Substances in a Global Context* (Ashgate, 2009).

MICHELLE MIAO is currently a Postdoctoral Global Fellow at New York University School of Law. She conducted research on the topic of penal populism and human rights as a Howard League postdoctoral fellow at Oxford University's Centre for Criminology after completing her DPhil in law at Oxford University in 2013. Her doctoral thesis studied the politics of China's recent capital punishment reform. She has published several articles and book chapters on the death penalty in China. Her research interests cover the following areas: human rights, Chinese law and society, comparative studies, capital punishment, and incarceration.

SUSAN TREVASKES is a member of the Centre of Excellence in Policing and Security at Griffith University and an Adjunct Director of the Centre for China in the World at Australian National University. Her main research interests are in criminal justice, punishment, and courts in China. Her recent books include *Courts and Criminal Justice in Contemporary China* (Lexington Press, 2007), *Policing Serious Crime in China: From "Strike Hard" to "Kill Fewer"*

(Routledge, 2010) and *The Death Penalty in Contemporary China* (Palgrave Macmillan, 2012). She has also published a number of articles on anticrime campaigns, private security, public security, drug crime, public shaming events, and death penalty reform.

YUNHAI WANG is professor of criminal law of the Graduate School of Law at Hitotsubashi University in Japan and the president of the Society for Legal Culture Study in Japan. He received his education in both China and Japan and earned his LLM and PhD degrees in Japan. He also conducted research from 1999 to 2000 at the Law School of Harvard University as a visiting scholar. His main works on the death penalty include *The Death Penalty: A Comparative Study of China, America and Japan* (Seibundou, 2005), "The Death Penalty and Society in Contemporary China," published in *Punishment and Society: The International Journal of Penology*, 10(2) (2008), and *When Does China Sentence a Bribery Offender to Death?* (Kokusaishoin, 2013).

MOULIN XIONG is assistant professor in the Law School at Southwestern University of Finance and Economics in China. He was a visiting scholar in the Sociology Department at the University of California, Irvine, from 2010 to 2012. He has an interdisciplinary background, and his major research interests include quantitative criminology, criminal law, and sociology. He is working on a number of projects, including China's practice of the death penalty, a global study of criminal fines, sentencing disparity, crime and offenders in the life span, global crime definitions and standards, and criminal law crisis (including overcriminalization and decriminalization). His research has been published in such journals as *China Social Science*, *Tsinghua Law Review*, and *Juvenile Delinquency Issues*.

ZHIGANG YU is professor of law at China University of Political Science and Law. He was a visiting scholar at Oxford University from 2004 to 2005. He has published 12 books and over 200 articles in such journals as *China Social Science* and *China Journal of Law*. He was named one of the 10 outstanding young legal scholars in China in 2010.

NING ZHANG is associate professor in the Department of East Asian Studies at the University of Geneva and a member of the Research Centre on Modern and Contemporary China at Ecole des Hautes Etudes en Sciences Sociales (EHESS), Paris. Her research focuses on the history of Chinese legal culture. She has published many articles in English, French, and Chinese on the institutions and practices of the death penalty in both imperial and contemporary China.

She also served as a guest editor of two special issues of academic journals on the death penalty in contemporary China: "The Debate on the Death Penalty in China Today" (*Contemporary Chinese Thought*, 2005) and "The Debate on the Abolition of Capital Punishment as Applied to Economic Crimes in China" (*Chinese Sociology and Anthropology*, 2009).

INDEX

Abolition, viii–x; domestic debate (over), 24; movement, xii, 1, 23, 98, 156–157, 160–162, 175, 327, 334; outright and immediate abolition (in China), 12; unique circumstances (in China), 13, 20. *See also* Death penalty: abolition
Adjudication, 50, 52, 75, 190–191, 194, 204, 211, 343, 345–346, 348
Aggravating (extreme/serious) circumstance, 37, 38, 81, 114, 118, 144–145, 197, 200, 202, 206
Amnesty International, xi, 12, 14, 17, 19, 21, 37, 214–215, 220, 233, 312–313
Anticrime campaign, 3, 14, 17, 124, 127, 134, 137, 147, 237, 345–346. *See also* Strike-hard campaign
Anti-Rightists, 87
Appeal, 3, 9–10, 49–50, 53–54, 90–91, 116–117, 193, 199, 203, 215, 216, 218–219, 232, 281, 283, 287, 293, 305, 307, 310, 328, 330; right to, 46, 48, 336, 339
Appeasing the feelings of the public, 12. *See also* Public opinion
Appellate courts, 9–10, 14, 16, 117, 280–281, 289, 292, 343; open hearings, 9, 215. *See also* Intermediate People's Courts
Appellate review, 8, 16, 40, 49, 230, 330, 338. *See also* Trial: of second instance
Application cases, 189
Armed enemies, 64
Arrest, 2, 11, 17, 40–42, 78, 82–84, 86–87, 116, 193, 197, 200–202, 232, 328, 332, 334; large-scale, 72–74; warrant, 43, 45–46, 53, 55

Assault, 10, 25, 31–32, 128–129, 133, 135, 145, 166, 225–228, 230, 236, 253–255, 328; aggravated, 110; intentional, 166, 253; resulting in death, 129, 145
Assembly line, 9, 346
Attorney-client privilege, 46
Authoritarian society (state), 267, 283, 293, 316–317

Bail, 16, 42
Balancing leniency and severity, 5, 17, 24–25, 116, 124–125, 137, 141–144, 151
Bandits, 63, 67–68, 70–71, 73, 158
Barbarity, 265
Basic court, 40. *See also* Trial: of first instance
Beijing model, 86
Beijing Municipal Party Committee, 66, 70
Bense Group, 331–333. *See also* Wu Ying
Bo Xilai, 17, 91
Bribery, 110, 112, 178, 217
Bribe taking, 34, 36, 179, 347
Building a Harmonious Society, 108, 114, 142
Burden of proof, 49, 337, 340
Bureau of Public Security, 86

Campaign style for enforcing the criminal law, 109. *See also* Strike-hard campaign
Capital punishment, 6–7, 25, 63, 83, 123–124, 149–150, 160, 163, 194. *See also* Death penalty
Cash for clemency, 26, 114, 276, 286, 288, 292, 294, 308, 311, 346

Charging, 39–40, 45–46
Checks and balances, lack of, 9, 57, 343
Chen Gang, 327
Chen Jianyang, 209
Chen Xilian, 2
Chen Yi, 72, 76
Chiang Kai-shek (Jiang Jieshi), 62, 83, 303, 321
Chinese Communist Party, 2, 15, 49, 51, 59, 63, 65, 71, 74, 79, 85, 102, 127, 175, 268, 283, 286, 288, 301, 303–305, 307, 316, 319, 344
Chinese enhanced due process, 116–118
Chongqing, 17, 28, 71–73, 91, 221, 292
Class-struggle theory, 103–104
Closed-court review, 16
Communist revolution, 62, 79, 320
Commutation, 193, 198–203, 339, 342
Confession, 8, 43–44, 47, 173, 193, 197–198, 210, 316; coerced (forced), viii, 15, 18, 45, 53–55, 166, 317, 337; voluntary (self), 9, 142, 287
Confucianism, 101, 112, 247
Conspiracy, 80, 317
Conviction, 8–11, 51, 54, 56, 58, 206–211, 214, 240, 332, 337–338, 345; error, 51; rate, 15, 45, 56; wrongful, viii, ix, 8–9, 54, 58, 164–165, 209–212, 214, 240, 269, 270, 310, 338, 345
Corruption, 44, 59, 178–179, 217, 238–239, 253, 255, 310, 344, 351
Counterfeiting, 35, 81, 226, 228, 230, 232, 240, 255
Counterrevolutionary, 2, 62, 69, 71–72, 89, 159, 217; offense (crime), 6, 13, 24, 63–64, 68–69, 74–75, 77, 81–84, 103
Crime campaigns, 19, 21. *See also* Anticrime campaign; Strike-hard campaign
Crime severity, 262, 265
Criminal defense, 5, 16, 46, 56, 337; right to confront witness and evidence, 14. *See also* Defense rights; Legal representation
Criminal investigation, 39–41, 43, 45, 53, 57, 317

Criminal Law: 1979 Criminal Law, 3, 6–8, 64, 79, 90, 104–106, 124, 126, 169, 188, 217; 1997 Criminal Law, 3, 13–14, 105–106, 113–115, 128, 169, 188, 217–218, 308; 2011 Eighth Amendment, xi, 5, 15, 22–23, 31, 36, 105, 113–115, 147, 169, 200–202, 215, 237, 311, 335
Criminal Procedure Law: 1996 Criminal Procedure Law, 4, 14, 16–18, 39, 47–48, 64, 84, 90, 118, 218; 2012 Criminal Procedure Law, 10, 14–16, 31, 147, 206, 339
Cross-examination, 49
Cultural Revolution, 2–3, 13, 88, 126, 304, 307, 317
Custodial summons, 41, 53–54
Custody, 33–34, 40–43, 45, 77, 328

Deadministrationalization proposal, 344–345
Death penalty: abolition, 98, 156, 159, 163, 167–168, 170, 172, 175, 194, 248, 314; approval power, 6, 8, 9, 13–14, 16, 57, 218, 230; eligible offenses, 3, 5, 13, 14, 31, 34–36, 37, 105, 115, 157–158, 160, 217, 236, 308, 333; exemption (minors; pregnant women; seniors), 15, 335, 341; retention (of), ix, 12, 25, 123, 156–181, 236, 247, 314, 319, 335; review (procedure; final review), 24–25, 50, 78, 85, 88–92, 115–116, 130, 168, 171–173, 177, 180, 191, 201, 208–210, 215–216, 218–219, 225, 229–238, 240, 288–289, 292, 333, 339; worldwide, 37, 39, 233
Death row inmates, 15, 18, 19, 51–52, 309, 341
Death sentence, viii, ix, xi, xii, 2, 5, 8, 11, 16–17, 21–25, 33–34, 44, 45, 50–54, 57, 76–77, 79–80, 82, 85–86, 87, 89, 90–92, 97, 98, 108, 110, 111, 112, 114–116, 117–118, 123, 124–142, 144, 147–151, 159, 164, 172, 180, 192, 199, 209, 215, 216, 217–219, 221, 223, 225, 226, 239, 269, 270, 286, 287, 302, 306, 308, 310–311, 316, 329, 331, 332–333, 335, 337, 339, 340, 342; number of, viii, ix, 1, 13–14, 16, 25, 37–41, 67–69, 105, 346;

suspended, ix, 14, 24, 63, 90, 115–116, 125, 130–133, 135, 137, 138, 147, 154, 166, 168, 170, 173, 177–178, 201–202, 208, 218–219, 223, 229–233, 308, 310–311, 341; with reprieve, 24, 89–92, 123, 131, 134–135, 234–235. *See also* Execution

Decentralization, 14, 16, 24, 85, 87, 305–306

Defense rights, 16, 39, 46

Delocalization proposal, 344

Deng Xiaoping, 7, 84, 92, 104, 126, 137, 150, 268, 302, 304

Detention, 40–43, 45, 81, 116, 295, 329

Deterrence, 25, 134, 136, 163, 215, 248, 253, 256–266, 314; effect, 18, 163, 231, 268–270

Dezhi, 98, 101

Disputes: civil, 37, 114, 135, 172, 196–197, 200; family, 37, 114, 131, 138, 139, 170, 193, 195–197, 231; marriage, 37, 114, 139, 170, 196–197; neighbor, 37, 114, 135, 138, 139, 141, 195–197, 199, 202, 231

Dissenting opinions, 15; lack of, 20

Dong Wei, 10–11, 20, 171

Dongyang, 331–333. *See also* Wu Ying

Double jeopardy, 336, 339

Drug offenses, 146

Du Peiwu, 8–10, 18, 26

Economic crimes, 14, 22, 24, 88, 91, 146, 215, 218, 233, 237, 239, 253, 308, 332

Economic reforms, 31–32, 111, 124, 126

Embezzlement, 42, 110, 112, 178, 253, 255

Empirical data, studies of, ix, 21, 23, 161, 216, 237, 239, 341

Engels, Friedrich, 102

Espionage, 34, 69, 80, 159, 255

Evidence, xi, 10, 14, 27, 47, 50–51, 53, 56, 71, 125, 132, 134, 141, 158, 161, 292, 337; admissibility (of), 5, 9, 57, 192, 203–211, 310; confession, 9, 15, 18, 43–44, 46–47, 54, 305, 317; illegal, 5, 9, 15, 18, 43, 118, 147, 337, 345; law, 5, 15–16, 117–118, 337–338, 341, 345

Exclusionary rules, 5, 338

Execution, viii, xii, 1, 5–6, 8, 9–19, 21, 23–28, 37–40, 52–53, 67–69, 72, 76, 83, 86–87, 91–92, 97–98, 104–105, 108, 110–112, 114–117, 129–139, 157, 163–164, 207–208, 223, 260, 262, 265–267, 286–289, 301–302, 304–309, 311–319, 321, 331–332, 335, 337–339, 341–342; extrajudicial, 304; halt procedure, 5, 10–11; immediate, viii, ix, 6, 9–11, 14, 25, 37, 41, 50, 57, 114–116, 123–125, 127, 141–151, 166–173, 177, 180, 191, 218–220, 225, 229–240, 274–275, 280–282, 291–296, 328–329, 346; means of, 4, 18, 308–309, 339; moratorium, 315, 319; number of, viii, xii, 13–14, 19, 37–39, 64, 97, 124, 214–216, 306, 313; policy, 302, 309, 314; rate, 89, 306–307, 312–316; wrongful, 164, 208, 262, 265–266. *See also* Death sentence; Lethal injection

Exploiting class, 103, 159

External interferences, 15, 17, 344

Extrajudicial interventions, 17, 343

Fazhi, 98, 100

Five Antis, 85

Five-Year Reform Plan, 15, 17, 57, 344, 348

Fixed sentences, 33

Fraudulent fundraising, 332–333, 346

Gao Minxuan, 160, 202

Globalization and information era, 107

Gongjianfa, 9, 346

Great Repression, 70

Guangxi Committee, 86

Guiding cases, 25, 187–192, 211–212, 290–291, 346

Gu Kailai, 91

Habitus, 91

Han Shuzhi, 75

Heavy penaltyism, 24, 140

High People's Court, 8, 11, 193, 203; Liaoning High People's Court, 2; Shan'xi High People's Court, 10; Yunnan High People's Court, 9

Homicide, 138. *See also* Murder

Hong Kong, 26, 301, 312, 314–315, 319, 321

Hooliganism, 7, 13, 217

Hua Guofeng, 84
Hu Jintao, 106, 137, 142–143, 268; administration, 59
Human organs of the executed, 18
Human rights, viii, 25, 88, 100, 119, 159, 162–166, 270, 306, 315–316, 319, 321, 335, 341; concept of, 162; consciousness, 165; dialogue and seminar, viii; movements, 239; organizations, 13, 19; record, 346; status, 215
Hunan (Province), 11, 67, 70, 74, 163, 221, 225, 281, 327; Reeducation Committee (of), 330

Incapacitation, 248, 253, 256–262, 265, 270
Inhumane treatment, 15, 18
Innocence, 6, 9, 27, 48, 57, 269, 281, 336, 338, 339, 341
Institutionalization, 62, 65, 89, 143, 283, 285
Instrumentalism, 341
Intermediate People's Courts, 27nn8–9, 332; Changsha Intermediate People's Court, 11; Kunming Intermediate Court, 9; Yan'an Intermediate Court, 10
International community, 1, 13, 159, 161, 237
International standards, ix, 20, 26, 88, 214, 327, 334, 339, 340–342, 345–346
Internet, 11, 22, 160, 165, 174, 179, 180, 274, 281–282
Interrogation, 5, 8, 14, 16, 41–44, 46, 51–52, 54, 68, 118, 143, 146, 289, 337
Investigation, 39, 40–41, 43–46, 48, 49, 57, 71, 116, 188, 210; custodial, 53; supplemental, 53
Issuance procedure, 190

Jiang Jieshi. *See* Chiang Kai-shek
Jiang Junjun, 328
Jiang Qing, 2
Jiang Zemin, 106, 307
Jin Xing, 76
Judiciary: decision-making, xi, 56, 97, 171, 284, 287, 294, 309, 331, 334, 340, 342–344; independence, 51, 345; interpretations, 196, 208, 330; jurisdiction, 176, 310; reforms, 57, 108, 345–346; transparency, xi, 16–17, 179–180
Just deserts, 201, 311
Justice: miscarriage of, 240, 309, 336, 338; procedural, 11, 147, 330, 337; substantive, 330

Kangsu, 204. *See also* Protest
"Kill fewer" policy, 21, 238. *See also* Balancing leniency and severity
"Kill many" policy, 21
Kuomintang, 68, 77, 83, 92, 321

Lan Xiaoqiang, 328
Law: civil, 48, 187, 283, 339; enforcement, 43, 49, 65, 108, 334; in book, 44, 58; in practice, 44; written, 188
Law Yearbook of China, 31–33, 45
Legal compliance, 336, 348
Legal consciousness, 12, 176
Legal representation (counsel), 16, 46, 48, 51, 336, 340
Legislature, xi, 26, 194, 267, 275, 308, 340–342, 346
Leniency, 44, 123, 124–125, 130, 136–139, 144, 172, 201–202, 233, 311, 332; policy, 42–43. *See also* Balancing leniency and severity; Cash for clemency
Lethal injection, 4, 15, 18, 308–309, 318, 339
Li Fei, 187, 193, 198–203
Life imprisonment, ix, 2, 5, 16, 32, 34, 44, 69, 78, 80–81, 118, 173, 177, 181, 191, 194, 201, 209–210, 216, 219, 225, 249, 251–252, 258–259, 328–329, 337, 340
Lin Biao, 2
Lingchi, 21
Liu Run, 328
Liu Shaoqi, 2, 65–66
Li Wuqing, 10
Luo Ruiqing, 65, 70, 73, 84

Maintaining social stability, 12, 148, 344
Maoist period, 62–63, 304
Maoist theory, 62, 123, 136, 307, 312, 316, 320

Mao Yuanxin, 6, 64, 78, 83–84, 90
Mao Zedong, 62, 88, 91, 168, 267, 302–303
Market economy, xii, 32, 104–105, 107, 111–112
Marx, Karl, 102, 316
Massacre, 82, 236
Mass rallies (sentencing), 89
Mass social order, 108
Mass trials, 24, 73, 89
Media, 10, 13, 22–23, 26, 56, 164, 166, 189, 281–283, 293, 329–332; report(ing), 2, 15, 20
Microblogs, 22, 329. See also *Weibo*
Military court, 69, 82, 85, 221
Military crimes, 255
Ministry of Civil Affairs, 19
Ministry of Justice (MJ), 5, 18, 120, 142, 205, 208
Ministry of Public Health (MPH), 5, 19
Ministry of Public Security (MPS), 5, 18, 55, 79, 142, 149, 169, 205, 208
Minors, 14, 36, 331
Misjudged cases, 343
Mitigating circumstance: discretionary, 130, 197; statutory, 138, 172, 197
Monetarization, 104
Monetary benefit, 106
Murder, 3, 7, 8–10, 14–15, 25, 27, 31–32, 35, 51, 53, 99, 110, 117, 128–129, 138–139, 177–178, 197, 225–236, 238–239, 251, 253–254, 281, 288, 292–293, 308, 310–311; case, 55, 141, 164, 227, 284, 292; offender, 114, 231, 256, 259, 263, 286; rate, 32

Nationalist revolution, 62
National People's Congress (NPC), 3–5, 7–8, 46, 105, 107, 112–113, 117–118, 126, 147, 217–218
New China, 11, 113
Nian Bin, 52, 59, 337, 344–345
Noncapital crimes, 41, 226, 310
Nonchanges (of death penalty practice), 108, 113
Nonrandom samples, 249–250, 267
North Korea, xii, 26, 266, 301, 314, 316–319, 322

October 10 Directive, 65–66, 85
Offenses of endangering state security, 6, 13, 64
Old Five Punishments, 248
One-party ruling, 107, 111–113
Opium, 111
Opium War, 111, 304
Organ donation, 15, 19
Organic Law of the People's Court, 3–5, 8, 124

Party Revolutionary Committee, 2
Paternalism, 97
Penal populism, 276–294
People's Liberation Army, 6, 79
People's Republic of China (PRC), vii, 1, 31, 64, 98, 158, 218, 248, 267, 300, 319
Poisoning, 35, 52–54, 59
Police: abuse, 54–55; interrogation, 8, 14, 46, 143; recording or videotaping interrogation, 337; investigative power, 44; misconduct, 9; supervision, 336; torture, 18, 54, 143, 337
Politicization, 63, 78, 83
Popular will and support, 15
Postarrest investigative detention, 42
Postexecution challenge, 12
Postsentencing phase, 39, 52
Posttrial phase, 40
Precharging phase, 44
Presumed innocence, 338–339
Pretrial: investigation, 46; stage, 116, 118, 146
Prison Law, 187
Probation, 33–34, 130, 311
Procedural law, 31; 1928 provisional law, 83
Procuratorate, 9, 27; agencies, 40–49, 53, 55–57, 189, 209–211, 328, 330, 337, 345–346; charging, 39, 45, 76–77
Property crime, 149
Prosecution, 18, 40, 46, 49, 116, 189, 283–284, 337, 339
Prostitution, 4, 36, 225, 255, 328, 330–331, 346; organizing, 255
Protectionism, 50, 59, 330–331, 334
Protest, 2, 46, 48, 49, 138, 203–204, 207, 210–211, 281, 328–329. See also *Kangsu*

Provincial levels, 220; basic court, 40–41; high court, 40–41; intermediate court, 40–41
Provisional law, 63, 81, 83
Public indignation, 51, 134, 164. *See also* Public opinion
Public opinion, ix, 20, 22–23, 25–26, 51, 119, 161–162, 164–166, 169, 170–171, 174–180, 194, 212, 219, 247–249, 251, 266, 270, 274–276, 279–283, 285–286, 288–289, 293–294, 314–315, 320, 344
Public outrage, 77, 91
Punitiveness: in incarceration, 262, 265; in sentencing, 262, 265

Qin Bin, 328
Qin Xing, 225, 327–329
Quasi-laws, 188
Quotas, 24, 63, 305, 317

Random sample, 250, 267, 269
Rape, 31–32, 35, 37–38, 110, 117, 128–129, 131, 138–139, 145–146, 201, 210, 220, 222, 225–226, 228, 230, 310–311, 330; gang, 37, 328; of minors, 37, 225, 253, 328; public, 37
Rational choice theory, 44
Reactionary groups, 67
Recidivist, 200, 202–203
Reeducation, 90
Reform, 1, 124–126, 138–143, 162, 214–216, 218, 236, 238, 327; agrarian (land), 66–67; economic, 7, 31–32, 124, 126, 150; legal and judicial reform, 44, 51–52, 57–58, 149, 165, 188, 212; measures, 1, 9, 12–17, 23, 25–26, 167–170, 178–180, 282, 285, 291, 307–309, 311–312, 320–321, 333–334, 340–346; sentencing, 138–143. *See also* Reform and openness
Reform and openness, 104, 108, 111–112
Regulations, 15, 19, 63–64, 69–70, 72, 88, 90–91, 158, 179–180, 187–190, 343; 1951 Regulations, 64, 70–85
Rehabilitation, 8, 88, 90, 253, 256, 258–266, 270
Repression, political, 24, 65–74, 83–87, 91

Reprieve, 24, 89, 123, 131, 134–135, 234–235. *See also* Death sentence: with reprieve
Retrial, 9–10, 27–28, 50, 53–54, 56–57, 76–78, 142, 193, 199, 204, 289, 310, 328–329, 339
Retribution, 134, 164, 215, 231, 236, 239, 248, 253, 256–257, 262–268, 268, 286
Revolution, 62, 79–80, 301, 302, 320–321
Revolutionary legality, 64
Robbery, 3, 17, 25, 31–32, 34–35, 55, 75, 78, 99, 110, 117, 124, 127, 129, 133, 138–139, 145, 149, 201, 209–210, 220, 225–226, 228, 230–231, 236, 253, 255, 308, 311; aggravated, 128, 149
Rule by law, 98–99, 101, 106, 176
Rule by virtue, 98–99, 101
Rule of law, xii, 7, 88, 100, 105–107, 119, 175–176, 344, 346

Safeguards, vii–viii, 8, 39–40, 47, 52, 309, 334–337, 339–340, 345
Sannan, 337. *See also* Three difficulties
Search warrant, 42–43, 45
Seizures, 41, 45
Self-incrimination clause, 43
Seniors, death penalty exemption, 15, 341
Sentencing guideline, 22, 31, 37, 146–147, 180, 310
Severity, 45, 80, 124, 127, 129, 136–137, 141–145, 150, 163, 193, 262, 265, 275, 310–311, 320. *See also* Balancing leniency and severity
Sexual abuse, 253–254
Shang dynasty, 248
Shanghai, 63, 68, 71–80, 82, 87, 220–230, 233–235, 240, 280, 314, 344
Shen Deyong, 212
Shen Junru, 80
She Xianglin, 9, 27, 280
Singapore, 26, 219, 266, 301, 311–314, 316
Socialist popular justice, 18
Socialist system approach, 98–99
Social terror, 89
Standing Committee of the National People's Congress (SCNPC), 3, 5, 7, 8, 46, 217–218. *See also* National People's Congress

State Compensation Law, 338
State Council, 19, 87
State-planned economy, 32, 111
State-power-based society, 24, 97, 99–104, 108, 110, 113, 118
State secret, viii, xiii, 13–14, 16, 23, 58, 128, 147, 222, 239
Statute of limitations, 3, 116
Stay of execution, 10
Strike-hard campaign, 6–8, 14, 17, 26, 55, 85, 88–89, 91, 109, 138, 140, 149, 169, 212, 217–218, 232, 237, 240, 306–307, 312. *See also* Anticrime campaign
Subjective culpability, 191, 193, 196
Substantive law, 31, 136
Summons, custodial, 41, 53–54, 125
Sun Wangang, 9
Supreme People's Court (SPC), 3–6, 8–13, 16–19, 24–25, 37–38, 40–41, 45, 47–48, 50–53, 57, 114, 116–117, 124–126, 137–149, 172, 179, 187–190, 192–194, 198–200, 204–205, 207–208, 210–212, 214–215, 218–220, 223, 225–226, 230–232, 236–238, 240, 275, 284–285, 289–291, 293, 306, 309–311, 329–334, 338, 340–346; fourth Five-Year Reform Plan, 17, 344; review and approval authority (power), 3–6, 8, 16, 22, 50, 116–117, 124–126, 141, 198, 218–219
Supreme People's Procuratorate (SPP), 3, 5, 18–19, 25, 38, 45, 51–52, 142, 187–190, 203–208, 211–212
Surveillance, 71–72, 85; residential, 42
Systematization, 89

Taiwan, 26, 82, 301, 312, 314–316, 318–319
Tang dynasty, 98–99
Tang Hui, 38, 327–330, 332, 334–354, 337, 341, 344, 346, 347
Terrorism, 124, 149, 253–254, 318
Theft, 32, 34, 79, 99, 105, 145, 217, 237, 308
Three Antis, 85, 90
Three difficulties. See *Sannan*
Tianjin, 2, 70–72, 74, 89, 146, 221
Torture, 2, 5, 8, 9, 15, 18, 43, 45, 47, 54, 91, 143, 215, 289, 305, 317, 337–338, 345. *See also* Police: torture

Transparency, xi–xii, 14, 16–17, 179–180, 215, 220, 239, 346
Trial: of first instance, 40, 47, 117, 232; of second instance, 9, 40, 49, 180, 207, 210. *See also* Appellate review
Two Hands Principle, 112
Two-trial finality system, 116

Unarmed enemies, 64
Uniform sentencing guideline, 22
United Kingdom, vii, 111, 267, 296, 320
Unpardonable crimes, 99

Victim, 8, 26, 37, 48, 53, 64, 73, 82, 128, 133–135, 138–142, 146, 165, 172–173, 192, 195–203, 207, 212, 222, 225–226, 231, 236, 274–294, 344–345; advocacy, 276–278, 280; family (of), ix, 56, 193, 197–198, 200–203, 274–276, 278, 274–294, 311, 330; fault, 148, 172, 196–197, 231; precipitation, 10; rights, xiii, 114–115, 167, 170, 193, 196, 285–287
Vietnam, 26, 266, 301, 314, 316–319
Violent crimes, 11, 25, 32, 34, 55, 105–106, 110–111, 138, 144–145, 149, 177, 201, 218, 220, 225, 231, 232, 236, 237, 239, 276
Visitation, by family members, 5, 15
Voluntary cooperation, 339
Voluntary surrender, 142, 172, 197, 202, 287

Wan E'xiang, 248
Wang Jingwei, 63
Wang Junbo, 8
Wang Lijun, 91
Wang Shengjun, 164, 237, 340
Wang Xiaoxiang, 8
Wang Zhicai, 187, 192
Wang Zongfang, 7
Wang Zongwei, 7
Wan Keqin, 75
Weibo, 22, 329. *See also* Microblogs
Wenhuibao, 73
Wen Jiabao, 268, 332–333
Wen Yaomin, 75
Wenzhou, 332–333

White-collar crimes (offenders), 11, 232
Working class, 103, 159
Wu Ying, 232, 277, 327, 331–335, 337, 341, 346, 347

Xia dynasty, 248
Xiao Yang, 114, 116, 138, 268, 275, 285, 288, 340
Xi Jinping, xii, 106, 346
Xin Yuanlong, 187, 203

Yanda, viii, 7, 109, 124, 149, 153, 217, 305. *See also* Strike-hard campaign
Yao Shushi, 67–68, 72, 74, 87, 92
Yuan, 27, 232, 293, 328, 330–333

Zeng Chengjie, 11, 18, 20
Zhang Gaoping, 210
Zhang Hui, 210
Zhang Wentian, 76
Zhang Zhixin, 2, 13
Zhao Zuohai, 9, 27, 165
Zhou Qiang, 268
Zhu De, 6
Zhu Guohua, 6–7, 13
Zhu Zhanping, 10

GPSR Authorized Representative: Easy Access System Europe, Mustamäe tee 50, 10621 Tallinn, Estonia, gpsr.requests@easproject.com